Somersaults

Rovings, Tears & Absurdities –
A Memoir from the
Fringe of Journalism

by
J. J. Hespeler-Boultbee

CCB Publishing
British Columbia, Canada

Somersaults:
Rovings, Tears & Absurdities – A Memoir from the Fringe of Journalism

Copyright ©2017 by J. J. Hespeler-Boultbee
ISBN-13 978-1-77143-296-2
First Edition

Library and Archives Canada Cataloguing in Publication
Hespeler-Boultbee, J. J. (John Jeremy), 1935-, author
Somersaults : rovings, tears & absurdities – a memoir from the fringe of journalism / by J. J. Hespeler-Boultbee. -- First edition.
Issued in print and electronic formats.
ISBN 978-1-77143-296-2 (pbk.).--ISBN 978-1-77143-297-9 (pdf)
Additional cataloguing data available from Library and Archives Canada

Cover artwork (fish and ship) and design by J. J. Hespeler-Boultbee
Cover artwork (water tropics illustration) © rolffimages | CanStockPhoto.com

Photo credits: All photos contained herein are copyright J.J. Hespeler-Boultbee.

Extreme care has been taken by the author to ensure that all information presented in this book is accurate and up to date at the time of publishing. The publisher cannot be held responsible for any errors or omissions. Additionally, neither is any liability assumed by the publisher for damages resulting from the use of the information contained herein.

All rights reserved. No part of this publication may be reproduced, stored in a retrieval system or transmitted in any form or by any means, electronic, mechanical, photocopying, recording or otherwise without the express written permission of the publisher.

Publisher: CCB Publishing
              British Columbia, Canada
              www.ccbpublishing.com

To the memory of my brother

Also by J. J. Hespeler-Boultbee

A Story in Stones:
*Portugal's influence on culture and
architecture in the Highlands of Ethiopia
1493-1634*
Foreword by Richard Pankhurst
©2011 – ISBN 9781926585987

Mrs. Queen's Chump:
*Idi Amin, the Mau Mau, Communists,
and Other Silly Follies of the British Empire,
A Military Memoir*
©2012 – ISBN 9781771430296

I wish to express my gratitude
to my son, Michael,
and to my friend, Danny Ziegler,
for their computer skills and suggestions,
and to Margaret Erskine,
for her help and scholarly input.
My wife, Alemie,
has been a source of
constant kindness and patience
during the months it has taken
to write and prepare this work;
without her assistance it would
likely have remained far longer
in an embryonic state.

Contents

Part I – Roadside Notes 1

Part II - Penmanship 145

Part III - Smorgasbord 231

*What do I know about what I shall be, I who do not know what I am?
To be what I think? But I think so many things ...!*

Fernando Pessoa writing as Álvaro de Campos in "Tabacaria"

PART I
Roadside Notes

Part I – Roadside Notes

Lemma 3
Bloody Casino 5
Global Gallop 7
Chums 13
Dapple 17
ANZACS 19
Seven Shillings 24
Wonks 27
Pacific Run 30
Social Whirl 37
Scurvy 41
The Commute 52
Québec 55
New York 73
Last Spanking 74
Eberstein 76
Tappie 82
Blighty 84
Sam 96
Mr. Cope 104
Nick 111
The Moat House 119
Big Finn 122
A Tudor Voluntary 126
Per Sapientiam Felicitas! 129

Lemma – Telling Stories

Now that the narrative leap-frogging and dodging that constitute this work have been more or less knocked into shape, I return to its beginning to write this lemma.

People who write well are frequently poor speakers; similarly, people considered great raconteurs are as frequently hopeless writers. It is difficult to say where my own talents might lie according to this thinking, but not approaching the level (by my own standards) of a gifted raconteur – yet anxious to say my say – writing gets the nod in this case, but not always.

I love drawing, and also consider myself a ceramic sculptor. Many times when I might have preferred to express myself in clay, there have been frustrating limitations – of medium, space, tools or opportunity.

However, there are those who see clay as mud – and who love nothing more than to throw it. This tends to force me to write. With writing an audience is given licence to read what has been written, or to close the book and put it away – even hurl it into the furnace.

Choices – and maybe it is easier, after all, to close or destroy a book than to turn one's back on a boor who's standing in your face and throwing mud.

Since childhood I have written things down, often coded in note form. Much has been lost or tossed over the years, but rifling through files and old scrapbooks, a trunkful of tatty little notes, I have discovered snippets of poetry, abstract thoughts and stories by the hundreds – a great deal of it so unpolished it is embarrassing to read over. Yet these notations jog memory – and so record something of a passage through the years.

"What do you write about?" is a frequent query. "Me," I reply, invariably invoking embarrassed chuckles. "The first book was *Me*, the second *More Me*, the third *Me Again* …" It is a stream of journalistic memoir inasmuch as I was once a news reporter, kept journals for years, and thus possess a substantial fount of subject matter to write about. It may not be to everyone's liking. There is nothing noteworthy in this, except for my awareness that my own passage has led me through a string of unusually colourful bazaars, and for years I have felt it almost a duty to record what I can. In this present work I have started at the beginning – common, though by no means the rule in an opus of autobiography. I worked as a journalist, after all, so if you do not tell me a story, I will tell you one.

Actually, the "rule" is broken in some measure because there already exists a published autobiographical account of the two years in which I was

Somersaults

compelled to serve in the British Army.[1] By itself that constituted one gigantic somersault – one that has eclipsed almost every somersault I have turned in the years since. This present account, then, covering a period of some thirty years, has been divided into three parts. Chronologically, the details contained in the military memoir would slot into place between Part I and Part II of this book's narrative.

If my creative and archival energies persist, it is possible that other volumes of somersaults will follow. A further volume describing the extraordinary adventures and delights of my life in Portugal might be one. Like Álvaro de Campos sitting in his room across the street from the tobacconist's, I have in me all the dreams of the world – the more concrete ones I have managed to record might be seen as somersaultic. (Occasionally it is fun to create words as well as stories.) Another volume might logically describe how those events led directly to my deep connection to Ethiopia – some aspects of which have already been recorded.[2] Time and energy: an octogenarian must consider limitations.

What follows is not history in the strict sense – although the drum roll of history does thump along in the background, as it does with anyone's memoir. This work is no more than my best recollection of the rocky road I travelled from childhood to about the age of thirty – at which point I began another life altogether.

The reader may discover the sequence of the stories in these pages has been altered in a few instances – a device employed in order to leaven both the telling and the reading of the tale. The alteration is slight. In many instances quotes are recalled; although their sense is accurate the precise phrasing may not be, and I have been obliged to fill the gap using my keenest imagination. I make no apologies for this: it is, after all, a frequently used contrivance in storytelling.

Here and there a few names have been altered or changed altogether. This is in order to protect the innocent from unintended injury and myself from unwanted prosecution.

---

[1] See J. J. Hespeler-Boultbee's military memoir, *Mrs. Queen's Chump* – CCB Publishing, British Columbia, Canada, 2012.
[2] See J. J. Hespeler-Boultbee's historical work, *A Story in Stones* (2nd Edition) – CCB Publishing, British Columbia, Canada, 2011.

Bloody Casino

Since infancy, indeed almost from the elemental time of my first consciousness, I have felt an obligation to make connections – to create lines, and measure the spaces between the lines, the causes and effects of connections in time and the events that occur during those times. It was due, almost certainly, to the acute consciousness that very little, if anything, happens in isolation – a notion that helped burnish the creativity of a colourful and unusual childhood. I was encouraged by my mother, who had a penchant for looking sideways and backwards, yet always forwards when it concerned her whims. The sideways were her glances at others, which could be cattily evil and have unpleasant consequences; the backwards was nostalgic, when she felt the need to draw on example from revered family – which was pretty well all the time, and very often accompanied by tears. I watched her and learned from her. Her encouragement, along with a constant stream of opinion and comment, helped me to develop a curiously quirky memory, a love of history and story which, as I developed and started to ponder what I might do for a living (once released from the army) helped spark the idea of journalism. Mama's view forward was a constant rationalization, a conviction that what she imagined would be best for everyone – particularly her sons. For me, she opted for the world of the arts. She imagined me a renowned painter, or maybe an architect. (Not a great irony, as it turned out, for a little later in my life, I was to spend a great deal of time living in Portugal and working in the country's rich milieu of architectural history.) Some of Mother's artful whimsy must have rubbed off. Although I eventually went to art school, my preferred option – at least in the beginning – was for journalism. Journalists, as opposed to artists, were paid for their work, I reckoned. I could be whimsical, too; the photo-journalist sitting next to me on my flight back to Canada in 1956 was a persuasive fellow, and might even have convinced my mother had they met …

Doors never opened easily for me, however. They had to be pushed – sometimes hard. There were demands, mine and others, and a great deal of scepticism: fantastic dreams were at first considered, later requiring profound and logical re-thinking – which naturally demanded some of the wilder notions be shelved altogether. Perhaps you will meet the Flim-Flam Man.

A garrulous child, breathless jabber-mouth with a never-ending story to tell ("… little children should be seen and not heard …" went with the constant instruction to sit down and belt up), I demanded and was given a constant supply of pencils, crayons and large sheets of paper in order to be kept content. It usually sufficed to ensure a moderate level of peace. My older brother and I were constant rivals.

"Be quiet and draw something!"

Once it had been made known and brought into the house, the malleability of plasticine was an exciting alternative. Such supplies would keep me occupied, happily alone and silent, for hours on end. When I could not, or was forbidden, to tell whatever compelling story was bubbling between brain and mouth, there was always a stock of material with which to produce a two-dimensional description on paper or even, on occasion, a three-dimensional model. In many cases these efforts were more effective than any amount of insistent and incomprehensible yammering. Thus, years later, when the call of journalism seemed to lose its shine (as eventually it was bound to in my case), it was the most natural thing in the world for me to revert to the visual and plastic arts. I built myself a house in Portugal – thinking all the while it was no more than large sculpture – and added a ceramic studio alongside it ...

That is jumping ahead too quickly. There is narrative sufficient to fill many pages twixt this point and that, and I mention the fact up front and now merely to evince how the narrative came to be in the first place both visual and tactile.

Fate: very early I grasped that every event in our lives is linked to every other, at least through our own witness. Individual places, people and events are joined together through our own senses and understanding of them, and thus become fragments of our overall education and understanding. When telling a story or committing to the written word it is, more than anything else, the organization of random knowledge into a cohesive stream that enables us, or not, to draw pictures or present and describe conclusions. The lines may be ragged or clear, but connections there are – and sometimes strong ones – so that what might at first appear to be a most erratic course, in reality has its own pattern, its own special precision. It is inevitable, especially, when Fate takes the lead in some crazy dance. Often times it has been precisely after participating in some haphazard or traumatic event, when I am still shaking my head and wondering how I managed to survive it, that I come to a comprehension of the choreography, the metaphysical *brincadeira* of the pantomime I have been coerced to enact. Though often of a mind that I wrote the music myself, set the stage and summoned the actors, I'm eventually obliged to admit the movement of the dance was never a thing I could manipulate once the orchestra had done with its overture and the curtain had gone up.

No matter how chaotic the journey may seem, or how well rehearsed, there is within the logic of any action a Truth that manifests itself to those who seek it. An Australian companion journalist, who once negotiated with me the long portion of an agonizingly corrupted by-way, summed up – in the sardonic drawl to which Australians are prone – both of our takes on the adventure we had been sharing:

"It's all a casino, mate. Just a bloody casino!"

Global Gallop

Although born in Vancouver, British Columbia, in 1935, I left when I was two. There was a brief period during the Second World War when I lived with my mother and brother in eastern Canada – but I did not return with my eyes wide open enough to actually see my birthplace until November, 1956. I had just spent the previous year-and-a-half on active military service with the British Army in the jungles of Kenya and Malaya, and my "homecoming" was unusual in that my father's house had never been my home. My father came to meet me off the plane when it landed at Vancouver airport; he was accompanied by his brother-in-law, my uncle, and in the moment of arrival I did not know which one of them to call father. I was not yet twenty-one, and knew neither of them.

Today there exists a name for the condition with which disturbed soldiers so often return to their families, but in 1956 such medical designation was unacknowledged. Besides, Canadian servicemen or women had not returned from any conflict areas since the end of the Korean War, so there was little need to know. At that time there had been virtually nothing for servicemen or women in the way of rehabilitation and certainly not for someone who had served in a "foreign" army. I laid off most of my strange sensations to the itchiness I felt at joining so cheek by jowl with a family I had never known – a father I had been told I met as an infant and could not now remember, a step-mother and five half-sisters – and being expected to treat it with unaccustomed amity. (Product of a split family, my mother had had custody of my brother and myself throughout my life to that point which, excluding portions of time at boarding school and in the army, would have involved generous sessions of maternal brainwashing. Dear Mama – there's another book!)

When society's level of toleration or embarrassment at any given individual is judged too great for it to bear, there had always been the lock-up or the looney bin – a permanent rest cure in some out-of-the-way sanitarium. But it is different with family. I suppose had we discussed or been constrained to discuss the subject at all, we might have found this to have been one approach in my case – but in the mid-fifties there remained, large and looming, the "stigma thing," the shame.

I have made several starts to this treatise. Quite apart from stuttering on the "me-myself-and-I" requirement for memoir, I found myself growing immensely tired, straying off-theme and growing increasingly distant from the protagonist of my story – which in an autobiography was me, after all.

As if stretched upon some psychiatrist's couch rabbiting on about my most fragile and innermost confidentialities, and after having written some ten or twelve thousand words, one might assume I would have been well and truly on my way, my computer purring along in high gear. However, it finally became imperative to admit that although I could not avoid use of the first person to round out the story, the child who became the man was now fading to a dim mirage. He no longer existed. I had known him intimately, of course, but now in a manner somewhat disconnected from him I was seeing in him a young man I had known once, but from whom I had since withdrawn so far that I stumbled, not at all confident as to how he would look upon – or judge! – the me of now. Certainly the person he was should not be muddled with the person he became. Yet I knew the story I wanted to tell was predicated on the transformation of that boy into the man who now presumes both to prance and lumber through these pages. Surely this cannot be the first time the writer of autobiography has been presented with such conundrum?

Therefore I must say it right at the start: if ever there appears here the disembodied voice of the inquisitor, or even of the mere narrator, think of him, kindly, as the tremulous voice of Great Uncle Menace shaking his chains like a Dickensian ghost and scaring the hell out of a small boy.

So my father was unknown to me. He had seen me as an infant, of course, but I did not meet him until right before my twenty-first birthday. It took very little time for us both to recognize (if not exactly acknowledge) our dislike for one another. I have mulled and munched over the details of this many, many times – as well as the singular background of family, my upbringing, my early schooling. All or any of that alone might have been sufficient to drive any man round the bend. In my state of clouded mind and almost perpetual fantasy, I have searched for "answers" – and by now know as well as anybody there are none. Confused, as some have judged, I have gone back and forth, "searching my heart" (silly expression, but apt in this instance), and the one thing of which I am certain is that there are no certainties. What is done is done, there is no safe retreat – so one must move ahead with whatever comes next. It is a good thing I possess the humour of an idiot optimist. Some would say its manifestation demonstrates I am on the cusp; but I know, as others do not, such humours have more than once saved me from zipping straight over the edge. For all the existence of this whacky humour, I cannot laugh at it. It permits me to burn a fuse slowly prior to an explosion, so I am thankful for it. Among scores of literary heroes, I read over and over Jorge Luís Borges and Fernando Pessoa. Visually I relate well to the Bruegels, Bosch and Gaudi. Picasso and Escher make wonderful and good sense to me. These are sombre names for sombre-minded whackos, so I never mentioned any of them to my father. I know my creative soul, and I'll be a survivor till it's time for me to quit. My father would have dismissed such rot.

After their marriage my parents set up house in the Kerrisdale district of Vancouver, an affluent neighbourhood that at the time separated the city's southern rim from a diminishing area of farmland. But for all their considerable privileges it was not a happy marriage.

Mother
on her wedding day

Even now, in my eighties, I have an excellent memory, and daresay it goes back further than most people's. My first "memories" – dream-like impressions – are of the house to which I first came home as a child from Vancouver General Hospital, and where I lived for the first two years of my life. The place is foggy in my mind's perception of it, to be sure, but it's there: warm carpets covering the flooring, a giant pram in which I sat like a maharaja, a wide lawn in front of the house – delicious green grass that, when I was scooped up and plonked down in the middle of it in my white dresses, brought big brown curly-haired dogs loping around the corner of the house to slobber over me and set me giggling, lick my face and push me over. Irish water spaniels, my mother later told me. A wooden trellis supporting colourful flowers concealed a large portion of the white front wall of the house. I was not old enough to recall or understand the rancour that went on in the kitchen and living room, or in the master bedroom – acidic quarrels, I later came to understand, that quickly eroded a marriage and destroyed a family. When I was old enough to assess such details my mother told me my father was a violent and jealous man, quick-tempered, controlling and always ready to lash out with his bitter tongue and hard fists. She told me it was for these reasons she left him. And reasonably fair-minded man that now I am, I have been left to suppose that although her accusations were probably true (I have no reason to doubt my mother's word) it did not exonerate her from traits – "we all have faults, dear" – that had been bred in her from earliest childhood. At various times I heard my mother described as feisty and spoiled, and even a she-devil. None of it is of consequence now. However one may have wished to describe her, Mother was not one to take orders from a man the likes of my father, who seemed to find it so necessary to issue them.

My mother was in her early twenties when she married. Both of her parents had died – her mother when she was thirteen, her father when she was nineteen. Apart from the guardian her father had appointed for her at the time of her mother's death, a distant and adventurous lady cousin who had been living in Canada but had latterly chosen to live in Britain, Mother was pretty much on her own.

One aspect of her complex personality was an extraordinarily sensitive, open and generous nature; polar opposite to what often presented itself as a capricious selfishness. She was artistic – gifted in drawing, painting and music. She possessed a deep appreciation of literature and poetry, a great deal of it initially learned as a quick and most precocious child in the lap of her mother, and at the knees of her doting father and grandfather. I have a photograph of them all together when Mother could have been no more than a few weeks old. As a single child her early associations were mostly with adults, her parents and their friends – an erudite and cultured group of Old World immigrants. Her early sentiments and perceptions were further honed at an expensive private boarding school in Vancouver, and still later at an even more expensive "finishing school" for young ladies in Switzerland. She would spend her holidays in England with her guardian, who was a mere half-generation older than herself. They would have made a team as they took on the delights of London and went for holiday trips about the English countryside or onto the Continent. There was nothing "professional" about Mother's education, however. The so-called professions were not especially in vogue for young ladies in those days. Nevertheless, she received a well-rounded schooling – an education considered more than adequate for the time. Before her marriage she had already travelled the world extensively.

But she was volatile. Her wilful temperament, combined with a strong pride in her family and its considerable means, almost guaranteed it. She was fiery and confident, excited by a thousand ideas that would have fitted poorly into the social scheme of parochial-minded western Canada. A young lady of Mother's spirits might have been seen as "difficult" by others, perhaps especially by someone like my father. If he thought her "a handful" and "spoiled," as later he allowed his family and friends know he considered her, he was also the type of brash young man who would have relished taking on the challenge of taming such a woman – as one might tame a bear, maybe. "Quite the filly," in up-country parlance. She was beautiful, after all, and rich – a "catch." But he failed. Monumentally. That was when he would have started calling her spoiled instead of spirited, an unrealistic dreamer, the handful that he derided. Then, by Mother's account, came the moment when one beating was one too many; she upped and left him with nary an instant of hesitation once she had made up her mind. That was shortly after my second birthday. My brother would have been not quite five when she made the move. She took the two of us, along with our beloved Nanny, to live in Australia.

It is difficult to say whether Australia was the intended final destination. On a previous trip there before her marriage Mother had had a boyfriend, so I imagine she may have thought she could have linked up with him again. I will never know, but if she had been thinking in those terms she certainly took her time getting there. Our route was hardly direct. Australia appeared on our horizon after numerous stops and stages, some of months duration.

Somersaults

Aboard ship somewhere in the
South Atlantic, bound for Australia:
Nanny Grace with
her two charges on deck

For the initial burst of our escape from Canada, Mother took us by car from British Columbia south to Ojai in California. When she had caught her breath and thought about what she wanted to be doing next she returned to Vancouver, packed what she considered necessary for a long journey, made arrangements with her banks – and rejoined us and our Nanny, by now in Los Angeles. From there we travelled by ship around to Panama City – but the climate was abominable, so Mother claimed, and we all moved on to Kingston, Jamaica. It was here, on a port dock, that I first saw a black man. He was huge and I was frightened. I began to cry, nervously picking at a colourful label pasted onto a steamer trunk. Mother stormed up under a parasol, examining me as she might some irritating insect.

"Do not remove the labels from our luggage, dear. If you rip them off they won't arrive where we're going. Wipe his nose, Nanny!" she commanded, pursing her lips and studying my wet and crinkled face.

She turned and walked away to attend to other important business concerning our luggage, for we had not only a heap of suitcases and trunks, but crates – numerous gigantic boxes that contained all of our antique furniture (much of it family heirloom) and household goods. It travelled as deck cargo. I remember tea chests packed with Mother's porcelain carefully wrapped in straw and paper shavings. Big dark men everywhere, regiments of them, it seemed, were singing and shouting to one another as they hefted our belongings onto trolleys and wheeled them into distant warehouses. Mother supervised, very busy under her parasol.

It was easy to take ship from Jamaica across the Atlantic to the England about which she had developed such romantic notions during the holidays she had spent there – but we did not remain long. The cousin who had chaperoned her through her school years was still living in London, but she had her own busy life and Mother needed something else. For a time we settled on the island of Jersey, English but close to Mother's romance with France – then it rained and she had a re-think. She spoke no French, had set her sights on sunshine – and at that moment the sunshine was in South Africa ... However, when we arrived, it appeared that did not suit either, so from Cape Town we continued by boat to Perth in Western Australia – which was only a wide continent away from Sydney. That involved a train ride any youngster would remember, including a stretch on the widely-publicized *Spirit of Progress* service between Melbourne and our final destination. Mother had friends in Sydney, so it was here we found the sun and hung ourselves out – for a time. A little more than four years, as it turned out. And it was here I first attended pre-school. For a child spanning three-to-seven, the years were long enough to allow development of some first precious associations and solid memories, to learn to jabber with my chums in that Aussie twang I can still mimic at will – my first real words. (These came minus the jargon which, at such tender age, was a wallop too salty for a little Joey to know about.)

Chums

It was while we lived at Manly that Christopher Thistlethwaite came into my life, my first, my dearest playmate – the first friend I can remember. And what a friend!

My brother had his bicycle and a cricket bat, neither of which I was then able or allowed to touch, let alone use, and on our long excursions to the park he would cycle off to the cricket nets, leaving me to play by myself on the merry-go-round, or on the down end of the teeter-totter. Valiant Nanny Grace would swoop in with joy and rough-and-tumble sufficient to satisfy all the infant urgings for attention that a spoiled little boy could wish for – except for the real delight that comes with a playmate and friend like Christopher Thistlethwaite. Being just over two years older than me, my brother found me to be as I was – an inept four-and-a-half or five-year-old, and no fun at all to play with. He was already able to swing a straight bat and ride his bicycle far faster than either Nanny Grace or I could run. Christopher Thistlethwaite was different. He stayed and played.

I have painful memories of my own timid nature in those days, a reticence that was to hold me for years in check, and which doubtless left its traces on my temperament. I would shrivel in the presence of others, a combination of awe at what I believed were their exceptional capabilities and firmness of conviction, along with my own assumption (before even trying!) that I could not possibly – anything. My big brother would wither me into stupefied silence when, for instance, Nanny Grace would take us to an ice-cream booth, and he would state clearly and with absolute authority precisely what he wanted. I would never know what I wanted. Usually I would choose the same as my brother, or the last item of a long list parrotted by a waitress who, rattling out the menu, had completely lost and confounded me, the ultimate word alone sticking in the gumbo of my brain. Nanny Grace would never fail to perceive this fluster, and I was sensitive enough to note her concern so that if she came up with some kindly suggestion on my behalf, it was easy to submit. Besides, she had an uncanny way of selecting for me exactly what I wanted.

Which is why I believe, now, she struck up a conversation with Christopher Thistlethwaite's nanny when we all came together by chance one day at the wasteland rim of the sandbox. In a trice Christopher Thistlethwaite and I conquered the great loneliness imposed by my brother's stewardship of bat, ball and bicycle. Suddenly there was this little individual dumping bucket loads of sunshine at my feet, enough to push my shadow round to the back of me where I couldn't see it. He asked for nothing; he ran and laughed with me, treated me for all the world like a pal, and I loved him with a fierce loyalty for the joy he brought to me. No competition. Battles countless we fought, but side-by-side, from sea-wall to sand castle, and every day we managed to condemn dozens of grizzly pirates to walk the plank at the end of the park bench.

I had asked his name and when he replied that it was Christopher Thistlethwaite I believed him and never sought to alter it. I always referred to him by his full tag, and when I returned home at the end of a buccaneer voyage around the grandstand, and my mother solicitously asked what I had done with my day, and with whom I had been playing, my answer was always the same. I had been, I would tell her, with Christopher Thistlethwaite.

It did not sound exactly like that because Christopher Thistlethwaite is, I suppose, quite a mouthful for a five-year-old to get right, and my earnest reply amid sniffles and sobs would likely have sounded more like:

"I bin playin'ith Quith-tof'r Thith-ill-fwait," which would invariably send my mother into hoots of mirth; not exactly unkind, but which puzzled me.

"Tell us where you've been and who you were playing with, dear,"

Mother would exclaim for the entertainment of her afternoon tea guests, and unsuspectingly I would cause them all to smile and cluck what a dear little, sweet little, shy little boy I was.

"You can't even say it right!" my big brother would catch on, pointing a finger and laughing derisively in my face.

I would attempt to argue, reasoning that an attack against me was an attack on the sacredness of my friend and friendship. Often my expostulations would only make matters worse.

"I can tho!" I would be close to tears, and Nanny Grace would start to rise from her seat with her arms stretched referee-like between us.

"Say it then!" my brother would taunt. "Say it! Say it! Say it!"

Chin quivering, I would splutter:

"I was'ith Quith-Tof'r Thith-ill-fwait, tho there!"

Howls of laughter! Floods of tears!

"Oh! You're so over-sensitive!" Mother would tell me impatiently.

Driven by a sense of desperation and the weight of such derision I clung to my little buddy with the tenacity of an undying friendship – a loyalty and affection which, upon more adult reflection, I have reserved for very few throughout my life. But these are sentiments I have ever since sifted separately from the sludge of the myriad feelings in which we encase our lives – the essential but selfish "me" – the "me" with whom we live daily and claim to understand. The truth of committment in friendships requires the highest grade of loyalty, and securely fastens bands around an individual's kernel. If one feels a loyalty one cannot skirt it; if one suffers because of a disloyalty, the injury is devastating. At the age of five I did not understand the fallacies that can be hidden in false friendships or loves, but the pain was a quantity I could measure even then. Over the years it is entirely possible I have learned not a whit from the brutal knocks of experience, nor grown or developed a useful thickness of skin. I remain "over-sensitive." Loved ones die. Friends go away and one neither sees nor hears from them again. These tragedies are painful, but are elements of Life that are not incomprehensible. However, the falsity and hypocrisy of friends who are not friends at all – this is betrayal akin to death. It happens all the time, but is a hard lesson at five.

"Are you my friend?" I asked Christopher Thith-ill-fwait one day as we sat by the shore throwing rocks at the tide. I felt good with him, but I suffered. Uncertainty. Fear.

Sure he was, and he showed me a little knife that he carried in his pocket and which his father had given him earlier that very day.

"Mummy!" I would cry out later, blurting full-breath news in a way that made my brother sneer contemptuously, and which caused me to feel like bursting into tears in sheer fright.

"What is it, dear?" my mother would coax, always a trifle impatiently, and I would hang my head, drop my voice away from my brother's laughter, and struggle not to cry.

"Quith-Tofr Thith-ill-fwait says he's my friend, an' he's got a knife wot his daddy gave him an' everything..."

"My! My!" my brother exploded. "Ach! He's not your friend, and anyway I saw his knife and it wasn't a very big one. I could have a bigger one than that!"

At last my tears would come and I would sob uncontrollably at being so humiliated, and I would try to tell in jerky, unintelligible gasps that I knew Christopher Thistlethwaite was my friend because he had said so and he meant it.

And my mother would smile because she noticed how I could never seem to refer to my little friend as Christopher, or even Thistlethwaite, but always by his full tag – or at least my rendering of it.

"Do be quiet, now, dear!" She would say at last, exasperated by my emotion and not quite knowing how to deal with it or even what had caused it.

"What are you crying about? Why all the tears?"

"Quith-Tofr Thith-ill-fwait – *choke* – my friend – *sob* – said – *gasp* – his daddy – *sob* – an' I – *choke* – saw it – *gasp* – an' it was – *big breath* – a beautiful knife – *sob* – and my brother – *sob again* – said it wasn't ..."

None of it made sense, and Mother would flutter her eyes in utter exasperation.

"Do stop crying!" she would scold. "Here, take this hanky ..."

"Cry baby! Cry baby!" came the taunts from the play room, my brother pulling apart the caboose of his electric train. And I would howl in misery until my mother, by now distraught, her eyes flashing left and right for a way out, would order Nanny Grace to take me to the quiet sanctuary of the bathroom.

"Wipe his nose, Nanny!"

Dear, sweet Nanny Grace. She of course understood everything because she was a friend to Christopher Thistlethwaite's nanny, had been with us in the park and by the water's edge. She could say my friend's full name without smiling or making fun of him, and so in the bathroom, there, she would dry my tears and talk soothing words, hold me to her crisply-starched apron until my sobs choked themselves off, and she would promise me that tomorrow we would go again to the park and there I could play to my heart's content with my best, my only buddy.

Christopher Thistlethwaite was at the centre of my existence for a long time – but whether it was for weeks or for months or even a year or more I could not now say. One day my friend told me that he would be moving with his family and his nanny to Brisbane – a place that sounded to me then as if it lay on the other side of the world. And then he was gone. It must have been a sad time but I cannot remember the sadness, and no doubt the emotions I felt were cushioned and dulled by the attentions of Nanny Grace. It seems to me sadder now when I try to think back to what it must have been like, the trauma of the moment dulling any specific memory. But I never forgot my little friend. I would talk about him endlessly long after he had left, Christopher Thistlethwaite this, Christopher Thistlethwaite that.

It brings on a smile, trying to imagine what he might be like now. I'm in my eighties; we'd be about the same age. I wonder if he made it this far – or if he even remembers the sandbox in the park at Manly?

Dapple

Recollections of Canada and the bulk of our travels to Australia come to me bathed in a soft pinkish mist; for years I resisted acknowledging that my first clear lineal memories were of Australia, not my native Canada. This fact caused me some infantile bitterness. I had absolutely no knowledge of Canada, but being Canadian was an element of exceptional childhood pride, and maybe still is. It was always the one clear quality that set me apart from my brother, who was born in England. Ha! Ha! I could tell him in my squeaky Aussie raw-meat twang, I'm a Canadian and you're not! He would flip me a bird, and ride off on his bicycle.

Language; I could have identified neither its importance nor unimportance to me in those long remote and hazy times. I was learning to converse in the same Aussie drawl I now recognize sounds like the banter of the drovers who congregated most mornings at the kitchen door, out at the Ritchie station. There were no differences then. No us, no them. The Ritchie station was the sheep farm way off in the New South Wales Blue Mountain boondocks where we were taken for several of our more exotic holidays. I was sure I had never seen so many sheep. Mother had been a friend to Margaret Ritchie from the time of her pre-marriage travels through Australia.

There were always hordes of children when we went for holidays at Ritchie's. We all had pet rabbits or pet 'roos, and we all had ponies to ride. I rode Dapple, a diminutive but chubby pony; my brother rode Bluey, somewhat larger and clearly having made the transition to horse – the difference between a tricycle and a bicycle. In my infant pride, and in view of the perpetual sibling rivalry that guided my infant brain, I was sure that eventually Dapple, too, would grow into a full-blown beast that one day would beat Bluey over the meadow and up the hill track to that kitchen door where the drovers hung about. The household's maids would daily swing on the kitchen bell summoning the kids to come up for their "elevenses" – orange juice freshly squeezed, served to us along with delicious little crouton squares of toast. We would all gallop across the lower meadow, the drovers laughing and shouting out their encouragement. They loved a good Derby.

But Dapple was always last and, coming up at the end, I could never be sure that the other children did not get more croutons than me. I was not big enough to sit upon him properly, my legs sticking straight out at the flanks at near right angles, and flapping like a couple of loose leathers. I was not able to grip his ample girth between my knees, or to tickle his ribs to make him go any faster. I tried, and poor Dapple tried his best too, I'm sure, but as a team we were not quite up to par. The drovers would smile and say never mind, but the others would laugh their derisive insides into a collective storm as Dapple and I flopped up, always last to the cookhouse door. The mockery and scorn was altogether too great a burden for my sensitivities, and so I would take my orange juice and toast and ride away to the bottom of the near pasture where I could sit alone in my misery and cry quietly at the enormous injustice of it all... Dapple, never you mind, I'd tell my mount. One day your legs will grow and then you will bring me in first to the cookhouse door and I'll show those other mean kids! It was not entirely clear to me exactly what I would show them, but doubtless it would be clear enough when I did. In the meantime, tears were the easiest and surest form of expressing the frustrations I felt.

"You are too sensitive!" my mother would scold as she was powdering her cheeks to go into dinner with the Ritchies. "Be a toughie!"

I would try to be a toughie and my brother would bloody my nose. Nanny

Grace would be there promptly to soothe my hurt feelings and I would stifle my sobs in her lap. Dapple, she said, was a good pony, but he would never out-run Bluey, so I would just have to live with the utter defeat of it. Did I want an extra portion of toast? Another glass of orange juice? Oh misery! I was appeased.

All in all, I must have been an insufferable kid – but for all that probably no worse than most.

We would return to the city after such adventurous weeks away, and always there was the nearby park at Manly, its edge running along an outer stretch of Sydney's harbour. There was a long promenade, and some trees and a children's play area with swings, the teeter-totter and the sandbox I shared with Christopher Thistlethwaite. Some way back from this, there was a large field where bigger boys, and men I suppose, would set up to play cricket. Batting nets were on the far side but I seldom walked over there.

ANZACS

We moved to a large house in Point Piper where the yew trees in the narrower part of the garden between the front of the house and the street were a special delight for me. They had been planted in a line that ran along the low property wall in front of the house, and grew to a substantial height. Our house and front yard were several metres lower than the level of our street. While the yew trees definitely appeared as trees on our side of the wall, from the street-side they appeared as a tall and bushy hedge rising several feet above the level of our garden wall. They completely blocked any view of the house. From the sidewalk it was impossible to see anything at all of our front yard. Entering at the gate, there was a long flight of stairs leading down to the level of our front doorway, the extent of the drop well concealed by the yews. Our roof was the sole portion of the house visible from the street.

It didn't take me long to discover I could very easily climb up inside these yew trees and, by pushing my way into the tops of them, bring myself to a point higher than anybody walking by on the sidewalk above the property. I could lie back, cradled softly in the upper branches as if I had been in my bed, and turn the cloud formations over my head into a thousand dreamlike adventures. These perches were my great secret. No one could see me, and I told no one where I had gone.

The war was summoning Australia's young men to fight in the North African desert, and grey troop ships were frequently in the harbour in front of the house. Among them were the Queen Mary with three funnels, and the Queen Elizabeth with two – the fastest ships afloat, we were told. I had seen pictures of both of them in glossy magazines, brightly painted black, white and red. Now they were grey like all the others – but huge and imposing anyway. From our veranda, or the bottom of our garden which ran all the way down to Seven Shillings Beach, we could see them as they sailed out below the famous bridge and continued till they were out of sight. I knew they were headed off to war, their decks crowded with slouch-hatted soldiers looking back at their sun-drenched city, shouting, shouting, shouting their hurrahs and Hitler's eternal damnation.

> *We are the boys from way Down Under,*
> *Marching to victory!*
> *We're not afraid of Hitler's thunder,*
> *We'll put him where he should be!*
> *The Poles, the Czechs and Germany itself,*
> *Will fight to put the Nazis on the shelf,*
> *For we are the boys from way Down Under,*
> *Sons of the ANZACS are we!*

The words did not mean a whole lot to me then, but I remember the song still, and its sentiment. Thinking of it, coupling it with the numbers I now know never returned, I am staggered and almost brought once more to tears. No doubt there is an infant nostalgia to my memories, but there is also an infinite remorse when I think of the heroic stupidity of it all. Perhaps it is an example of that over-sensitivity my mother was always so quick to note; possibly it remains a sentiment well mixed with what I later learned of war and killing.

In my yew retreat I watched the clouds rush away across the Pacific, wondered if anyone aboard the two queens could see in them what I saw – galloping horses, continents under smoke and thunderous gunfire. Some great lady was shaking a spear as she watched the troop formations from the top of a high hill, safely out of range of the war that raged somewhere beyond the promontory of Darling Point. In those days I never really knew who that lady was, but she seemed terrible and I did not like her. Now I think I know, but I am somewhat wiser and vastly more experienced.

The war was very real to me at five years of age. I was an early war artist, and had a scrapbook collection of fighter planes and khaki tracked vehicles. My drawings were of aircraft (I was familiar with the silhouettes of most of the major equipment on all sides of the conflict) and warships bristling with guns and spitting fire, and soldiers with soup-plate helmets. Ambulances with big red crosses on their sides raced up and down the hills I imagined, which in turn were covered with acres and acres of stick-like crosses, one for every man fallen. In my infant mind it was impossible to distinguish the difference between the cross on the side of an ambulance, and the cross that marked the site of an ambulance's futility. Mother's friends came by the house in uniform, and occasionally I would be allowed to don their hats, peaked, slouched or wedged. One of the men (his name was Michael Eisdale) bought one of my drawings for sixpence. It was my first art sale – and about the last of any significance for a few years.

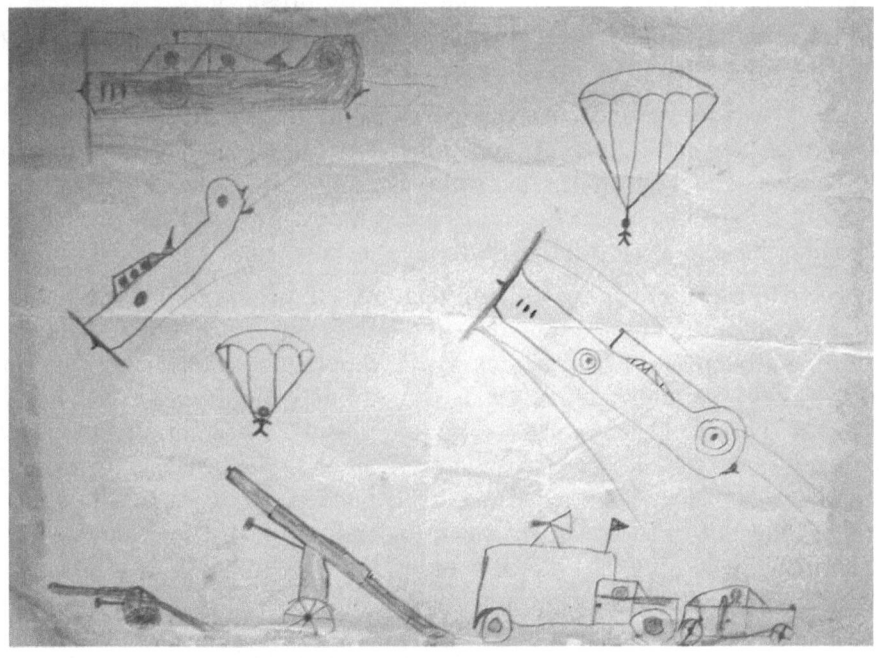

Early war artist –
telling example of what occupied a child's mind in 1942

One hot afternoon, lying on my back in my yew bed, I watched the war lady form herself into a squally black anvil. Chunky hail stones, big as marbles, pelted down from the skies like bullets to drive me indoors and chip the paint off our buff-coloured car (it had an orange-red stripe painted along its sides about ten centimetres below the level of the windows). The hail turned to downpour and bubbles appeared then burst on the deck of our sun porch. A sailboat had capsized about fifty metres from the bottom of our garden, its occupants floating in the sea and hanging onto the side of the hull. The craft floundered helplessly. The sharks, I suppose, had been frightened off by the white sail that now lay in the water, but I watched as one crew member struck out for the beach right below our sea wall, evidently thinking he could make it to shore. He had progressed only a few metres away from the boat, the sun now shining on him, the waters a deep calm blackness. He still had a good way to go when I saw the flash of a shiny wet grey fin cut the surface. It passed close to the swimmer, then returned and the man disappeared below the surface of the water. Not a sound penetrated the sanctuary of the glassed-in portion of our sun porch. With the sun now bright, it was as though the storm, the hail, the wind, the swimmer and the shark that took him had never really been there at all – a dream vanished.

Death was the ragged beachcomber who built a fire outside his haunt at the end of Seven Shillings Beach. One day we children discovered him putting rocks and a bunch of kittens into a gunnysack that he swung about his head and flung from the rocks. We found it at low tide, and never went near the man or his end of the beach again.

The Howden boys, my brother and myself occasionally met up in a nearby vacant lot with other children to play cricket – one bat, one ball, three stumps, a broken set of bails and everyone shouting at everyone else because nobody knew the rules but everybody thought they did. Everybody but me. I never had the least idea of what was going on, and didn't think I really needed to. In any case I felt like a guest at these affairs and I did not want to suffer the embarrassment of getting kicked out for being too uppity, or told to shut up for speaking out of turn. My brother usually fixed it that he would win the championship because he was the oldest and the biggest and it was his equipment. He stayed with the leg pads, at all times, and he cut a dashing figure in them for all that they hampered his running and his movements. Because it was difficult for him to move, he would very often stand with his arms outstretched and call orders for others to run and fetch the ball out of the scrub where someone had whacked it.

I was content to be included in these games when they were on, even though I did not understand what was happening or what I was supposed to be doing. If I could get away with it without being shouted at, I would wander off to somewhere about mid-field among the weeds and buttercups, a safe place to wait until someone would hit the ball my way. They seldom did, so I was apt to become bored and sit down. A little neighbour girl named Judy Brown often played with us, and I had taken a fancy to her. She was the best reason I could think of for enduring the boredom of a game I did not comprehend.

Disaster struck one sunny afternoon when I approached her at the wicket.

"Judy Brown, will you marry me when we grow up?"

"No!" she replied, whereupon she pulled a stump from the wicket and whacked me across the nose with it.

Everyone roared as I stood there howling and bleeding like a slaughtered ketchup bottle. Apart from the rejection, which must have altered my perceptions for life, I still carry a faint scar.

From this moment I became a recluse, if not an abject social misfit. I began talking to myself more than usual, and my perch at the top of the yew trees, always a secret I guarded jealously, was put to use daily – sometimes for hours at a stretch. At first I would mutter my complaints about how the world was treating me. As the symptoms persisted and I tended to bring them into the house with me, some of the grown-ups became alarmed. They would ask me what I was saying or to whom I was speaking. This embarrassed me considerably and, when I could, I would seek out quiet corners and shadows, go for walks by myself – or wait until no one was looking and climb up into the yews. I don't believe my hiding place was ever discovered.

The truth was I had found myself another playmate, and I kept this a secret from my family, too. The "talking to myself" was no more than conversation with my friend Christopher Thistlethwaite. He had not returned from wherever it was he was living at present, but I pretended he had – a trick I performed whenever I needed to play alone. It seemed to me my brother would only play with me if he was told to, and then on the strict condition he would win. I found him a threat, so often preferred to be alone and in that way could get together more easily with Christopher Thistlethwaite if I felt the need. I imagined the two of us running and throwing rocks, riding up and down on some extended bough of a monkey tree – and of course he shared with me the secret of the yews.

But one day, sneaking away unseen from Miss Moore's kindergarten, I found myself down on the beach with a pocketful of toys I had stolen earlier from her classroom. I might have been caught had I returned home too early, so decided to build a castle near some footprints that came up the sands of Seven Shillings, clear of the water. I set the toys round about.

"Who are you talking to?" asked a small boy coming between me and the sun.

"To my friend Christopher Thistlethwaite, but he's gone away with his dad to Brisbane," I replied, squinting.

The boy said nothing but dropped to his knees and helped me dig a channel through the sand. He had gangly legs and skinny arms, and a mop of tousled sun-bleached blonde hair. He screwed up his nose a lot.

"My dad's gone off to the war," he said unemotionally.

"So has mine," I lied. "What's your name?" I asked him.

He pronounced it clearly. I heard it correctly the first time and have never forgotten it.

"Gundagai McGinty," he said.

Seven Shillings

My fertile imagination ran like the silver ribbon of a canal, long and straight into a distance that I knew about but could not yet see. I was immortal, then, and there would always be time to travel the canal in its entirety, know all its waters intimately. In all weathers it ran, this canal of my imaginings, and it knew both the heat of summer days and the bitter cold of mid-winter snows and all that passed between one and the other. This imagination knew dawns as still as the bedroom of a child not yet woken; it knew mid-mornings bright and exciting like a busy market street, noons as blustery as an autumn football field, and late afternoons that lingered in a heat haze of the anticipation of evening – an evening maybe filled with the clatter of dense city traffic and the tense promise of colourful theatre marquees. Nights were filled with demons and fairies, dark broodings and fears, delights in the depths of shadows emerging like photographs coming off a newly-developed print paper, and the silken-handed caresses of the ghosts of histories. But the single thread that ran through all, like a tramline paralleling the silver canal, was the infallibility of my immortality. It was this, after all, that permitted the daring exploration of everything, absolutely everything. It permitted flight over all barriers, a fearless, unfettered and entirely unencumbered form of astral travel (had I known what that was) that I could use (and invariably did) to go everywhere. No laws. Jungles I ran through intimately, paths and ferns and snaking roots deep under a dark canopy that lifted for me alone to reveal all secrets hidden beneath it. Glaciers and mountain tops, valleys and deep caverns I knew and travelled, as simply as raising the fingers of my hand and turning them in the air before my eyes. I ran the course of all rivers, plunged over falls and cataracts, and sailed to every shore of every quiet lake. The seas, too, did not escape my investigations and these I knew from the fetid stillness of the Saragossa to the blasts and swells of the North Atlantic (had I known their names!) – the expanses around the Horn, or the mirror stillness that can be Malacca. Desert trails I followed till they petered out in dunes, and still I followed on to the fringes of great oases where arose palaces of cold white marble and the tents of nomad traders. Every people I knew: white man's calculation, black man's honour, red man's mystery, yellow man's inscrutable delicacy. I journeyed to their cities, knew their songs, whispered with them the confidences of a brother. In my great imagining, armed with the force of my immortality, I clasped hands with all men and was held like a loved one in their eyes and the eyes of their families.

Years after our first meeting, when I recounted these things to him, Gundagai McGinty laughed quietly, for he had felt rather the same, he said, and I had mirrored very well those things that had passed through his own mind. His gaze penetrated to the centre of me when he had something serious to say, and his laughter, too, at certain times was emitted in all seriousness. He felt the world of which we spoke was for him the same as for me – or for any man, for that matter, who reached out and took hold of it. Even if there was nothing new on the face of the earth, any man had it in him to find the newness of life and all it contained if he would merely allow himself to be reborn into the adventure of what had been given him. We both laughed then because it seemed our ideals were so parallel, and we vowed between us to maintain this grand thinking as a manifesto, one by which we would try to live out our lives. With a knife we slit the heels of our thumbs, and we clasped hands and became blood brothers.

Playing with me and the toys I had stolen from kindergarten that morning and had set up around the sand castle, I knew right away that I had found another playmate I could trust to the same degree as the boy who had been taken away to Brisbane by his father. As we heaped up the sand, dug the channels and patted down the walls of our construction, I could not help but notice the footprints Gundagai stomped into the damp beach closely matched those of my other friend – those coming up out of the water towards the castle no different than those I had seen in the sandbox in the park. And certainly the prints on the beach had been made by my earlier friend because I had only just then been talking to him ...

Childhood memories have a way of slipping back and forth between reality and fantasy, and it would be reasonable to assume that at times reality appears to be fantasy, or is forgotten altogether, and it is fantasy that is remembered as fact. Such is the sweetness of a child's confusion: smelly-toothed uncles become jolly zephyrs bearing ice cream cones; mere shadows are remembered vividly as fierce dragons.

And about my new friend I confess more than the usual quantities of memory confusion, for I am certain that the early reality of him was his ability to step right into my fantasy world and fill it entirely. And likewise what I fancy about those early encounters with him are precisely those things of which I have a clear memory – running on Seven Shillings Beach; marching along the sidewalk, swinging our arms bravely to the level of our noses as Australia's sons trooped off to war behind a regimental band that wound its way through the streets of downtown Sydney; sitting behind the steering wheel of the family sedan, taking it on stationary (but important) expeditions to the furthest reaches of the outback. For hours I would lie back in the wide branches of the yew hideaway watching the clouds form pictures overhead.

Christopher Thistlethwaite left and I was neither to see nor hear of him again. Perhaps it was this separation, forced on me by grown-ups too busy to stop to consider a child's unreasonably childish pain, that decided me to keep my new friend a secret from everyone. My mother and brother did not know about him, and to this day I have never spoken of him to any member of my family. Nanny Grace, even if she suspected something, knew nothing of my yew tree refuge, and in any case was not about to admit to her employer that she did not know where I was at all hours of the day. I know I never told her of the name Gundagai McGinty.

I learned that my new friend had been born in Australia. His father was of Irish extract, and although I never met him I was certain in later years that this man must have had a whimsical humour coupled with his sense of alliteration, for he named his son after a mining town made famous around that time by a popular song. The lyrics told the story of a miner and the faithful dog he ordered to guard his lunch-box at the entrance to the mine shaft while he went to work. There was a rock fall and the miner died; his workmates knew what had happened when they came along and found the dog still ferociously guarding the lunch-box. That was good stuff to sing about:

"The dog sat on the tucker-box ninety miles from Gundagai ..."

If the lyricist was not Banjo Patterson himself, it was someone who must have thought just like him, but then the Australians were always good and sentimental balladeers.

I also learned that at least one member of the McGinty family had been forcibly landed on Tasmania in the early 1800's. Gun was proud of that, and as he was proud of it I thought it quite permissible for me to feel proud too. Somehow this dark ghost put a very special stamp on the most special person in my life right then. Such things were important.

In time, of course, there was another separation, but this time we were both a little older and ready for it. After the Japanese bombed Pearl Harbor they swept south through the Philippines, Malaya, Singapore, Indonesia, and the islands to the north of Australia. Then they bombed Darwin and other northern communities. That caught everyone's attention, especially us kids.

Wonks

Sydney turned out to be an ethereal final destination for our little family. By this point of my already somewhat irregular childhood Mother had remarried an American citizen working in Australia. Whatever the plans she and our step-father might have had for a continued residence in the country, they were rapidly blown apart by the maelstrom of events in the Pacific.

So far this saga has nudged me to the cusp of my seventh birthday – a truncated history, but not inaccurate. It is funny how what one person considers "normal" another will judge to be unseemly chaos. I suppose it depends on environment, what one comes to know. For my brother and me at the time everything seemed copacetic.

Somersaults

Brothers

Years later, in northern British Columbia, I came to this precise point in explaining my background to a prospective employer. In what seemed a relaxed sort of conversation he had asked me to talk about my childhood. No harm, I thought; I was not long-winded about it, but I didn't hold back. People ask questions; it's silly to play coy, so I answer them to the best of my ability – but it invariably gets them into a fearful tangle:

Where are you from? *Vancouver.* You don't have a Canadian accent. *No, because I finished school in Britain.* Oh? How come? What did your father do? *He was a rancher in the Caribou.* Really – so you did all your schooling in Britain? *No, most but not all of it.* Oh? Where else? *I started in Sydney, Australia. Continued in California, Ohio, New York, Montréal and Toronto – then Britain.* What did you do when you finished school? *British Army ... Mau Mau ... Malaya ...*

The questions tend to tumble out a bit faster than the answers.

On this occasion my inquisitor had appeared genuinely interested, but at the juncture we have arrived at just now, he held up his hand, ending with a word that sounded like malarkey. It was unclear to me, but it appeared he thought I was trying to make a monkey of him.

As I rose to leave his office he said:

"You've either had the most extraordinary childhood adventures of any man ever to walk in here seeking such a low-level job – or else you're the Flim-Flam Man!"

I didn't get the job, so guess he must have reckoned me the Flim-Flam Man.

I had barely begun my tale, but it was enough to breach his concept of normal. The fellow couldn't handle it. In this his problems were greater than mine.

But to demonstrate another side to this coin (for all it may be judged arcane penny thriller), while taking a break from writing this very page I became engrossed in conversation with a young lady in my local coffee shop, and she told me details of her own story – circumstances very different from mine, but with convolutions so familiar it will serve for me to make a point: she described another family, her own, in a state of more or less permanent metamorphosis – more nomadic than most yet in unorthodox ways the better for it. She had been born in Montréal, she said – Irish father, Filipino mother – school in Istanbul. Her family was close, nevertheless – "hung together" well. The father was currently on his way to a teaching post in Iceland, the mother was headed off to study techniques of Andean *artesenato* in Bolivia, and my new friend was herself shortly headed to Japan to work in a traditional ceramic studio.

Bravo! I liked it. Conventional normalcy, hardly; her story was thrilling. One should take heart, I thought, for her description of what others might consider an example of familial disconnect was charming, refreshingly wonky. Nomadic or tribal idiosyncrasies exist all around us, thankfully, and are by no means uncommon. It has been that way for centuries; this sort of lifestyle has always been acceptable – albeit by a minority on our scrubbed-clean-sweet-smelling-all-Canadian home turf. The great mass of a bland population, sorrowfully the phlegmatically well-ordered and well-sheltered western mind of another normalcy – blunted to the point of mortification – finds it difficult to get around their unusual. To the acquisitive, a man is abnormal if his path through life abjures the standard protocol for the making of money and the paying of his bills.

But there is poetry in the difference, and no amount of coin could either buy it or write it another way.

The real abnormality is that the nomads I describe are not more widely recognized for the most precious cargo they are (and cargo is, frequently, exactly what they are!) for they can contribute to this whirling orb zaniness sufficient to twizzle the minds of those who do not dare themselves. If people could look at – and see – the rich fabric of our lives with knowledge and toleration it would facilitate great robustness of spirit, egg all of us on to live amazing stories with all manner of fascinating warps and weaves. How to run past greed and envy, stick-in-the-mud idiocy? Remain close to, or imitate, a wonk.

Sceptics are common – and dull.

Pearl Harbor was attacked on December 7, 1941. The Japanese conquest of the Malay States and Singapore followed, and had been completed by mid-February, 1942. On February 19, the Japanese bombarded Darwin and followed up with nearly one hundred additional air raids. Both the city and, indeed, the remainder of Australia were poorly defended. Most battle-ready units of the Australian army were fighting the Italians and Germans in North Africa, so it seemed there was little to prevent an invading Japanese force from sweeping south across the great interior desert. We were told Australia's homeland service personnel, spread coast-to-coast in a line crossing the continent, would have presented a Japanese onslaught with no greater defence than a solitary soldier every three kilometres.

Pacific Run

It was all happening that close – a long way from where we lived in Sydney, but close enough that Mother thought it best to return to North America, if possible. Leaving our step-father to follow on behind, our mother and Nanny bundled my brother and myself onto one of the last American passenger ships still in port.

Mother had her own truly harrowing account of her family's wartime crossing of the Pacific Ocean. Over the years it grew more frightening with her every retelling, but the passage of time has also permitted me to filter out what happened. My brother and I both assembled our own sets of memories, and we often found ourselves comparing notes; my own have been filed away in obscure recesses of my yet fairly active and fertile mind these past years. Every now and then I have taken them out and buffed them up; even without Mother's prompting and filling out of detail, there had always been numerous elements that could be tucked away – a personal picture indelibly scoured into the imagination of the near seven-year-old I was by then.

There was more besides, I was to understand later:

The ship on which we sailed was named the S.S. President Grant. An American passenger vessel that also carried some cargo and mail, its regular run was between Los Angeles and Manila in the Philippines. However, the Japanese invasion of the islands had been so swift that the ship had been caught in port with more than half of its crew absent on shore leave. The captain had the slimmest opportunity to bolt for the open sea, a necessary chance he felt he had to take if he wanted to avoid having his vessel captured, or bombed at dockside. He held off as long as he could; some of the crew were able to return as the bombing of the city was in progress, and with them came a group of frantic nuns from a local convent anxious to escape what they were sure would be their certain evil fate if caught by marauding Japanese soldiers. With few charts for the seas he now found it necessary to navigate, the captain picked his way through the myriad islands that dotted the Celebes Sea, the Straits of the Moluccas, then the Banda and Arafura Seas. He made Darwin but, instead of entering port, decided to head east then south off the Queensland coast. There he had to manoeuver the length of the Great Barrier Reef in order to bring his ship safely to Sydney; here he was permitted to replenish some scarce foodstuffs, but not to acquire the charts he needed to make his way back to Los Angeles. These last had been in short supply. In the end he achieved the entire feat – Manila-Sydney-Wellington-Los Angeles – with little more than the assistance of a school atlas and the overlap of charts he had for his customary Los Angeles-to-Manila run.

We nearly ran on the rocks as we approached Wellington, New Zealand, and were so close to them we could make out, through the thick mist that hung over the channel, hundreds of seals at play along the shoreline. The entire ship's company was summoned to boat stations where we lined up quietly on the deck ready to abandon ship when the order would be given. It never came, but I remember breaking the electric silence by throwing a well-calculated tantrum; I insisted on taking along my favourite teddy bear, a koala glove-puppet sewn of kangaroo hide. I had named him (in my mind he was a masculine entity) Frankly. At first Nanny had insisted I leave him in the cabin along with my other toys, but I kicked up such an embarrassing rumpus my exasperated mother snarled:

"Oh, Nanny! For God's sake let him have the damned thing!"

Nanny returned to the cabin and fetched Frankly. Clutching him desperately to my life jacket I made up my mind that, come what may, we would share together whatever fate befell the two of us.

More than once thereafter I had occasion to remind my mother of her unkind and offhand words. To the entire family's utter consternation and bewilderment, Frankly and I were inseparable until I was into my teens, by which time he was little more than a worn and shapeless but fanatically defended leather glove. I wonder if adults ever really stop to think of the importance of a child's Number One Teddy Bear. It will never do to be offhand or callous about such things.

Significant impressions crowd my mind from our wartime Pacific crossing; it was a journey that any child would remember, as a child remembers, but the details came later – and rather soberly – augmented by Mother's imaginative explanations. The most dramatic episode involved outrunning the unfriendly attentions of two Japanese submarines.

Our on-board radio operator was from a Japanese immigrant family living in San Francisco. He spoke the language fluently and was able to pick up chatter between two enemy submarines searching specifically for the President Grant – an American passenger ship they correctly deduced was heading from Wellington to Suva on a more or less direct route to its home port of Los Angeles. The destruction of a ship named for one of America's most illustrious presidents would doubtless prove a mighty propaganda coup. It might be assumed they knew nothing of the unscheduled precious cargo we had taken on board at Wellington – one hundred and twenty pilots of the Royal New Zealand Air Force, all aiming to get to Canada for the completion of their flying training. Or perhaps they did know about them.

Stranger, how had the Japanese known the name of the ship, or that we were in those waters?

From the time we had left Sydney two little Dutch sisters travelling with their parents had been collecting the ship's lunch and dinner menus – scores of them snatched off the dining tables at the end of every meal. Neatly printed up each day on the shipboard press, they were complete with colourful headings revealing a picture of the ship, its name, company logo and, tellingly, the date. As we left New Zealand behind, however, the girls decided they no longer wanted their by now unwieldy collection of table cards, so they heaved the whole lot overboard. Our alert radio operator sounded the alarm when he learned from the conversations between crewmen of two Japanese submarines that numbers of the cardboard menus had been found floating on the surface of the sea. Clearly we were in the area; all they had to do was find us.

The ship was blacked out at night. All port holes were covered by stiflingly thick cloth curtains, some were painted black or boarded up. It was forbidden to turn on the dimmest of lights without the cabin first being inspected by a member of the crew. In addition, now, a frantic call went out for total silence. No one was allowed to talk above a whisper, socks were worn over shoes, and ship's personnel patrolled regularly to ensure these essential orders were obeyed. The President Grant sailed like a ghost ship, only her engines thump-thump-thumping her constant hydro-sonic tocsin over the stillness of a sultry sea to signal our whereabouts as she attempted to cut her mad escape. There was a sense of dread that lay over us in those days after we had left Wellington, a tension that spread across the decks of the ship and filtered down her corridors into the salons and every cabin – the sort of silence all lively children find threateningly incomprehensible. It was an alarming and meaningless adult thing – deliberately and harshly imposed to spoil our fun – for all the adults were suddenly aware we were now the target of merciless Japanese combatants who had made known their intent to kill us. The specific threat never quite penetrated my intellect, but the heaviness of foreboding is a thing I can recall in an instant.

The captain had immediately changed course on hearing of the subs, heading his ship almost due east into the vast anonymity of the South Pacific, somewhere between latitudes 30 and 40. After what seemed like the passage of weeks we sat dithering at anchor off Pitcairn Island, anticipating a submarine attack, but fearful of going ashore in case the place had been infiltrated with Japanese agents – two days or so of fruitless radio communication, and then we struck out towards the coast of northern Chile. There a turn to the north took us into Peruvian waters where authorities at Mollendo refused permission for us to dock, and we were unable to load by now desperately needed vitals.

The sudden influx of over one hundred air force personnel at Wellington, all of them requiring sustenance, had thrown the ship's galley into confusion, but a decision had been made earlier – forlorn optimism, as it turned out – to stock up with fruits and vegetables on our arrival at Suva, only a few days north of Wellington. As we never arrived there we were now faced with an insufficiency of food to cope with the greater number of passengers now taking part in this prolonged dash for the ship's home port of Los Angeles.

Our sudden right turn into the expanse of the Pacific Ocean, abandoning the Suva stop, brought about colossal shortage and hardship, and I recall numerous meetings of the adults in the ship's main passenger lounge when the children were confined for long hot afternoons in the dining salon. For endless days a scorching sun remained on our port side, and a lassitude seemed to overcome everyone on the ship. The adults set up a roster in order to cope with children who did not know what to do with themselves – some of whom, indeed, were starting to become nervous and quite ill. It was only the older minors who were even vaguely aware of our collective predicament; the younger ones understood little – mostly that what passed for meals became one hideously extended complaint.

"Fish – again! Y-euh!"

The ship's cook and his helpers did the best they could, but by halfway across the ocean everyone was subsisting, in the main, on a bilious diet of flying fish. At sun-up every morning and sun-down every evening these strange creatures would rise from the surface of the glass-calm sea, gliding sometimes for hundreds of metres. Lots of them would smack into the side of our hull and fall back into the water, stunned or dead; others would be fortunate enough to complete their phenomenal aerial journeys, sometimes inches above the surface of the water, then plop back in to commence the sport all over again; yet others would fly high enough clear of the water to soar over the ship's foredeck altogether. There were those, such was their fate, that would smack into the ship's superstructure and fall flopping to the deck. On occasion, and causing great consternation when it happened, one would swoop in through an open port hole. Cookie and a couple of the swabbies (or anyone else for that matter; it was not unusual to have one land at your feet while pacing the deck, or even to be hit by one) would scoop them up and take them to the galley.

In addition to quantities of fish Cookie's pantries also stocked what seemed to be a limitless supply of canned corned beef. Unfortunately, after a few days this proved to be no pleasurable gastronomic alternative. We grew sick of it about as quickly as if the cans had been filled with flying fish. There was no fresh water. For the children there was a large supply of powdered milk; this was mixed with a brackish liquid filtered from the sea through a condenser and which, with the occasional oil slick on the surface, we were assured was the purest of waters. It tasted foul no matter what quantity of milk powder was added to it, but it was the only "refreshment" available for minors so we drank it by the gallon anyway. Shipboard diet, for everyone, including children, was this abominable choice between the fish or the canned beef – three meals a day, no bread or vegetables. For a few days after leaving New Zealand there were potatoes, canned peas and carrots, but these luxuries were quickly exhausted. So was the flour with which the cook had been able to bake bread during the earlier days of our ordeal. Many passengers chose to skip mealtimes, preferring instead to tap into the bar in the ship's lounge where there was no shortage of every variety of whate'er's your pleasure.

Boredom was a big factor for everyone, but mostly for the children. They didn't understand it. For a time there was a superhuman effort on the part of all the adults to entertain not only the children, but one another as well. There would be soirées once we were well out into the open ocean to which all children were welcome. Some of the passengers would dance or sing, some would play instruments, or perform conjuring tricks. The airmen we had picked up in Wellington were an upbeat and jolly crowd. They performed the Maori Haka on a couple of evenings, scaring the living daylights out of the kids – to the degree that someone suggested it would be a good way to induce us all to leap overboard and thus be out of their hair. It is hard to believe there was a single adult on the ship who was not heartily sick of us – our perpetual high jinks, yelling and whining, demanding attention. The adult roster of minders worked to some degree, but as time wore on their attentions wavered. Several of the airmen offered to help, but they themselves were hugely afflicted by the tedium and numbers of them preferred to care for us from their barstools.

But then one day there was an extraordinary occurrence – and by chance it was one of those things destined to trigger within me a benefit that has remained a constant throughout my life.

In the midst of this wearisome phase of the journey, when the onerous monotony had well established itself and it seemed as though the ship would be sailing forever, like some slow comet crossing eternal space, who should come to our rescue but Cookie – the ship's head cook – a quiet fellow who generally remained in his quarters and seemed to talk mostly about fish and canned corned beef. He made model airplanes, and agreed to put on a show of them in the ship's dining salon. The children especially were enthusiastic, so Cookie gathered all sixteen of us together and raised his finger in warning. His models were his treasure, he said, his greatest pride. He admonished us to look, but on no account to touch. He made a point of getting our solemn agreement, then told us that tomorrow morning, after breakfast, we were all to retire quietly to the main lounge and wait while he placed his exhibit on the dining tables. He would call us in by two's or three's with our parents, and there was to be no misbehaviour, no pushing or shoving – otherwise he would close it all down on the spot.

As a child, I do not believe I was ever so enchanted as I was by this extraordinary exhibit of Cookie's model-making talent. His models were big, beautifully executed, a veritable Farnborough Air Show of his exceptional talent. They were assembled from scratch, using old boxwood, paper, cardboard and wire – whatever he could find by rummaging about in the bowels of the ship during his long trans-Pacific crossings. He kept his collection in his cabin, in a not-much-used storage room off the galley, and on various shelves and in nooks and crannies in the deep dark and forbidden (to children) secret recesses around the galley area. Some of these models had wing spans that surely reached sixty centimetres – their found materials cut and shaped and shaved, then most delicately painted. From the cheap wood used to box fruit and grocery supplies he had fashioned squadrons of aircraft of every sort, design and colour – and not merely little knock-offs. They were substantially-sized replicas of the airplanes of both past and present – and from lands most children had never heard tell of. There were racers and fighters, bombers and liners, seaplanes and bi-planes, some from the earliest days of flight, others models of the British, American, German and Japanese fighters of the current war. This amazing factory was Cookie's passion and what he did all by himself during his off-hours. He was showing us his collection of about forty of them – a privilege I could recognize even at the age of seven.

Almost every table of the salon had at least two airplanes on top – superb models of craft I had never imagined. My eye was caught by a three-engine transport plane that Cookie told me had been used to fly across oceans in earlier days. Then there was a lumbering flying boat, maybe the biggest model of them all, with its wide hull and outriggers. A Catalina. All these planes, fighters and trainers or aircraft from the First World War, were complete with decals and markings. And of course there was a replica of the bright red three-winged fighter aircraft flown and made famous by Baron von Richthofen ...

The best part came at the close of the show when Cookie told us we could each keep one model for ourselves. This was better than Christmas. That morning he gave away sixteen models that must have taken him hours of care and patience to build, and we were free to choose which. I chose what I thought was the best of the lot – a replica of a Sopwith Camel, the First World War bi-plane. For hours after that day I would hold it aloft in my hand, swooping it and diving it – but looking at it from every conceivable angle. I was intrigued with its shape, its struts and stanchions, but especially by its various perspectives as I made it fly across my vision, or towards me or away from me. I didn't know it at the time, but I would use my artistic eye to poke around behind it, to discover it in each of its three-dimensions. I was intrigued by the way it changed shape and line – and to this day I firmly believe this was my entry into the world of three-dimensional thinking. Artistically I have always thought in three dimensions, and I believe this was manifested for me at this point.

Invisible to us children until now, Cookie had suddenly become a godsend – a model-making Pied Piper. He knew how to charm the children aboard the President Grant and, by doing so, ingratiate himself with all the adults as well. Somewhere between Pitcairn Island and the Chilean coast, the fellow had performed a small miracle. He succeeded with the children where every other adult had begun to fail miserably. Up to this point almost everyone on board had been ready to serve Cookie's head on a platter in retribution for the collapsing quality of his cuisine. Now all was peace and joy, mountains of goodwill and gracious understanding – though the meals did not change a jot.

Cookie paid dearly for our silence and co-operation, for he had given away a great deal of his finest labours of love. But from that moment on he was our hero – and he had no trouble whatsoever getting us all to do precisely as he said. Never mind that he was in cahoots with our parents, who were in turn greatly aware from that day forward till the end of the voyage they owed him dearly. They were more than happy to let Cookie call the shots with the kids.

Social Whirl

Mother told us years later that shipboard life was just the same sort of a social whirl in wartime as might be expected in peacetime – perhaps, considering the cruel fate of the war, a bit more reckless. There were not that many ladies on board and certainly Mother, Nanny Grace, and the few others were given a vigorous run by numbers of the one hundred and twenty young pilots with whom we travelled. Whatever Mother's faults (I was not counting them in those days, but in hindsight I have to acknowledge she probably sported a few) she tried to maintain a certain sense of propriety and discretion in her personal conduct in front of servants – not always successfully.

Although "one of the family," Nanny Grace was expected to know her place. (How often I heard that phrase!) She was considered a servant and treated as such – very often not well. At this time Nanny Grace was a good looking young lady, a conscientious, faithful and considerate employee, responsible and, from what I can remember, even a little prim and naïve. She was a good Christian girl with a high moral sense of right and wrong. Although a very different creature, Mother would have recognized and respected all these qualities in Nanny Grace and, indeed, was very likely even intimidated by such an open display of innocence coupled with a complete absence of servility. Moreover for the greater part of each day Nanny relieved our mother of most of the burden imposed by two highly active little boys, and our dear Mama was not one to pass up such a good thing when it came her way. Her face towards Nanny Grace, then, was a theatrical quick-change combination of discipline, cajolery, sweet reason and haughty demand, all of it leavened with the not entirely self-serving traits of a kindly confidante. From Mother's stance, as she explained to me quite matter-of-factly in later discussion, it was a question of maintaining face, and involved no small measure of acting skill and blatant hypocrisy. It was quite simply the way certain things were accomplished by that generation of "haves," a performance akin to "colonial" dominance – but at a time when colonial attitudes were a commonplace of the current ideas of class difference. Among those practiced in the deceptive arts, such duplicity was quite acceptable.

Although aware that the more boisterous New Zealanders aboard gave each of the shipboard ladies a whirl, I am quite sure that Mother's innate conservatism confined her socializing to the far fewer senior officers rather than the young pilots. But she was a graciously social person by nature, so on amicable terms with everyone. Often I heard her express her admiration for these spirited and gallant young fellows on their way to make war against Hitler.

The pilots, though, gave poor Nanny Grace barely a moment's peace. I have photographs of her, and she was a lovely young woman. It is hardly surprising she turned the heads of so many bored and ship-bound young men. Maybe, being the innocent she was, she posed them all a considerable challenge. There was no small amount of ribbing involved, some of which I suspect I might have understood even better than Nanny. At last, though, these constant attentions became too much for her, and in confusion she appealed to Mother for help.

Mother merely waited until the evening cocktail hour and spoke directly to the air force commander.

On deck parade the following morning the men were collectively told to cool it. There was a moment of clamorous good humour. A mighty groan went up, and a voice from one of the back ranks piped:

"Chrikey! The war's over already! The enemy is asking for mercy!"

"Your enemy is my bosom buddy, mate!"

Laughter, but they cooled it.

Our special friend among the New Zealanders was a fellow we called Winkie. Always polite, considerate, good-humoured and willing, he had become a particular friend to both Mother and Nanny Grace, and most of our contact with the other pilots flowed through him. He and some of his friends graciously agreed to babysit, giving Mother and Nanny Grace – and others – a welcome break from constantly trying to entertain irksome shipboard children. Youngsters confined for weeks on end to the deck and cabin space of a ship can become mightily obnoxious. Staff, parents and pilots did their utmost to produce some sort of programme for us, but there was not a great selection of activity on board that could stretch to all of our waking hours, and neither could any adult's singular stamina.

Winkie had his own special sort of programme. It was spontaneous and all the children loved him for his sense of fun and childlike playfulness. He must have come from a large family. Strong, fair-haired, with eyes flashing and the seeming ability to look out of the back of his head, Winkie was always good for a romp, a practical joke or a game of chase. He got people laughing quickly, and knew when to cut off so there were seldom any tears. And when from time-to-time there were tears, he was the first to pick a child up, show precisely the correct measure of sympathy, and jolly everyone back into good humour.

One day I came on deck to find Nanny Grace talking to an airman I disliked. I was jealous of him, protective of my Nanny – especially from him. Winkie and a few of the other pilots were standing in a group some distance off, and they signalled me over.

"Hey!" said Winkie conspiratorially. "Looks like Tiger over there is bothering your Nanny. Better chase him off."

I looked over, thinking of running at the fellow and kicking him on his shin.

"Use this!" said Winkie winking, and he handed me a long-handled wooden games mallet, about the size and weight one would use for croquet.

Without hesitation I grabbed the weapon, swung it over my head, and flew at the unsuspecting pilot. He really could not have seen me coming, and I smashed the mallet down on his sandaled foot with all my force. As he danced away in pain I swung again, this time catching him a mighty crack on his arm at the side of his elbow. I raised the hammer above my head for a third blow but he saw it coming and turned. Even so I hit him, very hard in the small of his back, and by now he was only trying to get away from this little demon. Winkie and his companions were screaming with laughter, but Tiger was in serious pain and by now trying desperately to put some distance between us. He hobbled off down the deck as fast as he could, clutching his injured elbow and dodging the further blows I tried to rain on him as he fled. He ran down a companion-way to the deck below, tearing off the heel of one sandal on the top step. I held it aloft like a trophy and turned triumphantly to Winkie for approval.

"Catch that little bugger and disarm him!" the injured pilot called up from the lower deck. "He's bloody hurt me, for Christ's sake! I think he's broken my arm."

Nanny Grace was horrified and she told me to stay with Winkie and company while she raced down to the lower level to assist the poor man. Neither one reappeared right away and Winkie became a little alarmed. He left me with his friends and went below himself to see what was the matter.

Nanny Grace came back an hour or so later. Saying nothing she took me to my cabin and ordered me to stay there. She was upset, but not overly angry with me.

The following day, on deck, I again ran into a group of the pilots standing at the rails. Among them were Winkie and the pilot I had attacked. I held back, afraid, and Winkie came over to me.

"Don't be afraid," he said. "It was my fault. Game got a little rough. Here! Come on over and talk to Tiger. He's really not such a bad fellow."

He led me over to the pilots, and all of them were smiling at me – except the one I had attacked. Tiger had a twinkle in his eye, which put me at ease, but I also read something in his look like bemusement, even surprise. I noticed he was wearing bedroom slippers, and limping; his right arm was in a sling across his chest.

"Well!" he said. "Looks like I've been wounded. You're going to have to fight my war for me!"

Obviously this was a lad not to be trifled with.

Winkie was to receive an unpleasant injury himself before our journey was complete and I was implicated in that event, too. My brother and I were visiting with him and his cabin mates one afternoon and, as usual, there was a deal of horsing about. I was sitting on an upper bunkbed wearing an American sailor's hat that Winkie had somehow acquired. Winkie was playing as if to take it away from me, making a grab for it. I was defending myself and the hat I now claimed was mine. I whacked at him with a heavy military web belt every time he approached.

Winkie could see I meant business and did not mean to get hit. No doubt he had my treatment of Tiger in mind. He paused looking away from me till I was off guard, then suddenly lunged. But he caught his knee a mighty crack on a piece of metal that was part of the lower bunk, and he rolled on the floor in agony. I leapt down on top of him beating him on his shoulders with the belt, but his cries were of genuine pain and his cabin mates hauled me off and calmed me down.

Winkie's knee swelled to twice its normal size. We watched it grow.

He wound up with his leg in a splint quite a bit more elaborate than the one on Tiger's arm. For much of the rest of the trip he could not leave his cabin, and that was the sad end of our rompings together. Months later, when we had eventually arrived in Montréal, Mother received a letter from him. His kneecap had been broken and he had been grounded. We did not hear from him again after that, so never learned whether or not he got to fly in the war – or if he survived it.

Scurvy

Few portions of our Pacific crossing could have been more indelibly registered with me than, at journey's end, when our ship steamed into the sanctuary of the port of Los Angeles and several of the passengers (my brother and myself among them) were promptly hospitalized. The run from Wellington to Los Angeles had taken thirty-eight days, and several people were ill.

Big ugly bruises the size of my hands covered my legs, my abdomen, my flanks and upper arms. I did not feel ill, though I was told I was. But I did feel my whole body had become fishlike – my bruises not so different from the colour of the flying fish that had smacked into the ship's superstructure and fallen to the deck, stunned and squishy. The fish that was my body looked as though it had been several days out of the water, soft and putrid. There was a smell ... I assumed there was some connection between myself and the fish I had eaten – and, in a way, I suppose there was.

My brother had the same symptoms, but somewhat worse, and he had been running a fever. I was pleased with myself, smug that I should feel so well and that he should feel and look so rotten. Both of us were put into hospital in Santa Monica to undergo intense observation and care – a curious experience for two young boys who really had no idea of the gravity of their situation. We were attended by rounds of curious doctors and nurses.

Scurvy. One man had died of it on the trip, we were told. In the meantime Mother rented a cottage in one of the valleys up behind Santa Monica, not far from a dam.

My brother was confined to his bed for a period until his fever abated. I never was, and was permitted to prowl the corridors of the hospital in my white dressing gown, making friends and chatting to staff, doctors and other patients. There was a sun room in which I spent long hours at play with a variety of paper cut-outs, blocks and toys – but the chief toys of them all were the Sopwith Camel given to me by Cookie, and my adored Frankly, the koala glove-puppet. The Sopwith Camel was important, right up there with my buddies Christopher Thistlethwaite and Gundagai McGinty; but there was nothing in the wide world dearer to me than Frankly.

Early one bright morning, while we still lay abed in our ward, my brother and I heard the long and distinctive roar of approaching airplane engines. They were low and screaming – two single-engine aircraft hurtling right over the hospital. We heard them from far enough away that we were able to leap out of our beds and run to a window across the corridor. There was a large courtyard garden behind the hospital, and we could see the planes as they appeared to clip the tops of some far palms and disappear from view. Wing-tip to wing-tip, each of us was sure we had seen red discs painted on the undersides. Later we were told they had been Japanese Zeros, that they had flown over the coastline dropping pamphlets, and that this had been the unique time the defences of the United States mainland had been breached. True or false? Who's to say?

On the occasion of my brother's sixtieth birthday – which would have made it some fifty years later – I happened to be having dinner with a group of Americans who were staying for a holiday in a hotel near my home in Portugal. For some reason I recounted this childhood event. One of the guests was an engineer and a scientist, a man of precise and efficient confidence – a man of knowledge, I assumed, but a talker and a poor listener. He accused me of lying, assuring me that no foreign planes breached the security of the United States mainland during the Second World War.

"Nice story, but not a word of truth in it," he said brusquely.

"I'm not sure you are entirely correct," chimed in one of the ladies present, trying to rescue me from being bullied. "I remember when I was in Oregon there was a town party in one of the communities – celebrating the return of a Japanese flyer who had been shot down and landed there by parachute during the war ..."

"He didn't come by parachute," interrupted one of the diners at the table. "He arrived by balloon. Famous incident. He was taken prisoner, of course, and for years after the war he would return to visit the community where he was treated so well. Occasion for an annual festival, I believe."

So many "barrack room lawyers!" My first inquisitor continued to explain to me why my story had been such hogwash.

"If they were Zeros they had a range of no more than three hundred miles, and so would have had to have been carrier-based, which means the carriers would have had to have come within at least one hundred and fifty miles of the American coast. I can assure you no Japanese ships got that close ... I expect what you and your brother saw were two U.S. planes. There was – still is – an airfield at Santa Monica. My guess is that a couple of them flew in low – maybe one of them was in trouble ..."

So maybe I wasn't a liar – only mistaken.

"Maybe that nurse who told you they were Zeros dropping pamphlets was playing a game with your little mind ..."

Could be. Still, it is never good to mess with the memory of a seven-year-old.

At this distance in time it is hard to be certain of what I remember, or to distinguish between reality and what I am sure I remember being told. Childhood fantasies and certainties are not easily explained. It is also quite possible that my ungracious acquaintance was himself in error. Some years after this dinner party I had occasion to check a few facts: the Japanese Zero was modified numerous times during the Second World War for different types of operational use, but the basic A6M series, commonly in combat use from 1940 to 1945, was designed as both a carrier and land-based machine. It had a range in excess of 2,600 kilometres – or more than 1,600 miles.

A young nurse who often came to our room and seemed to take a liking to us volunteered the information one morning that the ward a few paces down the hall from ours was occupied by a badly injured Japanese pilot whose plane had been shot down.

Later my brother and I tiptoed to the door of the pilot's ward and peered inside.

It was a big room with the customary trappings of a hospital ward, and a solitary bed off to one side. The occupant was so swathed in bandages and silence that we really could not tell whether he was Japanese or a Viking.

Silence as we stared – but neither of us was entirely sure what it was we were staring at.

There was an almost imperceptible and laboured revolution underneath the bedding, a slight realignment of traction apparatus. A bandaged head revolved slowly on a pillow, and from the depths of the white folds two eyes peered at us with the same burning curiosity as we peered at them.

Nothing was said – a long moment of pain that created a tension between the three of us, staring. Then we ran, and our scampering footfalls in the corridor broke the spell.

"Is he really Japanese?" my brother asked the young nurse.

"Yes," she assured us.

"Why don't you kill him?" my brother demanded, for small boys who had heard so much propaganda could not reasonably be expected to think in any other way towards such a despised enemy.

"Oh no!" said the nurse. "We are going to treat his injuries and save his life, not take it."

"But why?" my brother pushed. "If you had a pistol you could shoot him..."

"Stop talking like that!" scolded the nurse. "Even if he is an enemy, he is a gallant soldier – and he is sick and in pain. Don't talk that way about a man who has tried so hard to do what he feels he must!"

But my brother was not convinced, and when the nurse had left the room he tried to convince me.

"I'd kill the dirty Jap!"

I cannot remember my reaction, but I probably agreed that my brother's logic was correct. He could be pretty persuasive.

Our neighbour in the Santa Monica cottage had been made a war widow during the bombing at Pearl Harbor. A good looking but frail and mostly silent woman in her forties, Mrs. Sanders was perched tightly on our living room sofa in tears one afternoon when I entered the house. My mother sat silently with her, arm comfortingly around her shoulders. Mrs. Sanders looked very old that day, my mother contrastingly youthful. I did not know what had happened, but I felt awkward so left the room again to wander alone in the orchard between our two houses. I was aching to go indoors again, maybe with the excuse to collect a toy, to ask Mother what the matter was. But I felt frightened of other people's miseries in case they were somehow transmitted to me. I would have helped, had it been possible, but my motivation would have been entirely self-serving. By assisting to clean up somebody else's mess I would be trying to make certain their bad medicine was not passed on to me. Compassion was not a sentiment I had really grasped as yet. Mine was a very childlike logic, but as I could not be absolutely sure of it I remained outside, confused and hiding among the tree trunks and the tall grasses that surrounded them.

Presently Mrs. Sanders came out of our house and cut through the orchard towards the garden door of her own home. She saw me and came over before I could duck out of sight. Bending down so our heads were level she took hold of one of my arms and looked into my eyes. She was still crying but trying to put on a brave face and smile through her tears. I frowned.

"Don't be sad, Mrs. Sanders," was all I could think to say.

She said nothing in reply, but hugged me and then turned and ran quickly to her back door. I knew she was trying to hide from me a fresh flood of tears – a flood that welled up from very deep.

"What's wrong with Mrs. Sanders?" I called to my mother as I marched back into our living room – but Lord! Mother was sobbing too.

My brother had been out all afternoon with some of Mother's friends but later that evening, after he had arrived home, we were both told to sit down in the kitchen. Our mother had something important to say to us.

"You know that Mrs. Sanders' husband was killed at Pearl Harbor last year, don't you?"

We nodded seriously.

"Well, Mr. and Mrs. Sanders had a son who was a flyer in the navy," Mother continued. "She was told earlier today that her son, also, has been killed."

Being killed did not mean anything to me at that age. But I did understand the concept that killing was one of the consequences of war; I could not quite get a handle on the significance of death, the permanence of it. Did it hurt as badly as getting my ears boxed by my brother? If I got killed would I lose the war? I clammed up and looked at my brother. He would know about such things and could explain to me later.

My brother was bigger than me and I lived in mortal fear of him. I could never quite bring myself to trust him fully. I had learned that when he could he would defeat me – even hurt me – and in any case defeat was a great hurt. A jab or a jibe, my brother seemed ever ready with one or the other.

So I said nothing, but now as I looked at him I saw fear written on his face. Listening to what our mother was saying he looked pained, stunned. His eyes bulged as he stared at our mother, and they turned red, blood-shot. But he did not cry. I could sense then he understood something I did not.

Looking back to that incident over the intervening years I find myself thinking not of the immense sorrow felt by Mrs. Sanders, nor of the pain of death suffered by the two people she loved most in the world. She is certainly dead herself, now, and that small nuclear family as a whole is no more than a puff of smoke, a story nobody knows anything about anymore. Maybe there is some writing on a piece of paper somewhere, or a name chiseled onto a plaque. But the whole incident, in retrospect, concerns my brother at that moment in the kitchen.

Two men had died tragically, but it did not evoke in me anything like the impact I can feel even now at realizing my bully brother's vulnerability at going-on-eleven. The deaths of two men he never knew, whether he later remembered the matter or not, hit him hard when he listened to our mother talking in the kitchen that day, and I guess I was affected, too. At that moment I could weigh my brother's pain more easily than I could weigh the pain of our neighbour, and I remember feeling a tremendous empathy for him. I wanted him to be sure I was right there beside him.

A milestone passed. Despite our dreadful squabblings and quarrels I think it was that day I learned to love my brother.

J. J. Hespeler-Boultbee

A week or so after this Mrs. Sanders appeared at our house again and spoke to my mother. Would the boys like to see her son's toys? We walked beside her to her house and entered through the garden door into a rumpus room in which a gigantic billiard table had been set at one end.

Laid out on the green baize of the table-top were two mighty armies of tiny painted lead soldiers – the one side dressed in the dark blue jackets of the American Civil War's northern troops facing their opponents in the grey uniforms of the southerners. There must have been a hundred pieces on each side. In the front were the action troops – soldiers lying down aiming their rifles, or kneeling; some charging, some tossing grenades. There were infantry men, artillery men and a colour party with flags unfurled. There were stretcher-bearers, canons and mortars and their operators, and a sizeable cavalry charging their opposite numbers arranged at the other end of the table. Drawn up to the rear of these action troops were ranks of soldiers in formation – some standing at attention, others marching, and still more cavalrymen on parade. There were generals in beards and medals and dress uniforms, some on horseback, some on foot; there were bugle boys and drummer boys and musicians, and nurses and scouts and even a few civilians whom we took to be recruits or regimental hangers on. Every piece was painted in exquisite detail.

My brother and I were enthralled, and walked round and round the table.

"Don't touch!" Mrs. Sanders said, and we had to hold our itching fingers behind our backs. We put our noses to the edge of the table and studied every piece. What a treat!

Of course we were tempted to ask, "Can I have one?" – and probably did, knowing how unashamedly forward we were. The answer, we knew it of course, had to be no. The set was complete and perfect in every detail.

"I've decided I'm going to give it to a museum," Mrs. Sanders told us. "That way more children will be able to see them and enjoy them, the way you do. But I won't be taking them to the museum right away, so any time you want to come over here and look at them, why you have only to ask me."

She ushered us out and we went home; but we came back – several times over the next weeks, and she always said she was happy to see us. I liked her. She has popped into my mind countless times over the years. Courageous and kind lady she was. From her I learned something about courage and gentility – and in this way was introduced to nobility.

Once safely ashore Nanny Grace decided she had had enough. Working for Mother would have been an intense assignment; she needed the break. She had taken care of my brother and me since the day of my birth, cared for us as if we were hers. Now, despite Mother's most self-serving arguments, I am sure Nanny wanted nothing more than to return to the normalcy of her home in British Columbia, marry her beau and raise a family of her own. She vanished from our lives.[3]

Without Nanny's uncanny skills, her soothing and diplomatic patience, Mother was soon out of her depth. Her progeny were demanding and noisy, more intent on defeat than détente, seldom neutral. My brother and I were two unaccommodating little hellions who fought and yelled continuously. It was law, true, but anyone knowing our mother at that time might have been forgiven the conviction that she enrolled her two brats in junior school not because of any sense of responsibility she might have acknowledged as to preparing us for our respective futures, but in order to be rid of us for the periods of peace and quiet she could snatch during school hours. She bought each of us a pair of boxing gloves and ordered us to remain in the orchard area outside the house she had rented.

It was an after-school experiment in the tough love my big brother heartily enjoyed as he chased me around the trees, flailing his arms like a mine-sweeping battle tank. His fists may have been padded, but they hurt and reduced me to humiliation and tears all the same.

---

[3] Nanny Grace and I were to meet again when I moved to Victoria, B.C., some twenty-five years later. She saw my "byline" in the local newspaper, recognized my name and left a message at the editorial desk. A piece of paper was rolled into my typewriter: "Jeremy, call your Nanny." I visited her home in Esquimalt where her walls were festooned with photographs of her journeys, and those for whom she had also worked as Nanny. My brother and myself had been held up as examples for her own growing family; it was hard to read mischief in our framed baby pictures. From then on, no matter where I travelled for my work, Nanny and I remained in touch for the rest of her life.

We had both attended a private school in Sydney, and now we were signed into the public system in Santa Monica for a few months. It did not last long. Mother soon had us on the move again, this time by train across the country to Ohio. It took forever.

"Look, dear! There's the Mississippi …!"

"So? Where's Mr. Sippi?"

The query entered family legend.

We moved, *en bloc*, so to say, into the home of our step-father's family in Middletown, and for several months were enrolled at one of the local public schools there. The idea was to remain in Middletown until our step-father returned from Australia. We caught the tail end of the summer term and stayed until the New Year. I remember very little about the school itself, except that it was built of red brick, the boys and girls entering by separate doorways. I particularly remember a small but very unpleasant boy who was known as a bully. He took exception to our Australian accents, so muscled up to us. His name escapes me. Nobody at the school liked him, and even my brother walked around him. Everyone shunned this boy, but the more he was shunned the more obnoxious he became. Other children were frightened of him, and I was also except that I was curious enough about him to try to be friendly on one occasion – over our lunch boxes. He took an egg salad sandwich and a sausage from me, then walked away jeering loudly. I learned my lesson and from then on shunned him the way everyone else did.

School got out for summer vacation and we idled away the days in slow heat until one morning at breakfast we learned from the local newspaper – Mother read it out – that there had been a tragic drowning in the nearby river. Some boys had been playing on a raft, one had fallen off and been caught in a whirlpool. His body was found a day or so later washed among some reeds at the water's edge.

"It's dangerous down by the river," Mother told us. "I don't want you to go near there without me."

The boy who died was the bully from school. There was a picture of him as well as of his distraught parents. Why should they cry for him, I wondered, when he had been such a horrid little boy? I figured that had he been somewhat pleasanter he might not have been drowned. This, I was sure, was God's punishment for a bad boy – and God thenceforth stood a bit more prominently in my everyday reckonings, which is no doubt why I have any memories at all of such a brief stay at that school.

Our step-father arrived from Australia late in the fall, and was with his family that Christmas. His brother, David, was well-known for the rich tone of his voice, and sang in his local church choir. He would be singing a solo at the midnight mass, a big event the entire family would be attending – even our wheelchair-bound step-grandmother.

We all piled into the car and drove through deep winter snows to the church. On the way there, though, someone thought they smelled smoke. By the time we could all smell it, there were flames flickering onto the road from under the car's engine.

All out. Even Granny. I am not sure what it was that was burning, but we were still a long way from the church and would be late for David's solo if we could not be on our way quickly.

"Everyone make snowballs!" someone ordered, and by throwing the snow under the car and into the engine compartment we managed to smother the fire and soon be on our way. The solo was in progress as we arrived at the church.

David's voice soared to the roof rafters. I had never heard anything like it before. It filled every nook of space inside the church. Young as I was, I had not the least doubt this was a Christmas message being sung especially for me. David's voice was inspired, every note crisp like the tinkle of crystal.

When the solo was ended, and with the choir singing in unison other well-known hymns and anthems, I found I could easily recognize David's voice filtering through the others – a baritone I can hear still if I close my eyes and think of that Christmas midnight. The interior of the church – the space, the people, the white surplices of the choir, even the ceremony – it all runs together as part of the adventure we had had on the road getting there. It was the first white Christmas I can remember.

Middletown was to mark my first conscious encounter with God, conscience and the Great Hereafter – but the revelation managed to accomplish little in the way of modifying my behaviour, or that of my brother. I knew, and remember understanding, that in those months we were driving everyone nuts. We did not care. All that Ohio summer and winter my brother and I rearranged our step-grandmother's living room furniture to build forts and barricades. We used every cushion in the place to construct tunnels and hiding places. We tormented the aging sausage dog whose preference was to pass the entire day baking his brains under the front room's radiator. We would tug him and push him until, in desperation, he would flee to the backyard – and there we would throw sticks for him. If he failed to pick them up (he always failed to pick them up), we would throw the sticks at him until one of the maids would scream at us from the house and rush out to rescue the miserable animal. Silly mutt sausage, he would promptly return to baking his brains under the radiator. I am not sure if God saw any of that, but He probably did.

When the tin trays we used to slide down the carpeted stairway were taken away from us, the sideboard was ransacked for the household's rather more precious silver plate trays; they were more robust and made less noise, but it seemed this was not the main reason there was objection to our use of them. Once bent out of shape they were nowhere near as easily repaired as the tin ones. Re-plating them proved expensive.

And then there was the yelling and screaming … Mother called on God a few times about then, I seem to recall, but He was not paying her any attention. Maybe He felt she deserved what we were meting out.

One day after we had left Ohio and were able to reconstruct our moments of turmoil in conversations with Mother (our abhorrent behaviour was no doubt being held up as a lesson) she recounted how, had she possessed the equipment to monitor such things, she might have been able to log – from the moment of our arrival – a graph to show the daily levels of the family's exasperation. She claimed a palpable degree of relief descended over the household once our bags had been packed and we showed signs of moving on – and out. Our step-father worked at management level for a wartime steel production firm; once home he was never able satisfactorily to explain any of us to his Good Christian family. The wider complaint may have concerned all of us, our mere presence; but once he had arrived from Sydney the whole family singled him out for the Brobdingnagian share of blame, poor fellow. There was a collective sigh when he was posted (it happened quickly) to his company's head office in Manhattan – an epoch (it felt to be all of that) in which my brother and I were packed off to a boarding school first in Montréal, later to another one close to Toronto. The Holy Bible then became required reading.

Somersaults

The Commute

Precise chronology around this time remains a confusion. Our various moves were memorable, but I have mislaid the order in which they occurred; the dates and times are lost to me. I have tried to figure out a logical chronology that would make sense, but then "logic" and the rationale of Mother's ability to think on her feet (she was an impressive dancer) present an awkward scenario when squeezed side-by-side into the same paragraph. There are stretches of the imagination more believably witnessed than described. In fairly rapid succession my brother and I were enrolled at a boarding school in Montréal, then a public school in Montréal (its name eludes me), then a public school at Pelham, New York. After that came the boarding school outside Toronto where we remained enrolled for a full academic year. Our residences over this period were in Montréal, Québec; Old Greenwich, Connecticut; Pelham, New York, and finally Manhattan itself. In addition there were at least two long summers at the Seigniory Club at Montebello and a couple of winter holidays at Shawbridge – both of these places located in the province of Québec. Although not able to put every locale and event in its precise order, some pretty strong memories do poke themselves up – like blossoms out of season.

Of the Montréal boarding school, for instance, I recall that the headmaster's name was Mr. Mack, and that the wallpaper in the small boy's dormitory – an overall shade of blue – was decorated with airplanes, trains and cars. Cupcakes delivered daily by van to the school were what turned the misery of the place into a moment of treat (yellow blonde-cake and vanilla icing). Occasionally black and white films would be flickered onto a classroom screen, old newsreels which provided me my first images of war. It was mostly winter when we attended this school, though I also have images of playing in the muck of a spring run-off. We wore herring-bone knickerbockers and toques when there was sufficient snow to go tobogganing on the slopes of Mount Royal. The thaw and warm airs during the days brought on certain odours I can still recognize, oil on the roads and the smell of rivulets running through the mud at the sides of unpaved lanes. I played at building dams and sluices with muck and mud, channeling the run-off. The evenings were chill. Memories – but barely an individual soul.

While we were at this boarding school Mother took a small house in Old Greenwich, and would collect us there for holiday breaks. There were river flats nearby and on its watery maze of channels I paddled my first canoe-like boat. It was painted Cambridge blue on the outside, Oxford blue inside, and was ecumenically christened *We Two* – presumably because my brother was to have the same rights to its use as me. But he had a bicycle that took him off on whatever adventures pleased him, and in fact I had *We Two* mostly to myself. It became my vehicle of solitude, for I was content as a loner. I quickly became expert at guiding the little craft about and, although I could never have been far from home, it seemed to me I travelled miles through those waterways, among the marshes and estuary mud flats. There were islands I am sure no Robinson Crusoe ever set foot on. Huck Finn would have understood my joy. In my imagination Gundagai McGinty came aboard frequently. He and I stayed out in the channels from lunch till evening supper hour, day after day. The little craft was well-named. It was apt. *We Two* we were – but Gun and me, not my brother, especially when he wasn't even there...

It was in the sea at Old Greenwich that I learned to swim. There was a pier. My brother used to run off the end of it with his buddies, everyone holding their noses, and of course I was envious that I could not join in. I used to paddle about in shallow water with a life jacket on, but one day, taking a deep and courageous breath, I slipped out of the jacket and dog paddled after it, pushing it in front of me until my toes no longer reached bottom. Like this I made it the full length of the pier where there was a ladder. I clambered up, triumphant, and announced my accomplishment.

"If you made it out this far, you can make it back," said my step-father, who had been watching my progress and met me at the end of the pier. He took away my life jacket, picked me up and flung me back into the sea. I glub-glubbed to the surface, then managed to chug all the way back to shore.

Knowing how to swim gave me great confidence in myself. Socially I had problems – I never knew how to conduct myself in the presence of others. I was shy and withdrawn, allowing those who might have been my peers to step over me, talk me down. I was physically quite strong for my age, and I was not a coward. Swimming gave me the added ability to understand my body instinctively, to feel and know its limitations. *We Two* and the ability to swim did that for me. In time I was to learn the confidence that comes through the ability to use my hands creatively – but my aloneness never left me. It was in my dealings, at any level, with other people – no matter how "close" – that I felt myself on shaky ground. This is something that has persisted throughout my life and has thrown me for more loops than I care to number.

Mother baked her first cherry pie in Old Greenwich. It was a disaster but it, like Mr. Sippi, also made family legend. We broke the knife trying to cut into it, so my brother fetched a hatchet and shattered the thing into glass-like shards. Helpless with laughter, we all sat around the room sucking and chewing at what little bits of pie remained behind on the kitchen table.

To my knowledge this was to prove my mother's only culinary casualty from that point forward. I came to appreciate fine cuisine as the years rolled on, and to acknowledge that Mother had managed to turn herself into a first rate cook. She was compiling a cookbook at the time of her death.

From Old Greenwich we moved into Pelham, a large yellow house high on a rock bluff at 109 Corlies Avenue. Out of curiosity I searched the address on Google Earth and was delighted to see a picture of the house, much as I remember it – and still painted yellow. The house was within walking distance of the school where we were enrolled for a term. I have clear memories of this school and a class photograph to confirm it but, alas, the picture does not show the face eternal of my great love of the time, a young lady a year or two my senior by the name of Josephine Fieroy. The photograph shows the faces of all my classmates and little friends, but not the beautiful Josephine who turned my head and set my heart thumping so hard I thought it would burst.

Josephine was older and in another group. I gave her a present – some stamps, I think – and recall packing whatever it was into a match box I had decorated especially for her. She accepted my gift graciously, writing me a thank you note which began, "My dear little English friend..." She was notably taller than me, which accounts for the "little." "English?" – well, a girl from Pelham, New York, could not reasonably be expected to know the difference between an English accent and an Australian accent ... I suspect I was thrilled to receive any recognition at all. The fact that we seldom saw one another, and I was so breathlessly in love it was impossible to speak, was of no importance. I was enchanted. Sweet Josephine gave me a gift, too – a bunch of odd playing cards, all of different sets and back designs and by no means a deck. Utterly useless, but the gesture swept me into an extended period of lovelorn bliss.

Our great passion never progressed beyond that auspicious beginning. We never stole a kiss. We never even held hands. Affairs of the heart have ever left me dumbfounded.

Pelham was summer. I have no recollections of a winter there. Hot weather, Captain America at a local cinema on Saturday afternoons, and shoplifting little plastic model airplanes from a local five-and-dime store. I was caught. Mother was horrified, or said she was, but we got off lightly. All the toys were returned and we had to make a most abject and humiliating apology to the store manager. For sure I would never graduate from Fagan's school of skulduggery. I was an inept thief.

J. J. Hespeler-Boultbee

Québec

Mother felt comfortable with exclusivity, which is why we spent at least two summers at the Seigniory Club in Montebello. One of her acquaintances our first year there was a certain Mrs. Hood whose two sons, Guthrie and Shirley, were boarding at the same school my brother and I began attending in the winter term of 1944. In the meantime, and for most of that summer, the children were turned loose within the club. Guthrie was an upright and sensible boy, older than the rest of us. But young Shirley became the undisputed leader of the little brat pack. We were quickly apprised of the fallacy of such seemingly feminine a name, for Shirley (boy) was a ruffian like few nine-year-olds I have known, and well qualified at that time to show the rest of us the knotty ropes of pre-teen delinquency.

The clubhouse itself was a magnificent log chateau on the north shore of the Ottawa River, some sixty kilometres east of the capital city. The place represented the last word in gentrified elegance and luxury with its golf course, tennis courts, stables, swimming facilities, and a small orchestra playing Strauss waltzes during the supper hour. But for children it was a paradise, an adventure in unparalleled liberty. There must have been at least a regiment of kids, phalanxes of unruliness – while the one thing all our parents craved above everything else was to be shot of us, and left alone and in peace. There was a babysitting service for the tiny ones, but for the slightly older hell-raisers the parents established a roster – one or two adults being responsible for all the children through any given day so that the rest could enjoy their time alone or with each other. Some parents were stricter than others, but by and large we got away with almost anything we wanted.

Riding horseback, we could go off for miles along the trails through the forest, or out around the golf course. If there were no grown-ups in the vicinity, we discovered that the fairways were perfect for galloping and races. We would try to stay off Cumberland-turf greens and out of sand traps, but even so we were capable of throwing up some extraordinarily large divots. Children always think that they are getting away with such crimes, that they cannot be seen. So when authority descends like a thunderstorm it is invariably a surprise and the cause for righteous expressions of injured innocence.

Somersaults

There was a note on the club notice board one morning:

WILL PARENTS KINDLY INFORM THEIR WARDS THAT GALLOPING HORSES ON THE GOLF LINKS IS DANGEROUS, DESTRUCTIVE AND PROHIBITED

We were out for fun but like most children we were not too aware of our boundaries, the fine line between playfulness and demolition.

One evening the children were to be shown a film – the story of Buffalo Bill; it was intended to keep us occupied while the adults enjoyed a formal dinner and dance in the main dining hall. *"Excluded"* – what might an intelligent adult expect from forty boisterous delinquents if not a little adolescent bumptiousness?

Shirley launched into a conspiracy before the film began: each one of us made five or ten paper airplanes. Considering the number of children, it was one formidable air force – and it was a well-kept secret. Not a word to any outsiders or adults. In the interval of the film, presumably when the projectionist was changing reels, we stole out of the theatre and gathered on the fourth floor balconies that ringed the great dining hall and looked down into it. Far below, our parents and seniors were enjoying their dinner to the soft accompaniment of the orchestra's rendering of a potpourri of Viennese waltzes.

On a given signal we launched – and kept launching from every direction – a veritable barrage of paper aircraft, an insistent invasion against the poor diners below. When they looked up, startled, they could not see us; they were dazzled by the glare of an enormous chandelier.

It was sensational! Giggles of delight as the little aircraft and darts dived into the soup tureen and one of the bassoons, landed on the platter of roast beef, collided with the waiters or settled on top of the salad bar. More than one hairdo was attacked. Members of the orchestra were so taken aback that the waltz they were performing was instantly transformed into a cacophony – then came to an abrupt halt when the musicians started shouting at one another.

The following summer when we returned to the club for the second time, we noticed two or three dusty paper aircraft lodged in the crystal embrace of the dining room's chandelier. It would seem the ladders had not been tall enough for the cleaning staff to pluck them out.

What a party it had been! We laughed and laughed and ran about like little savages before being ushered back into the cinema for the second half of the movie.

One thing bothered me about that evening, looking back on it. When I peeked behind the large movie screen I could find no sign whatsoever of Buffalo Bill or his horse. I was convinced I understood how movies worked, a sort of real life projection of magic and lights from behind the screen.

Had to be ... no?

Many times we were on the river in canoes. Young as we were we would travel long distances, sometimes for a couple of days at a time. There were numerous secondary streams that flowed onto the main river, often so shallow we would have to get out and drag our canoes behind us to higher waterways. There was a stream of mineral water from which we drank because we believed it to be an elixir that would give us long and healthy life. Slightly salty. (Here I am past eighty, so it must have worked.)

Coming back, if the wind was right, we would lash the canoes together side-by-side and rig a mast with sticks or a spare paddle. An old tarpaulin or a blanket would serve us as a sail, and we would cast into mid-stream a long way from either bank where the wind would cut the surface of the stream into a frisky chop and fill our sail like a Viking long boat. There was no adventure to equal it.

Mother would make a great noise about being "so worried," but I do not think she ever was – not really. At least she never grounded us. We would tell her we were sticking to the north bank all the while, going only a little bit upstream and always really close to shore. And "of course" we always wore our life jackets. We had found a place really close where we loved to camp, we told her, and we filled her with wondrous stories of our adventures and fun – making sure all the while that our stories were not too exaggerated and kept more-or-less within the bounds of what she thought was safe and acceptable. I do not know if she believed us, but I have to think she did, or at least wanted to. We had even picked out a spot about four hundred metres up from the boat houses where we could take her if she ever insisted on seeing our camp. We told her it was difficult to walk there through the forest and that the best way of reaching it was by canoe, but she never insisted. She felt a certain confidence in us, for sure – and for the rest, I guess, it suited her to believe we were camped close by.

One of our number who ran at the fringe of the pack, so to say, was a little German girl named Muthgard. None of the children liked her because of her nationality and the way she spoke with a German accent. We tormented her as malicious children know so well how to torment other children and, though she ran with us, when she stopped she would remain on the outside of the circle looking in. Unfortunate girl.

Mother had befriended Muthgard's mother, and pleaded with us to be more loving, generous and friendly. But we had nonetheless concluded among ourselves that both Muthgard and her mother constituted the "enemy," and we made war in our own cruelest fashion. The mother spoke with a heavier accent than her daughter, so we were content with our certainties. We renamed the girl Mud-guard, and chanted at her: "Mud-guard! Mud-guard! Mud-guard!" We were cowardly; we would chant it at her only when we were in consort with one another, and she was not with her mother. In the end we would drive her away in tears, crying to her mother. We did not have the courage to meet her one-on-one because in fact we knew little Muthgard had a fiery temper and a strong tennis arm. She could serve up a mighty wallop if she could catch one of her tormentors alone. I came to know this firsthand one day after she had gone through a prolonged bout of torture. Perhaps I wrestled with a guilt thing or, what is more likely, was sanctimoniously conscious of not being one of her immediate persecutors on that particular occasion.

Spirited girl – she would have none of it when I approached to make some effort at apology for what my friends had done to her. What I thought of, or intended, as contrite repentance she accepted as an obvious demonstration of hypocrisy.

In a trice she had put me on my back on the ground, then sat on me beating at my head with her clenched fists. It was a most unfortunate reaction on her part, for I was instantly persuaded it was safer by far to be her enemy than to risk being her friend. To approach her at all in future one must come at it from the secure position of strength in numbers, I reckoned, and a strong survival instinct told me the numbers at my back would never permit me to befriend her. Had I ever entertained the notion that Muthgard was not really such a baddie, after this beating I now became her staunchest enemy.

Shirley and his family had taken a room at the end of one of the longest and darkest corridors in a remote wing of the huge log chateau that was the main residential building of the Seigniory Club. I was too afraid to go to his room. I would hang back looking at the souvenirs in the lobby gift shop while he ran upstairs to collect a sweater and change into his running shoes, and then we were off – running pell-mell along the forest paths to the boat house to collect our canoe and head off upstream. A short outing, this afternoon ...

Shirley was my pal, and it was the most natural thing in the world that we should get together again during this time of adventure and exploration. We were good canoe partners, as we were good partners at raising hell. Prow or stern made no difference; we were perfectly suited to either position and we were strong paddlers on both sides of our craft, so from the very beginning of our canoeing together we could concentrate solely on accommodating to the other's strengths and actions. Paddling in tandem in a canoe is a complementary thing, the pair constituting a single motor that has to function with precision, timing and strength. Each has to think like the other and, when it works that way, there are seldom surprises or upsets. Throughout our weeks on the Ottawa River we had practised together almost daily so that there were few in the club to better or even equal us.

We flew like an arrow across the boat basin and cut into the stream, then turned into a low-lying area at a point where a lesser tributary entered the main current and formed a wide area of shallow water and tall reeds.

"Smack'em with the flat of your paddle blade to stum'em – not with the edge, otherwise you'll kill'em!"

But Shirley knew what we were about and hardly needed the caution.

In the slack waters, dipping no more than the tip of the blade, our canoe sliced silently though the reeds like the shadow of a cloud. To left and right giant bullfrogs sat on lily pads or tufted grass clumps, or perched on broken tree limbs floating half-submerged, croaking deep-throated warnings to one another. We were so good at our paddling, so silent, that we could sneak right up on them without raising the alarm.

Whap!

The flat of the paddle would come down on one poor creature smacking the water about him into a splash. Shirley in the prow would hit them, I would grab them and plop them into an old potato sack.

"Another one over there!" And we would glide in to the capture – croak! – whap! – grab! – stuff! Within minutes we had bagged about a dozen and figured that was enough. The gunny sack was fair squirming with alarmed bullfrogs, each one all legs and belly bigger than two fists.

Job complete we raced back to the boat basin, docked the canoe and hauled out our catch. It was heavy, took the two of us considerable strength to muscle it up to the footpath and drag it along to the chateau. Unnoticed, we hoped, we entered the main building by a door at the end of one of its wings.

Each bedroom door off the corridors of the chateau had a transom window above it, and I had taken particular note before our expedition that the window above the door to the quarters of Muthgard and her mother was ajar. Like terrorists well-rehearsed in their plan we unloaded the sack of stunned and squiggling bullfrogs onto the floor of the corridor and quickly lobbed them all through the transom window.

We did not wait for the screams, nor did we know whether Muthgard or her mother were even in at the time. We scampered off down the hall as quickly as furtive and guilty assassins, and waited till suppertime to see if there had been any reaction. There must have been one, but we did not see it and neither of us ever learned what it had been – or if ever there was one. Neither stout-hearted Muthgard, nor her even stouter-hearted mother, was about to oblige us with the least satisfaction of knowing whether or not there had been a reaction, and we could hardly have enquired without revealing our part in the plot.

To this day I have felt a twinge of guilt. I have long since learned to live with it, but have never been able to think back on that incident, its utter meanness, with anything other than a kind of embarrassed horror. The cruelty of the escapade was indicative of another complex part of some adolescent resistance to being pushed into the shadows – that and, I suspect, the ostentatious narcissism. The action had about it some prevailing Machiavellian tendency to ensure that whenever there was a message to be delivered, even when redundant or totally incorrect, it should be concise and clear to the point of searing. Often I have wondered how my companion in this particular act of skulduggery has looked back on the incident – or if in fact he has any memory of it.

We were rascals, no doubt, and must have driven the powers-that-be in that club to the furthest limits of their patience and distraction.

Late that first summer – and this is when Shirley's name was indelibly etched onto my psyche – we the children burned down the club stables. It was with the greatest difficulty that the ostlers and other hotel staff were able to save the lives of some twenty horses.

I was present, ran with the gang that did the deed, so must admit my guilt through association – although my presence was as observer on that particular occasion, not participant. A number of the older boys (a very young Shirley had been among them) were hiding in the loft above the stalls smoking cigarettes. I had been with them at first, but there are great differences between a boy of eight or nine and boys of ten, eleven or twelve. When big boys – almost teens – are smoking they tend to look down on smaller boys as unreliable nuisances, maybe even snitches. In any case, little kids don't know how to smoke properly.

Thus dismissed, I was sitting outside the stables in the shade of a large clump of trees, probably feeling very left out and sorry for myself, when Shirley ran up, urgency to his step.

"You'd better tell someone the place is on fire," he said, somehow absent his customary self-confidence.

I was neither alarmed nor particularly inclined to go for help. Shirley was only a little bit older than I was, so I did not think I should take orders from him. In addition he had not been as excluded from this escapade as I had been, so I can guess that at least a portion of my attitude was pique – simple envy because I had been shunted aside. Even at that early age I was not entirely convinced messengers would not be shot; calling attention to a fire might get me in trouble. I hesitated long enough to see the first billows of smoke rise above the stable roof and to hear the first neighing of frightened horses.

Suddenly there were grown-ups present and I was relieved of the need to yell fire.

The alarm went out rapidly and in minutes there were scores of people running about fetching buckets of water. To no avail, as it turned out. The fire was quickly out of control. I watched several people run right into the smoke-filled interior of the building to drive out the horses from the wide doorway at the far side of the stables. Huddled under the trees I felt a certain fascination for the scene before me. The horses were led off a safe distance upwind of the smoke, and I stayed in place to watch the entire building reduced to a heap of ashes and charred woodwork. It could not have taken more than a half hour.

Somersaults

There was to be yet another memorable event at the Seigniory Club, this one in the summer of 1944 – even more traumatic for us than had been the stable fire. It circumscribed our lives as carefree children hell bent on seeking out the next adventure.

All of us, parents, friends, children, had gathered late one afternoon in either the chateau bar or dining room. It was a late tea, or perhaps Mother's cocktail hour. In whichever case I clearly recall a failing light, late afternoon or early evening. There was a large round table, with chairs circling one part of it and comfortable leather-covered window benches on the opposite side. The grown-ups were having a conversation, but on this rare occasion the children were included. A dashing young Royal Canadian Air Force pilot named Kit was holding forth on the joys of flying and I for one was enthralled. I think everyone was listening – not least his pretty fiancée, Marnie, a friend of Mother's who had rented a cabin for the summer in the forested hills a few kilometres up behind the club.

"It's fascinating to fly over this country," Kit was saying. "There are a countless number of lakes and rivers, so you really have to be on your navigational toes to find your way about – but you can spot the Ottawa from a great way off, it's so big. The landscape is so empty, perfect for low flying..."

"Can you do a loop-the-loop?" we asked wide-eyed.

Kit smiled.

"Tell you what!" he conspired with us kids. "Tomorrow before lunch I'll fly over the club and do a loop for you, right there over the river."

We were thrilled, and the following day my brother and I headed for the boat houses right after breakfast, deciding that the best place to watch the spectacle would be from mid-river. We paddled out and sat waiting in the canoe, scanning the skies for some sign of Kit's approach. We did not have very long to wait. We heard him before we could see him. The roar of his engine rose and fell unevenly, so that without laying eyes on him it was obvious even to two small boys that something was amiss.

Suddenly he seemed to pop up over the tree-tops a kilometre or so down the river, a great yellow Harvard trainer. He picked up a course mid-stream heading directly towards us. As he approached the plane rose and fell, at times nearly touching the water that flashed beneath him, and a plume of jet-black smoke streamed out from the cowling of his motor.

We were dumbfounded. We could say nothing. Was this part of the show? As the plane passed close overhead the engine seemed to surge with a newfound power. We caught a glimpse of two helmeted heads in the cockpit, then the plane leapt into the air and climbed to several hundred feet, only to turn and dive as though the pilots were trying to blow out the flames that by now were quite visible to us. But the engine was faltering again. Banking sharply to his right, the pilot skimmed his craft across the river to the north, barely clearing some trees that lined a bluff.

Marnie's cabin was on the slope some two or three kilometres from the edge of the river. We could see it quite clearly from our position in the canoe. By now a mass of flames and trailing smoke, the Harvard seemed to make a beeline for this remote cabin, but crashed into the trees a few hundred metres short of it. Before it went in we thought we saw someone jump from the cockpit.

We paddled directly to the shore, hauled up the canoe, and started through the forest in the direction of the crash as fast as we could run – which was pretty fast. At first we had to guess the right direction, but as we closed the distance we could see the smoke and flames. Trees in the vicinity had been set alight. It took us maybe fifteen minutes to arrive at the scene.

High in a tree, but close to the downed plane, we saw one of the flyers hanging in the straps and unfurled trappings of an unopened parachute. He was far too high up for us to reach, but he was not moving.

We approached the wreckage of the plane as close as the heat of the flames would allow, but there was nothing that two small boys could do. We caught glimpses of Kit sitting quiet and still in the cockpit surrounded by flames. Our view of him was obscured for long periods by the smoke, but when it moved aside we could see his face quite clearly framed by his flying helmet. We watched as it burned and pieces of his headgear peeled away as carbon. We backed off, stood there mouths agape.

Marnie came down from her cabin. She must have seen what happened and had a fire extinguisher with her. She played it on the flames, crying and sobbing and shouting at the two of us to stay back. But she might as well have used a squirt gun. The extinguisher did not extinguish anything.

I had never seen metal burning before and was surprised to see that it could flame up like paper.

Somersaults

There was a house in Montréal where we lived for several months during the fall and winter period prior to Mother's move to New York; there remain memories of a break from boarding school, a place with a small entrance vestibule, jumbles of snow boots, heavy coats hung one atop the other on wall pegs and a sleigh. We used to visit back and forth with one of Mother's old school friends, Barbara Gwynn, and her husband Quinten who, with their many children, lived in a huge house in the city; they also had a rambling old country farmhouse on the edge of a forest a few hours away from the city where they could all go for weekend retreats and holidays.

Weekends at this place – for we visited on several occasions – were the best of treats for active and curious children. It was the epitome of "be thyself," where we could play all day in the woods and its streams, leap over logs or climb out onto high boughs, and run through mountains of fallen leaves – for at this place it seemed always to be that time of the year. There was no end to the great string of adventures imaginative young minds could conjure. There were the two of us, and five of the Gwynns – plus a few extras...

One morning, when everyone else was yet asleep, I arose early from my bed and snuck downstairs to see if I could find something to eat. I was being quieter than a mouse as I crossed the carpeted dining room, for I did not want to awaken anyone, or to be caught prowling about. I guess I felt guilty – or perhaps I was continuing the stealth of the games we had been playing in the woods.

Peering through the serving hatchway cut in the wall between the dining room and the kitchen, my morning eyes clear and now accustomed to the faint shadows of early daylight, I could see a group of tiny field mice scampering about on the kitchen counter. There were eggs on the counter, and the mice wanted one of them – but it wouldn't roll properly when they pushed it.

Finally one of the mice opened his four legs wide, and straddled the egg. Then he rolled onto his back, with his prize cradled against his tummy and nestled safely within the cavity between his body and limbs. The other mice gathered about him – pushing him, and pulling him by his tail. There was a hole in the wall at the back of the counter and that is where they evidently wanted the egg ...

Now every time I tell this story, people's eyes pop open wide in amazement – then they smile because they can see the picture clearly, but then they tell me they don't believe a word of it ...!

Yet – and yet – I have this image, this memory, clear as if it was happening right before my eyes. It is firm in my mind.

"Arg-h!" they exclaim.

"Arg-h!" I say right back for, as I've said before, children who have certainties about such things care not to be scoffed at.

I have not told this story often because it is one for which I have been accused of exaggeration. Hurtful. I have to admit the possibility a small boy with an inventive imagination could dream outrageous things – and bring them magically to life. Though I do indeed have a distinct recollection of this extraordinary encounter, whether one believes it or not is not so important as the telling of the tale itself – so from this moment I resolve to recount it more frequently.

Two winters in a row – it must have been during Christmas breaks – Mother took her two sons to a small resort village in deep-snow Shawbridge, a village tucked into Québec's Laurentians some sixty kilometres northwest of Montréal. Canada's winter snows are not unique in the world, but I do not believe there is a Canadian alive who does not consider he or she has a deep personal connection with it. Despite the flare of colour, deep fall can be depressing, a dark and somber foreboding of shadows and a child's anxiety about when winter's snows will finally arrive. But deep snow is different – winter has settled in at last. I was not alone feeling enchanted by snow, whether looking at it through the window of some warm interior or stomping through it knee-deep and outdoors, swaddled in clothes akin to a bunny suit or knickerbockers. No matter where one lives in Canada, winter has to be dealt with – and snow is a part of it, sprinkled or dumped.

The difference was that with fall I was made aware of the chill. It can be uncomfortable because one's feet may get wet; or one's legs feel stiff, cold even through thick knickerbocker pant legs and long johns. An overcoat and scarf are not sufficient to fend off the permeating cold, and yet one could feel sweaty, encumbered and overdressed wearing more. In fall one is tempted to use pockets instead of mitts or gloves – and as a consequence one's hand and arm movements are restricted. Fingers can freeze carrying packages.

But a heavy snowfall is different. It may or may not be as cold as a light snow, but it looks colder. It is a psychological thing, and one is not seduced into wearing less than is absolutely suitable. There is the underwear, for starters, then snow boots, a warm sweater and a nylon outer garment – or a good parka instead of a flapping overcoat. A scarf, a toque, practical gloves or mitts for the hands, and you are set – totally comfortable even at thirty below ... it is not the cold that predominates, but the silence, the most exquisite absence of sound ever encountered. One will never hear a silence like it outside the snow zones. Robert Service understood the silence of deep snow. He wrote about it obsessively – and beautifully. In *The Call of the Wild* he sang of the Great White Silence. In *The Ballad of the Northern Lights* he talked of the world being purged of sound the length and breadth of a frozen continent and later, in the same ballad, of a vast white world where the silence of the sky communes with the silence of the snow. Writing of his Yukon life he comes back again and again to the deep silence of deep snow.

I recall once (I cannot remember exactly where) building a snow house, an igloo. We used blocks of snow the way we had seen it done in films about the Inuit – except that the house we built seemed bigger, with passages and inner walls and separate chambers, a veritable labyrinth of snow and ice and mystery. And I remember tobogganing where I could tell from the virgin whiteness no man had ever been before, down hillsides none knew about – or under the heavy hanging bowers of evergreens, drifts piled up against their trunks and into the very branches themselves, where secret caverns of snow hid me from the view of all the world. Years later, taking a winter drive through the mountainous country on the British Columbia side of Banff's National Park, I drove clean past Revelstoke – missed it even though I was looking for it. The deep snow piled up by the ploughs on either side of the highway hid the town so completely I had to go in search of it. The piles were high enough that houses and street lights, all off-highway access to the habitation itself, were totally obscured. Perfect camouflage.

If I had to come up with a single metaphor to describe the cacophony of winter, it would be the silence. A twig snapping in the snowy forest is like a thunderclap. Footfalls in the snow are like the march of an army of elves. Sleigh-runners over crisp snow hiss like a jet of water played into the depths of a fire. All these sounds intrude upon the great still white silence in such a way that God Himself would seem to be goaded into commanding, "Be still!" Even if orchestrated, a festival of noise in such a vast white landscape would be an embarrassment to nature.

Mid-winter taxi service in the Shawbridge we encountered (today it has been renamed Prévost, an amalgam of three villages) was horse-drawn, large open sleighs that could carry four to six people plus driver. We would snuggle-in under bearskin rugs, and in truth there were scores of sounds now to shatter the silence – winter sounds; we could not help but notice them. Over the continuous *schiesch* of sleigh or ski runners there came the regular clop-clop-clop of the horses' hooves, and the high jangling of hundreds of tiny bells sewn onto the harnesses that traced over each horse's shoulders, back and flanks, each separate tinkle insisting its own thin rhythmic syncopation. The other most notable of sounds that winter sojourn were wafted up to us from the railway – not from the station, or any part of the line that entered within the village confines, but from way off beyond the bounds of habitation, the far side of forests and the North River – as if in conversation with the packs of roving wolves and the bears that hibernated out there.

There was a toymaker in Shawbridge, a skilled carpenter whose workshop was a child's delight of wooden wheels and wagons, puppet heads and marionettes, horses with rockers, doll houses with façades that opened up to reveal interior rooms and staircases, and palaces and castles full of miniature furnishings. Some of the toys were painted and finished; others were made but as yet unpainted. Still others were in pieces – wheels in one pile, axles in another, carriage-bodies in another. Boxes, heads, torsos, legs and arms, pieces of this and that all stacked into heaps on shelves and ready for assembly. When he grew tired of making cars or railway engines the carpenter would put the pieces aside, and instead build a scooter or small dining set. He was a jolly fellow with a warm smile and kind eyes, a white-haired Geppetto who understood and enjoyed children. He could look stern if one approached the machinery too closely.

He became my friend, and he always welcomed me in out of the cold to huddle by his wood-burning stove, to savour the special smells of his wood chips and sawdust and to play with some of the toys he had put away on the shelves. This was real. Santa's North Pole at Christmas could not have been any better.

In the fall term of 1944 Mother enrolled her two sons at a boarding school near Toronto. I think she did this on the advice of two people – Mrs. Hood, Shirley's mother, whom we had met earlier that summer at the Seigniory Club, and an old family friend, Temple McMullen, himself an old boy of the school. Whether my mother sought Temple's advice at the time of our enrollment, or whether it had been proffered some years earlier I cannot say. Mother claimed he had spoken to her about his years at the school, and that he had said it was one of the finest in Canada.

Temple was my godfather, and a man who was shortly to die in the war. I recall vividly his photograph among those on the stairway of the senior school, a sort of running memorial to those old school boys who had been killed overseas. I would study his face closely and sometimes cry quietly to myself. I could not remember him personally, so in truth had no good reason to tear up – but I thought I did, and that was sufficient. Mostly I think it was because, as Mother kept reminding me, I was a sensitive and emotional boy easily prone to turn on the tap, and found some sort of release in doing so.

In general the schools I attended were conditions rather than entities with which I might find some comfortable identification. But this new boarding school was different in that it had an impressive collection of red brick buildings for which I could feel a clear empathy. The physical stature of the buildings was important to me for some reason – I have thought since it might have been an early indication I was later to become intrigued by architectural history. It was a Canadian school with its own coat of arms, and a uniform I liked, "an' everything." I was intensely proud of becoming a member of this august establishment, and of my Canadian-ness. It was the first school I had encountered in which I felt I had a place, and to which I could direct an identifiable and clear loyalty. I might not have been able to articulate my feelings very well, but deep down I knew what they were. I was extraordinarily happy to go there, and when I entered the elementary section at the age of eight, I was the smallest and youngest member of the school – also one of the proudest. I shared a tiny annex dormitory – "E Dorm" – with Edmond Price and Shorty Monroe, two young men who, along with Shirley Hood, became my bosom buddies – for all that we fought continuously. Seventy years on Ed and I are still in touch – not a great deal in common beyond the years we have known one another and kept in touch, but seventy years is already a lot. We have both followed our separate *caminhos*, but that early bond has survived, happily – and the survival itself became the bond.

I have a vivid recollection of my ninth birthday, when I had been enrolled at the boarding school no more than a few weeks:

My friend Shirley Hood for some reason refused to extend birthday good wishes to me, and I happened to take exception to what I considered a spiteful and unkind gesture. Very bad form, so I resolved to punish him.

He had gone out to play a game on the sports field, and his everyday clothing had been left hanging on a peg in the locker room. I took his knickerbockers, and spread a thick layer of black shoe polish on the inside seat of them.

Quite naturally, when he returned from his game, and after he had taken a shower, he needed to get dressed – but couldn't. The condition of his knickerbockers was reported, and it was discovered the damage done was so severe they had to be tossed out. There was a brief conference, the guilt of the offender quickly established, and I was duly summoned to the housemaster's study.

When he asked me why I had done such a thing to Shirley Hood's knickerbockers, I said precisely what had been on my mind: I was deeply offended that he had declined to wish me a Happy Birthday. I added that I considered my behaviour had been justified under the circumstance ...

"Well," said the housemaster, "bend over that chair, and we shall see if I can knock a little birthday sentiment into you this way ..."

He used a thin cane to whack me six times – hard – across my tender rear end. It hurt.

"Happy Birthday!" he said again. "Your mother will be presented with the bill for Hood's new clothing."

Up to this point in my young life I had attended such a confusing array of schools that the very word "school" induced in me a numbness of mind bereft of an image of actual place or set of buildings – and for sure I never equated the concept of school with "learning." I was not altogether certain what schools were for, and had long ago come to think of my attendance as a necessity in order to grant Mother the peace and quiet she so craved. Few incidents ever stood out vividly. There was the boy who had died in the river in Ohio, or Josephine, my beautiful heart-throb. And, of course, there was the matter of Shirley Hood's knickerbockers.

There had been a point of serious contention at the school in Pelham, for instance, one that had jolted my sense of justice: every morning I was being obliged to place my right hand over my heart and swear allegiance to the American flag. Even at such an early age I found this unacceptable, a repugnant distortion of a loyalty I did not feel. For several mornings in a row I would sit down if I could – only to be forced to my feet by my teacher's stern looks, or her inducement, using a degree of physical force applied to my ear. I had the wit to know I was not a citizen of the United States. More importantly I felt it was wrong to be obliged to swear allegiance to someone else's flag; my country was my country, sacred as the head that sat on my shoulders. To my cost, I failed to remember this object lesson ten or eleven years later as I submitted to being drummed into the British Army and sent away for a year and a half of jungle warfare.

It did not matter greatly to me that my mother's motive for enrolling us at a boarding school might have been her way of seeking resolution to the urgent problems my brother and I created for her. A teeny bit selfish, mayhap – but of her, or us?

As an adult looking back, it is clear that if my very existence – and my brother's, also – conflicted with Mother's preferred lifestyle, she did in fact have considerable difficulty in managing the two of us. Now I can claim a perfect awareness of the psychological proposition: that parents who send their children away to boarding schools are merely trying to palm off onto others responsibilities they themselves are unable or unwilling to tackle, with the added benefit that they are now freer to live their lives without the enormous encumbrance of growing, pushy, contrary and obnoxious children. It is a popular notion, quite in line with myriads of other popular myths expounded by modern explorers of the psyche, maybe even correct in some instances, but which in certain essentials is not true. Such researchers couch their opinions in expressions of great knowledge and authority, backed by the copious statistics drawn from years and years of studies and research; but they have to, otherwise they would be doubted, their professional status downgraded in the popular mind. It would play havoc with their income. In our case, and I am sure this would apply in other cases, too, Mother's problems with her offspring were very competently taken in hand by the school. Boarding schools do provide an excellent foundation for a child's adult years, and generally an above-average level of education. There are schools that fail their pupils as there are parents who fail their children, but by and large I believe the system works pretty well.

Mother would have given the matter of her children's education as rigorous a consideration as she was capable of, I am sure, and boarding school was an essential as much for the time as it was for her concept of our social station as a family. But I do not have any misconception as to how her reasoning was kneaded by her penchant for rationalization, liberally larded by her inability to cope with us. It was most probably this element that ultimately provided her with the clinching argument that boarding school "was necessary." She would fly into rages with us, or dither, and then with her brains quite sizzled by the confusion we deftly created for her, in the end willingly admit that she would happily see us gone for a time. Unfairly, then, we would have accused her of failing in her stated intent to take an active interest in our education. Now I am more willing to accept that in her desperate addle-pated way she really was doing as best she could "for our own good."

As a result of my own experience at boarding schools I spent years criticizing the system. But now in later life, and looking at the education bestowed upon my own children in a state system, I feel somewhat less able to point the finger. It is not classroom work alone that concerns me, but the overall product in terms of culture, taste, sense of quality and decency towards other individuals and society as a whole. I believe that if the directors and teachers within a private boarding school system enter into a close, conscientious and knowledgeable contract with parents and children, if all the possible idiosyncrasies of a particular student are taken into consideration, the time at boarding school can be extremely beneficial and enlightening, a thoroughly positive thing in a youngster's growing years.

In our own case, however, I do have the feeling that had Mother been encouraged to participate in our schooling (say through some sort of parent/teacher association) she would have been horrified and greatly inconvenienced. She would have enquired with indignation, I am sure, precisely why she should be asked to pay such astronomical school fees as well as being tapped to do some of the essential work. "Psychology" – the mere mention of it, let alone its practical application – raised ideas with which our poor mother would have had difficulty coping. She paid her money; the school provided a service (with implied – though not written – guarantees). With such an arrangement she would have considered the staff at school was, *en bloc*, a tutorial service hired to do a job – underlings, servants in a way, to whom she paid a wad for doing a specific job. A little feudal in her thinking, was our dear Mama.

Truth to tell, Mother was not an inconsiderable psychological study herself, though she would have denied it huffily and would have pronounced herself "perfectly normal" – apart, perhaps, for the admission of one or two little foibles to which a lady of her station in life was perfectly entitled. After all there was nothing so exceptionally unusual about girdling the globe with her *enfants terribles*, plus Nanny, bags, baggage and all the family furniture in crates ...

I visualize it as I write:

"This way, Nanny! Come along, children!" – *the parasol raised against some tropic sun over her head as she strides along an outport quay and up a gangplank, calling orders to all and sundry, navvies and stevedores, to treat her cases with the greatest of care. And should they crack the glass in the door of the grandfather clock she would bloody well clock them ...*

Perfectly normal. But I run ahead of myself; more of Mother anon. For the now we are two small boys enrolled in a great Canadian school.

J. J. Hespeler-Boultbee

New York

One could say these were confusing times for Mother; not to the same degree for her sibling hooligan offspring. Youngsters like us, as our mother had long since discovered, are nothing if not resilient when left un-coddled and to their own devices. We were of tender age, true, but had already become used to a certain level of chaos in our lives, and we managed to survive very well. After our Nanny's departure we had been left on our own a great deal, and were quite able to desist from our perpetual quarrelling and rousting about – when we did not have Mother to antagonize. We could even muster a fair degree of self-reliance and responsibility when it was required. Heads up and totally confident, between terms we would travel together by train (overnight from Toronto to New York) for our holiday breaks – a benign unchaperoned passage for children by now nine and nearly twelve years old. It would be an unthinkable risk for most parents nowadays, but for the two of us then it was a simple matter of imperative if we wanted to find welcome warm beds and dinners in the weeks while school was out.

There was never the least hint that our mother might come to collect us at the station when we arrived in New York. She would know the day but seldom the hour of our arrival and, in the event we might want to go somewhere else before heading home – a movie, for example – we would deliberately refrain from informing her. We came to know the train's regular coach porters, befriended them even, so were totally at ease en route as far as our destination. Once in New York, we were likewise quite at home on local buses and subways. For that matter it was a simple matter to take a cab to our apartment building downtown. The doorman, whose muscles were well disguised by his liveried uniform, would ensure the street toughs that liked to hang about the building, taunting and aggressive, would leave us in relative peace as we entered.

By now well used to travel we were both particularly adept at geography in our schoolwork, though neither of us was up to the level of our fellows in language studies and mathematics. History always intrigued me, but I was way behind in mathematics, French and Latin. Later, in high school, I failed lamentably at all the sciences, but excelled in my art class – and particularly enjoyed my art teacher. The similarities and differences of the important school sports – cricket and baseball, rugby and ice hockey – caused me consternation, so I attempted avoidance of any sports that were compulsory. Later, though, I was to find my niche in individual sports – gymnastics and boxing, middle-distance running and swimming. I had not learned about boxing from my brother so much as I had from the necessity of beating back the attacks of the ruffians watching for us as we went in and out of our apartment building on those occasions when our doorman was off duty. Somehow is seems intimidating to say one learned to fight in the streets of New York.

Our excursions back-and-forth between Canada and the United States lasted a little more than a year. Mother, ever the supreme Mistress of Rationalization, had always been able to assess (quite cleverly, I thought) the absolute necessity for anything she fancied, her impulses always as insistent as they were strong – and invariably costing bundles of money. Now, as soon as the fighting had stopped in Europe she wanted – "had to" – be on the go again. She had been on the move since her teens, was by now an inveterate traveller and well along in her programme of teaching her two sons to keep up with her. The restrictions imposed on her movements during the war years, though she flouted most of them by crossing the Pacific mid-turmoil with all of us in tow, had counted as little less than a confounded nuisance.

Last Spanking

During the summer break of 1945, when we were all surviving the heat in a two-bedroom apartment in New York's Lower Manhattan, my brother and I succeeded in testing Mother's nerves to their fullest. Having come down from Toronto, the two of us found ourselves confined and bored stiff. We were intent on being as unmanageable as we could be, and I am sure our mother had endured about all the rambunctiousness from us that she could take. One of our favoured antics was to drop paper water bombs from our living room window onto people passing in the street below. We were easily spotted, of course, and it was not long before the police were knocking on our door and issuing cautions.

The war against Germany had finished just a month or so before, and we were arranging to go to England to visit with Mother's dear relative and guardian, Tappie, who had been trapped in London throughout the blitz. (Her correct name was Tabatha. My brother and I were let in on a family secret: that, in seeking a good childhood nickname for her, Tappie's close family had decided "Tabby" was like naming her after the household cat, and had decided for the sake of simplicity to turn the b's upside-down.) With the tight regulations in effect at the conclusion of the war, and the sheer quantity of bureaucracy involved in getting across the Atlantic, I think our mother might have been on the brink of leaving us behind. Two bumptious, noisy and quarrelsome boys had an unfailing and most unsympathetic way of commanding her attention. We were merciless.

From our shared bedroom my brother and I could look down one of the city streets and, maybe six or ten blocks away, we could make out the enormous tower of the Empire State Building – at that time the tallest structure in the world.

Knowing the two of us usually awoke fairly early, our mother said one Friday night:

"Tomorrow is Saturday, and I intend to sleep late. I want no rough-housing, shouting or pillow-fighting from you in the morning, is that clear? If I hear even so much as a peep out of you, I'll come in there and whack the daylights out of both of you. Do you understand?"

Mother had a way of talking tough, but the two of us had her fairly well sussed-out, and were pretty good at gauging her. Sometimes she meant what she said; sometimes she was a marshmallow. On this occasion, however, we reckoned she meant it. We knew we had been pushing the limit.

So early the following morning, quiet and innocent like bunnies, my brother sat in his bed arranging his stamp collection while I had my knees propped up and was doing a drawing. There was a heavy summer fog over the city, and the streets were unusually quiet.

Suddenly there was an enormous crash from somewhere outside, and my brother and I looked at each other quizzically.

In the next moment the bedroom door flew open and in stormed Mother like an avenging hornet. She took me by the ear, walloped my little bum till it burned and pushed me into the bathroom, locking the door. Then I heard my brother yowling as she laid into him.

"Not fair! Wasn't us! Didn't do anything!"

"Gr-r-r-r!" Mom growled, and stomped back to her bed.

After a few minutes my brother unlocked the bathroom door and let me out. We did not know what had happened, but whatever it was we were sure we were not guilty. Unfair! Mutter-mutter, pouts and tears. What outrage! What persecution!

Later in the day the tabloids were delivered and we found out what had happened. A United States Army Air Force B-25 Mitchell bomber had flown into the side of the Empire State Building. Some fourteen people perished in the disaster.

Mother was beside herself with guilt and remorse, and of course my brother and I made the most of it. For years afterwards the two of us remained about as impossibly high-spirited, and no doubt we continued to give her numerous good reasons to wale the tar out of us. But she never did. In fact that morning, 28 July, 1945, marks the date of the last spanking either of us ever received from her. We arrived in England one week later.

Eberstein

Despite all the kerfuffle surrounding our antics and misbehaviour, and with dear Mama so erroneously considering herself a Princess of the Blood Royal (as scarlet as yours or mine, notwithstanding), we were by any measure most favoured children. On so many occasions we shared the warmth of intimacy and laughter, often with Nanny Grace, and often as we were being tucked into our beds for the night. After Nanny left and there were just the three of us (four again when our step-father was on the scene) we would sit around the kitchen table and Mother would read to us, or tell us stories. She was well-versed in the Greek, Roman and Norse classics; she loved stories of French and British chivalry, or of the Russian boyars and Cossacks. Then there were the stories of our family, and mother's childhood in the Okanagan.

Our mother and father had both come from exceptionally privileged family backgrounds: his from early Alberta oil production and Vancouver real estate, hers from Old World money and the development of lands, railways and hotels across Canada's western provinces. Mother's grandfather, Wilhelm, descendent of lines of minor Bavarian and Hungarian aristocrats, was a diplomat representing his Fatherland in the New World during Bismarck's political machinations hammering Germany together. He was later to become a politician for Winnipeg and Rupert's Land, served as Commissioner for Immigration responsible for bringing the southern Russian Mennonites to Manitoba and, in his later years, was Speaker of the Manitoba legislature. His son, Alfred Æmelius, Mother's father – who had refrained from marriage until he was into his fifties – had made his own fortune as a mining engineer, owning coal mines in China and tin mines in Bolivia. After his marriage to English-born Matilda Jermyn, he settled down to fruit farming in the Okanagan Valley. Mother was born an only child, the last of the family in Canada to bear her father's surname.

Born at the ranch in Summerland, she told me numerous stories about the place – so that, unseen, I came to think of it as I might my ancestral home, the family seat, so to say. Hers were always summer stories; I could never imagine the place under snow in the winter. On the other hand I could smell the dust of a hot interior British Columbia summer. I have a faded photograph of my mother as a baby in the arms of her mother. Grandmother Matilda is seated on a cushioned wicker rocking chair, my mother spread across her lap and gazing open-mouthed at the unseen photographer. Next to them, relaxed, smiling and holding a partially-smoked cigar, is Grandfather Alfred – and next to him, also seated and favouring a cigar, is Great-Grandfather Wilhelm, a dapper wide-brimmed fedora perched crown-like (he is the patriarch, after all) on his head. Mother is definitely the centre of attention for what is surely one of her very first photographs. The three adults are all looking at her. The picture was taken on the veranda of the ranch house – no shadows, so it is not hard to imagine a hot Okanagan summer afternoon.

By 1909, the year of mother's birth, Alfred and Matilda Hespeler were well-known throughout the length of the Okanagan valley. One of the reasons for their notoriety was because of the size of their barn – by far the largest for miles around and well-suited for the community market days held there once the snows had gone, and for the barn dances frequently organized by the locals.

Matilda was a hard-working and gracious hostess at these functions. For days ahead of an event she would busy herself in her kitchen and chase her small staff and volunteers into action – baking breads, or cakes and cookies, and in quantities sufficient to please a ravenous group of maybe two hundred guests, or more. Though a child, my mother was eventually given her share of chores to perform, running messages, sweeping, or washing and rinsing pots, pans and cooking implements.

Somersaults

Eberstein Ranch, 1909 – Mother as a child in her mother's lap
with her father, Alfred, and grandfather Wilhelm looking on

The barn dances at Eberstein Ranch were well known and well attended. Young hands from farms up and down the Okanagan Valley came in on horseback, arriving with their girlfriends on buckboards or in traps and wagons. Some would arrive a day early in order to lend a hand with sprucing the place up, last minute preparations and decorating, trimming the hedges and lawns. The extra food they brought in, combined with what Matilda had prepared, would ensure there was sufficient to feed a small army. An impromptu market would be set up under awnings surrounding the house, with the sale of everything from vegetables and preserves, to small farm equipment, fabrics and handicrafts. For days before the event the place swarmed and buzzed. The major influx of guests started on the morning of the big day itself. Riders coming from the north end of the lake would stop by farms on their way south, picking up or escorting other guests along the way so that, when they all arrived together, there might have been a bloc of as many as seventy or eighty of them. Some would come in from Kelowna and Penticton; the mounts of all of them would need water and fodder and a paddock in which to pass their time for a few days. The buckboards and wagons would be parked around the perimeter of the paddock. Space would be cleared on the barn's earthen floor for dancing. In fine weather the barn's double doors would be flung wide open to allow for revellers both inside and out; the band – and sometimes there would be several musical groups – would set up in the hayloft. On the rare occasion when it was raining or the weather was not too obliging, spectators would back up against the interior walls of the gigantic structure, or pack themselves into the loft next to the musicians. There was always extra space up the loft stairway, on hay bales that lay scattered about the floor, or perches on the gates and divisions of the animal stalls.

So it went year-in, year-out – and several times a year. As well as these essentially social affairs, Eberstein was also well-recognized as a working fruit ranch, the soil there well-suited to orchard production, especially to the cultivation of peaches. Produce and play were both prime, and people enjoyed their time there.

One of those who habitually showed up at these functions was a young man by the name of George. He came up from Penticton, which was not a great distance away – always alone, a painfully shy fellow. He would hang back against a wall and watch everyone else having fun. Matilda spotted this and decided to try to draw him out. One day she caught him by his sleeve, led him into the kitchen, and gave him a plate of sandwiches.

"George," I would always imagine her cajoling voice when Mother would tell me this story. "Be a dear and help me distribute these …"

Taking the plate, George would work his way among the guests offering them the sandwiches or drinks. The action made him feel useful and accepted. After the first of these affairs George became a regular at helping out. It seemed to break the ice for him somehow, and plainly he adored my grandmother. Nothing she requested of him ever seemed too great a trouble.

His feelings for Matilda were not unreciprocated. Grandmother was a gentle person, acutely aware of the sensitivities of others, and I think she had an innate understanding of young George's personal agonies. She would seek him out and always make sure he was comfortable in his surroundings.

However, there came the day when the idyllic world that had been created in this far away loyal valley blew apart. In the last half of summer of 1914 war was declared in Europe, and the entire Empire rallied behind England. In those days western Canada was populated in great part by first- or second-generation settlers from Britain, people who possessed strong feelings for the causes for which England was prepared to go to war and would not hesitate to sign up; the Motherland called them and they went. The farms of the Okanagan were quickly depleted; a huge percentage of the young hands unquestioningly agreed to go and fight.

George was among them. He came to say goodbye to Matilda and Alfred – and then he was gone, an eager young fellow in his baggy duds and rumpled wide-brimmed hat who, despite his shyness, knew (or thought he did) what his duty was.

Months went by and no one heard from him. Some of the local boys signed on in Vernon, at the north end of the lake; others were shipped down to the coast at Vancouver to undergo their basic training. Few of them ever had the money or the opportunity to return to their homes in the Okanagan Valley to spend a last leave before going overseas. From Vancouver they were sent east by train to await embarkation from Montréal. No doubt George went with them. He did not write.

Weeks turned into months, months into years. News came slowly to the valley, and it was usually bad. One has to imagine (but it is not terribly hard) how it was for families all across the country to hear that their sons, their brothers, their fathers or husbands had died in a war so far away, and which few at home could understand. The agonies were intensely personal in every case, to be sure, and yet were common to all. It was particularly appalling around the time of the Battle of Passchendaele, the terrible conflagration that consumed Canadians in the main – the Fields of Flanders in April, 1918. Hundreds – thousands – died. It was Canada's awakening to the huge responsibilities of nationhood, and it was a price paid by her youth.

On a sunny morning early in the summer of that year, my mother was awakened by the distinctive sound of her mother's bedroom door closing firmly. Time to get up, she thought, and bounded out of her bed. Still in her nightdress she was confronted by my grandmother coming out of her own bedroom, also dressed in her night attire, and pulling a robe about her shoulders.

(At this point I am re-remembering my mother's telling of the story; the quotes she used are now of my own imagining.)

"George is back! George is back!" Matilda cried excitedly and, with that, the household was aroused. Alfred appeared from his own quarters.

Everybody went downstairs, but George was not there. My mother went out into the yard, then over to the barn – no sign of George. My grandfather pressed his wife for clearer details.

Matilda explained:

"He came into my room. I didn't hear him enter, but I awoke to find him standing at the foot of my bed and smiling."

"What did he look like? How was he dressed?" my grandfather asked.

"Well, it was certainly George, alright," said Matilda. "I'd know him anywhere. He was still in his military uniform – pack on his back, cross-straps and pouches in front. He had, puttees wound about his legs, even his rifle ... And he was wearing his steel helmet."

Grandfather checked:

"Are you sure of those details? Rifle, too ...?"

"Yes! Of course I'm certain. I saw it all quite clearly ... Then he left, closing my door behind him."

"It was the door closing that woke me up," said my mother. "I heard Mummy's door closing; I know the sound it makes ..."

"That was not the military dress he would have been wearing when he embarked," Grandfather commented. "You are not describing how he would have appeared while travelling to go east by train, and from there by boat to England. He would have been in uniform, but not battle dress. You are describing how he would have looked on the battlefield ..."

But George was to be found nowhere on the premises and, although the incident was hard to ignore, or comprehend, in the days that followed everything quickly went back to normal. Matilda had had a dream; that was the most reasonable explanation ...

Two weeks passed, and one morning a buggy drew up in the courtyard, an elderly couple seated on the bench behind the horse. My grandfather greeted them politely, never having met them before, and when they were descended from their rig and comfortably seated round the parlour table, they revealed their identities.

They were George's parents, they explained, and had come to Eberstein on their son's specific written instructions to them.

George had been killed in Flanders two weeks previously, the father said gravely. Before leaving to go overseas he had left a letter with his parents, with the plea that they open it only in the event they received news of his death. They did as he had asked. They put the letter away safely at the back of a cupboard – and it remained there until two days ago when they had cause to open it. Among the personal expressions of a son's love for his parents, George had specifically requested they go in person to Eberstein Ranch and notify Matilda and Alfred of his death.

"Somehow I think we all knew ..." Grandmother Matilda began to say.

My mother remembered her mother's truncated sentence – how she had managed to avoid mentioning to the elderly couple she believed she had seen their son at the moment of his death.

Tappie

Not so surprisingly, of course, and as an impressionable teenager, Mother had become inordinately fond of her second cousin, Tappie, the guardian and companion who had been prepared (and paid) to indulge Mother's every whim so generously while she was attending school in Switzerland. Tappie, it seemed, had been quite prepared – to encourage Mother to think of herself as a little princess; it was fun, and maybe even profitable. There was not a great difference in their ages and, as the years went by, they found they were well-suited companions, one for the other, and established a strong bond. When my brother and I eventually entered the picture, Mother encouraged both of us to call this dear soul "Auntie" Tappie – even though, living our early childhood in Australia and North America, we had scant notion of who she was. Mother taught us that this auntie, now dodging the bombs of wartime London, was a courageous "internationalist." As we grew older and better equipped to understand some of the intricacies of life, we were able to add other details – and we learned, for instance, that Tappie had really been quite a swinger in Vancouver society between the wars. It vexed and embarrassed our grandfather to no end, which was most likely why he had been so anxious to see her on her way – and pay for her generously to remain away while she was performing the useful function of keeping an eye on his daughter. (Promises of good behaviour might have been taken seriously in those days, one must assume, but the stipend would have helped.) Tappie was no dowdy old aunt, to be sure. She had been a ravishing beauty in the flapper years of the west coast's 1920's, and had acquired a string of admirers who might have filled a modest telephone directory. She had been, my brother and I guessed, a pretty liberal-minded chaperone for our mother.

Precisely how Tappie had finally snagged her love-match was a bit of a mystery; it was a story to which we were not privy. Before the war members of her extended family had apparently expressed their collective relief on learning she had finally made her choice to settle down, albeit so far from home. No one had met her beau; no one knew anything much about him, and no one thought to make too extensive their enquiries once they understood his august rank in His Majesty's military – for the object of Tappie's fancy was a retired admiral of the Royal Navy, gallant and square-jawed in his uniform as he glowered from the photographs she kept of him on her mantle and beside her bed in her small London flat. Somehow he had captured her giddy and roving heart. Possibly with motives of upward social mobility, perfectly logical when mixed with passion, Tappie had been prepared to move halfway around the world from her cozy origins in British Columbia to make her life in pre-war London and, as so often happened in those conservative days with a limiting and dogged sadness, to accomplish little more than keep a secretive affair percolating when no doubt she might have hoped for marriage – for the bounder was already married. Though Mother, to us, tut-tutted her take on the mores of the day, her own life, as we had already begun to understand it, was hardly so exemplary that our acquired convictions outweighed our sense of intrigue. As for Tappie's nefarious liaison, we kept it as muffled a secret as we could. Really, the exercise served most to stoke the prurient minds of two adolescent boys. We remained as hush-hush as we were requested, but the matter to our callow thinking seemed a silly exercise. We tended to look on our Auntie Tappie as an elderly lady whose capacities for great passion had long since been filtered out of her life. We simply could not understand that she had loved the man dearly for years.

Tappie had moved into her apartment just off Sloane Street before the outbreak of war, and there she waited for her admiral to divorce his wife. (Over a period of time my brother and I had extracted from Mother a mass of titillating history – concerning Tappie as well as others. Most of it came in muted whispers during intimate closed sessions with her. The two of us were nothing if not adept at winkling information out of her, and anyway she could not keep secrets from us for very long.) We understood the idea of divorce caused the admiral considerable hesitation, perhaps not necessarily because of conflicted feelings for his wife and family, but more for the strategic defence of his pension and lagging fortunes. In any case, divorce was a messy business and carried a severe social stigma. But Tappie was determined to stand by him, which she did by stoically remaining holed-up in her little flat throughout the blitz. By the end of hostilities in 1945 the intrepid old sea dog was ill and on his deathbed. No fool, his wife had had more than enough of him by the mid-war years. She could suffer his inattentions to her no longer so both booted him from her bed, then abandoned him altogether once she had somehow secured the lion's share of his pension for herself. Then she refused him a divorce. In the end he was left to the ministrations and comforts of his long-time mistress who, fast becoming a guilt-ridden and bent little matron, murmured petitions for forgiveness from an array of saints and angels, and everywhere toted a string of prayer beads and her Holy Bible. To her credit Aunty Tappie was devoted and faithful to the man she always called "The Admiral." She alone was at his bedside to bring him his final comforts and close his eyelids.

Hearing of the admiral's demise, Mother, whose concerns were no doubt genuine but whose practical assistance mostly involved hiring someone else to do the whatever necessary, nonetheless decided she needed to "be there" for her guardian. Our sudden removal from school and flight to England was well enough organized in the summer of 1945 that she was able to dump Husband Number Two without causing either of her sons undue alarm, although both of us had actually become quite attached to him. The exercise was so smooth he himself likely had little idea he was being dumped. He would follow on later, as he had from Australia, we were told. We were pretty astute, though. After a few weeks in Britain, when we queried her on the matter, it became clear we would not be seeing him again. He had deceived her, she explained. He was no more than a dishonest con man, she said, a thief who had robbed her of some of her most valued possessions by removing them from storage in New York and selling them. To "spare our feelings" she thought it best to deceive her children, also. Somehow we were made to understand there was to be no more than what there was – and that was that.

Blighty

The three of us had arrived in Britain aboard a trans-Atlantic flying boat, relic of the pre-war sixteen-hour "clipper" service – a lumbering comfort from Baltimore to Pool (via Botwood and Shannon) that went into demise quite quickly following the war.

Seeing us off, our step-father had given each of us a dollar bill.

"This is your *short-snorter*," he said.

On the flight, he explained, we were to collect on each bill the signatures of everyone else on the plane, crew as well as passengers. Everyone had to write their names pretty small – but as it turned out, there were only sixteen passengers, plus about eight crew, so there was ample space on the bill.

The short-snorter was a custom thought to have originated among bush pilots in 1920's Alaska, but made popular by trans-oceanic flyers – mostly servicemen – during the war years. It was a quaint superstition, tongue-in-cheek and never intended to be taken seriously, that required anyone crossing an ocean by air to collect on a specimen of paper money the signatures of all those on board the flight. Thereafter anyone learning of your voyage would be able to challenge your veracity, demanding proof of your journey – which, of course, would be the signed short-snorter. Failure to produce such evidence would indicate a bullshitter and so incur a penalty: a round of drinks for everyone on the challenger's side at the time the proof is called.

Mother went along with the gag as well, so on the flight all three of us busied ourselves asking our fellow passengers and crew to sign our bills. They did so matter-of-factly and most willingly, which to me seemed convincing evidence the short-snorter was a valid form of air travel etiquette, if not insurance against bad luck – or being called upon to pay a round of drinks for a gaggle of people I may not know or like.

The custom has faded with the advent of modern air travel; two and three hundred souls aboard at a time, hundreds of trans-oceanic flights per day ... A quaint procedure, indeed, indicative of an earlier period in the romance of flight. Even so, for years afterwards I faithfully carried my crumpled short-snorter folded into my wallet. I think I even had it on me when I landed back in Vancouver eleven years after my flight in that old clipper flying boat.

We landed at the seaplane harbour in Pool in the early morning, and from there Mother had to shepherd us up to London from the south coast. The war with Germany was over and London was still in joyous shock, but the wreckage of bombed-out buildings was everywhere to be seen – piles of masonry bulldozed into mountains on every street ready to be carted away. Khaki-green jeeps hurtled about London's busy narrow streets transporting Tommies and GI's to urgent duties here and there – or, as seemed at least as likely, parked outside clubs and pubs. Most of the British Tommies were back home or held in barracks prior to their release from the military; the soldiers we saw roaming the streets and celebrating were mostly GI's – not well-liked by their hosts. It was the first time I heard that adage: "over-paid, over-sexed and over here" – but I hardly understood what it meant. I did notice, however, that lots of them would step out of doorways in an effort to talk to my mother. I thought they were being friendly – as I thought my mother was being unnecessarily unfriendly when she shrugged them off or told them to "get lost." Those GI's who weren't tearing about in their jeeps seemed to lounge long hours in doorways or seated on roadside curbs and stairs. People were prepared to acknowledge the Yanks had been of immeasurable service in defeating Nazi Germany, but beyond that they had few good things to say about them. They were too numerous, I would hear people say. They were too insensitive, too brassy, too loud.

Amid all the city's shattered infrastructure and chaos, and the shortages of everything – particularly decent accommodation – Aunty Tappie had managed to procure a small apartment for us on Pont Street; its bathroom had black accoutrements – black floor tiles set square, black wall tiles set diamond pattern to a height above my head, black tub, black sink, black bidet, black toilet, and even a black handle to the black tank's pull-chain. Black, black broodingly funeral black. Colour of war, I thought – and within days the bomb was dropped on Hiroshima. We all stood outside Buckingham Palace and cheered with an exhausted and battered multitude the day the war was finally declared over – and since that time it has been impossible for me to enter a black-tiled bathroom without thinking of the horrors of Hiroshima.

What on earth are they going to put in the newspapers now that the war is over? It was my most consuming thought. Not quite ten, I was already interested in "the news."

The first difficulty to arise once we were on English soil was that, the war having so recently ended, Mother experienced difficulties having her monthly allowance sent over from Canada. We were not destined to remain long at the Pont Street apartment; we had to find cheaper accommodation. But one of our guests at Pont Street who made a special impression on me was a man named Mack McInerney, Uncle Mack to us boys (not to be confused with Mr. Mack, our headmaster at school in Montreal). He was an American, had known our mother and step-father in New York, and was one of the designers for Lockheed who had helped perfect the enormously successful P-38, the twin-engine, twin-tail, twin-fuselage fighter known as the Lightning. The plane had been used to great effect in all theatres of the war, but particularly in the Pacific against the Japanese.

I do not know why Uncle Mack should have come to England when he did, so soon after our own arrival; his presence had a business connection in addition to whatever pleasure we all derived from his company. His job entailed a great deal of travel; he would come and then go again, sometimes with extraordinary stories of devastated Germany, sometimes of Italy, or of how he found the pace of recovery in France or Norway. Always he was a highly entertaining and jolly companion, taking us boys about London to Kew Gardens or Madame Tussauds wax museum or, best of all, to the famous science museum. My first commissioned art sale was to Uncle Mack. He encouraged me in my drawing and one day, at his request, I drew and coloured for him a picture of a donkey pulling a cart. I used as a model a small porcelain figurine which was on our living room mantle. He was charmed by my effort, or so he said at the time, and gave me sixpence – same as my (non-commissioned) sale to Michael Eisdale in Sydney some years before, so I guess sixpence was about the going rate for one of my early masterpieces.

But one day my brother and I came home to find Mother in tears. There had been an air crash in Scotland. Uncle Mack had been returning from one of his European trips; everyone on board had died in the fire except him. Somehow he had been thrown clear of the plane at the moment of impact. His unburned but lifeless body was found several hundred metres away from where everyone else had died inside the plane.

It was a traumatic event. It stayed with me, and I still recall how I felt at the news. At near ten I could not have had a deep understanding of its impact on me, but I know that for weeks I felt overwhelmed, crushed and very small. I had seen the violence of an air crash before, at the Seigniory Club two years earlier, but it had not involved someone for whom I had had such strong personal feelings, nor could I imagine a catastrophe capable of snuffing out the lives of so many people. Mother's tears registered with me, as did the gap that was left because Uncle Mack wasn't there anymore to fill it.

Time worked its magic; the tears dried, the gap closed. Even I recognized my young life had been eventful. I choked a bit, but the event passed. Uncle Mack has come to mind many times in the years since the crash that killed him, and always when it does I am a near-ten-year-old again who can do nothing with the information.

I think if they were honest, adults would have to admit they are closer to their own childhoods than they care to let on.

My brother and I were packed off for our first term at boarding school in Northamptonshire, and when we returned for our Christmas holiday Mother had already moved into a cramped single room somewhere close to Paddington. We tried to keep white mice in cages, but when they escaped Mother screeched loud and long – not at all, she hastened to assure us, because she objected to mice, but because the premises was far too small for family-plus-pets. We knew otherwise, of course, that she was repulsed at the very thought of mice and was only able to maintain a modicum of composure by convincing herself that ours were caged. We knew she was making a super-human effort to be a good sport about our new passion for rodents. My brother had hauled his out of the cage by its tail to put an identifying mark of India ink on the back of its head; it wriggled and squirmed, dropped onto the floor and ran for cover. Mother squealed. In the melee I let mine go too, and there followed a frantic half hour – Mother on the bed alternately behaving like a schoolgirl about to wet her knickers, or shouting orders like Sergeant Major Brittan and throwing pillows. My brother finally caught one mouse under an inverted saucepan; Mother caught the other with the help of a long woolen sock. In that instant, I do believe, she cured forever her phobia for rats and mice.

Our school uniform consisted of grey flannel jackets and shorts, grey knee-socks and black shoes. Our shirts were also utility grey flannel, and we wore neckties of bright yellow. Raincoats (one cannot contemplate the vagaries of English weather without considering both raincoat and the ubiquitous umbrella) were of dark blue gabardine and, to top things off, a bright yellow school cap to match our ties. Mother would come to see us off aboard the school train at the beginning of each term, and we would gallop up and down the platform greeting our buddies and showing off. Mother said we always looked like a bunch of twittering canaries; dressed in a severe suit to create the correct and somber image of a caring parent, she herself looked like a war refugee. Platform farewells are awkward things; thinking about them gives me an itch to go somewhere.

By our first Easter break Mother had moved again, this time into another single room – but considerably bigger. Anticipating our arrival for the holidays she had decorated the place as best she could with the landlady's bits and pieces. She had cleverly arranged a comfortable sitting and dining area that converted into sleeping space for me at night. My brother had a cot along one wall that was a seat in daytime. Mother's bed was in an alcove, divided from the main area by a curtain of coloured burlap. She had hung a few pictures on the walls along with a bright poster of some event at Earl's Court. It was home for the time.

"You wait till our belongings arrive," she said more than once. "We'll find a decent apartment and have our own things about us again. I'll be able to fix up a proper home, you'll see ..."

The present place was located in West Kensington not far from Barker's department store where my brother and I used to enjoy browsing about, possibly casing the joint for items to steal – although I'm inclined to think our thieving days were done. We were by now fast becoming proper little London gentlemen. I seem to remember once suggesting how we could heist some item or other from a local store, and being severely chastised by my senior sibling – who explained in words even a dummy like me could understand that he had made the decision to go straight. I do not believe I ever had the temerity to raise such matters with him again.

Our quarters had a balcony that gave onto a quiet inner-city backstreet; it gave us a pleasure far greater than hanging out of a window. There was a small public garden right across from us, the green canopy of its trees reaching above the height of our windows and so rewarding us with a panorama of the city's natural bounty – shrubbery, flowers and birdlife. The balcony gave us a perch one floor above life at street level, and from here we could look onto that other world passing dreamlike just below us, critically examine the passersby without them having the least idea of what it was we were able to see. There was a sense of exhilaration, even power, in this simple exercise. We enjoyed going out there to play with a soapy liquid that had newly come on the market – a solution into which we could dip a wire ring at the end of a handle. A filmy diaphragm formed across the ring and we could blow it out, gently, to form series of light floating bubbles.

In those days milk was delivered daily by horse-drawn wagon, the dairy company's name gaudily displayed on painted boards on the vehicle's sides.

Customarily, in our area, the milkman left his rig in the street about two houses down from where we were playing on our balcony, and it so happened that one day the breeze carried our bubbles down to cross before the blinkered eyes of the bewildered milk horse, and then burst – pop!

The startled animal evidently decided it would be best to get out of there. The brakes could not have been applied very firmly. With determination and an effortless heave Old Ned set the wagon wheels in motion. By the time the milkman stepped down off our neighbour's porch his wagon with its cargo of jangling milk bottles was turning the corner of the garden at the bottom end of the street.

My brother and I spluttered with laughter. Infinitely better, we agreed, than tossing water bombs from our New York window onto the unsuspecting pedestrians below; once the bubbles had popped, no evidence!

I do not believe the harried milkman was able to turn Ned's head around. Very few on our street received milk that day.

Right next to our building was the bombed-out shell of a building the authorities had not yet demolished. There were such scars on every street in London. A sign outside read:

DANGER – KEEP OUT

"Don't go in there! It's unsafe ..." Mother warned darkly.

So of course we went in and explored the place from top to bottom, climbing as far as the shattered stairs would allow, poking about in whatever rooms were still accessible. One never knew – we might have discovered an unexploded bomb, or the remains of a German pilot lodged in a hole in the roof.

Mother came onto the balcony and called us in from the street for supper. By a stroke of luck we had only then left the ruined shell and she had not seen us in it. As we sat at our evening meal there was an almighty rumble from outside, and clouds of dust rose in the street to the height of our windows. We ran onto the balcony. The entire four-storey façade of the forbidden building had fallen forward into the street. In doing so the remains of the roof, and all the floors from the top down, concertinaed into the building's basement. In an instant there was nothing left at all at the side of our building except a huge space filled with rubble.

My brother and I looked at one another with huge eyes.

"Well, I'm glad that for once you both had the good common sense to listen to your mother and not play about in there," Mother commented matter-of-factly, ushering us back to the meal table.

"Now finish your soup quickly. I've made a delicious shepherd's pie."

A frequent visitor to our humble quarters in those days was a young man described to us as a distant "cousin" by the name of John Hillery. He wasn't a cousin at all, actually, but the explanation served for my brother and me. In fact John's parents had been close friends to Tappie, and Mother had met the family years before when she was on holiday from her Swiss finishing school in the 1920's.

John had flown Spitfires for the Royal Air Force during the war. He had been taken prisoner in 1944 and ended up in Colditz, the camp for incorrigibles – those prisoners who had attempted escape from other camps. The place was said to be escape-proof and, indeed, for John it was. He had been held there until his liberation after the allied victory in the following year. He had suffered a broken leg at the time of his capture so was hardly in his best running-and-hiding form. When we first met him he walked with the aid of a cane, limping stiff-legged.

John was fun, regaling us with stories of his war exploits. We sat listening to him for hours, plying him with questions when we felt he had been short on detail. He seemed so dashing, hobbling about on his stick, and when he was comfortably seated with a cup of tea, or a glass of Mother's "little something" in his hand, he would use his stick as a prop for whatever point he was making in his story. Sometimes it would be a joystick, sometimes the wings of

Somersaults

his aircraft, or sometimes the entire plane as it swooped across the sky. He could turn it into a canon in his wings, a rifle, or even Hitler's ridiculous moustache. He was quite an actor, was John, and a great storyteller.

Two of his yarns left strong impressions:

The first concerned the occasion when his fighter was badly damaged in a dogfight over France. His engine conked out and he was forced to get ready to bail out. As he told it, the best way to leave a stricken Spitfire was for the pilot to undo his seatbelt, haul back the canopy, then roll the plane over onto its back so that he would drop out still seated on top of the cushion of his parachute pack.

On this occasion John commenced to roll, but when he was at about ninety degrees his engine fired up again. So he righted the plane, but in doing so the engine stopped a second time. Cautiously he rolled over, and once more the engine sputtered to life. At this point he realized his carburetor system was playing up, that he could obtain fuel feed only when he was way over on his side, or even upside-down. So he closed his canopy, secured his seatbelt, rolled on his back and power climbed. When he felt he could not climb more, he righted himself and glided – then rolled, climbed, righted and glided – rolled, climbed, righted and glided – all the way back to Britain.

A former Spitfire pilot might be better qualified to say whether or not that's a likely story, but to a ten-year-old it was gospel – and to this day that's precisely how I have retold the story. You know how it is: some stories are always good for an extra mile or more, whether right way up or upside-down.

But the yarn about John Hillery that still intrigues me the most concerns his capture, his wound, and what happened subsequently.

He had found himself in a dogfight with a Messerschmitt 109 somewhere over western Germany, and in this he met his match in flying prowess. His aircraft was set ablaze, and shrapnel cut into his leg. He was further badly injured when he broke the leg parachuting to the ground and in failing to land properly. German defenders spotted him as he came down and he was quickly captured. He was well treated, however, and was taken to a nearby town where the municipal buildings had been converted into a hospital. There doctors treated his wound, set his leg in a cast, and he was confined to bed – unable to move and of necessity a model prisoner.

A few days after he had been downed and was stretched out in bed in the makeshift hospital a young Luftwaffe pilot paid him a visit:

"Are you the Englishman who was shot down near here last week?" asked the German in perfect English.

"Yes, unless there were others," John replied.

"No, there were no others. Just you. I was the one you were flying against. I learned only yesterday that you had survived and were here ..."

"So it was you! I lost you when you led me into the sun over that cloud bank. Didn't see you turn ... thought you'd gone off to my right."

"No, I stall-turned to the left, dropped below you like a stone, and then a power climb up on your left tail. I knew you hadn't seen me..."

The two young flyers talked for a half hour, the German sitting at the foot of the Englishman's sick-bed. Of course they talked about flying, re-fought their dogfight and compared notes as to what they did or should have done.

"I'm glad you pulled through," the German told John. "Look, I have to go now. There's an operation on tonight and I'm part of it."

"Good luck!" said John.

"When I get back I'll bring you some cigarettes."

John thanked him and they parted, shaking hands. Neither of them said "if..." but it was certainly in both their minds.

Sure enough three or four days later the young German showed up again. He brought with him some old English-language magazines, and several packets of cigarettes.

"Your people are very active now," the German commented at one point. "You are picking up in strength, and we are being pressed. I have to go up every day, sometimes several times in a day. Our leaves have been cancelled, of course. I don't think this is going to last a lot longer ..."

The German expressed himself in a matter-of-fact tone, pragmatically courageous. John heard him out but said little. Loss of confidence or hope could have been as certain as a death sentence, and John wished him no ill. The war would run its course and both of the young men would come through it or not, as Fate decreed. Bad Karma has a way of falling on the shoulders of those who wish others ill.

They talked about girls. The German had a fiancée living in Gratz, but he had not heard from her for months.

"It's not a good time to plan for the future," he said.

"No. Anything can happen," John replied. "But it's a shame not to dream."

"Dream? Ha! I dream alright. I have the sweetest dreams, but I don't dare plan. If you make plans they'll go wrong. Better off with no more than the dreams. Dreams cannot do any harm. If they are sweet they make you wish to fall asleep again – not as exciting as flying, maybe, but better than war!"

Theirs was a bitter laughter for two men so young, and once again the German took his leave.

He returned a few more times and the two of them, caught up on opposite sides of the quarrel between their nations, somehow soared above it all in their flights of fancy and their love of flying. And yet both of them knew that fraternization with the enemy is forbidden; so outwardly, especially in the presence of doctors or nursing staff, they treated one another with a certain formality. Both men, without saying it, recognized what fraternization was, and they probably very well understood why it was considered dangerous and forbidden. Yet both also knew to what a false circumstance the notion related, how little their encounter had anything fundamental to do with the prosecution of the war – for the war, truly, was a lesser thing for each of them, in the main an abrupt and unwanted intrusion into their unusual comradeship.

John never learned his new friend's full name – and then almost inevitably the German did not come anymore.

"He's bought it," thought John.

With the reserve defence mechanism warriors maintain deep in their psyches for the loss of people they come close to, he soon put the German pilot into a recess of his mind. His leg began to heal. He tried to escape from the hospital, but was easily caught. He was sent to a prisoner camp, tried to escape again, and was caught again – this time being sent to Colditz. Here he remained until his repatriation by the allied victors.

We had encountered John Hillery in London close to a year after he had returned home. He held back on many of the details of his story, never really saying more than that he had met the young pilot who had shot him down, and that he had actually quite liked him. As with other young people who had fought hard in the war, John could not settle down. About 1947 he went out to Australia to try to build a new life for himself. He returned to visit family three years later, and that is when we were able to round out his story.

One of his first jobs in Australia had been as a travelling salesman, his assigned route taking him on the nine-hundred-mile stretch of "the bitumen," the highway that runs from Alice Springs in the centre of the continent, north across the desert and barren ranges to Darwin. It is one of the most desolate and forbidding highways in the world. The rule in those parts was that if one happened to see another vehicle pulled over on the side of the road, it was obligatory – not to say a simple courtesy – to stop and render assistance if required.

John stopped. A large Holden had been pulled over, its hood up and its driver with his head pushed down into the engine compartment.

"Can I help you?" asked John.

The German pilot straightened his back ...

For John Hillery it was the start of another story.

The Hillery family lived at Little Missenden, a village not far from Aylesbury in Buckinghamshire. We spent one or two early holidays there, even rented a house a door or two away with the auspicious name of The White House.

It was here, at the age of eleven, that I discovered clay while on one of our walks, and I brought a bucket of it back to the house. To me it was a form of natural plasticine, but more pleasing to the touch. There was no one to tell me how to use it properly so I experimented, pushed it into all kinds of shapes – mostly ships with sticks for masts and paper for sails. But the stuff warped easily and was never such a pleasure to me when it was dry as it had been when moist and malleable. I made a few plates and jugs and bottles, but could never figure out how it was that they could be made to hold liquids. I tried varnishing or painting the interiors, but without great success. I discovered that by burnishing leather-hard clay with the back of a spoon it took on a sheen and became a little more impermeable; water might remain in a vessel ten minutes rather than pass right through (and take the bottom out of the piece) in two minutes or less. I made a model of the church at Little Missenden, and was terribly proud of it. I kept it, blanketed under a moist rag, beside my bed until I had finished it in every detail. Then I carefully placed it on our balcony to dry in the sun. But I overlooked the vagaries of English weather. There came an afternoon of rain, and my hours of painstaking modelling were reduced in minutes to a heap of mud, eventually becoming no more than an ugly stain on the balcony deck. Early and painful experiments.

No one told me one had to fire clay in order to preserve it. It was years before I was to learn the term "terracotta."

Sam

Little Missenden was the place where my brother and I came to know Sam, a merry old codger whose smells and habits seemed to offend everyone but us. For the two of us Sam was the epitome of adventure – a combination of Popeye, Tinker Bell, Walter Mitty, Rip van Winkle, Trader Horn, Man Friday, and the ugliest hobo forward of the caboose.

To call him a character would be understatement. A pithier description of the fellow would require usage of a dictionary of the most pungent phraseology. Up to that time of my life Sam was the single most extraordinary person I had met; certainly the most colourful. More than sixty-five years on I can recall few to match him. His craggy face and stubbled chin were the visible structure around the slash of his twisted-lip mouth that worked as though he was about to spit betel juice, but that held an assortment of yellowing and broken teeth. The squint in his glinting eyes, along with the droop of his tear-filled lower lids, was the result of his constant smoking of a rancid concoction of tobaccos – in a pipe bowl minus its stem. This forced him to grip the stub-end of the pipe's firebox between his lips and what was left of his teeth so that the smoke and fumes would puff straight up into his eyeballs, resulting in facial contortions that must have become permanent when the wind changed. The image of him is as clear to me now as though he had this moment sidled up beside me at my writing desk. And even if I failed to see him, I'd know the rank smell of him the instant he drew abreast.

He was a wheedler and a wheeler-dealer, but mostly he was a crafty poacher, always just one jump ahead of the bailiff. He lived in a decorated Gypsy-style wooden caravan that looked as if it had been rolled out of the circus. The horse that pulled it into its present space had long since died, or bolted, so the rig stood on the grounds of the public common that extended from the bottom of the Hillery garden, in a corner behind a shield of trees and shrubbery concealing it from general view. But for all that his camp and the independence he seemed intent on redefining could not be seen, it was surely given away by an almost constant whiff of wood smoke. If it had been wood smoke alone it might not have been so bad. The trouble was Sam liked to experiment, a sort of ruby-dub alchemy in which he attempted to transform bits of this and that (anything – rubbers, plastics, resins, liquids or flora) into a goop which he would use for any number of purposes, ranging from soup to glue, to "the best darned bait there is" for catching rabbits, stoats, foxes, squirrels, owls or an unsuspecting neighbour's chickens.

From time to time the stench from these obnoxious concoctions would roll up the garden path on a gentle air and fairly overpower Mrs. Hillery's tea guests. The hostess might quietly explain the source of such intrusions, usually with a flavour of tolerant English humour, but would never dream of marching in on one of Sam's experiments with a view to calling a halt to it. She would wait till a more propitious moment after the guests had gone, brew up another pot of tea, set out another large plate of her delicious home-baked cookies, cakes and thin cucumber sandwiches, place all of this plus two cups and saucers, sugar bowl, cream jug and dainty silver spoons, upon a lacquered tray and carry it down her garden path to serve Sam her daintiest – "and have a little chat."

And Sam, like Barcus, was always willing. Good-natured fellow that he was, he invariably expressed enchantment about Mrs. Hillery's own good nature. Theirs was a symbiotic relationship, and I think they were genuinely fond of one another. One has to imagine what was said. Within a day Sam's place would look like an extension of the pages of English Country Garden. Window boxes and potted plants would be set about the caravan as though a flutter of well-intentioned fairies had descended on the place. An unsightly accumulation of Sam's bits and pieces – bicycle frames, automobile fenders, old wash stands and a poor replica of Eros – would be hauled away, or at least concealed from view, and on one occasion the old reprobate was even coerced into repainting his home along bright carnival lines – yellows, reds, greens, blues and whites, with border panels done in flower patterns and painted lattice.

The whole charming effect would last a month or so before the sheer power of Sam's lifestyle gradually came to dominate again. Plants would wilt because of neglect or the noxious gases rising from some new experiment or culinary effort. The weeds would soar in increasing profusion, their strength to resist the local ambient being somewhat superior to their primrose, begonia and sweet pea cousins. Brambles, thistles, nettles, crab grasses and rag weeds would rise to heights unscaled in botanical lore and work overtime to cover the pretty paintwork on the sides of the caravan. About four months was the outside limit before Mrs. Hillery felt constrained to brew up another batch of tea and goodies, and join her neighbour for further amiable conversation.

Sam's abode occupied two levels. There was the caravan itself, and then the space under the caravan. Behind the great wooden wheels (which, remarkably, still had all their spokes) he had tacked up a sort of barrier, or partition, of boards and canvas strips to provide himself with a crawlspace storage area under the level at which he lived. Here, if one dared to crawl in, one would find all the treasure of Sam's long life, for ancient he certainly was – at least to me. Suitcases tied up with ratty string contained old garments – suits, sweaters, shoes, and bits and pieces of First World War uniforms. It seems he discarded nothing, that everything was put by for some rainy day that might happen sometime. In cardboard boxes he had bits and pieces of crystal set receivers, electronic gadgetry from Bomber Command, piles of odd cracked porcelain plates, cups and cutlery, presumably in the event that he decided to throw a dinner party. There were old pots, pans, surgical equipment, lawn mower parts, wheels, tires, a pram, a ladder, extra blankets, a broken chair or two, an old electric stove (in case the municipality ever strung wiring out to his complex and included him on the grid), a His Master's Voice crank gramophone with an accompanying collection of old hits on disc – 78 r.p.m. – and a sword (rusted and certainly ancient) which he swore had been waved aloft by a wild Highlander during the Battle of Bannockburn in 1314. Gumboots came in eight different sizes, some being duplicated lefts and rights. Rabbit skins, dried and stretched on makeshift rack frames of sticks, were haphazardly treated with salt and alum. They stank, and the hair was dropping out in clumps. Hose pipe he had – kilometres of it – and wire, and coils of rope and balls of old string, hammers, saws, paint cans full of rusting old nails, several picks, several shovels, old metal tubing, a couple of garden-room or greenhouse doors with broken glass, a barrow minus its wheel, mattresses, straw bales, a quantity of bricks, a pile of "good earth" for his plants, planks, bolts of cheap cloth, chicken wire. And mice.

Mrs. Hillery said she didn't mind the mice, but she asked Sam to please keep them in the vicinity of his caravan and not to let them approach the house at tea time where they might alarm her guests.

That was the lower level. It took a deal of courage for a small boy to crawl into it, but Sam said it was part of the ritual. I never discovered the full meaning of the ritual, and Sam didn't explain.

The upper level, Sam's living quarters, was less disorderly and, it should be admitted, a little less repulsive – though where one draws a line between one sort of repulsiveness and another would be a qualitative consideration. He lived like a rooting animal (a pig comes to mind), but there was a certain consistency and even orderliness about his sty. His dishes were "washed" in water he changed but once a week or so, when it was clear an added dash of soap powder would no longer suffice to suds-up the liquid that by now had turned a battleship grey. He explained his practice:

"'Slong as I can work up a bit o'suds, the water's still good for washin' ... it's the suds wot does in the dirt, 'n's long as I got suds I got hygiene. When ye can't get no more suds, might as well chuck water out, feed cabbages with it. Start again."

Pursuant to this logic his rinse water was always fresh. His "tea-towels" were his collarless shirts due for laundering "... I use the tails o'em for me dryin' up. Tails 'ave been tucked in me trousers, see, so that part's clean – probably cleaner than any tea towel 'anging up there beside the stove collectin' dust..."

His bed, actually a wooden shelf, was a tangle of smoke-rancid blankets, topped by an ancient army greatcoat. His pillow, without slip cover, was a battered heap of feathers encased in material that had once been printed in stripes of blue, pink or grey. One could not easily tell which colour was which because all was by now blended into one contiguous mass, the impression within that dim-lit place now being "stripe" rather than any more specific colour of stripe.

"No point in 'avin' sheets," Sam explained. "They has to be washed – an' besides, it's the warmth I needs, not the silky comfort ..."

His clothes, hanging in an alcove behind the chipped enamel stove, had likewise been transformed into a uniform grey colour, his shirts, jackets and trousers all about the same hue as his dish water. His bare feet ("... don't like socks; I only wears 'oles in 'em") were stuffed into unpolished black boots without laces, loose "so's the toes can breathe," he explained.

In fact Sam could explain most things. His darting eyes missed nothing, and from his crooked mouth he spouted out an explanation, a commentary or a philosophy about everything his nimble mind could light on. Others might consider his world somewhat circumscribed, but he didn't.

Sam was a poacher of considerable ability and daring. He was widely known in the district, recognized and tolerated – even admired – by most of the squires and landowners within a considerable radius of his roost beside the common.

"I'm not greedy. I never takes more than wot I needs for the pot, and I give away wot I can't use mysel'. I 'unts on lands where I knows me welcome – usually. It's rare, mind, but if I'm marched off a piece o' property an' so knows I'm not welcome, well – I'm extra careful! I won't go back where I know I'm not wanted – unless I really has to, o'cors ... Generally I respects others if they respects me."

All of this explanation was accompanied by a staccato burst of winks and nods, so that it would have been quite impossible to tell whether old Sam was having us on, or just reacting to the nervous ticks he had acquired through years of skulduggery, artfully dodging uncomfortably close inspection – or by smoking his pipe like Popeye. His mouth was so kinked it was difficult to know what was a smile.

In various corners of Sam's caravan were sundry firearms. Each piece was antique, and all were flint-lock shotguns dating from the mid-XIX century. Their owner never said where he came by them. He must have had at least six of them in working order, and he spent hours oiling and cleaning them so that for all that each one was of great age, they sparkled and shone as though still on the shelf at the gunsmiths. Indeed, in that grimy place, amid the confusion and general blight, these ancient firearms stood out for their pristine perfection.

"Here! Try one out," said Sam, arranging a couple of old tin cans on top of a stump.

I had never fired a gun before.

"Let me show ye, boy ... First a little powder, tamp it down with the stick. Then take, say, a quarter-page o'newsprint, make a dry wad, so, and bung that in place. That ensures yer powder won't run away. Tamp it down, not too 'ard – now, a small handful of yer shot ..."

He poured it from the funnel of a leather bag.

"Now we 'olds all that in place wi' another wad o'paper. Tamp it – that's the ticket ... Not too tight or it'll knock yer bleedin' shoulder off when ye fire confounded thing ..."

Now it was ready to carry, he said. To fire, pull back the flint hammer till it catches – settle yer firin' cap a-top ... But now ye hav't' be careful. A little jog an' t'whole thing could go off ... Now, a little line o' powder into the breach...

I aimed at the tin cans from about forty metres.

B-O-O-M!

Both tin cans disintegrated. The kick from the firing pounded my right shoulder and threw me onto my arse.

"There, ye see," said Sam, like a science professor. "A mite too much powder ... an' ye didn't need quite such a lot o' the shot. Ye tamped it down a little too 'ard, p'raps ... Y'aw'right? Here, try't ag'in ..."

Touch of powder ... newsprint, tamp it down just so ... little bit of shot ... more paper, tamp it down ... back with the hammer, settle the cap, pour in a line of powder...

W-H-A-A-M!

I picked myself up again, rubbing my shoulder, so bruised it felt worse than one of my brother's pummelings. I didn't want to try firing the gun again.

"That's the ticket! Ye'got it! We'll make a fine poacher out'a ye!"

Sam was all encouragement ...

One evening we were brewing up a paint-tin of tea over an open fire in front of the caravan, the smoke curling up lazily between the tree branches and impregnating our clothes with that unmistakable aroma of The Great Outdoors. Sam sat at the top of the little stair that mounted to his front door, the pipe bowl shoved into his angular mouth and clamped so that the hot wooden bowl was no more than a centimetre or two from the tip of his nose. He squinched up one side of his face to prevent the heat from the firebox burning his eyeball.

"Tomorr'as we goes a-stoatin'," Sam announced. "I wants y'alls a'here by five o'clock mornin' time ..."

Instructing his cohorts so conspiratorially, it occurs to me there was likely more Fagin in him than either Popeye or Walter Mitty.

"What's a-stoatin', Sam?"

He produced two small cages, a white stoat in each – beautiful sleek-furred creatures that looked to me like miniature otters or mongooses.

"Can't put 'em in the same cage. Both males, and they'd likely fight to the death ..." said Sam with exaggerated drama.

"To the death?"

"To the death, lad. They're vicious little brutes, but not with me. Look!"

He pulled one out of its cage and it ran up the inside of his sleeve to emerge from under the collar at the back of his jacket. From there it climbed nimbly onto his cor'blimey and sat there staring at us, sniffing. On top of Sam's head there would have been plenty to sniff.

The following morning, without a word to Mother, we rose silently and stepped from the cozy warm quiet of our house out into the chill morning mist of pre-dawn, making our way to the caravan on the verge of the common.

Sam was already up and bustling about. He offered us each a warm mug of tea, then handed out the equipment we were to carry – a tangled bunch of netting and something heavy in an old sack – and we were off across the fields, Sam leading with the confident swagger and brisk short steps of a young city businessman about to make a killing. At least he seemed to know where he was going, first over rolling hilly common, then cutting off into a wood and through shrubbery so dense that without our guide we would have become lost very quickly. Because of the mist visibility was down to no more than six metres, and Sam's grey-clothed figure had an uncanny way of blending in with the undergrowth so that we would have lost him in a jiffy had we not trotted right along.

"Sh-h-h-h!" he cautioned, and presently we came like shadows into a forest glade with a high bank on one side. On top of this were tall oaks and elms, their tangled roots breaking through the lower surface like varicose veins on the legs of a stout old woman. And among these roots were a dozen or more rabbit holes. A gigantic warren honeycombed the earth below the trees, and Sam went quickly to work with deft fingers.

He took the nets from us, and plunged his arm into the gunny sack to take out dozens of roughly cut wooden pegs. In minutes he had secured nets over all the rabbit holes on the face of the bank. Then he reached into another sack that he had been carrying and took from it one of the caged stoats.

"Watch this!" he whispered, and held the eager little animal to one of the holes. The excited stoat sniffed and squirmed, and appeared to know exactly what was expected of him.

Lifting one of the nets, Sam placed the creature at the entrance of the hole and the animal raced inside, almost instantly out of sight.

We put our ears to various of the holes. There was pandemonium inside the deep earth, squeaking, scurrying feet. In no time rabbits scurried to the exits of their warren and became entangled in the nets, terror behind, terror now in front of them. They thrashed about in the nets trying to escape, but then they lay still and awaited their fate.

Sam moved quickly, with his strong fingers reaching into the nets and breaking necks.

"Here! You do this!" he said to us. "I've got to get me stoat back..."

He started whistling and calling gently at one of the holes, and in a few minutes his little white demon appeared and he took hold of it.

I found I could not break a rabbit's neck. Instead I found a small one with wide, terrified eyes, and I lifted it out and held it close to my chest. It wriggled, but I secured its front legs firmly and presently it settled. I stroked the back of its head gently with my fingers, and wanted to keep it.

"No," said Sam. "He's a wild one, an' yer shouldn't pen 'im up. Let 'im go. He'll turn into a right fine buck, an' breed a whole lot more like him – an' I'll be able to make a rabbit stew next year an' the year after ..."

I put the little creature down. For a moment he stood there, hesitant, and then in a flash he was gone.

Sam smiled his wisp of a smile. He had caught and killed six adult rabbits. Others he had turned loose, females and young.

"That's the way yer do it!" he said proudly, popping the dead animals into a spare sack.

"No noise, no fuss. No bangs to alert an angry squire or gamekeeper. Good dinner for me – yous too, if yer likes. An' the good lady Mrs. Hillery."

"And when we skins 'em I'll show ye how to make yerselves a nice pair o'mittens ..."

We came home close to lunch time and found Mother in the kitchen.

"Where have you boys been?" she asked suspiciously.

We might have said, "canoeing" – but that would no longer fit. Neither of us wanted to tell a lie, so instead we said in chorus:

"Out!"

Mother eyed the two of us from under arched brows. We both looked as though we had been dragged through the forest backwards. My brother pulled a dead rabbit out from behind his back and held it up for closer inspection.

"Caught a rabbit!" he said, looking for Mother to clap hands and dance a jig.

None of it. She pulled back, her hands automatically shielding herself from any protracted vision of the wretched thing, the horror of it, as though she had been invited to examine the contents of his fishing worm tin.

"Very good!" she said. "We'll talk about what to do with it later. Now go get ready and wash up. Lunch is on the table ..."

My brother put the dead rabbit on the kitchen counter, and we both rushed upstairs to the bathroom to pee and wash our hands.

Good. No further questions.

Somersaults

Mr. Cope

We were "good boys," my brother and I – inasmuch as we were polite, washed our hands and scrubbed under our fingernails before sitting down to dinner, had been well-trained in when to say "please" and "thank you," and how to slick down our dishevelled hair when company was coming over. But we were far from the good boys our dear mother envisioned. When we thought we could be neither seen nor heard, we fought like a cat and a dog trapped together in a carrier basket – an ever-present sibling rivalry that took its toll on Mother's nerves, especially on those mornings after she had spent the previous evening entertaining at cork-popping speed.

It was not only a matter of the quarrels that developed between the two brothers of divorced parents – the one like his father, the other like his mother. That would have been bad enough. Our mother was well able to see how her two sons faced off against one another, and she was astute enough to understand that much of our bickering was directly related to her own behaviour and failure to cope. She understood that a great deal of our acting up was a way of addressing her, and that she could not answer it without facing her own demons. In front of others we were the very models of dutiful attention to our mother. When she was alone we ganged-up on her ferociously to let her know we had noticed the callousness and selfishness of her inattention and absenteeism. On the cusp of our teens we were not sophisticated or mature enough to define our resentment in quite the terms I use here, but we were masterful at performing our frustrations. Thinking we were trampling on her, Mother fought back – thus helping to perpetuate the nucleus of bedlam that had become a part of our family a considerable time before we had set foot in Merrie England. Matters soon came to such a pass that, realizing she was out-gunned, Mother finally called for help from none other than her solicitor – a long-time friend to both Mother and Tappie – a firm but stern man who went by the name of Geoffrey Silverwood Cope. We had been instructed to call him Uncle Geoff.

"Perhaps Mr. Cope can cope," said Mother, sucking in her breath and trying bravely to make some headway with her pun.

"Tsch!" My brother and I contemptuously turned our backs.

In due course, however, we were summoned to, and dutifully appeared at, Uncle Geoff's chambers in Lincoln's Inn, an austere and intimidating warren of passages, caves and law offices in the heart of the City of London, all of it most craftily designed to frighten two young toughs out of their wits.

"Come in, boys – sit you down, put your hands in your laps, don't swing your legs, and be silent!"

We did as we were bid.

Uncle Geoff sat behind an ornately-carved desk of quite enormous proportions. In his lap he held what looked to me like the head of a drum covered with a canvas cloth. He was poking a needle in one side of it, out the other – drawing a coloured line of wool through it in the same way I had seen Nanny work at stitching up the holes we wore in our socks. His fingers worked diligently, his shaggy brows all the while fluttering up and down like little white butterflies as he concentrated on the pattern he was making on the drumhead.

"Do you know what I am doing, young Jeremy?" he asked, seeing me staring at his work.

"You're sewing?" I suggested meekly.

"This is called *petit point*," he explained. "I have worked at this sort of thing since I was a boy about your age. Now I'm pretty good at it, but it has taken me years of practice. This piece is to be set in a frame ..."

He held it up so that I could see the design – an intricate, almost mathematical, pattern of colourfully stylized flowers.

"... And in due course I shall present it to the queen. It's a long way from completion, but hopefully I will have it ready to give to her as a Christmas present."

"Isn't that a lady's hobby?" I chipped in rudely.

My brother snarled sideways, but Uncle Geoff smiled his toleration.

"Well, some ladies seem to be quite good at it – it relaxes them. And I think that if it relaxes them, it might relax me also. Which it does. I don't think of any work, or a hobby for that matter, as being strictly for a man or strictly for a lady. If you enjoy doing something creative, then you must do it ... and always be sure to do it well."

Uncle Geoff was an unusually tall man, slim and with silvered hair. He stooped as he moved about his chambers slowly and with great caution, as though he expected the floor boarding to squeak. Mother had told us he had a way of ignoring silliness and saying no more than what was important for the moment – so I paid close attention to what he was saying, all the while pondering the attachment he exhibited to his *petit point*, and why it was so important he have it ready to give to the queen by Christmas. Of course Christmas presents were important; I knew about that. But we were a long way off Christmas ... He reminded me of Alistair Sim, the film actor with the astonishingly well intoned voice of reasoned authority. Frightening.

"It's my tea-time," he said, laying the drum to one side on his desktop. "Would you boys care to join me?"

It was a command, not a request, and neither my brother nor I could find voice to respond either yea or nay.

Geoffrey Silverwood Cope picked up a tiny silver bell that rested atop his desk, and shook it once. A voice from somewhere under our chairs gave immediate response.

"Sir ...?"

"Tea and biscuits for three, if you'd be so kind, Satchell."

"Of course, sir. Right away, sir!"

Satchell, as we were about to discover, was Uncle Geoff's "Man Friday" – butler, file clerk, research assistant, messenger and all-round dog's body. We were assured no day's work in that office could be completed without the fellow's invaluable services and attentions. During office hours he hibernated in a dingy cave-cum-archive below the deck of the chamber, sorting through everything from papers to Uncle Geoff's formal court attire, wigs and unpolished shoes. At the tinkling of the little silver bell he would mount to the office above via a creaky wooden spiral staircase that was almost invisible behind a table in one corner of the office, over against a dark wooden bookcase stacked with ancient legal tomes. Presently a wizened and balding little man appeared from the deep shadows. He was dressed in a high collar shirt with black bowtie, black waistcoat and a black apron hiding most of his pinstriped trousers. The sleeves of his white shirt were held halfway up his forearms by metalled expansion garters. He carried a large silver tray that bore a steaming silver teapot plus three teacups and their saucers – a set of exquisite Staffordshire porcelain. A larger plate that matched the design of the cups and saucers, held six biscuits. He placed everything on the desk in front of his employer.

"Would you like me to pour, sir?"

"No, Satchell. I'll do that, thank you ..."

And with that Satchell disappeared back down the spiral stairway into the blackness of his cave. Uncle Geoff prepared to pour the tea, a ceremony to which he had become well accustomed over the long years of his occupancy of these chambers.

"Milk?"

"Yes, please," in unison.

"Sugar?"

"No thank you!"

"Good. Sugar is rationed. You may each take two biscuits – one at a time."

The clock on Uncle Geoff's shelf ran one hour fast in order to un-nerve clients who tended to overstay their welcome and so crowd his time.

By now my brother and I were cowed. We had to get up from our seats to accept the proffered full teacup on its saucer, then gently sit down again so as not to spill the contents. The manoeuver had to be accomplished with one hand in order to leave the other free to take the proffered biscuit and, once back in our seats, we had to balance everything on our knees. And remain silent.

Geoffrey eyed us both from under his twitching brows; he also said nothing. Awkwardly and without passing a word between us, we all finished drinking our tea, blisteringly hot, and eating two biscuits. Then Satchell mysteriously reappeared and took everything away again.

More silence.

Geoffrey held up one finger, drawing our attention to it by no more than his action.

After an interminable moment he said:

"Good. It seems you are both quite capable of remaining silent. Why is it I hear otherwise from your mother?"

We were too embarrassed to answer.

"Never again do I wish to learn from your mother that you have treated her badly. No fighting, no answering her back, no loud noise. Do I make myself clear?"

"Yes, Uncle Geoff!" again in unison.

"Mark my words, kindness can work wonders. Be kind to your mother. No matter what you may think are your problems, they are small beside hers. Treat her with kindness. Always – kindness. Do you hear me?"

Somersaults

"Yes, Uncle Geoff!" Sheepish.

"Hm-m-m – do you boys have any plans for this evening?"

We looked at one another and shrugged.

"Good. There's a concert on tonight just around the corner from where you are living with your dear mother. So – both of you – tidy up. You will accompany me to the concert this evening. Go downstairs and Satchell will show you the bathroom. Take a pee, wash your hands, and return here right away. We don't have a lot of time. Quickly – go!"

We leapt from our chairs and ran to the spiral staircase. At the bottom we got to see Satchell's cubbyhole, another tiny office with an attached kitchenette – and lines of filing cabinets. We avoided pushing and shoving one another when we were behind the closed door of the bathroom, and then raced back up to where Uncle Geoff was pulling on a pair of pigskin gloves and preparing to escort us outside. He wore spats. Waving a walking stick in the air, he hailed a taxi and we rode in it all the way across central London: Covent Garden, Charing Cross, down The Mall, around Buckingham Palace to Hyde Park Corner, then on to Knightsbridge and Kensington Road to the Royal Albert Hall.

"Quick! Don't dally! We have to find our seats." Geoffrey marched ahead, and we broke into a run behind him.

From the outside the Royal Albert Hall looks to be every bit as massive as it is. From a distance it resembles a spacecraft visiting London from another galaxy, squatting like some alien giant red-brick toad under its dome on the south side of Kensington Road. We raced towards the entrance. Geoffrey suddenly stopped to turn us about and look back at the Albert Memorial right across the street.

"The Nazis managed to obliterate huge sections of London, but unfortunately weren't able to demolish that wretched thing!" he cursed.

He shook his stick at it.

"Without doubt it is the ugliest structure in London. The Nazis were never very friendly, but we knew they were our enemies when they failed to target that awful thing."

So saying, he turned us about again and marched us to the front doors of the hall.

My brother and I passed this auditorium nearly every day, but neither of us had ever been inside quite such a place before. We had once attended a boxing match with our mother at Madison Square Garden when we were all in

New York. It was difficult to compare size – a rectangle as opposed to an oval – but even if the New York stadium had been bigger (the old MSG was replaced in the mid-sixties) it was nowhere near so impressive as the Royal Albert Hall, completed in 1871. My memories of MSG are of gigantic utilitarian space; my memories of RAH are not of space alone, but of sumptuous late XIX century elegance and décor – a venue far more upscale than its New York counterpart.

In the wake of Uncle Geoff's coattails, we were wafted to seats right up under the stage. We did not have the least idea what spectacle we were about to see – until we were each handed copies of the evening's programme.

A singer. Shucks!

We looked at one another. My brother pulled a face. Probably one of those fancy operatic heavies who sang Italian gobbledygook on the BBC. I didn't know what to say, but I was surely disappointed. I looked at my shoes. This was punishment, alright. Sorry, Mother!

On the cover of the programme was a photograph of a black man.

"Who is he?" I whispered so Uncle Geoff wouldn't hear.

"I dunno. Paul Robeson. Never heard of him."

We soon learned. It was especially exciting when this very tall black man popped his eyes wide like saucers, stared straight down at us and jabbed a finger in our direction in time to his admonition:

"…Tote dat barge!"

Robeson sang his whole concert without a microphone, his deep, deep voice bouncing off the auditorium walls and ceiling. At several points between his songs he stopped and asked the audience if they could hear him at the back.

"Yes!" came back a thunderous response from hundreds of voices.

The atmosphere was charged, and the two young lads seated up front right under the performer couldn't have been having more fun if they had been dragged away to the circus instead.

Mysteriously, Robeson sang every number with his right hand cupped behind his ear. It bothered me some, but I was later able to find out why he did it. Saying nothing to us, it turned out Uncle Geoff was on the committee that had arranged for Robeson to come and sing in London that evening, and during the interval he took us backstage to the concert hall's green room. Paul Robeson was talking to a number of people, but eventually spotted our small group and came over.

"I've seen you two boys right down there in front of me. You seem to be having fun tonight. Are you enjoying the show?"

Oh yes! We were having fun alright.

"Please, sir," I asked him. "Why do you keep your hand behind your ear when you're singing?"

The great man bent down and let me in on his secret.

"The hall is very, very big, and I'm singing without a microphone. Also, I am none too sure about the acoustics – how good they are. If I don't control it right, my voice could echo in that space, so I have to listen to myself very carefully. Now, I don't just have my hand behind my ear, but I'm actually blocking my ear – completely – by pushing on the lobe at the back. That way I can hear my own voice, know exactly where my pitch is, out there in that huge hall. In this way I can control my pitch perfectly. I close the ear by pushing on the lobe from behind because it would look ridiculous if I stood there the whole evening with one finger in my ear! Here, you try it …! Put your hand behind your ear, and push …"

To Uncle Geoff's great amusement, his two charges did as the singer told them. We each blocked one ear.

"Now sing out, doe – ray – me … Ol' – man – riv – er …"

We tried it, and laughed. It worked. We each heard our own voice.

"Now, when *you're* on stage at the Royal Albert Hall, you'll know how to control your voices in every corner of the auditorium – and you won't need a microphone," Robeson laughed.

As Uncle Geoff was leaving us outside the Albert Hall after the concert he said, "Give my love to your wonderful mother, tell her I shall call on her within a day or two. Both of you, try to be as good to her as she is to you."

He strode away with a wave of his stick, and we headed for our home in the opposite direction. From the way he treated us, no real reprimand at all, really, I believe my brother and I learned a strong lesson in giving and tolerance that evening. Geoffrey was not obliged to give us anything; he simply did it, and showed he was happy to do it. Introducing us to Paul Robeson had been a splendid gift. There had been a firmness and gentle kindness from both him and the singer that stood in contrast to our recent bad behaviour towards our mother. I think we could both see it – an alternative to our rowdy belligerence and selfishness.

During the walk back from the Albert Hall (for we lived only a few streets away from it) we found ourselves pacing along side-by-side in silence. My soul was humming; I think my brother's was, too. There was a lot for us to think about. The two of us had been certain we were going to Uncle Geoff's office for a caning. What a thrashing it turned out to be! From that time I think the two of us indeed became a little kinder to our mother

Almost by-the-by: at various points in my life I have found myself teaching language. One of the most useful little gimmicks I have employed to get my students to listen to their own voices, and thus tune themselves to correct pronunciation, is precisely this ear-blocking technique taught to me by Paul Robeson. It works.

Nick

Earlier I wrote of the occasion in London when Uncle Mack bought one of my drawings. The drawing itself likely did not last very long. He might have kept it for a time, but after his death it in all probability found its way into a wastebasket. That would have been of no consequence, really; the triumph at the time was the sale and the strong vote of confidence that accompanied it. Yet, had it survived and been returned to me I am sure it would have become one of those meaningful personal keepsakes that eventually would have wound up in my treasure chest. For when he bought the drawing Uncle Mack had spoken to me earnestly, insisting I had signs of talent sufficient to continue some form of artistic pursuit. He urged me to think about it. I was not quite ten years old, so to hear that form of positive assessment made me feel pretty important. His advice has ever been part of an association of ideas that started with my reaction to Cookie's Pacific Ocean model aircraft show, some three years before our arrival in London, and the strong effect it had upon me. These two events merged in my mind with yet another that was to occur when I was about eleven and still attending the boarding school in Northamptonshire: the adventure of clay.

At first, neither my brother nor I fitted the ranks of great scholastic achievers. We settled into our new school with difficulty. The curriculum itself was complex and new to us: never before had we come to significant grips with Latin, French, the sciences, English literature or English history. As a consequence when holidays came around we both had to spend long hours cramming to catch up, the spectre of failing our "common entrance" exam looming realistically over our heads. It was the test all prep-schoolers had to take in order to progress into a chosen public school.[4]

My brother took the possibility of failure very seriously, and worked hard; I was two years behind him, and did not. I seemed incapable of taking anything too seriously. Life for me was like moving through a dream-mist from which I was sure I would awaken in time to discover everything had been just fine, turned out precisely the way it was supposed to ... I had no idea how this result was to come about. It seemed only a wistful and constant need for what I thought to be "adventure" would churn my grey matter. Serious classroom studies did not cut it. Only something that pumped the adrenalin would get through to me. Until I encountered well-taught history (my early history teachers offered little that extended beyond a sawdust-dry version of *1066 And All That*) I had come to the conclusion the dull life of the classroom was never so interesting as that which I could conjure in my mind. Instead of history texts I discovered historical novels, and they spoke to me realistically. My main interest was playing in the nearby woods, building a better gang house than my fellow students (two or three levels up a tree), or what I called "flying my desk" – an escape that allowed me to turn my classroom desk into an airplane and soar in my head over the roofs of the school buildings and through the mists that hung between the trees of the copse that surrounded St. Augustine's – the Anglican church we were obliged to attend on Sunday mornings. (Snoopy, the cartoon air ace on his doghouse-cum-Sopwith Camel, only presented himself to me many years later, when I was an adult. I could hardly believe what I was reading: it seemed amazing to me that this delightful little character, figment of his creator's whimsy, had also discovered my favourite airplane! I have felt in total harmony with him ever since.)

Like many kids with a whacky but fertile imagination, I was a nut about flying. Perhaps this had something to do with the fact I had been given a model Sopwith Camel, an exceptional gift, some years before by the cook

---

[4] A public school in North America differs from a "public school" in Great Britain. In the Americas, "public" means public. In Britain, "public school" refers to an exclusive form of extremely expensive private schooling. Confusing – but absolutely in line with the Englishman's exceptional ability to say the exact opposite of what he actually means. (i.e. "You're a jolly good chap!" signifies the speaker considers you a] a wonderful fellow, or b] a total son-of-a-bitch, and that he likes you not at all.) A "public school," then, is a private institution for highly privileged (often snotty-nosed) Little Lord Fauntleroy's, with a well-deserved reputation it takes about a lifetime to work off. The "common entrance" exam was a terrifying system of selection and, ultimately, stratification. The whole system went through mammoth re-vamping and improvement in the 1960's, but the nauseating air of snobbish exclusivity persists.

aboard the S.S. President Grant. Indeed, it was my finest toy. More, I think, my fascination was linked to my very secret and special degree of romanticism, a sort of air-headed liberalism that buzzed my brain whenever I looked up into the clouds, or thought deeply about what others might now glibly refer to as "freedom." My way of dealing with this trance-like state was to "fly" with complete abandon, a headiness that permitted me to envision myself at the controls of my airplane. My machine, of course – my desk – was a replica of the beautiful model the ship's cook had given me – an open cockpit biplane, complete with struts and guy wires. In my ecstasy the fields and towns lay far below me as I soared and swooped, zooming between banks of thunderous clouds, or diving out of them, my head (leather helmet and goggles) peeking around the perspex windshield. Where this bout of schoolboy imagination most gripped me was at the desk in my third form classroom. The room itself was my hangar, and my school desk was the biplane I flew – just as Snoopy the Great War ace flew his Sopwith Camel – except that my fanciful experience was considerably before Snoopy's comic strip creation, so I was not privileged to know him.

When the classroom was empty of my fellow classmates, when they had all screamed outside to play, I would remain behind at my desk – and then I'd take off. I would keep a book open in front of me in case anyone came into the hangar so that, if necessary, I could pretend I was reading and could thus save myself the embarrassment of explaining my weird behaviour as I went through the contortions required to fly my desk. In the high airs of my invention I was freer than a condor, totally content in my sky high absorption.

Some years later when I entered a more senior boarding school and was obliged to join the corps of cadets, I naturally opted for the air contingent and, in time, actually took lessons in flying. The reader can only imagine my delight when first I climbed into the front cockpit of a Tiger Moth, the pre-world war biplane then still very much in use as a trainer. Buckled into my seat atop the cushion of my parachute, I could look down on the landscape precisely the way I had when I had been flying my prep school desk. The only barrier to my complete joy was the instructor seated in the rear cockpit. I wished him gone so that I could enjoy all of this elation entirely by myself, and thus know again the sanctity of my high solitude. But by this time in my life I was also learning something about pragmatism, and so realized that without my instructor I might have some trouble getting my feet (and the Tiger Moth) back onto the ground.

Meanwhile I had discovered Robin Hood, D'Artagnan and his fellow musketeers, the Count of Monte Cristo, Robinson Crusoe, Allan Quatermain,

Huckleberry Finn, Lord Jim and a host of other characters, all of whom spoke to me of history and its multitude of faces and actions – my take on historical comprehension.

More worrying to the school staff (I thought it was my secret from them, but it wasn't) I would very often slip from my bed after lights-out to make secret nighttime forays into the school's corridors and classrooms, or outside into the kitchen gardens and woods. One of the teachers told me he had seen me once at dead of night on the lawn below the main school building; he was inside, looking out through one of the windows at a ghostlike creature some distance away. He had thought I was sleep-walking and refrained from waking me out of fear I might be frightened. By the time he had gathered his wits and come outside to bring me back in, I had eluded him, and managed to make it back to my dormitory unseen, so that when he came up to check on me I was already snuggled down, eyes closed. I was not able to assess it then, but can certainly understand it now: the school staff had one weird little boy on their hands, and were desperately concerned. They reported their worries to my mother, of course, but by the time I met with her during the holidays, when we might have talked about the matter, the whole thing had disappeared, slipped her mind. That suited me.

Edgy, restless, curious but also immensely unsure of myself, adventure real and imaginary became my motivator, but it was something I kept to myself – like my yew tree hideout in the garden of the house in Sydney. Yet I was daring, using what I thought to be creative ingenuity, and I had bags of courage. Usually (not always) I managed to get away with things. Few of my schoolmates were prepared to take the risk of getting caught, or to suffer the severe beating that would surely ensue – but I always took risks, lots of them, and there were times I had to accept heavy penalties. Corporal punishment – flogging, in one form or another – was *de rigueur* in English boarding schools of the day. When I was caught in the wrong, breaking the rules, I was caned – and caned so many times I lost count. These punishments seldom curbed me; I was artful. They ensured my maximum craftiness and cunning. Through various escapades and the consequences they brought down on me, I quickly learned the necessity of acting alone, relying on no one but myself. My buddies were more astute; they would hold back.

A small river ran along the bottom of the field that lay to the side of the main school building – no more than a creek, but known as the Great Ouse. At no place was it any deeper than my knees, in most places not even that. An old stone bridge crossed this creek separating the main school grounds from our football and cricket fields – and below the bridge a local farmer kept, tied up and used from time-to-time to collect river rushes and grasses, a small punt with its quant pole. One afternoon I stole this punt and pole. Climbing aboard and crouching down so my head would not show above the river's embankment, I allowed it to drift downstream out of sight from the school. I held the boat in check with the quant pole.

    I don't suppose I had drifted and quanted more than a couple of kilometres, but at the end of this stretch where the creek entered a wooded area, there was on the left a high bank of grey mud. I knew immediately what it was, for I had encountered clay earlier that summer in Little Missenden, and this was a lode of exceptionally fine quality. I squished my fingers into it deliciously. It was like plasticine – so, right there and then, I squatted down on the floor of the punt and started modelling with a lump of it. My fingers modelled various objects, but the very first was a little dog – a cocker spaniel. I made him as accurately as I could, setting him onto a flat clay plinth and placing a bowl at his front paws, a collar about his neck; I used a fine stick to inscribe both with his name – "Nick."

Nick

Somersaults

After a while, and when I was satisfied with what I had made, I carefully placed Nick on the thwart in the prow of the punt where I wouldn't step on him, and made my way back upstream to the stone bridge. There I secured the craft the way I had found it. Maybe I would want to use it again; this little boat, this stream, this clay bank – would be my secret alone. I never told anyone.

Nick dried out in my desk back in my classroom. He became a delicate light grey in colour, almost white, and the black paint I had at hand seemed to take well to his surface. The collar with his name and his dinner bowl I painted brown, the plinth on which he sat green.

The headmaster saw me working on Nick, and he sat with me for several minutes to watch me at work. He seemed pleased, asked me no questions as to how I came by the material; of course he considered me a "difficult child." He did not say so, and perhaps he really did not know how I had acquired the clay; it would have been of absolutely no significance to him. I was no fool; I could sense his unease about me. I was constantly acting up, breaking out at night, raiding the kitchen gardens for carrots, prowling about and getting into mischief. As I was never caught, so I was never punished for my escapades; but the headmaster and the school staff had a pretty good idea what I was up to and I knew they were alarmed at the direction I was taking. Now I am absolutely sure the headmaster was thinking – more likely hoping – this experiment in clay might somehow "get through" to me. He returned several times to my desk to watch what I was doing with the clay, and he encouraged me to do more of it. He said I should enter Nick in the upcoming arts and handicrafts exhibition and contest – so I did, and won the trophy.

Suddenly, and again, I was in my rightful place. Clay has the power to centre the person who has been thrown out on a tangent. I don't know if working with clay was responsible for improving my grades, but it was an activity that hooked me. I started to settle down, and eventually passed the exams that permitted me to go on to public school. There was something about working with the material – mud – that was elemental, humbling. It is Mother Earth in your hands, the most basic of the sorcerer's creative materials; it possesses the means of establishing how we can stand on this world's surface.

Nick went to my mother as a gift and soon, under the pressures of an active schoolboy life, I put him out of mind. Unknown to me she had carefully wrapped him up and squirreled him away – and she kept him for the remainder of her life. She had been living in the south of Spain, and after she died it was necessary to go there and sort through her belongings. She had placed Nick carefully in a tiny box and wrapped him in cotton wool and tissue. It was touching to see him some thirty years later, to encounter that sentimental side of my mother so soon after her death, but I was pressed for time so placed the little box in a steel trunk with numerous of her papers. In the course of time the trunk came into the possession of my eldest son back in Canada.

To conclude this anecdote it's necessary to leap ahead to an evening in 2013, nearly thirty-five years after Mother's death, and an occasion when I was talking to my son about the ceramic studio I had operated in Portugal, and how I had become so involved with clay in my early childhood ... He slid out of the room, returning with Nick in his box – a dried up chunk of un-fired grey clay, a bit chipped and broken, but still quite recognizable more than sixty years after I had made him.

Our reminiscing could mark the end of this little anecdote – but not quite. In my absence from the family over the years, my children had been living with their mother and going to school on Vancouver Island. Not knowing anything of the model I had made when I was eleven, the family had given a home to a little black Cocker Spaniel – the joy of their household – and the children had named the pup Nick.

Serendipity?

Life has a way of pulling loose ends together. It is seldom possible to divine how or why, but there is significance in all happenstance. Childhood flirtations with "art" – Cookie's airplanes, the sale of two sixpenny drawings, the creek's clay bank and Nick – are in small fashion a confirmation to me of a whole world of creative fantasy that actually exists. Unseen forces are constantly at work, constantly pushing an almost vertiginous perspective of every object – for me invariably an exercise in three dimensions.

It is possible to love drawing and painting, and the whole range of two-dimensional representation. The freest drawing, for me, has always been in some way an attempt both to view and portray the three dimensional; a quizzical eye that insists on trying to look around to the other side of everything. This has been both a useful and privileged stance to adopt for, on a purely personal plain, it has helped me lay claim to the skills of ceramic sculpture and, later, stonemasonry. It has provided an overall assessment of whatever appears as "sculpted," or formed, and by logical extension has included architecture itself in all its concepts – design, use, aesthetics, structure, history. As if by chance, there has emerged before me a unique world in three-dimensions, in no way derived from any previously-examined two-dimensional experimentation and depiction. This has laid out before me a

Somersaults

whole new world, and I have spent a lifetime examining it.

Serendipity, fine – and a rich revelation.

Anyone recalling Britain in 1947 will remember winter that year was exceptionally cold, and the snows lay unusually heavy on the ground.

The school was situated on low ground in something of a valley, and for several days the drifts were so deep that we were cut off from the nearby village of Brackley. Supplies were running low in the kitchen, and we were especially short of bread.

It was not a long distance to Brackley – about two miles, if I remember rightly – but getting there by car was out of the question. The headmaster decided to call for a work team to trudge in over the snows with a toboggan. It was intended as something of an adventure, and one of the resident teachers – a Mr. Kelsey – was selected to go with us. There were six of us altogether, the master and five students – my brother and myself among them selected, I can only guess, because the two of us were Canadians and perhaps someone had had the notion we would feel at home in the snows.

Well wrapped against the cold, the team was cheered along by several of the teachers who came out to see us off; the headmaster waving cheerfully. Our bright intent was to return with as many loaves as we could lash onto the toboggan, and for this purpose we took along a length of stout cord.

As it turned out, the snows were much heavier than we had calculated. Drifts were deep and progress was slow. We were just entering the outskirts of the village when, without warning, Mr. Kelsey let out a loud groan and collapsed into the snow. Immediately we realized he had probably suffered a heart attack. Apart from a few groans and broken words, he was totally incapable of giving us the least assistance.

Hauling him onto the toboggan, we used the length of cord to ensure he would not roll off, and in this fashion managed to drag him as far as the village bakery. Adults took over at that point, and the baker's wife made sure we had a full load of bread for the return journey to the school. Despite the drifts, the telephones worked. Help was soon on the way and a grateful Mr. Kelsey was back at school within a few weeks.

The Moat House

High school, in the form of an English public school, lasted the five-year period from Christmas term (September), 1949, to summer term (July), 1954.

Mother re-married an Englishman – we called him JB – during my first Christmas term. He was a highly intelligent, quiet-spoken man – a poet, a scholar of the Greek and Roman classics, and was possessed of an uncanny photographic memory that gave him the ability to find his way in numerous foreign languages, as well as spout long passages of both prose and poetry – in English, or any of the other languages and dialects he happened to have stored away in his extraordinary mind. He never "forgot" anything. Indeed, he memorized our considerable home library in its entirety.

One of his great pleasures was to take a Finnish folktale in its original language, for instance, and write a poem about it, or compare its structure, its form, its nuance and libretto to, say, a similar Arabian folktale in its original Arabic. He spoke Finnish and Arabic, had an encyclopaedic knowledge of ancient Greek and Latin, and this helped him learn other European languages – modern Greek, Italian and French. He learned sufficient Russian to be able to converse in it (this while travelling by train from Leningrad, as it then was, to Baku in Azerbaijan). He also managed to pick up a "smattering" of Farsi. His Arabic came as a consequence of his military service during the Second World War when he was an officer on Field Marshal Montgomery's intelligence staff in the North African desert. He studied German for three weeks by memorizing a German grammar book we had kicking about the house – then took his newly-acquired family on a trip to the Tyrol where, by chance, his language was proficient enough that he was able to replace the group's tour guide when the fellow collapsed with food poisoning.

JB was first, foremost and always a Londoner. His work in the family business in the centre of the city provided a necessary income, but it was clear he found it an interruption to those elements of a classical and artistic life he considered of at least as great import. He claimed to know every statue in the city's hundreds of parks, public places and along its streets; and the streets he knew better than most taxi drivers. Often when he had hailed a cab he would engage the driver in friendly conversation, occasionally offering up tips on short cuts. However, he and Mother decided they would prefer to live out of

London, and so finally purchased a house on about six acres of property to the west of the city, not far from Windsor. This extraordinary place became our home from the time I returned at the end of my first term at public school until I was released from the army in 1956 – a total of seven years.

It was named the Moat House. The main portion had been constructed in the XVI century as a parsonage farm, its moat a defence against the religious purges of the era. Thankfully one of the previous owners had drained away the stagnant waters a century or so before we took over, opening up and levelling a stretch of land in front of the house where was planted an apple orchard that extended over one hundred metres up to the front gate. The dry moat, now a large horseshoe-shaped earthwork at the rear of the house, formed a delightful walkway lying inside a ring of lofty elms that surrounded the house and marked the limit of our property.

The building itself was a solid brick structure with an elongated two-storey brick façade, and an unassuming front door in the centre of its ground floor. All of the windows were of leaded small panes – most of which must have been of the same vintage as the house itself. Its main roof structure was of two massive twin gables that reached from side-to-side, one behind the other, right across the full width of the building. Beyond the entrance hallway and its broad oaken staircase, there were fourteen rooms on the ground floor, eight on the floor above, and three attic rooms tucked up into each of the twin gables – the three across the front a small suite for my brother, the three across the back a studio and storage space for me.

Mother had arranged a small and very comfortable suite for a live-in maid at the top of a rear staircase, but it was used instead by our gardener, George, who multitasked as house guard, butler and Man Friday to JB when needed. A bit of a chameleon, George was always kind and attentive to my brother and me, able and willing to cover the tracks of those of our more innocuous escapades when we felt details would best be kept from JB or Mother. He was knowledgeable concerning the garden and its array of blooms and lawns (he helped Mother develop a prize-worthy rose bower), and built up a kitchen garden that kept the household in fresh vegetables the year round.

With his language capabilities, a part of JB's workload was to host frequent dinner parties for his firm's business associates from Finland, Eastern Europe and Scandinavia, and on these occasions George would come inside the house, wait at the dinner table and serve the wines. He was excellent at it, impeccable. Both JB and Mother were immensely proud of him.

We were equally fortunate in finding a lady from the village who would come (sometimes with her daughter as her assistant) to clean and vacuum the house, take care of kitchen and laundry chores, and all the general interior workings of a large house. Mrs. Wiggins was her name; she lived in a council-house with her small family and said she would prefer to come daily instead of accepting the quarters at the top of the stairs.

The arrangement worked out very well. Five days a week, Mrs. Wiggins would get off the bus at our gate and trundle down the driveway with armloads of bags and parcels and an umbrella rain or shine, walk around to the vestibule door by the kitchen – divest herself of all her kit and caboodle and call out a cheerful "Good morning!" with the optimist's certainty that someone within the bowels of the house would hear of her arrival. Unfailingly cheerful, always meticulous, she quickly became more of a confidante to my mother than a low-wage employee; the two of them together would set about planning how the household should be operated – then putting their plans into action.

"Be tight with what you pay for goods at market," JB said more than once. "But be generous with those who give you service. Try to pay them more than even they think they are worth."

So the Moat House became home, our first and only house in England. What I did and thought during those developmental years as a teenager was done either there or from there. It was the important image of home space I carried with me throughout the time I was away at boarding school and in the army, a very solid rock around which I could wrap my otherwise shortened anchor chain. After bobbing around the world like an adrift and hollowed-out fishnet float for the early part of my life, the house – more than the people who occupied it – represented terra firma. This is looking back, of course; it is not a concept of which I would have been aware at the time. When we moved into this magnificent old place Life had been winding up the key in my back for fourteen years.

Big Finn

JB's business interests took him to Finland several times a year. Because of this there were occasions when the Moat House appeared to be overrun by visiting Finnish businessmen, government bureaucrats, parliamentarians and sundry ranking ministers. They were invariably highly impressed with the place, a parsonage farm that had been in operation at the time of the Tudors. Mother and JB were attentive hosts, always happy to take their guests on tours of the property – always including, as a sort of *pièce de résistance*, a descent into our tiny cellar to inspect the entranceways to two passageways that led off to left and right below the level of the moat – secret escape hatches, so local lore informed, for monks fleeing for their lives before the religious persecutors of the epoch. We had been told (intriguing tales, but we were never able to prove their veracity) that one passage surfaced at Heathrow airport, a few kilometres away, while the other came up somewhere within the bounds of Windsor Castle. That said, both "passageways" were closed off within a few feet of their entrances. My brother and I caught hell from JB on one occasion for attempting to un-brick one of them. Removing a chunk of wall, we found nothing on the other side but earth and rubble and roots – so that if these were truly the commencement of passages they had most likely collapsed years before somewhere under the moat. We were promptly ordered to replace what we had torn down. That cellar was a constant source of curiosity to the two of us, and likewise never failed to appeal to the imaginations of those who came to stay over at the house.

An important government official visited us for a long weekend – an extremely tall man, probably close to two metres. All round, he was size large, and very probably close to three hundred pounds. He spoke not a word of English so that Mother felt obliged to smile ridiculously non-stop for the entire period of his stay. She thought it was the best way of showing off the gracious side of her nature. I believe his name was Per – and I also believe Minister Per very much liked his schnapps.

"There used to be twelve – and look! There are only eleven now ...!"

Mother was standing in front of the liquor cabinet. Its interior was painted bright scarlet. It had been dubbed the Temple of Bacchus. She was holding a silver tray in her hands on which (we counted) were eleven tiny schnapps glasses, each one a recognizably different colour from the others.

"See! Only eleven. The Big Finn's glass is missing ...! He must have swallowed it when everyone was singing round the piano last night. Just threw it into the back of his gullet, schnapps, glass and all ... Gulp!"

Her eyes popped clownishly as she pronounced for me the simple logic of her argument.

We laughed. The night before, Mother and JB had thrown a dinner party in honour of our houseguest. They had also invited their close friends, Prince Paul Levin and his wife, Margot Homer-Dixon, an old school friend of Mother's who played coy about being addressed as princess, but liked it anyway. Paul had been a schoolboy in Moscow when he and his nursemaid were obliged to flee the Bolshevik revolution and seek asylum in Switzerland. A massive man, he had become a Canadian citizen prior to the war, joined the Canadian military at its outbreak, then fought his way up the length of Italy with the commandos. He was badly wounded, lost an eye and almost his life – but had been revived by skilled military medics whose ministrations had been augmented by Margot's newly-developed wartime vocation as a nurse. It was the start of their romance. In earlier days Margot had been known as a popular Vancouver socialite and great beauty; now both of them likewise very much enjoyed their schnapps, and almost any excuse for a party. Paul could not read music, but nonetheless played the piano by ear and with such exaggerated and sentimental gusto that he brought himself close to tears. He would roll his enormous head on his shoulders, his glass eye glistening in its soggy wet socket, as his giant hands flashed up and down the keyboard. Now and then he would remove the false eyeball altogether and stick it on top of the piano where it could watch him. He was totally uninhibited at not being able to see very well, either through his partial blindness or the effects of the schnapps, and through the evening had regaled the household with his repertoire of mournful Russian ballads. The Big Finn clearly enjoyed himself now that the war was over and everyone could be friends and get roaring drunk together.

Mother was chuckling as she stood that morning in front of the Temple of Bacchus. Whether or not her explanation of the missing schnapps glass was true, her imagery was going to stick and become our little secret, something impish between just the two of us – for the moment. In time it was to become the wad of yeast to give rise to one of a select list of family tales that would never die as long as we were on hand to keep them alive. Now we both laughed, side-splitting hoots that brought tears to our eyes. We imagined the Big Finn as he paced about the premises, taking it all in – until sometime, maybe later tomorrow, when he would have to exercise his natural inclinations – and so, possibly, return Mother's little schnapps glass ...

"If it survives the journey, I'll be sure to wash it well," she assured me. "Alcohol should ensure its purification."

Somersaults

In fact we never discovered a satisfactory ending to the incident. Mother felt it was not the sort of enquiry one could politely ask a government minister, even had she had sufficient knowledge of his language to be so bold. The following day he left and we were never to see him again.

The Big Finn pulled JB to one side as we all stood in the driveway beside the car that had come to take him away. He smiled and nodded his head, several times clapping his host of the last few days on the back as he spoke in friendly and sonorous tones. He clicked his heels and bowed to my mother, his words no doubt expressions of gratitude. Then we all waved goodbye as the car wound its way up the driveway through the orchard to the main gate. Everyone smiled.

"What did he say to you?" Mother asked JB.

"He said that he was very happy to have met us all, and that he wants us to visit his home outside Helsinki one day – perhaps next summer. He was very complimentary. I really think he had a very good time."

"Nice man," mother commented as we entered the house. "He seemed to enjoy Margot and Paul …"

"And the place. He was very taken with our home. Only one criticism – he thinks we should install a flag pole …"

"A flag pole?" Mother scrunched up her nose.

"Yes – a flag pole. Quaint idea. The Finns love flags. Very nationalistic. They all have flag poles outside their homes. Flags everywhere you look …"

That was the end of it. Life went back to normal, and my brother and I returned to boarding school at the end of the summer.

It must have been at some point in the spring of the following year that JB received a telegram from the Big Finn.

"Flag pole on the way," it read (in Finnish).

"Good God!" exclaimed JB, a staunchly British conservative who really was not all that fond of the showiness associated with the waving of flags.

Promptly, and conveniently, he forgot about the matter – until the summer, at which time there was a phone call from the dispatch department of British Rail. A flag pole was resting quietly in the waters of the BR dockside in the Thames estuary. What would he like them to do about it?

"Well, send it over of course!" barked JB, not unreasonably irritable.

Towards the end of our summer holiday a British Rail truck made its laboured journey from the east end of London through to the narrow streets and alleyways of Slough and then the village of Langley – and so to the Moat House. Exasperated and exhausted, the driver and his mate arrived at our gate shortly after lunch. It had taken them since five o'clock in the morning to negotiate their way.

"We got your bleedin' flag pole, Ma'am," they told Mother. "Where do you want it put?"

"In the orchard beside the driveway will do," Mother replied matter-of-factly, as though that was the obvious place to put flag poles. We all went outside to look at the thing.

It was most of an unpainted and very tall tree. The pole itself (we measured it at the time, but I have quite forgotten its actual dimensions) was close to the full length of the front of our house. Then there was an additional length to mount it – the portion that needed to be set into the ground embedded in concrete. It alone must have measured an additional five metres.

It took the driver and his mate, blaspheming like a full team of surly and drunken stevedores, all of two hours to manoeuvre the damned thing off their transport's flat-deck onto the ground of the orchard. It lay next to the apple trees until the following summer. Every time JB walked past it he scratched his head.

"Apart from the bloody thing itself – and I want you boys to paint it – a flag pole that size would look utterly ridiculous were it used to fly only the standard-sized bunting ..."

Whereupon he ordered up – it was a special order – three flags: a Union Jack, a Canadian ensign, and the national flag of Finland. Each was the size of a double bed sheet.

Eventually we managed to have the pole properly erected, but even then it hardly suited our muted penchant for flamboyance. Finns would come to visit every now and then, and expressed their enthusiasm and contentment at finding their colours flying above the English countryside, high over the canopy of the trees in our orchard.

Somersaults

"Whazzat, then?" someone asked in passing our gate, pointing to the sign of Finland at the top of our pole. "Dryin' out yer bleedin' laundry?"

"That is a gift from the government of Finland," JB remarked. "So far it has cost me the greater portion of a year's wages ..."

"And I don't suppose I will ever again see my missing schnapps glass," Mother huffed.

A Tudor Voluntary

Queen Elizabeth II was crowned on 2 June, 1953. It was an occasion of great celebration, quite deliberately intended to help lift the spirits of a tired and battered Britain after the long, dark and dismal days of the Second World War. Being a Canadian, Mother was able to obtain tickets to good seats along the route of the coronation parade, in a section of the Mall reserved for visitors from Commonwealth countries.

By now we had been living several years at the Moat House in Langley, Buckinghamshire – a life not entirely composed of affluence and ease, for there were numerous shortages that seemed to hang on for years after the war, and money for pleasantries and extras was in no way easy to come by. For all that we could board a train and be in Paddington well within an hour, we lived an essentially frugal and quiet rural existence. It was not difficult to convince ourselves of our entitlement to the comforts of a measured gentility.

Hundreds of thousands of people would be headed into London to watch and celebrate the coronation, so routes into and from the city were carefully worked out by the authorities and police. JB called his small family together for a dinner on the eve prior of our drive up to London. We would have to be ready to leave the house at first light. He wished to apprise all of us concerning his approach to the city, where the car would be allotted parking space and what we were to do in the event that any of us became lost or separated. Having moved this essential information out of the way, he raised his glass and proposed a toast to Her Majesty, at the same time making a memorable little speech – which, we suspected, was the true motive for his summoning us to this familial huddle.

One of the more distinctive marks of the reign of Elizabeth I (1558-1603), he said, had been the loyalty she had shown her servants and the common man; how along with this sense of duty there had been an accompanying and widespread celebration of decency, courtesy, and chivalrous good manners that had ultimately left an indelible stamp on that epoch of England's history. It would be a good thing all round if these fast-fading elements of Tudor integrity could be renewed and upheld throughout the years of the new Elizabethan age, he said.

My brother and I, still incorrigible roustabouts who had spent considerable energies over the last few years corrupting the morals and behaviour of JB's own son, our young step-brother, looked deep into our soup plates as this stern Englishman delivered what we were pretty sure constituted words of deliberately-nuanced wisdom that none-too-subtly camouflaged a well-deserved scolding. While in a manner historic, his remarks were pointed, intended to impress, and not without effect – despite the fact that all three of us had learned from our history lessons at school that the goodness in Good Queen Bess had been somewhat questionable, her good years on the throne tempered by spasms of terror and torture, bloodshed, beheadings and general mayhem. Not in fact such a jolly period of the Merrie English saga. We all listened, intently solemn of face but rather blank of mind; I do not believe that any of us – Mother and JB included – were shining examples of correctness in all matters pertaining to decorum.

Our car – an ancient delivery van with rear side windows – was a disgraceful clunk, an unsightly relic of rural abuse more accustomed to the transport of apple baskets and potting paraphernalia in its after portion where the seats could be folded flat, than in conveying a family of gentle folk to the capital to pay their respects to the queen. But JB had had it serviced and washed for the occasion. At five o'clock the following morning, with a heavy fog lying over the fields beyond the elms that surrounded the moat of our house, we piled aboard and started on JB's chosen road to London. Mother wore a cream crinoline dress, with a flowered hat on her head wider than the lid of a dustbin. My little step-brother wore a dark blue suit and tie, his hair slicked back like a choir boy. JB and I sported morning dress and grey top hats. My brother, on leave from officer cadet school, was in his best regimental bib and tucker. We expected to run into heavy traffic, but we were largely alone during the early stages of the journey, and in any case had to take heed of the poor visibility. But at a country crossroad far from any main highway there loomed a vehicle even more decrepit than our own. It was leaning sideways at a precarious angle due to the camber of the asphalt at the side of the road. Closing the distance, we could see a diminutive and elderly man in a shabby raincoat bending over to examine a flat tire. His wife, grey-haired and wrapped up in a motoring blanket, stood helplessly beside him. She was scowling and no doubt ready to blame somebody for their embarrassing predicament.

JB brought our car to a halt beside them, stepped out and doffed his topper.

"Good morning!" he greeted them brightly. "It seems you have a problem. May we be of service?"

Clearly JB was recalling the meat of his lecture to his family the previous evening – the bit about kindness and good manners.

"Oh, that's frightfully kind of you," squeaked the old duffer. "As you can see, we have a flat tire, and I'm not quite sure how to change it, or even if I can …"

"Never mind! Never mind! That's easily fixed … *Jeremy* …!"

Thus summoned and clearly designated master of the jack and wheel wrench, I removed my top hat and morning coat, rolled up my sleeves and got to work (on my pinstriped knees) changing the tire of what looked to me to be a 1927 model Austin Seven. It did not take me long, but while I was squatting beside the vehicle, I heard the following conversation between the old man and JB.

Old duffer: Are you going to the Abbey (Westminster Abbey) too?

JB (one-upped): Ah, no …! Not the Abbey, exactly – but we do have very good seats in the Commonwealth section of the Mall …

OD: Oh! Well, you see – I have to be at the Abbey by six o'clock …

JB (a bit piqued): *At* the Abbey, or *in* the Abbey …?

OD: Well, actually *in* the Abbey. You see, I'm supposed to be playing the organ …

From the inside of our car we all watched the elderly couple chug off in a pall of smoke, on their way up to London in their little tourer. The old fellow must have had his foot to the floor, for we soon lost sight of them. His wife appeared to have swathed herself in another blanket against the cold.

"Good Lord – of all people, the organist!" exclaimed JB. "You'd think the Privy Council overseeing the coronation would have been anxious to have nothing happen to him on such an important occasion – that they'd have the pair of them wrapped up in cotton wool and mothballs, camped through the night right next to the bloody organ ..."

A little later in the morning, once we had taken our places in the bleachers on the Mall, we listened to the service being broadcast over loud speakers. When we heard the organ strike up we wanted to congratulate ourselves for saving the day. It was only later we learned there had been three organists on duty for the coronation service, that our noble contribution to the success of Queen Elizabeth II being anointed and crowned did not quite merit mention in the palace gazette.

Per Sapientiam Felicitas!

My fellow students used to compare our time in public school to being locked into a prison. Schoolboy exaggeration, but in one respect accurate: friendships were akin to conspiracies. I made wonderful friends at public school; lots of enemies – it was my nature – but mostly friendships.

A great deal has been written about the English public school system, but perhaps the most significant thing about it was that it went through a period of radical alteration in the 1960's – long after my time – that took on a set of staid and dried out imperial principles based on bullying and sheer cruelty, turned them upside-down and instead concentrated on delivering exceptionally fine education. Elitism, for which the system was also renowned, has been the English way for centuries, but even that belatedly (and hopefully) is petering out.

Racking their imaginations and with the counsel of close friends, Mother and Aunty Tappie had lit upon a well-known boys' school located in Worcestershire where it nestles up against Herefordshire, little more than a stone's throw from the Welsh border. To ensure placement in such exclusive schools parents were usually obliged to register their children for enrolment shortly after bringing them into the world, and later to fork out its exorbitant fees. In our case, however, Providence intervened. During the war years the school body had been ordered to evacuate, and the entire campus had been taken over for the creation of a communications centre (the Telecommunications Research Establishment [TRE] developed secret electronic and radar systems) – which was operated in large part by the Royal

Canadian Corps of Signals. After returning to the original site and re-opening the school at the end of the war, the headmaster decreed in a magnanimous gesture aimed, one would think, at bolstering Commonwealth relations (and, it might be suspected, to garner a knighthood if he could work it right) the school would now inaugurate a "new tradition" – to accept Canadians into its ranks and, if at all possible, attempt the uphill task of modelling them into respectable gentlemen. That took care of enrolment. Now all Mother had to worry about were the staggering fees. She held out hope that one or the other of her offspring might one day warrant a bursary or scholarship, and thus lift some of the burden from her shoulders. It never happened. For each of us the curriculum posed a continuous daily slog, not just to master each subject area to which we were introduced, but to overcome the imposition of social and cultural factors that, to say the very least, were at odds with how we had thus far come to see the world – like living in a colander through which we were unable to filter ourselves, even with the "assistance" of the school. This austere establishment was our high school education, and we were to remain at it until each of us in turn had reached the age of eighteen. It is not the kind of thing teenagers like us were easily able to assess, but our schooling was costing our mother a fortune, and she was seeing rather meagre return on her investment. In every respect her two sons were proving a heavy financial burden.

Boredom – the excruciating boredom that accompanies rote learning in the classroom: in terms of our studies neither my brother nor I were especially challenged. We were both floundering – and yet our individual performances while at the school were more than offset by what we were able to achieve in the years following our departure. Perhaps it was the overall experience of the school itself that later enabled us, though I am inclined to doubt it. We both felt, and strongly, there were real problems with the school and the manner of its harsh and traditional teaching; almost to a man (there were no female teachers whatsoever) the entire staff had progressed through the same system a generation earlier. They were part of an outdated way of thinking which, right after the traumas of the Second World War, hardly applied anymore. And there was precious little or no space for two boys who appeared a trifle early on the historical timeline, confronting all the norms. I believe both of us were "special cases" – hardly the sort of stable family material school masters thought they could best be moulding within their classrooms.

Scholastically, the years at public school were years of agony for both of us. Report cards would be sent to our mother at the close of each term, and routinely they reminded us that we needed to "pull our socks up" if ever we hoped to pass our General Certificate of Education (GCE) exams. Monsieur

Le Grand, laconic French teacher, whose intellect, patience and cultural certainties were daily assailed by recalcitrant students (and neither my brother nor I were the dimmest!) was instructor to both of us at different times. He must have been at the point of capitulation when he penned on my brother's report card: "A deathbed repentance could not raise Boultbee Major (I was Boultbee Minor) from the lowliest of French scholars." At least it gave Mother a chuckle. Here was one member of the college staff who was not so squeamish as to avoid informing her she had two boneheads for sons – but she reckoned, and possibly absolutely correctly, the comment told her more about our French teacher than about her boys. She stuck out her chin, sucked in a deep breath, and backed us as only an undaunted and loving mother would – and should. Indeed, we gave her no other choice. Seeing the two of us sweating and straining through hours of tuition and cramming during the holidays, must also have been painful for her – emotionally and financially. (She was forking out as much on extra schooling as she was on regular school fees.) Even so, progress remained painfully, laboriously slow. By the time each of us had squeaked through our exams, Mother was as dried out as last year's prune pudding. I think she realized that whisking us about the globe as she had, good for our sense of worldliness and geography though it may have been, nonetheless had a detrimental effect on the stability necessary for the head-down nitty-gritty of concentrated school studies.

Sports were, and still are, seen as enormously important at all British public schools – but in the years of Empire they provided a surreptitious form of brainwashing that very well suited the larger picture of force and domination. It was not for nothing it was claimed "the Battle of Waterloo was won on the playing fields of Eton" – indication it was in the rough and tumble of brutish contact sports that one developed tenacity and fight, promoting and developing the Old Boy network along the way. On the cricket pitch one was supposed to develop those other concepts of British refinement: the garrulous "jolly-well-played-Sir" sort of insincerity that emphasizes class over sordid scrabble; the comment is portrayed as just acknowledgement for fair play and sportsmanship, when its actual intent is to draw the enormous us-versus-them difference. The fight: brutishness, genuine insincerity – qualities at which the British still tend to excel while attempting to convince themselves they possess all the goodies in more lavish quantities than anyone else.

Team sports were never my thing. In the area of individual sports I was good at gymnastics and boxing, enjoyed long distance running, and was especially adept at competitive swimming and diving. One day my housemaster thrashed me for carving my initials into the wooden top of my classroom desk. "If you want to be remembered, laddie, give us a performance worthy of your name so we can inscribe it on the honours board." So I swam like a fish, and my name was duly inscribed in gold on the honours list.

We had a divinity class on Thursday mornings, right after our bout of physical training in the house yard, and before going into breakfast. The class was given by the school chaplain, Rev. Richardson – or RevRich, as the students irreverently dubbed him.

To relate this incident properly, it is necessary to understand the school's basic geography. The roughly six hundred students attending the school as boarders were divided between ten houses (numbered one-to-nine, with a tenth School House) that ringed the main school campus. RevRich held his Thursday morning class in the upper room of a little red brick building that lay on the southern rim of the circle near the science block, and reachable from the five houses closest to it via a fairly well-concealed back pathway.

Students attending the class from the more distant houses were "disadvantaged," inasmuch as they were obliged to dress themselves completely after their bout of morning physical training before crossing the school grounds to get to the little red brick building. But this was not the case for those students coming in from the five closer houses. Numbers of them chose instead not to bother dressing themselves for the class, but would appear in their dressing gowns and slippers – and seldom on time. They would drift up in their ones and twos through the doorway at the bottom end of the classroom, sleepily taking their places at their desks lined-up in rows extending out on either side of the centre aisle that led up to the teacher's dais.

Members of the class had discovered remarkably quickly (gangs of boys can be like that) RevRich had no capacity whatever to teach class. Absentminded and kindly, he would blink at them through his spectacles and smile beatifically. Then he would clear his throat and call out in weak voice:

"Be seated, boys. Be seated. Be seated. You really should try to get here on time, you know ... Now, open your Bibles to the seventh chapter of Deuteronomy ... 'When the Lord your God brings you into the land ...' Read on, please, Mr. Hawkins ..."

There would be a great commotion at the back of the class as Hawkins would start reading and tin plates were passed around. Someone had brought a small gas stove into class and was pumping it up in order to brew a nosh of baked beans. The cutlery clattered against the plates.

"Boys! Boys! Do quieten down! I'm sure Hawkins' voice cannot penetrate clearly to the back of the class …"

Hawkins would then begin bellowing Deuteronomy Seven …

"Please, sir – can we open a window …?"

"Yes, yes. Do open a window …" RevRich would respond reasonably.

But the "we" making the request for the open window would be a cabal of pushing and heaving thugs – who would treat the "we" quite literally. Five boys would rise from their desks and advance with intent on a single window. There would be a mêlée around it, and one of the boys would wind up being pushed through the opening ...

"Boys! Boys! Do, please, come now and resume your seats. You are being most unreasonable in light of Mr. Hawkins' valiant efforts …"

Eventually class would resume, and Hawkins would drone on about the Lord's great love for His chosen … His blessings for obedience … demand for the utter destruction of the Hittites … the Canaanites … the Amorites … the Jebusites …

I am very sure RevRich was a good Christian, with evil in his heart for neither man nor spirited and obnoxious schoolboy, but unfortunately he had no idea how to maintain discipline in a class of wild animals in need of their first feeding of the day, and who had no wish to learn the chosen curriculum he had been instructed to teach them. Week after week we continued to treat him abominably, at whatever time it was when we finally reached his classroom ...

But one day we were surprised. Unknown to members of his Thursday morning class, poor RevRich had been involved in a traffic accident and was confined to a hospital bed. The headmaster decided to take the class in his stead.

On our way up the back pathway some of us were met by others who had gone before us. They were flying back downhill in their slippers, their dressing gowns streaming behind them.

"Crikey! It's the headman …"

By the time all of us had received the awful news, hardly a soul arrived in class on time and the headmaster, raging like a tornado, obliged us to read

Deuteronomy Seven again, and said he would be testing us on it. We settled noses-down into the flimsy pages of Holy Scripture. Silence as we swatted.

About fifteen minutes from the end of the class, the door at the back of the room creaked open a crack, and an umbrella was poked through; whoever it was pressed the button and popped it open with an audible snap …

We all caught a collective breath, one eye over the edge of the Holy Scripture to watch the headmaster – standing legs akimbo, hands on hips and glowering with the wrath of – well, Deuteronomy Seven.

One of our classmates was so tardy he had failed to hear the news, and clearly had no idea he was to be facing anyone but RevRich. In pajamas, bathrobe and slippers, and bending low to conceal himself behind the canopy of his open umbrella, the wretched student crept up the aisle giggling to himself at his prank and, finger to lips with a conspiratorial "Sh-h-h-h!" made his way to the foot of RevRich's dais. Suddenly lowering the umbrella, he burst out:

"Boo!"

The headmaster eyed him from under very dark brows.

"Boo to you, laddie!" he said.

The student crumpled to his knees in an effort to conceal that he had pissed himself, the rest of us gripping our noses and covering our mouths in a collective effort to stifle our laughter. The head was not amused. For sure the offending ruffian was to be caned mercilessly; I never did find out how many strokes he received.

In the end, however – and for good measure – the entire class was caned. It gave us a taste of the dire consequences mentioned in Deuteronomy Eight – and Nine.

My brother and I went to Italy during the summer before he entered the army, ostensibly to spend a month studying Italian at the University of Venice. Insofar as the language was concerned, I don't think it was a great deal of use. Both of us found more interesting diversions than sitting in a hot classroom trying to make sense of a language that seemed to us, at that time, about as obtuse as the Latin we had been wrestling in school. I am not sure what my brother got up to in the city; I asked and seldom got answers I could decipher. As for myself, a pretty young Italian girl happened my way; she was working in the university canteen to earn enough money to cover her tuition when fall classes got underway. She spoke excellent English, so there seemed little point in me trying to stumble along in unintelligible Italian. Dreadful waste of a scholastic opportunity; charming way to spend a portion of my sunny idleness.

At the end of the university course my brother and I headed up to Torbole at the north end of Lake Garda for the final two weeks of our Italian escapade. We stayed at a small resort that had recently re-opened following the war; it was inexpensive, the food was ample and good – and one of the perks was a fleet of small sailboats that guests could take on the water for minimal charge.

They were open dinghies. Both of us had spent several Easter holidays learning basic sailing on the Norfolk Broads, so one afternoon, when there was a good breeze, we took one of the dinghies and set off for the far side of the lake. We decided to examine how the *strada*, the lakeshore road, hugged the western side. We could see that the mountain came straight down into the water, so the construction of the roadway, as an engineering feat, was a mystery to us. The steep cliffs prohibited housing, but the *strada* had been carved into the sheer cliff face. In places, as it circumnavigated the lake, it tunnelled its way through large spurs of the almost vertical mountainside.

Looking back towards Torbole, the entire coast sparkled jewel-like in the late afternoon sun. However, we had sailed into the shade of the mountain that dominated the lake's western shoreline. As the afternoon had worn on, a great shadow spread across the enormous face of the mountain so that we were totally free of direct sunlight. This meant that although we were sailing into a setting sun, there was no glare in our eyes and our vision was unimpaired. As we made our way up under the lee of the cliff, we could see there was very little traffic on this coastal road. A few cars went by, some appearing to slow down in order to get a better look at the two of us in our tiny sailboat.

But suddenly we heard the fast approach of a car, its engine and its tires screaming, the driver blasting on the vehicle's horn. The overall sound of the approach rose and fell as the car navigated through the tunnels, the racket so loud and in such contrast to our tranquillity out on the water that our attention could not help but be drawn towards it. Some impatient driver was in a frantic rush.

We were close-in under the cliff, no more than fifty metres from it. Both of us looked up in time to see the car – a red sedan – fly out of a tunnel and slam into the roadside guard wall at a right-angled bend. It hit with such force that the wall shattered. The car careened out into air clear of the roadway, seemed momentarily suspended – then plunged into the lake.

We did not have far to go. We navigated over to the spot where the vehicle had hit the surface of the water. By the time we arrived over the spot, not a half minute later, there was not even a ripple to indicate where it had gone in. No bubbles, nothing.

It took us a while to get back to our hotel, and we immediately notified the manager.

"Ah! Probably another suicide," he commented. "I'm afraid it happens all too often. The war, you know ..."

He told us he would notify the police. But then he said he was quite sure the police would be unable to do anything about it. It was not the first time this kind of thing had happened. The water was extremely deep in that spot, he said, and any vehicle falling into it would have carried its passenger – perhaps there had been more than one person inside – straight to the bottom. Not a hope of recovery ...

It had seemed impossible for me to devote myself to serious studying during my final year at school, so I concentrated instead on having fun (even more than usual is an admission of sorts). I was supported in no small measure by, of all people, my art teacher – Harry Fabian Ware.

Etiquette and the "insistence of distance" (an Englishman understands that time-honoured master/pupil law like none other) demanded that I should call him "Mr. Fabian Ware," and I would never have thought to do otherwise. Yet, though master and pupil, we were friends in every sense. I had never suspected it would be possible to become friends with one of my teachers, but in hindsight I think there is no other possible way to describe how we were with one another. He maintained his status as *maestro* without exhibiting any pretensions whatsoever. He was so incredibly good at what he did, and was able to pass along his knowledge with such clarity and gusto that there could never be any misunderstanding on the part of any student of his meanings or his requirements. He was a master of his craft, and as such he needed to teach.

I loved the man, and am sure I absorbed more from him – in all subject areas important to me – than from any other teacher in the school who had attempted the task of instructing me. In my final two years at the school Harry Fabian Ware was instrumental in securing permission for me to abandon those subjects that came across as total gobbledygook (math, sciences, Latin), and I was able to spend virtually my entire time alongside him in the art school – a series of studios tucked up under the pitched roof and gables of the school's main building. In addition to studio work I studied both art and architectural history, and was ultimately permitted to sit for a combined Oxford and Cambridge diploma course in this area.

Nearly twenty years after I had left the school I was travelling in England and had the chance to return for a visit towards the end of a summer term. There were still a few familiar faces I recognized; one of the junior teachers during my time there had now been promoted to master of my old house, another was now a venerable doctor of geography. But of course I wanted to see my old art teacher, so drove up to the home where I had visited with him and his wife so often in the past.

The house was a Victorian Gothic monstrosity in a tangled garden a short walk from the main college building, so I drove up and parked. It so happened I was making this leg of my journey in company with a beautiful girl I had known at university in Canada. It was an exceptionally warm day, so I was casually dressed in jeans and a tee-shirt; the girl curled on the seat beside me wore little more than sandals and a slip.

We ducked and dodged the undergrowth on our way up to Harry's front door. By the time we reached it we both looked about as tangled as his front yard. I knocked on the big oak door.

"Who's there …?" demanded a gruff voice I instantly recognized.

I announced myself.

"Good heavens! Really? Come in! Come in!"

We heard the door being unbolted, a lock being turned, then it opened a crack and the fingers of two hands appeared as Fabian Ware pulled the door back against some heavy object on the inside. I know those fingers, I thought.

"Oh – oh – oh! I'm so happy to see you!" he said as he poked his head around the door, white-haired now but still the man I remembered so fondly.

"Usually I go round the back and come in through the French windows – but I've got this open now, so come on in …"

He ushered us through to the parlour, and on the way I caught a glimpse of his wife sitting in a made-up bed, a mattress on the floor of the living room, a colourful wrap around her head.

"Can't go in there," said Harry. "Wife's busy having a nervous breakdown. Come on through ... mind the paint pots ..."

Then he called out to his wife:

"It's Jeremy, dear. He's come back to see us. After all these years ... Brought a charming young lady with him ..."

"Hello, Jeremy!" squeaked Mrs. Harry. "So good of you to come! Who's the young lady you've brought with you? Not a wife, I hope – ha! ha! Harry, put the kettle on and make some tea for them ... There are biscuits in the jar..."

"Of course I'm going to make some tea for them ... No need to issue orders!"

The inside of the Fabian Ware house, giant barn of a place, was chaotic. The whole of the interior, top-to-bottom, was his studio, it seemed. Maybe his wife was an artist, too, and some of the wreckage was hers – but his was the work I recognized, and possibly (I was thinking rationally) the cause of his wife's nervous breakdown. There were canvases everywhere, three- and four-deep standing up and lining every wall of every room in the place. Hundreds of boards and canvases and sketches, many incomplete, were everywhere – pads of paper sitting on top of pads of paper. And tables with pots and brushes, stacked higgledy-piggledy in the open and in every corner, easels, plaster-cast busts and models of torsos and legs and arms and stuffed animals – and everything climbing the stairs to the floor above, and even the floor above that, in a mad-cap conga line of oil smells and turpentine and colour and bedlam.

Hardly a surprise Mrs. Harry had decided to have her breakdown on the floor of the living room. It was possibly the only space left to her. The girl accompanying me smiled and rolled her eyes at the scene. In silence she was notifying me she could glimpse a corner of my life by measuring this crazy corner of Harry's, but she was enjoying herself so there was no cause to worry about her or whatever judgements she might be making.

Harry sat us in his parlour, a comfy room off the kitchen, and we all gathered about a large table as our host warbled on in his staccato voice about news from the college since his retirement. His comments were none too flattering; it seems the school's demands on him got in the way of his artistic production. Every now and then Harry would leap out of his chair and run into the front room to see that his wife was comfortable and had everything she needed – mostly more tea. His voice as he talked to her sounded gruff and grumbly, though we couldn't actually hear the words – and her replies to him seemed chirpy and bright enough. After their long years of marriage the two of them appeared to have settled into a pattern of dealing one with the other, his being quietly solicitous no matter what one might have read into the tone of his voice.

At one point I told him my story about how the students treated Rev. Rich – and he howled. He thought that was the funniest thing he had heard in a year.

"Hang on a minute," he said. "I've got to tell that one to Mother …" and he ran out of the parlour into the front room.

My friend and I could hear the laughter in his voice as he gave his rendering of the story, and it was followed by high-pitched peels of delight as Mrs. Harry caught the drift. Then she called out to me: "Did you treat Harry like that, too?"

Harry was still laughing as he re-entered the parlour.

"Oh, you students were terrible," he said. "Imaginative, but terrible. All these good stories really should be written down, you know … But, then, that was what it was all about. Students have to buck the system. They get trapped in this bloody place for so many months of their young lives, they have to do *something* to lighten their loads, good gracious me …!"

The telephone rang and Harry answered. It was his daughter arranging to come for a visit the following weekend.

"Hold on a mo. I'll check with Mother …"

He placed the receiver on the counter and raced from the room to his wife in her makeshift bed on the floor of the living room.

Natter-natter-natter, gruff-gruff-gruff, squeak-squeak-squeak.

It went on, back and forth for several minutes. Then Harry came back into the parlour shaking his head.

"Oh-dear-oh-dear," he said cheerily. "She can be so difficult!"

He sat down and resumed talking to us for a few moments before he noticed the telephone was off the hook.

"Oh!" he exclaimed, as though someone else had put it there – and he hung up the receiver.

"Wasn't that your daughter on the line?" asked the girl sitting beside me.

Somersaults

"Oh – was it? Dear me, dear me! Well, never mind, she'll call back ..."

Which is exactly what happened next.

"... I'm having tea here with an old pupil of mine, and a lady friend of his... They dropped around to see us. Wonderful time we're having ... Reminiscing ... Such amusing times ..."

He finally made arrangements for her to come the following weekend ...

"Give Annie my love ...!" came a clarion squeak from the front room ...

"Mother sends her love ... So do I ... Bye-bye!"

Harry sat back with a sigh and a big smile on his amiable face. For all his age, he had a full head of hair – whitest white, and matched by the white of his moustache and thick and bushy white brows. There was a slight tinge of yellow to the tips of the whiskers under his nose – indicative that he still smoked his pipe.

"May I offer you a drink ...?"

The girl said no. I said I was driving.

"Smoke ...?"

The girl said no. I said I no longer smoked.

"Mind if I do ...?"

On the mantle above the fireplace there stood a large and ornately-carved humidor of a dark and well-worn exotic wood – maybe teak. Harry reached up and took it down, then sat back in his chair and lifted the lid as he cradled the thing on his knees. The room was suddenly filled with the unmistakably pungent odour of cannabis. Harry began to stoke his pipe with a liberal quantity of the dark greenish herb, nonchalantly tamping it down just so with a long and practiced thumb.

The girl and I looked at one another wide-eyed.

"You use that stuff?" I asked him

"Yes – herbal tobacco. Best there is," said Harry.

"Herbal tobacco? Why, I think maybe I'd like to try a little of that with you, after all," I said.

"Certainly," replied Harry, unhooking a second pipe from the rack of several that surrounded the humidor. "Here – help yourself!"

He passed me the humidor, and I started to fill the pipe he had given me.

"How long have you been smoking this type of herbal tobacco?" I asked casually.

"Oh, years!" Harry explained. "I used to buy it off a special dealer in exotic tobaccos when I was in London before the war. He put me onto a friend of his who carries the same line, works out of Worcester. I was very lucky to find someone so close ... Saves me from sending to London for it. I reckon over the years I've saved a bloody fortune in postage alone!"

"You mean this is the same awful-smelling stuff you used to smoke up in the college art school?" I was laughing.

"It certainly is! I haven't changed my brand in forty years ..."

The girl and I later made our way back through Harry's tangled front yard to where we had parked the car in the street. She had partaken of Harry's special herbal tobacco as well, so the two of us were feeling giggly. She clung to my arm, and ran her fingers playfully through my hair.

"Herbal tobacco, huh? What a wonderful old fellow! Didn't you tell me he was the teacher you loved most of all? I'm beginning to understand why...!"

On that same visit to the school, I happened to mention to Dr. Chesterton, my old geography teacher, that my girlfriend and I had been to visit Harry Fabian Ware a little earlier in the day.

"Oh, wonderful old man. Great friend. I haven't seen him for several weeks. How is he? How's his dear wife?"

Conversation naturally turned around this visit to Harry, and Chesterton laughed when we told him how my old art teacher's house had appeared more like a workshop than a stately Victorian home.

"That's Harry! He was always in a bit of a mess, paint under his fingernails," Chesterton said. "But he was hugely popular with all of us in the staff room – completely unconventional. You know, the Headmaster always hated him. You remember old G–? He was so prim, so completely organized, and he detested Harry's chaos. He'd cut him dead, refuse to speak to him ... We all knew about it. Even Harry would tell us of his encounters with the

Somersaults

Head, and the way the old man wouldn't have anything to do with him. It was the running story among the staff, a great and continuing saga …"

He related how one day Harry had come into the staff room in fits of laughter, and all the other teachers wanted to know why.

Fabian Ware told them how he had only a few minutes before encountered the Headmaster as the two of them were walking on College Road – converging, but on opposite sidewalks. The Head had called out and made a hand signal summoning Harry to cross the street; he had something he wanted to say.

For the first time in the dozen or so years he had been teaching at the school it crossed Harry's mind that perhaps the Head was making an overture, an effort to be friendly. He walked across the street in bright anticipation, and bid the Headmaster a good afternoon …

"Can you guess what the Head wanted to say to poor old Harry?" Chesterton asked me.

"I've no idea," I replied.

"When Harry reached him, the old man said: 'Mr. Fabian Ware, the fly of your trousers is unbuttoned.'"

Dr. Chesterton shook his head with mirth.

"Good old Harry! He and his art studio – he gave us all such a lot! The Head never understood quite why we liked him the way we did, crusty old bugger! But we all loved Harry Fabian Ware so very dearly, so very dearly…"

For several years after the end of the Second World War, Britain's National Service Act obliged all males over the age of seventeen and a half to register for military service – and this particularly applied to resident aliens, no matter their nationality. No doubt it was considered just payment for the privilege of living in Britain, so it was either agree to serve or leave and return to your homeland.

Although Canadians, my brother and I both elected to remain and serve. All of our school fellows were due to serve, a strong compulsion for both of us to do the same. It was the mid-1950's and no one had yet learned how to burn his draft card nor, indeed, even thought to do so. That anti-establishment act of defiance was to become popular a decade later.

Two years apart, first my brother and then I were duly commissioned as infantry officers in one of the home counties regiments, then seconded – lent – to serve in the King's African Rifles, a colonial regiment then fighting the Mau Mau in Kenya. In my own case, after almost a year in Africa, and by now fairly adept at jungle warfare, I was sent to fight the Chinese communists in Johore – the jungle-covered southern state at the tip of the mainland peninsula, now a part of Malaysia. Both the Mau Mau and the Chinese (CT's or Communist Terrorists) were designated "terrorists," which gave the authorities licence to hunt them down as if they were vermin-covered wild animals.

My brother thought this was alright. I did not – and thus was triggered a divergence between us that morphed into a major political break and was never satisfactorily resolved. With nuances that did not manifest themselves for several years, my brother's political views were swinging to the right, while I was engaged in a fairly hard turn to the left.

National Service for us came about in the middle of that post-war period when Britain was anxious to use spry young men like ourselves – willing, naïve and gung-ho for adventure – to hold together a badly-battered Empire. By this time Mother had married her Englishman, JB, who had served during the war in the North African campaign against Erwin Rommel.

Military service will be good for you, said step-father Number Two, imbue the pair of you with tenacity, discipline, responsibility and a sense of history and achievement. Fabulous opportunity to see the world, he said. Serve the queen and her great Empire, and so on and so on. His enthusiasm was infectious and neither my brother nor I had yet been inoculated against ideas like his. We both understood it as a duty and went willingly, an act of recognition by both of us that we had been honoured to feast at England's table during the years of our residence in the country and our schooling ... All of my school fellows were likewise un-bleatingly willing to accept the same royal shearing. In any case, it was the next great adventure down the road.

My brother was quite good at soldiering, as it turned out. He served with the KAR at the onset of the Mau Mau rebellion, and at one point was appointed bodyguard to the colonial governor, Sir Evelyn Baring. I followed him to East Africa two years later. By that time the rebellion was beginning to wind down. I had always thought, after the fact, that my own military career had been nowhere near as auspicious as my brother's, but it's hard to make comparisons. After basic and officer training I spent almost one year in Kenya, then closed out my two-year stint of service "with the colours" by taking part in the colonial war Britain had been fighting against the Chinese communists in Malaya since 1948. In both Kenya and then in Malaya I actually enjoyed the jungle – the outdoor exertion, the comradeship of the troops I commanded. Like my brother I might have managed to distinguish myself as a "good soldier;" certainly I made an earnest contribution – a year and a half of active service, patrolling and fighting in tropical jungles. But I had become aware of the implications of what I was being told to do, and was beginning to understand my profound disillusionment – a disgust at the privileges of Empire and at the sordid degradation of its inevitable collapse.

In the end, I probably wasn't such a good soldier after all. Too contrary. I was young to be so opinionated, but I was impressionable even so, and no doubt a little intimidated.

However, what seemed to me so obnoxious was what I considered to be the arrogance and racism of Britain and Britons, the tenacity and cavalier justification for their level of sheer cruelty that, as so many have been quick to point out and parrot, was really no more than the exercise of a corporate "colonial responsibility." My failure was in understanding – that it had been like that since the beginning of the colonial experiment, that it was one of the givens of a rampant and greedy capitalism, that things hadn't changed a whole lot over the years, and that my opinion was squat.

An honour, even a duty, to speak my mind, one might suppose – but who at any time would think to give a damn for the sensitivities of a twenty-year-old?

PART II
Penmanship

Part II – Penmanship

Canada Redux 147
Grounding Un-grounded 152
Manta Ray 160
The Editor's Demon 166
Fellow Traveller 167
Broken Logger 183
Cougar Story 184
St. Paddy's Night 186
Big Freeze – Regina 189
Art Critic 198
Micky Canter 202
Euro-Junket 208
Visuals Fey 212
The Captain's Table 215
Funerals 220

Canada Redux

It was October, 1956, when I finally returned to the Moat House, my family's home in Buckinghamshire, military service done and behind me. I had been badly shaken, but I was still spirited and felt sufficiently upbeat to tackle the next round of whatever Life was about to toss at me. However, immediately upon my return I was to discover all was not well with my mother. She was at the point of ridding herself of Husband Number Three. She was down and discouraged in a way I had never seen her before, and was by no means in any frame of mind to listen either to my plans or my doubts. My brother had left home and was now living in East Africa. Mother was alone and drinking, and I knew I could not remain with her. She knew it too. The two of us were sitting at the kitchen table one evening when she said:

"You mustn't be here to witness all this ... It's time you returned to Canada to meet your father ..."

There were certainties behind the words she uttered, and I knew them; even so the message rolled across my heavens like distant thunder. For years I had known this moment would come, but when the rumble finished and the bolt flashed, I was stunned all the same. Still unsettled by my military hitch, I was unable to think very long or hard or clearly – about anything. Assessing the deeper significance of my mother's words was nigh on impossible, but they hurt. I recognized the dismissal; I had spent the last two years learning all about dismissals, so knew them in every variation and what they sounded like. It took a month for me to gather myself together, but then I did as bidden. Returning to Canada's west coast (I had no solid memory of the place whatsoever) I was again hoping to discover "home;" the reality was that I had just been heaved out of the one nest I had known.

Maybe nowadays there would be someone who would know how to have dealt with the difficulties being experienced by this young man so recently returned to Canada, but at the time there was no one at all – no one reachable who was sufficiently qualified to know about the condition I was in, or to question whether or not, and to what degree, my head and whatever core values I thought I possessed had been scrambled. Like eggs, I think no one at that time would have known how to count them, let alone unscramble them when they had been so well-cooked. Maybe even today the so-called experts might be buffaloed. Back then, Canada's most recent war had been several years before my return, so even had there been medical professionals who knew about post-traumatic stress, there would have been few shattered soldiers for them to take a look at, to make the decision as to whether or not they were in need of help or reorientation. My guess is that they would have been reluctant to muck about with a soldier returning from a "foreign" conflict completely beyond Canada's experience, reality or responsibility. There was no one to assess the needs of a British military cast-off, and the fact he was a Canadian would likely have confused any bureaucracy involving itself in the issue. "*Canadian*? What were you doing in the *British* Army?" None of that sort of stuff was on the medical charts in 1956. The need was in no way acknowledged, and in any case there were no services available for spooks like me. I think of it all now with a smile: my chop-and-change childhood, the years spent in a Dickensian boarding school system, all of that topped off by a two-year hitch in the British army – laced with a year and a half of the jungle book.

In addition there was a genuine reluctance to admit there was anything wrong. The stigma thing – in reality the first hurdle beyond the trauma itself.

In all this there lurked a recipe for disaster: joining the military, any military, is hardly "normal." It's like submitting to an intense and continuous round of brainwashing. No one can be "normal" once he has suffered a boot camp drill sergeant screaming abuse at him from two inches in front of his nose, putting a recruit through the paces considered essential to "break and remake" him fit for soldiering. The method employs the screaming of idiotic obscenities at the recruit until the poor devil can no longer be certain as to who is the more imbecilic – the drill sergeant or himself. This extraordinary behaviour is such a well-known and time-honoured "tradition" that we laugh about it, make jokes about it. It is a treatment that will no doubt produce a soldier, to be sure, but it is also virtually guaranteed to assure anyone in possession of "normal" sensibilities a traumatic, even psychotic, episode before the term of basic training has been completed. The recruit may not recognize it. He likely will have been so badly broken – and so remade – that he will never again know his own mind. The trauma is increased if that formerly normal man – or woman – returns from soldiering to civilian life after a bout of active service. The degree of the psychosis will vary depending on the individual soldier and the severity of the service – but for sure Citizen Harry or Sally would be a well-trained soldier by the end of it, ramrod straight on parade, but mentally bent like a paper clip. Now a trained killer, that miserable creature would never be the same again.

That's the start of it. The longer one remains in service the greater the scrubbing – and there is no successful way of treating oneself, either, taking it upon oneself to commence a process of restoration. One cannot remain in service and simultaneously banish the demons. The one element defeats the other. It is impossible for anyone caught in this situation to "heal" him- or herself in a hurry – or at all – by retreating to whatever civilian life had existed before signing up. I have thought maybe it could be worse if he/she rises to the dizzy rank of general; by that time there'll be the need of a war to fight, otherwise he/she might feel professionally unfulfilled. (How about, as a way of putting an end to wars, making military service obligatory for all men upon attaining the age of fifty?)

What has become normal, though, is that the victim (by now totally off the wall) is utterly convinced of his or her normalcy, and that it is everyone else who is out of touch. Loopy? The one hope of ever mending such a mess, of levelling off, requires getting out of the service.

But if someone is put under contract to an army, what then?

Well – there are no excuses. Explanations, sure – but only lame ones.

I have often proclaimed my love for the canopy of the jungle. It was a sure sentiment. I think that was because the jungle was the unique place where there was shelter safe from people with clipboards and swagger sticks who told other people, like me, where to stand. True, the Chinese might have shot me, but at least they weren't playing with my mind. I knew the score. It never occurred to me that, had I met them, I would have been in doubt as to what I would have to do. The alternative to a Chinese bullet was the British harangue – this last a certain misery I was able to avoid so long as I could feel the preferred companionship of the men under my command, all of us together under the solitary covering of a dense foliage.

Returning to Canada there was no one available with whom I might discuss all these ideas, these conflicts and pitfalls. I returned to a home that wasn't my home, befuddled as a drunk following a ditch, qualified for nothing and with no clear plan as to how I intended to stay alive or make a living for myself. Perhaps my father would be able to proffer advice on that score. He had been a cattle rancher since the first time I could recall my mother talking about him. He bred prize Hereford bulls in the Caribou, though he had recently been forced out of business by the introduction of artificial insemination – a detail that provided abundant material for some of Mother's more savagely incisive commentary. But cattlemen were phlegmatic, no? He would come up with an idea …

After the ranch failed my father started running a small real estate and insurance office off the main street of Kamloops. Almost immediately I found myself out of my depth with him. I could not talk to him. He had strong passions for deeply conservative politics, so took his activities as a local businessman very seriously and had little time for weighty sidetrack issues that required explanation.

"You've got to get a job," he would tell me – thinking and meaning bricks, mortar, planks of wood, hammer, nails – paycheques.

"You've got to make a living for yourself. What do you want to do?"

I felt like the small Blue Boy standing before the Roundhead inquisition in Yeames' famous painting of the English civil war, "And When Did You Last See Your Father?"

I turned the question around in my head. I had no idea how to answer him.

Sitting next to me on the trans-Atlantic flight, and somewhat older than myself, had been a young man who told me in broken English that he was a photojournalist, and had fled Budapest only days before. Wanted by the Soviet Union's invaders of his country, he had said farewell to Hungary, and would now be seeking asylum in Canada. He opened a valise to show me photographs he had taken of revolutionary partisans shooting at soldiers in the streets of the city – dramatic close-ups of the uprising.

"I'd like to be a journalist," scatterbrain chirped to his most prosaic father, who was anything but amused.

What the older man meant by a job was exactly what the younger man had imagined – hammers and nails, shovels and hard hats, chequered shirts and big boots, maybe moving boxes around in the back of the local grocery store, maybe as flag-man for the municipality on the new highway running across the top of the town – maybe even selling insurance for him ...

Nothing wrong with any of it, but it was not exactly what I had in mind. If I had had a mind.

Disinterest and lack of enthusiasm for his suggestions irked the older man. He became angry and cynical. His face grew red, and his eyes bulged.

My stomach turned over, then, and thereafter it never again settled in his presence. The family bought me a cake for my twenty-first birthday, and my father flicked a cheque at me for fifty dollars. "Happy Birthday," he had said, and I felt utter consternation, as though lost, wanted to tear the cheque into shreds. But I needed the money.

I had a good contact, I told my father – a friend who was a photojournalist. He would help me ...

A paternal sneer, first of many.

"You've got more of your mother in you than you have of me!"

Not such a bad thing, I thought ...

My show of confidence (it was only show) did not succeed in convincing me, and it certainly did not convince my father. At first I resorted to an angry and immature belligerence. I was discovering how hurtful this man could be, and the level of my own resentment at the profound and bitter rage (he called it disgust) he continued to feel for my mother – and for me by extension, I thought. He had noticed my facial features resembled my mother's. Our limited history together was a given; perhaps it could all be overcome ... Not unreasonable was the consideration that, prior to my return to Canada, I had been involved in some extraordinary events; yet my father had asked me nothing – not a single question – about the years that separated us, my interests in art and architectural history, my schooling in Britain. My pattern of rationalization tended to resemble my mother's, along with my attention to everything within the realm of the artistic – and these he also both noticed and resented.

In particular he failed to ask me anything about the one thing I most needed to talk out – the active military service I had so recently left, fighting in the forests and jungles of Kenya and Malaya. One evening I came upon him thumbing through a school atlas belonging to one of my half-sisters – in an effort, I thought, to pinpoint exactly where I had been. He declared he had two areas of query:

The first – "Not sure of Kenya's exact location in Africa ... but I see it now ..."

The second – "... and the Chinese were trying to colonize Malaya ...?"

It occurred to me we came close to talking about it at that point, but we didn't. For a moment I had thought maybe he was interested, that this might prove some breakthrough to him, and so began offering answers to his queries... But his eyes wandered blankly, and then someone came into the room. It was not difficult to sense the great relief he must have felt at not having to listen to any lecturing by this young whippersnapper. The subject was never raised again.

My father scoffed when, some years later, I gained admittance to art school.

"How are you going to make money with art?" he sneered.

It took me a long time to acquire the courage to face him, learn how to work around his unkindness and taunts, but by the time I graduated I had ceased talking to him altogether. In those early weeks, however, when I had so recently been released from the army and after my arrival in Canada, I was perplexed by the way he pushed me away, held me at a distance. The uncertainty of it lasted a long time; I did not want to accept what I saw as rejection. It seemed to me he was angry because I needed help – in lots of areas, no doubt, though I would not have known it at the time. My father was, indeed, someone utterly strange to me. I returned to his household bringing with me something many returning servicemen bring with them – a murderous illness of ease, a scary impulsiveness, an anger and derangement that few people who might have known me before I joined the forces would have been able to recognize in me. But nobody in my father's household had known me, and he least of all. So who was a threat to whom?

There is a nursery rhyme Mother would chant to me as a child on occasion as she was wishing me goodnight and tucking me into bed. It was sometimes delivered with a conspiratorial little giggle that sounded like the tinkle of a bell. In fact it was wickeder than that. It took me years to comprehend her *sous-entendu:*

> *"Mama, Mama! What is this mess that looks like strawberry jam?"*
> *"Hush! Hush! My dear, it is Papa – run over by a tram."*

Grounding Un-grounded

By the spring of 1957 I had moved to Vancouver Island and started working as a general reporter at Nanaimo's only newspaper at that time. It was not quite the job I had envisioned from my conversation with the Hungarian photojournalist. I chased fire wagons and ambulances, covered magistrate's court proceedings and wrote up some of the thousand-and-one parochial items of which all Canadian newspaper editors are so unabashedly enamoured – dog shows, tea parties, kite competitions, after-lunch speakers at service clubs, nature rambles. There was a fanatic sailor building a forty-foot boat in his back garden with no hope of ever squeezing it out between his own and his neighbours' houses; (behind all their houses was a ravine, which was definitely not the way to go). Another fanatic, equally incongruously, was building an airplane in his basement – wings attached. He solved his exit problems by bulldozing his front yard into a ramp and smashing down the exposed concrete wall of his basement. The removal of such a basic structural component caused his front door and porch area to sag so badly the whole house had to be supported with hydraulic jacks. I know he managed to get the darned thing clear of his basement and re-build his mutilated house, but never discovered whether or not he ever managed to get his plane off the ground – or if he had ever bothered to acquire a licence to pilot it.

Identify a story – about anything – give it a bit of colouring and a twizzle, add a personality if one can be identified – name, age, address (people buy newspapers to see their names in print); consider the requisite "Who?" – "Why?" – "Which?" – "What?" – "When?" – "Where?" and "How?" – the essential questions all journalists are required to keep pasted on the ends of their inquisitive noses. Add a quirk or two, a smidge of drama ...

BINGO! We have news. Papers sell, boosting circulation. Advertisers are happy.

Little old lady crosses the street – not news. Little old lady crosses the street and someone pushes her under an oncoming bus – ah-ha! Definitely news!

The journalist is right there, "why-face" shoved prominently into the centre of the picture, playing his essential role in the democratic drama, whether or not his (her) observation of whatever is going down is essential, relevant, substantial, obnoxious, idiotic, a revelation or a cover-up. All the great men on earth revere him (her) because it is the journalist who maintains the great man's greatness, writing about him and seeing that his picture makes it into the paper; except when the great man is corrupt. Then the journalist could be a liar or a swine – perhaps both. And the little man dances the same jig, for he aspires to greatness and believes public exposure is the fastest route to his goal – and the fortune he seeks. If it doesn't work for him, then it's the journalist who is out to get him. Tricky business, journalism.

I understood none of this when I first started at the paper. Schools of journalism barely existed in those days. Of far greater consequence in the business was the "news nose," the ability to suss out a story, see its potential for garnering interest and then be able to write believably. Court – labour – crime – education – finance – sport. I found it hard to assess the weight – sometimes even the point – of the everyday news. One had to deal with it, to be sure, but if I had any strength at all it was in features writing, that element in any daily newspaper for which the journalist is permitted to take sufficient time to go into a story in depth.

Somersaults

Apart from the man who hired me, the first person I came to meet and know when I arrived in the city was a lumberjack. We got drinking together in a beer parlour that same evening. According to regulation or tradition (information I had for some reason previously squirreled away in my mind) he wore plaid shirts with the sleeves rolled up above a pair of spectacular biceps, woolly socks coloured warm thunder-cloud grey (a red band round the top of each sock), and fitted his feet into studded-and-steel-capped size fourteen boots. A pair of wide braces held up baggy non-descript work pants. When he stood up there must have been close to two metres of him to answer to the name of Larry.

We would see one another frequently after work. The beer parlour was across the street from the newspaper office. Drinking buddies would be about the best description of our relationship; the beer parlour was our common sod and the easiest place to make new acquaintances. I'm not sure what the two of us might have had in common apart from the beer, but we enjoyed one another's company all the same; I imagine our individual circumstances pricked the inquisitive in the other. He was a clever fellow with a bright humour – by no means someone I would pigeon-hole as an uneducated labourer. I lost touch with him when I left the city, but have always chosen to imagine him progressing well in his world as the years rolled on. He was an active fellow, interested in all life around him, so my imaginings about him have been positive. I was fascinated at encountering for the first time a real life and (at least to my mind) typical Canadian logger, a man engaged in an occupation that has been so widely romanticized in far corners of the world (like drovers in Australia or gauchos on the South American *pampas*) that there was absolutely no one I knew who had not heard of it and imagined men like Larry fulfilling its avocation. He nudged himself into the far recesses of my old world preconceptions.

Neither of us made a special point to call the other, but from time-to-time when we happened to meet in the street we would enjoy a catch-up session over a brew at the Commercial Street beer parlour where we had initially met. We would sit head-to-head over tall glasses of draft while he pumped me with questions and I told him stories – or vice versa. The stories he told me were no less dramatic than my own, but from a different warp. As he rolled out the events and characters of his everyday life I was spellbound by his matter-of-fact descriptions – of the woods where he earned his money, the landscape, the trees and the animals; of his home life and the closeness of his family. He told me his mother was as big as he was, which I found hard to believe – until the day when I actually met her. Larry and I were the same age. Both had come to that exceptional point in life: young men, energetic, curious and unbound, and trying to look ahead to see where we could go next. Larry had no father that he knew of, had lived at home with his mother and several younger brothers until recently, still kicked in a sizeable share of support for them but now had his own place. He had started work at the age of fourteen, but somehow managed to continue with his schooling and graduate from Grade Twelve. He had never been off Vancouver Island, was attached to the place as if a root to one of its tall trees – but his wit gave out a strong impression of optimism, that he was certain there would soon be a lot more to his life than he was encountering at the moment. He was fascinated by my descriptions of Africa and the Far East and wanted to go there tomorrow.

Larry had a perpetually dishevelled look about him, but I put it down to his size and the difficulties he might have run into finding clothes that fit. One could hardly have expected him to have tailor-made duds to go out into the woods to cut trees – and it would have been about as unreasonable to expect him to switch attire only because he might be coming into town for an evening of beer. He was a rough man, at least in appearance and humour. But to me, whom he had decided to befriend, he was extremely polite – occasionally to the point of showing anxiety as to how to address me, or explain me to his other friends. Now and then he would invite some of these people to join us at the table, and his manner of introducing me seemed deliberate, even insistent – explanatory. I was a journalist, he would tell them; I attended court almost every day and had acquaintances among the judiciary and the police; I had seen action as an officer in the British army. Without reeling off an extensive biographical list, he was able to make the statement to his friends that I was "okay" – for all that I might seem to be a bit of a misfit. It was his way of being attentive to me, a rough cedar bark charm. His friends took him at his word, treated me as a curiosity – a sort of woodsy politeness, I guess.

Inevitably we would drink to excess and our conversations would prod the necessity for fresh air and a change of scene, usually at an hour when there was little else to do in town but jump in Larry's car and ride up into the countryside behind the city. There the two of us would sit quietly, listening to music or else talking earnestly about what was "out there" for the two of us. One evening when we had been joined in the beer parlour by a couple of his work buddies, Larry suggested a cruise in his car along the town's main Commercial Street. An exercise in aimlessness.

The car in which we rode was a machine like none other I had seen. It was a gigantic Plymouth, its exterior painted a dark metallic grey, with terrifying dragons on either flank painted in flaming red, yellow and orange, with flecks of green and white. Their tails curled out from under the exhaust area, their bodies snaking up towards the wings and hood to protect the motor, wide fierce eyes popping out of their heads and their open jaws ready to swallow up whatever road lay in front. The car's rear end was jacked two feet off the road and sported twin chrome tailpipes that roared as they blew out billows of angry smoke. Both car and driver, in journalistic parlance, were "known to police," who would have recognized the vehicle five blocks away as it moved through the town. But few if any policemen would have experienced the car's interior – though they might have caught a glimpse of it as they bent down to the driver's window to proffer Larry the occasional ticket. Despite appearances, he was a careful driver. Although recognized by the police, he was never so stupid as to cross them. On the contrary, he seemed to know a number of them on a first name basis.

The car's interior was a masterful attempt to assemble all the essential elements of Lothario's boudoir. Still encumbered with bags full of strait-laced English reserve, I found what passed for decor amusing, seductive, titillating and embarrassing all at the same time, but not unpleasant once I was nestled back for my first joy-ride, Larry at the wheel. After all, I tried to tell myself, the décor of the exterior was just paint and chrome, and with a little labour I might have produced that myself, had my visual tastes nudged me that way. The interior, however, was nothing short of a work of garish genius. Everything, including the dashboard and floor coverings, even the steering wheel, was white – some of it sparkled. A leering white plastic skull acted as handle of the gear stick. The seat covers, the interior walls and ceiling were also white – in sexy-fuzzy mock fur. The backs of the front seats collapsed level with the rear bench to turn the entire space into a bachelor's sex-pen. All the windows – front, rear and sides – were trimmed with tiny dangling white pom-poms, the overall effect being the raised middle finger in salute to any who dared criticize a deliberate blaze of gaucheness. At the flick of a switch the car's horn would play the first four crashingly-conspicuous notes of Canada's national anthem. Inside, the sound system, hooked up to an array of speakers, was a high-powered radio receiver – a technological wonder for its time, able to tune in to any station broadcasting from Vancouver Island, the Lower Mainland or around the Puget Sound area. The choice of music, thumping loud or soft and smulchy-sweet (taste dependent on the occasion) was not at all to my taste, but I bent my head and lent an ear – and tried my hardest to comprehend a melodic cultural phenomenon that, until that particular moment, I had never been party to.

The first evening we decided to cruise the downtown area, Larry drove slowly and with an air of casual control, the elbow of his left arm resting nonchalantly on the sill of the open window at his side. What he termed his "cruise" was quite shark-like and was really more akin to a move from some dance on a dark stage – brute tango, perhaps, deliberate and with studied motion. As we moved along he singled out a young lady on the sidewalk and slid in beside her, talking in a sort of honeyed growl as he slowed the car to prowl at her speed. Every few paces she would stop – then Larry would stop too and there would ensue an instant of conversation between them, the words sliding so easily from Larry's throat, quips and sighs, smiles and gestures that treacled into the night air and might have prompted me to laughter, except that the ploy seemed to be working like the charming of a snake. I was so fascinated I durst not break the spell. At last she came around to the passenger door and I slid to the middle of the front bench to make way for her by the window.

"Jerry – switch places so we can keep the lady warm between us ..."

Larry's two friends sat like shadows on the back seat and said nothing. For a time we circled aimlessly about the town, all the while nothing louder interrupting the sound of the motor than the girl's incidental peals of laughter at one of Larry's suggestive saucies. Clearly the two knew one another. We finally returned to the point at which the girl had jumped into the car. Larry stopped, the girl got out and bid us all a good evening ...

"Nice girl!" I was tempted to comment after we had pulled away.

"My sister," Larry replied – a snort of subdued laughter from the back seat.

I was a little skeptical, except that the two fellows in the back did not say anything to back their cynical humour. I did not know what to think, and then one of them leaned forward and whispered huskily into Larry's right ear:

"'Nother sister up there in front ..."

Larry pulled the car over to the curb and slowed down so that I might have reached from my passenger window and tugged at her long hair.

"Go on, Jerry!" Larry urged. "Do your stuff ...!"

Evidently he wanted me to chat her up, but I was in such a quandary of embarrassment I had no idea what to say. It was not the first time my shy nature had caused me a terrified blockage; I was ill at ease, unequipped, untrained, totally at a loss as to how I could possibly mimic Larry's infallible patter. But I had to give it a go:

"Excuse me ..." I said to the lady on the street, at the same time realizing I had absolutely no interest whatsoever in this charade. In addition to the level of my stupidity, surely the lady herself must have twigged immediately to my essential disinterest. I felt ridiculous.

Had I possessed a hat to doff, I am quite sure I would have doffed it. Barmy!

"Would you care to ...?"

She had turned as the machine slid up to her, pulled herself to whatever regal height she could muster in her street flatties, and put away the lipstick with which she had been daubing a pair of tired-looking and utterly haggard smackers – but she most certainly did not anticipate having this particular gormless twit poke his idiot head out of the window of a passing car to give her the come-on.

She was ready, with an instant comeback:

"FUCKORF!"

I was wounded. My companions, for an uncomfortable instant, motionless and holding themselves in check, threw themselves to the backs of their seats and bellowed their laughter – a collective knee-slapping howl at my ineptitude. The poor creature moving away down the street could hardly have failed to overhear.

Doubled over and spluttering at my performance, and incapable of driving the car, Larry got out from behind the steering wheel and came around to my side.

"Here, Jerry ...! You better drive."

I slid over and took the wheel, and the conversation between Larry and his pals broke into a series of take-offs on my toffiness. Two blocks further on he gave me a nudge.

"Hey, Jerry! See the chick in that doorway ...? Pull up close alongside her..."

I moved the car over, slowed to a crawl to allow Larry the chance to perform his shtick. It will take him no more than an instant, I thought.

"Stop right there!"

I pulled up. The girl turned around and saw Larry hanging his arm out of the window. I expected to hear a string of honeyed patter. What I heard instead was:

"Hey!"

This was immediately followed by the sound of Larry clicking his tongue as if goading a mare to gallop.

An instant it was. Squealing her delight and reeking with the anticipation that lavish quantities of the cheapest perfume were intended to convey, she would surely have wriggled her way through the cavity of the window had not Larry opened the door for her.

It was delicious burlesque.

"Nice car …!" she gushed, indicating she had not seen it before.

"Another sister?" I queried – but Larry was hardly interested in my witty-cynicisms, though someone in the back seat sniggered. Already Larry's face was buried in the girl's hair, so it was possible he could not hear me. I was feeling such an acute sense of gormless embarrassment I huddled behind the wheel and pretended to be the regular chauffer.

"I'll drive us all back to my place and turn the evening over to you gentlemen when we get there …" I said.

We were close to my house so that within moments (Nanaimo was not a big town; one could be anywhere within its bounds within minutes) I was on the pavement outside the car in front of my home and bidding my companions a good-night.

It was then I overheard the chirpy voice of the girl, possibly thinking I was out of earshot, but also quite possibly not giving a damn one way or the other:

"Did you say that guy was Canadian?"

"Yeah," Larry responded as he slipped the clutch. "He talks funny; doesn't know a tree from a totem pole, but he's okay …"

Incongruous, I thought as I let myself in at my door. Only a couple of months before I had been in the company of young men and their ladies, all of us the same age as those in Larry's car right now, all of us aspiring to "rank" – officers and gentlemen filled to our collar dogs with the vainglorious airs of young squires-in-waiting, a tad shy of the royal blade tapping us on a heavily-braided epaulette. This evening had proven a decidedly gaudy juxtaposition to all that.

There must have been a lesson in it somewhere, I thought, but I was far too confused to be able to cope with lessons in anything.

Somersaults

Manta Ray

The editor of the Nanaimo paper – no need to give him a name – was demonic. Tubby little man in his fifties who had remained on his unexercised arse throughout his career, he wore a green sun visor that emphasized his baldness, arm garters that emphasized his dirty shirtsleeves, and chewed on soggy cigar stumps that billowed a putrid smoke – all the accoutrements, in essence, that would successfully parody his occupation. His glass-fronted cubicle at the rear of the editorial office (staff named it the "fish bowl") smelled foul, and its foulness oozed from the perpetually opened door to remind the rest of us he was present and watching.

For the most part it was an effort for him to rise from the chair behind his desk so that most of his beckoning and bellowing emanated from deep within the fish bowl and was quite unintelligible. On these occasions, when he thought he was being ignored – maybe several times in a shift – he would heave himself up out of his seat and, waddling angrily from side to side on a pair of exaggeratedly shortened and stumpy legs (they were hidden inside rancid pinstriped trousers that were never cleaned and stank as bad as his breath) he would hold onto the door-jam of his tank and shout orders at reporters and photographers alike. His language was derisive and mean. He had a formidable list of blasphemous curses and epithets, and used them liberally to punctuate his tirades. His voice would rise to an obscene screech for the photographers because they were usually behind the closed door of the dark room located in a far corner of editorial's otherwise open space, and he could seldom bring himself to wobble over there.

Staff members put up with the abuse because they valued their jobs, and knew how quickly this demon editor could turn on them, or order them from the premises (we were not a union shop). No one found him pleasant to work for; most merely tried to stay out of his way. Some, it might be said, learned to develop their ulcers in silence.

I detested the man. I could find no pleasure at all in being in the office, and found it daily more difficult to work there. My own scrappy disposition and aloof sense of independence, sure signs of a young man's budding immaturity, hardly fit with the editor's mean temperament. Luckily I was away from my desk for lengthy portions of each workday which made the job bearable. While my duties were as general reporter, my specific role was to cover court and the police beat. I made a note of what time, more or less, the editor left the office each day. If I worked it right I could often avoid being at my desk when he was at his – but his comings and goings were by no means regular and it was difficult for me to develop a systematic pattern.

Through my court contacts I became friendly with several stalwarts of the city. Ron McWhirter was a local lawyer whom I met most mornings in the courthouse where he appeared to defend a variety of miscreants fallen foul of the police for doing what they oughtn't. Lionel Beaver-Potts was the magistrate who gruffly scolded, fined and jailed a variety of unfortunates and numbskulls; considerably older than the rest of us, he was in reality a friendly teddy bear sort of fellow who liked to kibitz with those of us obliged to work long hours in the building. Frank Ney, a local realtor and a friend of Ron's who occasionally showed up at our coffee klatches, was destined to become mayor years hence – and I remember him chiefly for his prankish sense of humour. There was a Royal Canadian Mounted Police officer ever present, who seemed to be a part of this informal group but whose name now slips my mind. We would all assemble quite regularly almost every weekday morning in the coffee room of the courthouse.

In those days *The Vancouver Star*, published daily over on the British Columbia mainland, used to put out a special Vancouver Island edition. They stopped the practice years ago, but at the time it meant that a correspondent had to be maintained on staff in Nanaimo. Phil Jonder had been doing this job for several years and was a founding member of our courthouse group. He was a most affable fellow, a competent and very reliable journalist.

Phil's annual holiday came up about mid-point through the summer, so he took time off for a few weeks of well-deserved rest. His paper nonetheless required a representative on the island, so sent over another reporter – a man named Bill – for whom, unfortunately, the rest of the courthouse gang did not feel the same camaraderie as we did for his colleague.

Bill was a greenhorn at this particular job. He had been a journalist for a few years, but he had Big City ideas that were distinctly out of place for an underdeveloped geographical portion of Vancouver Island. Despite his expressions of confidence, he came across as clearly unsure of both himself and his sudden new surroundings, a juxtaposition that created an unnecessarily pushy sort of aggression everyone noted right away. It was nothing he could admit; we might have helped him in any number of ways, but he was a "teller," not an "asker," independent enough that he clearly wouldn't be seen seeking assistance from any of us. His bombast reflected an absence of even the least humility towards others who, had they chosen to do so, might have made his life a little easier. He displayed instead an irritating eagerness to bulldoze, presumably in order to score a "scoop" – as if that was at all likely during that somnolent island summer. His manner was abrasive, as though he was constantly on some personal quest to satisfy an urgent necessity – his story – that would bring to him the notoriety and fame he deserved. His intensity was decidedly irksome.

To us he exuded nowhere near the merry fun of the man he was replacing and it is to our shame that we judged him unkindly. When we might have assisted him we played tricks on him instead. We made light of misguiding and confusing the poor fellow. We would catch him feigning absentmindedness, but listening intently to our conversations in the coffee room; thus we managed, without giving the order, to send him galloping off in all directions on all manner of wild goose chases. Hints were dropped about developing stories in lumber and saw mills, marinas and boat yards all up and down the island. He would pick up on them, say nothing, but then race off to check them out.

It was mean, true. Cruel, even. But it is what we did, and we thought it funny at the time.

"Where's the story …?" the fellow would ask – and we would tell him.

But then one day some of us – McWhirter was present, and Ney along with the RCMP constable and myself – found ourselves out on the waters off Nanaimo in McWhirter's boat, somewhere between Protection Island and Gabriola Island. We weren't doing anything special except bobbing about on a beautiful weekend afternoon, laughing and having a good time. Someone had brought along a case or two of beer.

McWhirter looked over the side of his boat.

"What's this …?" he exclaimed, and with his boathook pulled up the remains of what used to be a fish. It had only then happened by, smelly even as it floated in the water, its eyes infinitely hollowed. Very dead.

McWhirter hoisted it up, holding it aloft for all of us to see.

"What was it?" someone asked. "Cod? Coho?"

"It's a damned good story, that's what it is …!"

He swept his free hand over the boathook and the fish it had snagged, across an imaginary banner headline of a newspaper's island edition ...

"*Manta Ray Caught Off Shores of Nanaimo* ..." he quoted dramatically, as though reading the bold type.

"'*It was too big to fit into the locker, so we had to toss it back into the chuck,*' said boat owner and expedition leader Ron McWhirter ..."

Ron was having fun, and he pulled us all along with him. Unceremoniously he tossed the dead fish back into the sea and we all drank a toast to it, laughing at the prank we imagined pulling on the unsuspecting and unpopular island correspondent of *The Vancouver Star*.

That was the end of the matter, I thought, until a couple of days later when I was sitting feet-up at my desk in the newspaper office. Part of my job was to keep abreast of what was being written in competitor newspapers. I flicked open the island edition of *The Vancouver Star*.

In a banner headline across the top of the front page:

MANTA RAY CAUGHT OFF SHORES OF NANAIMO

I couldn't believe it! I took my feet off the desk, sat up straight and read on. There followed a complete story: a group of Vancouver Islanders – us! We were all named!

We had spent a quiet afternoon cruising in Ron McWhirter's boat and trailing our lines when suddenly – after a wild fight – we managed to haul this frenzied monster over the gunwales and into the boat, there to discover it was a giant manta ray, its "wingspan" measuring at least a metre-and-a-half tip to tip ... We struggled to fit the thrashing beast into the boat's locker, but finally had to give up and toss it back into the briny ...

It was too big for the locker, McWhirter had explained ...

McWhirter, Ney, the RCMP constable, myself – we were all there, so the story went, amazed and aghast at the extraordinary thing we had witnessed.

Not only that; there were quotes from marine biologists at the University of British Columbia, asserting that such a catch was a strange occurrence indeed:

'... Very rare for that species to be found in cold waters such as ours ...' said Marine Biologist, Dr. So-and-So.

There could not have been a string of more reliable witnesses.

Sitting at my desk – mouth agape, eyes a-bug – reading this bunk, there was a sudden blow to the back of my head delivered by my own evil-tempered editor with his own rolled-up copy of the Star's island edition. I thought, or had hoped, that he had gone home for the day. He hadn't.

"Dammit, you incompetent nincompoop!" he screamed furiously, wobbling from stump-to-stump. "You were right there! Why the hell haven't we got this story in our paper …?"

I couldn't tell him.

"You want the story, you get the story …"

Immediately I set about feeding him what he wanted – scalping details from the Star's baloney to write up the baloney that eventually would appear in our own paper.

The editor grumbled at the Star's scoop, at his own reporter's incompetence and tardiness, but seemed content enough once convinced we had at least played catch up. Such a big story!

So I elaborated imaginatively.

By now, though, I had had enough of both the paper and its editor, and it looked as though all I needed was a slight push to motivate me, an excuse. A few weeks later I was sitting at my desk one afternoon, sorting through notes and copy, when the editor started screaming and cursing from inside his fish bowl.

This time his invective was aimed at me. A tumbler flipped over inside my head, and then nothing seemed to matter.

I stood up, picked up my enormous Remington typewriter, climbed with it onto the top of my desk. Striding from desktop-to-desktop, I made my way to the rear of the editorial room, to a position opposite the editor's fish tank.

He stared up, furious, chomping down so hard on the cigar in his face that it stood almost perpendicular and made him look cross-eyed.

"Gr-r-r-r …" he began to roar, but flecks of spittle gathering around the thing in his mouth, and at the corners of his lips, turned what he intended as a growl into a gurgle.

At that moment I raised the Remington above my head as if it were a football I was tossing back into play from the sidelines. The damned thing hurled well, shattering his plate glass window and bouncing from his desk into his lap.

"You'll pay for that …!" he screeched.

But by then I'd flicked my jacket off the back of my chair and over my shoulder, and was headed out the office door. There seemed no point in returning the following Thursday to pick up a paycheque.

Something wasn't quite right. I knew it but couldn't shake the nuts and bolts in my head to start the machinery working the way it should. I would have been the last person who could have assessed the problem correctly or dealt with it proficiently.

The incident has come to mind many times in the intervening years – almost sixty of them – and in learning to accept it philosophically it has also been possible to recognize the degree of Buster Keaton-style slapstick humour that went with it – and to acknowledge the sort of rationalization to which dear Mama would have adjusted (as she would have said) "in three shakes of a lamb's tail." No flies on Mama – she would have chortled with manic mirth, and argued my justification till doomsday before the sternest of magistrates. I have often thought that, had I been able to explain my action to her, she is the only person in my entire world who would have, without a shadow of doubt, defended me with the tenacity of an angry leopard. Mothers are like that.

Too bad I wasn't pushed there and then into the arms of a social worker; I might have opened up a notch. But it didn't happen. There was no one. Not in Nanaimo, not in Kamloops – likely not anywhere in the country. It's a wonder I was not picked up, charged with hooliganism, given lodgings in the hoosegow.

The Editor's Demon

(the curse)

No keener man with jaw a-jut has walked my varied beat,
Nor got away with quite so much (with quite so much conceit!)
But now I am an editor, and a good one. Pure as white,
And 'though the world may scream I'm wrong, I know damn well I'm right.
Yes, I'm an Editor, you see. It is my humble work
To probe and dig and rearrange, and sift through all the murk
Of stuff that's sent me day-by-day to clutter up my desk:
The doubtful prose, more doubtful verse, the scraps of humouresque.

I see it all and, with my pen, each random piece I mark
So when it's print I know for sure that I'm its Patriarch.
I know each comma that I write. Each phrase. Each mark of blue.
If you wrote the piece, you'd never guess. There's not a part of you
Left hidden in the mass of words that fill each page on page!
Ha! Ha! You're right! That's what I do, my Demon to assuage!

(the capitulation)

Each of us is cursed with it, this Demon of our skill;
And oh, but how we loathe him, 'though we cannot do him ill ...!
We bow and scrape, we can't escape; he's master of our mind,
And 'though we run a thousand leagues, he's still a pace behind ...!

I've had enough. I've given in. Come, Demon, take my pen,
And you and I, the two of us, we'll set to work again –
You work my mind; I'll work my hand – and when the writers scream
I'll tell 'em that the words they wrote confused the story's theme!

Demon, I'm an editor, and you're my Demon now;
So should you care to write a piece, I'll try to show you how ...

What's that you say? You can't abide a sombre critic's view?
Why Demon! That's tomfoolery! Now what's come over you?

Call me a knave, if that be your choice –
I care not a whit that you raise your voice ...!

Oh reader of this verse, look on! Your Editor has won.
For as you meekly scan these lines, my Demon is undone!
At last I've found his weakest spot; I've put him on the shelf.
Ha! Ha! Look! As I wield my pen – the Demon is Myself!

Fellow Traveller

Tony Hodd and I met on the main street running through Kamloops. In those days the city centre still had a boardwalk along some stretches, yet equipped with hitching rails. Tony was wearing a wide-brimmed hat – he called it his "semi-Stetson" – an open-necked shirt set off by a red kerchief tied loosely about his neck, khaki slacks and comfy shoes. He dressed like a man at ease, and lurched slowly away from the wooden post against which he had been leaning when he caught sight of me. He sauntered purposefully forward to introduce himself. There was the slight grin across his face of one who knows he is not recognized, but it was a smile at odds with the sad light in his eyes. No doubt he had some prior knowledge of a kindred spirit, but I was foolish and failed to see it right away.

"Hello!" he said, hand outstretched. "Someone I met yesterday pointed you out to me, said we should get together."

The man's upper class English-ness was immediately apparent despite his well-stitched quasi-western attire. His accent was unmistakeable, clear and crisp – fetching to the American ear, infuriating to the Canadian with a closer recall of the centuries of colonial control and ostentation. It might have been the primary element about the man most instantly identifiable, but more subtle was his stance, the erectness of his carriage and the way he held his head, tilted back slightly and inclined to one side. He stepped lightly and offered his hand, a firm and confident grasp. The whole apparition stamped him English even before he opened his mouth.

"Oh?" I queried.

"Yes, you have been working in news, I understand, and I'm anxious to get a job in that area, too – possibly with the local paper. What do you think of my chances?"

In those days there were no journalism schools in western Canada. If someone had half a wit and could scribble their name, there might very well have been a good opportunity to work in a newsroom. The bigger city papers had a system of apprenticeship for juniors – coffee-making and running errands, working oneself up the ladder rung by rung. In time the exercise could transform into writing up lists and minor reports, later maybe the more detailed stuff – fires, police, general news and events – and eventually interviews, labour, education, the courts and legislature. The senior and more able writers were the ones who wound up on the editorial page, with feature material and "think" pieces.

But the smaller provincial papers were always on the lookout for talent; it could be a dead-end trap, but not always. Sometimes it could be by far the best means of learning the news business.

"Reckon your chance is pretty good if you can write well," I told him. "You should get over there and give it a go. I'm writing for the local radio and television station, but I don't think there'd be anything for you with us. They are already well-staffed. The paper, though – that would be an obvious outlet. They have a turnover …"

Then I asked him:

"What have you been doing up to now …?" which elicited a move to the local coffee shop where we sat for an hour and got to know one another.

Tony had not yet been in Canada a full week. He had done his National Service about the same time as myself and, like me, had spent only a few weeks at his home in Britain before flying directly to Vancouver. His choice of Kamloops was not quite entirely spontaneous; he had read about the place in a photo magazine and liked the look of the surrounding countryside. He told me he was interested in horses and cattle ranching, but knew nothing about it. His family background in Britain had been rural and genteel, but he rightly figured he would be having to start at the beginning if he intended to follow through on a working country life in Canada. He figured the way he should go about it would be first to get to know and understand the community, some of its key players and personalities – and that he could do this best by becoming a reporter for a local news organization. It seemed methodical, not entirely naïve.

"I'm in no great hurry," he said. "If I could get on the paper here I might even find I like it. I'm a good writer – I could stay at that for a year or two, perhaps, then find work more rewarding. Ranching has always fired my imagination. What do you think?"

We had an easy connection, though I was hardly the one to give him advice. Over the next several weeks we met up with one another quite often. His toffee-English accent was the product of a private school education not unlike my own, and it further turned out he had also served as an infantry officer with the British Army in the Malay jungles. Whereas I had spent a year in Kenya before finishing off my last six months of service in Malaya – and that in the relatively calm southern state of Johore. Tony had had to endure a far harsher experience in the northern jungles of Kelantan for the entire one-and-a-half-year duration of his commissioned service. Our ease with one another stemmed from the coincidence of having Malaya as a common military background, except that Tony's service appeared to have involved a more rigorous and dangerous series of episodes than I had had to face. Although neither of us would have known or admitted it at the time, looking back I am sure both of us were suffering from similar doses of a post-service psychosis – the result of our schooling and backgrounds since childhood, of course, but all the more readily perceptible because of the intensity and the brutality both of us had encountered as soldiers.

Whatever it was the two of us had suffered (and we could hardly be expected to give a name to it when neither knew we were victims) few men can be aware they are in the process of sailing round the bend, and ought to shout for help. Once there, even fewer would happily admit to it; there was stigma involved, and it would have been quick to take hold.

We were not so exceptional, Tony and me – except in this place. We saw ourselves as two young men intent on making a living for ourselves. I wanted to have fun while doing it, if possible, but that was not quite Tony's perspective. It was not that he was incapable of enjoying himself when we met or when we got together socially with others our age, which we did from time to time; but there was always a distant seriousness about him – maybe even that sadness I had noted when first we met. He was a good looking fellow, and a number of girls seemed to enjoy buzzing around him. He fended them off with polite smiles. I wasn't sure whether it was because he didn't like any of them particularly, or whether maybe he simply didn't like women. I decided to say nothing and wait for him to launch into the subject in his own time. His mind was occupied, certainly, but shut to any personal intrusion I might have made, unintentional or otherwise. Tony was one to pick his own timing, choose his own moments of preparedness to meet others and speak his mind.

During the First and Second World Wars and again after 1945, during the years of National Service, hundreds of thousands of young fellows in Britain – no different from us – had had to endure all manner of abuse to their psyches, to their compassionate concepts of right and wrong. I have no reason to think either Tony or myself fell into any other category. Perhaps a psychopath would not be jarred by what he might encounter through army training or active service, but any moderate and thoughtful person subjected to such rigors will almost invariably suffer some form of catastrophic mental fatigue – the greater majority not necessarily knowing anything about it. Tony seemed to have all his marbles, held his act together pretty well, I thought. In hindsight I wonder if he himself felt so sure.

It was evident to both of us (we could sense it from the attentions of the people around us) we must have stood out in this interior western Canadian community like camels in a horse corral. I certainly was not savvy enough to know how to meld in easily. Nor was Tony, but he did not seem to want to try particularly. Saying this is not intended to rattle a drum, nor lay claim to some special status – it is simply stating the facts of that time: since the XVI century Canada has been populated by newcomers who probably felt about as bewildered by their new situation as we were, and every one of them had to face their spooks on their own. This hardly explained or lessened the sense of strangeness. Of the two of us I am sure I was the more socially unseasoned. So unseasoned, it seems, that I was totally unable to suss out the complexities of Tony's agonies.

We were young. I suppose both were unaware of the cut of our individual attire or any need to disguise it. Our wardrobes had been purchased, and for good money, in London prior to crossing the Atlantic, and thus they failed to match the form in which most men covered their backs or their feet in this western setting – either indoors or in the streets. As a result we were highly visible in a crowded beer parlour, the objects of quite blatant stares. The same held for our English accents which, no matter how we hushed our conversation, appeared to stand out across the silence of beer parlour pauses with substantial acoustic resonance.

However, not as well perceived but even more fundamental for each of us personally, had been our respective service in the military. In both cases, it was this that had pried open scabs on the surface of each of our exteriors. In some manner we both felt destabilized. Now, many years later as I write, Canadian soldiers have returned traumatized from war in Afghanistan, and young Americans from Iraq. Their unsettled condition has been identified and named: PTSD – post-traumatic stress disorder. None of this was known to us then.

Kamloops being farm and ranch country, Tony and I had walked into a society significantly dominated by men of the land. There were those who were considerably older than we were, set in their ways and neither cognisant nor interested in a lot more than whatever directly impacted their lives. Those we met of our own age were busy with their jobs, and had little or no concept of any world beyond Kamloops that couldn't be reached in a day of driving at breakneck speed in a pick-up truck. There were no younger and harder men who would have known any recent battlefields. Not knowing or perceiving the difference, it would have been quite possible we were regarded as two upstart Limeys who had set themselves apart. If this was the case such feelings might well have been justified, but I am sure neither Tony nor I would have been able to see or understand it. Integration was not a thing either of us would readily have considered necessary, even if it had been possible. It took time, but eventually I came to understand I was seen as an outsider, maybe even an oddball – "not-one-of-us." It was the same for Tony Hodd. We talked about it sometimes. Both of us felt as though we had been lumped into a separate mixing bowl, well apart – even segregated – from the society in which we now found ourselves. It induced in me an aloneness, a feeling of ostracism maybe close to a paranoia. It was never a pleasant sensation.

Tony was taken on at the Kamloops paper within days of our first discussing the possibility, and he settled in as a general reporter. We would meet less frequently, now and then at this or that function, or at the site of some story both of us were covering simultaneously. We were friends, no question, shared talk of our individual intimacies, but our get-togethers for lunch or dinner, or even a beer or two after work, were necessarily fewer. However, after Tony had been on the paper a year or so, and without warning, he suddenly announced his intent to move – from Kamloops to an area of the Shuswap Lake, about a hundred kilometres to the east. By this time he had acquired a reliable car, so he made arrangements with his boss, rented a small house in Salmon Arm and made up his mind to commute to work as the newspaper would require his presence. It was a substantial distance, an unusual move to my way of thinking, but there is no denying that the Shuswap is a beautiful lake, and that if someone hankered after an open air life there were few places in the world that could top its idyllic setting. As a consequence of his move we saw even less of one another; on the rare occasions when we did meet, he would always talk most enthusiastically about the merits of his new lifestyle.

"Come and see me!" he insisted – but another summer had come and gone before the opportunity arose.

"How will I find you?" I had asked him, to which he replied that it would be best if we met at a local café in Salmon Arm, one half of a local general store on the edge of town. There was a telephone there, so we could make arrangements by leaving messages for one another.

Today Salmon Arm is a substantial town, and Shuswap Lake a popular summertime playground, but at the time of my friendship with Tony the whole area was remote, the community no more than a tiny hamlet huddled into the three-point junction of a road system connecting Kamloops, Revelstoke and the Okanagan Valley. Shuswap Lake was a vast expanse of water that spread itself out into four arms conjoined in the middle and lying over towards a north-eastern wilderness like an *italic H*, running as far as the eye could see. Apart from the silver of the waters, the predominant colour was the dark green of the forests that blanketed the surrounding low mountains. In summer sunshine the place might have passed for some sort of Shangri-La – which I am sure is not far removed from the sentiments of the local residents.

I found the store without any trouble. To my surprise Tony showed up, not in the car I had last seen him driving, but in a pick-up truck. There were no other customers in the place, and I had time to finish drinking my morning coffee before he arrived. The lonely proprietor, chirpy now that he had someone to talk to, had been hovering in front of me at the counter filling my ear with what a great friend and good customer Tony had become, what a sterling citizen – that my friend was his friend, and one of the region's more notable characters ...

"It would be good to have more like him in the community ..."

All this had been in answer to my casual query as to whether he and Tony knew each other well, or at all. The fellow began to tell me about Tony's "encampment," giving me the notion of a man who'd never been there but badly needed to go – a prying curiosity, more ardent in pumping than imparting.

"Encampment?" I queried.

Thankfully at that instant Tony stepped through the doorway and the proprietor lost his opportunity for a more intense gossip. He and Tony exchanged greetings.

"Encampment?" I said again.

"Yes," said Tony. "If you're finished here, let's get going. Then I can show you where we're at – my lady should have a new brew ready about the time we get there ..."

"You have news to report, I see," I commented.

Leaving my car locked next to the general store, we drove in Tony's truck out of town on the road towards Sicamous and Revelstoke, along the southern section of the Shuswap's *H* – then took a dirt road down to the left that ran to the water's edge and skirted northwards again into deep bush country. Tony had sold his car and bought the light pick-up truck in which we were now riding. It was a practical vehicle for the country. On the way he told me a little of his new life in the area.

On the rare occasions I had seen him over the past year or so, Tony had come to town always nattily dressed, just as I had seen him during the period of our earlier encounters. But now he was dressed in rough work clothing – grubby pants, heavy-duty shirt and work boots. He smelled different, too – wood smoke, and earthy saplings. I had expected to find him lodged in an apartment or small house in Salmon Arm, but now I found him living in what he also described as his encampment, and there was a new lady in his life. I knew nothing of this, really had no idea what I might have expected, but clearly we were by now so far from any customary urban centre that "apartment" or "house" no longer would have applied. As we worked our way further into the bush I began to think tipi, or some sort of crude lean-to structure with a brush roof.

"What's the name of your lady?" I asked him.

"Sally," he replied. "And we have a dog called Kismet."

By now we were near his encampment, and the dog appeared at the moment his name was pronounced, running alongside the truck till we came to a halt at the side of the home Tony was sharing with his Sally.

He did not speak a great deal on the way out to his place. He answered my normal queries in monosyllables, holding back and not divulging more information than what I had specifically asked for. The place was a half-hour journey from Salmon Arm and he had to concentrate on his driving, especially when we turned off the main road, but even so he refrained from offering anything in the way of catch-up, answering my questions with grunts and minimum conversation. We would have plenty of time to talk, I reckoned, so refrained from pressing him.

We rounded a bend and there, a short distance back from the water's edge and well-camouflaged by a delightful grove of evergreen trees, was a small two-level cabin built of timbers and roofed by hewn cedar shingles. The footprint of the place was tiny – about six-by-six metres – with a wooden stair on the outside of the structure that led to the upper level, presumably a bed chamber, with a single window facing over the lake. A large deck had been built to cover the rocks at the front of the place, and one entered the cabin through a wide opening, its concertina door consisting of a series of small top-to-bottom glass panels. This all-glass door opened-up the entire lower front wall of the cabin to allow the wide span of nature to come inside; it was the sole source of daylight to the cabin's lower level, more than sufficient to see one's way around a tiny kitchen-cum-living area. It was here we found Sally leaning into an open fire pit, above which hung an enormous copper funnel that must have spread over fully an eighth of the entire space of the small room. It had a flue that poked its way upwards through the ceiling so that it passed into the quarters above – the cabin's heating system. In addition to the outside stair, there was an interior ladder against one wall and an open trap-door between the two levels. Furnishings were minimal: an enormous old sofa pushed back against one wall, a table and a couple of upright wooden chairs. There were shelves for a row of books, and a small cupboard near the cooking space.

Sally was in the act of peeling an orange and she threw the torn rind onto the fire. She was a First Nations member of the Shuswap nation. Her people had lived in the valley of the Shuswap and areas of the Thompson River since centuries before Tony had found her, and she seemed to fit most naturally into this tiny corner of the vast surrounding wilderness. She was seventeen, the confident owner of her space. She stood up straight as we entered, squared shoulders and back and taking full advantage of her height. She was as tall as Tony. Her clothing consisted of a simple flowered skirt and a loose blouse, her black hair shoulder-length and untidy framing a dark and expressionless oval face. She was bare legged, and wore no shoes on her dusty feet. In her hand was the orange she had just peeled and, as Tony introduced us, she took a pace towards me and held out a single carpel in welcome. I waited until she had popped one into her own mouth before I ate mine. With a slight bow, she took two more oranges from a large fruit bowl on a table and handed one each to Tony and myself.

The entire scene came as a surprise to me. I had to admit no particular idea of what to expect, except it was not this. Having always seen Tony in town wearing his casual London-cut "western" attire, talking in his slow and impeccable accents about the curiosities he was discovering as someone new to Canada, this scene jarred. He hadn't been in the country more than three years yet. I had been able to imagine him in a totally English setting, comfortable in the evening clothes of an English country gentleman, dapper squire to the well-chosen, pretty and witty debutante on his arm, taking her into dinner at some sumptuous estate within easy reach of the city. In my wildest imaginings I had not seen the layout of the scene before me now. I had never heard any mention of Sally. For that matter I had never thought to ask. I was embarrassed at myself because I realized my entire body of thinking about Tony was deeply his own personal affair – and with no right whatsoever I had somehow prejudged, then judged and misjudged him.

"Did you build this ...?" I began to ask.

"Yes. Sally and me together. Kismet kept the wolves and bears at bay while we worked."

Their cabin was an extremely well thought-out and well-built structure, its setting a slice of Paradise. In addition, it was clear to me the two of them worked well together as a team, that there was a deep affection and commitment between them. We sat in the warm late morning sunlight watching the waters, the trees and the giant landscape before us – not another person, not a sound anywhere to break nature's spell. Tony and I lounged on the deck while Sally sat on the stoop and worked at a piece of fabric.

"You're still working at the paper in Kamloops ...?" I queried.

"Oh, yes. Nothing too regular, but the paper pays the bills. I go into town as little as possible – sometimes twice a week, sometimes not at all for several weeks in a row."

"You're one of their reporters. What is there to report on out here?"

Sally chuckled, threw her head back and with the merest sweep of her eyes indicated the entire vastness of their existence, so greatly to her liking.

"This is it. We're in the centre. Lots going on around here ..."

Tony smiled, a little smug.

"The people at the paper know I live out this far, so they rarely give me evening assignments. When I get an evening assignment, I go in and then either sleep in the truck or come back here late at night. They get what they want from me."

"But that's a hell of a commute! I don't see how you can manage. I mean, how do you even get your copy into the office ...?"

"I can call it in. There's always someone on the re-write desk to take dictation. Either that, or I write it up out here, and take the finished copy to them when I go in ..."

Still I did not understand. Clearly my friend had developed a system, but I was quite unable to see it. It seemed best to hold back a little, to refrain from asking obvious questions. Things would resolve themselves for me during the course of my short stay. We ate lunch on the deck, and my two hosts began to open up.

"The paper is not my life," Tony explained at one point, perhaps irked at my ignorance of his sense of finesse. He spoke in contempt of both his own work and what he considered was his newspaper's role in the community.

"It pays for our lives – for the moment – but it is not a newspaper as I understand newspapers, and definitely not what either of us feel we need right now. The paper does not fill me; it empties me. Salary, yes, but for the rest it aims to hold me captive – and I cannot accept that. So I put my foot down as best I can – and for the present I can do this. I am able to. This is what I need, if I am not to burst asunder. Sally's what I need, this place, this life. This is my peace, not the silly little rat-race of trying to report on daily Kamloops. Right at this time of my life, I need this – not that."

He was trying hard to inform rather than instruct, as if it was a matter of course I should have been conscious and well aware of him and his delicate sensibilities.

"But how on earth do you manage?" I pressed him, referring to funding.

The deck of his cabin stretched over the rocks towards the water, far enough forward that it served also as a wharf to which a small short-masted dinghy was secured by a line. Tony had fitted his little craft for both rowing and gaff-rig sailing, but it also sported a fragile-looking Seagull outboard engine bolted to its port side gunwale to be used as an auxiliary means of propulsion. When not in use this apparatus remained raised and locked clear of the water. Tony ushered me aboard, and we cast off onto the lake, leaving Sally with her sewing. From our level, so close to the surface, the far shore appeared almost unattainable, a morose black slash between the expanse of the deep waters and the expanse of the green-treed hills. Such a position helps one to comprehend insignificance.

"We manage alright. This is where I like to come. I write most of my stories from out here. The news comes straight out of my head. I dream it up – or I dream up incisive think-pieces that seem to please my editor no end. I do quite a bit of work from out here, actually, write it all up when I return to the cabin. The greatest inconvenience is getting it into the paper when the editor needs it, but I'm getting that down pat, too. I try to put in an appearance at the office every week or so."

I listened to him talking, and I think I heard all he had to say. It was somewhat astounding for me to learn that a clever man could sit in a boat in the middle of a lake and dream up stories for his newspaper, but I could not be critical of such practice when I did not know his fullest reasoning, so I allowed my greater concentration to rest on the spectacular scene all about me. I suppose I was envious that I had not thought to do the same, or perhaps that he could get away with it. It was easy to believe there was a god given quality to the very air of this place, the enormity of the waters on which we now sat in this diminutive little craft, our entire puny universe bobbing along, flotsam, or like an insect being carried through time on the shoulder of another universe that had no need to pay the least attention to it. For an hour we sat and talked and, when the time was right, we headed back to the cabin for the evening meal Sally was preparing. The breeze was just right to hoist the gaff.

Afterwards we sat on the dock as before and watched a lazy sun amble its way across to the western sky. We spoke of our military service as Sally sat scowling critically and uncomprehendingly, for she could have had little idea of the vocabulary we were using – merely that we talked of war, and that was a subject she would have found even more obscure. Geographical place names didn't appear to mean anything to her, let alone the intricacies of whatever it was we had been doing in Britain's colonies. She perked up when Tony commented that most of the colonies would have their independence as soon as the British packed their bags and headed home.

"Here no chance that might happen ..." she commented dryly. "No packing bags; no heading home."

Tony pulled out a photo album of his time in Malaya and allowed me to flip through it – black and white pictures of Tony in the uniform of his regiment, proud at the start of his service; pictures of his friends as the service moved him out to Malaya; pictures of soldiers posing in their jungle uniforms, their personal weapons held in an assortment of positions showing their familiarity with them. Indeed these were photographs just like ones I had taken of my squad and of my time in the army. But then I turned a page and suddenly there were pictures of the horror we were so often required to face. Tony and a small group of his platoon posed beside the bodies of three Chinese men, one of them propped against a tree in a sitting position, his head thrown back, mouth agape and seemingly full of teeth. The bodies were shown in macabre detail, their uniforms splashed with their dark blood; the soldiers were grinning triumphantly as they leaned upon their weapons. Tony watched me as I studied them.

"What happened here?" I asked him.

There had been an ambush, he told me. It had been planned for days and, in the end, the Chinese Malays – communist terrorists or CT's for short – had walked right into it. A couple of them got away, he reckoned, but the whole group had been coming into one of the *kampongs* to collect food to take back into the forest. The British had been tipped off.

"I don't have photographs like this," I told him. "We shot, and got shot at, but never any proof of a kill. Not like you have, here. This is really gruesome

Somersaults

stuff."

"It's what happened. It was all part of it. Part of the record, the photographs. Awful, really, but you have to deal with it ..."

I knew how Tony was thinking about this incident, and maybe others. I could read his emotions in the blankness of his face – clear as words on a page. I knew well how easy it could be to re-live traumas like the one in these pictures, how just talking about such things, never mind re-examining them with the aid of photographs, can bring a trauma back, all of it, in a trice. Tony's face had become almost expressionless, his eyes gone dull and distant. Right now, and for a long moment he was back in the jungles, lost in his recollections. Then he turned to me, his brows furrowed.

"How do you deal with it?" he asked.

"I don't know, really. I don't even know if I'm coping with my own ghosts. It's something that happened, that's all. Now I'm expected to put it away, get on with whatever comes next ..."

"Yes, you're quite right. Get on with it. Except that for me what's come next is the misery of this fucking newspaper. When I first joined it I thought I could maybe use it as a stepping stone to greater things, but that was a pipe dream. The damn place is a trap. They expect you to work your arse off recording the most mundane crap you ever heard of, intruding into peoples' lives in the grossest way in the name of news. Some drunk in a car runs into a kid on a bicycle, and I'm expected to chase around and find out all the relevant details. Hello, Mrs. Snodgrass, your little brat is lying under the wheels of that drunk's car. Tell me, how does it feel ...?"

He became silent, closed his eyes – but his eyelids fluttered. Then:

"Any different for you at the radio station?"

"No. Could be worse. Different sort of writing, every bit as barren. There's a distance to newsprint we don't have on air, whereas radio is very much here and now. Mrs. Snodgrass won't be able to see the page-one photo of her child under the wheels of that drunk's car until the paper is thrown onto her porch tomorrow morning. Radio makes her take a look at him right now.

"No different with advertising, we have to write tight in order to sell a product in thirty seconds, sometimes a minute – awful stuff. Bullshit, all of it. Sell-sell-sell, buy-buy-buy – the essence of our capitalism."

"Yeah. Well, that's why I've come out here. I need to gather my marbles, decide what moves I can make next. Maybe stick around as long as I can. We're okay, right here, for now."

He glanced at Sally.

"I have a little money from England, but we need the paper's paycheques. I most definitely do not need whatever else that bloody rag represents. I don't know what eats at me more, my past, my present or whatever lies immediately in front of me. I'm constantly reminded I should feel obliged to my employers for keeping me alive, but I don't feel like that at all – no more than I would feel terribly obliged were I to find work in a lumber camp or an oil refinery. We do ghastly things for money, soul-less occupations that turn us inside-out and tie us in knots. Then we give it all away just to pay the bills."

I had planned to stay over at their cabin that night, and had brought a sleeping bag to roll out on a camp-cot. There was a chill off the water as the sun went down, so we moved inside and stoked up the open fire on which Sally had cooked our evening meal. Tony opened a bottle of wine and he and Sally nestled together into the big sofa they had set against the wall near the ladder to the loft. I sat on the end of a log close by the warm stones that surrounded the fireplace.

"I was in a lot of trouble before I left Malaya," Tony told me, continuing the conversation we had started earlier. "At one point I was facing a court martial."

I could smile at that.

"Same with me, my friend. I've been on that list. It never came down to it in the end, but I was surely in a whole lot of trouble."

We both laughed. It seemed another point of contact between the two of us.

"Why, what was your offence?" he asked.

I had been castigated by not one, but by two adverse reports, I told him. An adverse report was exactly that – a report card to the headmaster. It was the system by which a serving officer could be reported to the War Office for almost any variety of transgressions, real or imagined. In my own case, the first was for disobeying an order. The second was for telling my brigade commander I thought I was in the wrong army. Bad attitude, I was told – there is hardly a worse crime. The sum of two adverse reports qualified me for a court martial, I had been informed – and it was upon receiving this additional information that I revealed a substantially worse attitude. It came to naught in the end. After two harrowing years in the "wrong army," I returned to Canada, joined a militia unit and joyously retrieved my youthful but sagging military reputation.

"My case was a little worse than that," Tony explained. "I was charged with raping a rubber tapper who worked from the labour lines in the area my platoon was patrolling. She wanted money. I might have tried to help her, and her family – and I did help them as I could. I gave them money. But they wanted more, and when I said there wasn't any more money than I'd already given them, the whole family got nasty. She, or maybe it was her mother, or her father – I don't know – devised this awful artifice, and reported me to my commanding officer. He was obliged to look into it, of course – and then he felt he had to bring charges against me. Then the brass – once the brass got involved, the whole affair was blown out of proportion. There was an open and full enquiry. The whole thing was thrown out in the end, but it was a painful and destructive episode. It was largely because I had such a difficult time explaining it to my family that I've wound up out here ..."

He leaned forward and flicked through the pages of the photograph album, finally placing his finger on one of the pictures – a young girl, facially very beautiful but dressed in the shabbiest of clothes. Instantly I recognized the standard garb for rubber tappers throughout Malaya – bare feet and baggy trousers, shabby smock and apron. And a straw hat that flopped.

"That's her," he said. "I knew her family, wanted to help them, tried to help them. But they thought they could squeeze more out of me. Both she and her father testified against me at the court martial."

"So the court martial went ahead ...?"

"Oh, yes! It was quashed, as I told you, but it buggered me socially – both at my mess, and among the settlers in Kuala Lumpur. Everyone clapped me on the back, said how sorry they were – but no one would invite me to their homes anymore."

"Did you want to go to their homes?" I laughed. To my ears the harsh treatment he claimed seemed to smack of sending one's enemy into Coventry, an English schoolboy form of castigation.

We both laughed again, but Tony's laughter had a brittle edge.

"It was a lifetime ago ... But it was a painful thing. I could never understand the way my mother and father took it all."

Changing the subject to call my attention to an infinitely more pleasing topic, Tony told me about what he described as a "museum" in Salmon Arm, and said we should look in there the next morning so he could introduce me to the curator.

"He's a friend of mine ... old fellow by the name of Tweedale. We'll collect your car when we go into town, and you can carry on back to Kamloops from there. But you really should meet this man first. He has an exceptional collection. Everything under the sun."

The following morning we all drove into Salmon Arm for a breakfast at the general store, then set off for Tweedale's museum. His place was a substantial old house on a secluded street in an unassuming section of the town, but when we knocked and were admitted by the old man himself, it was plain to see his place was about minimum-sized for the spread of his gigantic collection. Had I had more time, or been able to return prior to the old fellow's death a few short weeks later, I would like to have asked him to allow me to make an inventory. He might well have had one, anyway.

From top to bottom, and in every corner, there was amassed a horde of artefacts the likes of which I have never seen in one man's home before. There were paintings and drawings and prints in frames, or else rolled up and stuffed into barrels and bins; there were sculptures from both local and distant North American First Nations peoples, sculptures from Hawaii and the Islands of the South Seas, sculptures from Borneo – Brunei and Sarawak – China, Japan, Russia, India, Egypt and most of Bantu Africa. There were collections of medals in cases, collections of rifles, pistols, spears, shields and boomerangs. In other cases there were collections of polished stones, stamps, coins and butterflies. There were books galore, old mantle and staircase carvings, stained glass and porcelain, and rugs, and tapestries, and wine barrels. My mouth dropped open. I would have needed a full day even to see a portion of it all – longer if ever I returned to catalogue all there was.

I stopped by a collection of Makonde wood carvings from northern Moçambique, examining them closely.

"If you are interested in Africana, you might like to see this," said Mr. Tweedale, pulling open the drawer of a small armoire.

He handed me a notebook, its black hard cover faded to a mottled purple, its yellowing folios ruled in almost invisible light blue lines, every line seemingly crammed full of finely-formed handwriting – and it, too, looked ancient. The words had been written in India ink which faded in and out of an iodine-tinted hue no longer jet – words that lined up like the carriages of a rickety train filled to overflow and now chugging its way across each page. When I opened the book's cover, I saw written on the very first leaf: "British East Africa – Joseph Thomson survey notes – Mombassa-to-Lake Victoria – 1883."

I knew about this man, the famous explorer and his survey of the trans-

Kenya rail link between the coast and Lake Victoria. It was a strange and humbling sensation, to be holding in my hands his personal account of that well-known expedition.

"I'd love to read through this!" I told Mr. Tweedale. "How on earth did you come by such a treasure?"

"I inherited it, I suppose," said the old man vaguely. "I'd be delighted to have you read it, even to transcribe it if you would wish. Come another day and we'll talk about it ... I'm sure it is, as you say, an important document."

The opportunity never presented itself. When a short time later I learned of the old man's death I wrote to the family and received a reply to say they were methodically reviewing everything in his house, and would keep a sharp lookout for the Thomson log. Never another word.

Tony Hodd and I met in Kamloops a couple of times after that weekend on the Shuswap. I was getting ready to leave the radio station and move on, and from his conversation when we did meet it seemed Tony was feeling both guilty and disenchanted with what he was doing. Clever ruse, but I suspected he was beginning to admit the way in which he had been making a living for himself – sitting in a boat in the middle of Shuswap Lake dreaming up far-fetched yarns he'd then peddle to his editor as hard news – was both difficult and dishonest.

On my short visit to their camp I had taken Sally to be a single-minded person. I would not have been surprised to learn she had been all along working out an alternate plan for her life, and that possibly those plans would not include Tony.

Years later I was travelling by car to eastern Canada, and passed through Salmon Arm. The place was greatly expanded in size, and there was nothing about it that felt at all familiar. I attempted to find the general store, but couldn't. No one could give me a lead on Tweedale, either. I asked a number of likely people if they knew the whereabouts of an Englishman ... No one had ever heard his name. I even tried to find the dirt road that led to his cabin, but was forced to give up.

It was as though Tony Hodd and everything that went with him had really been an auxiliary scene from Brigadoon, the village in the mists of the Scottish Highlands that wakes up once in a century. It's real, it's there, but you'll find it again only when you are far too old to care or try to catch up – when your mind has finally wandered into a zone in which it is far easier to shrug and allow complexities to settle into meaninglessness and uncertain memory ...

Broken Logger

My step-mother slipped on an icy sidewalk and broke her hip. I went to see her in the hospital and, on leaving, noted in the ward next to hers (the door was open) an unfortunate fellow trussed up in bandages – body cast and plaster of Paris all the way to the extremities of his four limbs, everything suspended by a contraption of ropes and pulleys and guy wires. I reckoned he had suffered fractures considerably more sinister than my step-mother. He could barely turn his head, for it and his neck were also covered in bandages. But our eyes connected as I passed so I stepped into his room.

"Good heavens, man! What on earth have you done to yourself?" I asked as cheerily as I thought he might be able to stand.

He replied with a simple answer and a wry smile.

"Logging," he said.

He seemed to suffer no pain by talking to me, so I asked him:

"How did that happen?"

He appeared to be happy that someone took the trouble to stop by and chat.

He and a shift of fellow workers had been felling trees in the forest, he explained, dropping their cuts so they were lined up in a uniform direction. However one of the men was less experienced than the others, and had made a serious misjudgement. He felled his tree at right angles to the general formation, toppling it across the trunk of another huge tree lying on the ground. Its long upper section, together with its numerous branches, lay on the ground; the heavier lower section was high in the air.

To clear it out of the way my new friend clambered among the branches at the narrower end of the poorly-felled tree, and started cutting away its limbs. He stood on the trunk, using his chainsaw to work his way towards the tree's crown which was now down-slope, and considerably lower than the tree's base-end. The base itself had been pivoted to a precarious height above the level of the logger working at the other end of the trunk – the high portion making, as it were, an unbalanced see-saw. The logger had almost reached the crown when his inexperienced co-worker, the same man who had made the initial error, dropped his next tree in the correct direction. His now perfect cut fell directly across the high base-end of the incorrectly-felled tree.

The result was predictable: the section of the giant trunk that had been lying on the ground, its branches now almost entirely cleared away, was suddenly flicked upwards. Standing on the tree trunk cutting its limbs, the poor logger in the bed before me was catapulted into the air as if shot from a canon.

"Both my legs were broken by the force of being driven upwards so suddenly. I went up so high I came level with the tops of the biggest trees in the vicinity – a hundred and fifty feet or more. I should have been killed when I landed, but instead broke both my arms and a few ribs, my neck …"

I got into the habit of stopping to talk to him every time I went to the hospital to visit my step-mother. He was still there when she was finally discharged, after which the hospital faded as a priority, and the necessities of my own busy life took renewed hold. To my shame I lost touch with this busted-up logger, and only later realized I had never asked his name.

Cougar Story

A little boy went missing in the Thompson River area north of Kamloops, and the sad story was picked up and used as headline material in one of the local area newspapers. It was the big story of the week when it first broke, and search parties were assembled to comb the thick bush and river banks in the vicinity where it was thought the boy might be. As the days wore on and the little fellow was nowhere to be found, the search parties came in shaking their heads – and the story was gradually relegated to the inside pages of the newspaper. As week followed week and there was still no sighting of the lad, less and less was written concerning the incident until finally it faded to little more than an occasional mention. It was thought there was no chance the boy would ever be found.

However, the parents of the child did not give up hope. Distraught, the mother and father continually begged all the district news sheets and radio and television stations to maximize their coverage of the story in order to keep the populace alert and informed. This way, it was hoped, someone somewhere would see something and report it to the authorities.

Days ran into weeks, weeks into months – and still there was no sign of the little boy. The local radio dropped the story altogether; then the television also gave up. Now and then a local newspaper would run a brief update to say search groups, although called off, were still on the lookout. Concerned police departments were anxious for every possible lead, but they also were having to admit defeat.

Several months after he had disappeared, there was a sudden flurry of hope. The parents had gone to the camp of a First Nations shaman to seek his advice and counsel. In great solemnity the ancient shaman listened to their mournful story, and he agreed to do his best to discover the boy's whereabouts. There might be a way he could help, he said, even if it meant no more than the assurance that the boy was indeed gone. He sat by his fire and willed himself into a deep trance. In the end his attention returned to the anxious parents. He raised his head and looked directly into the father's eyes. He said:

"Your boy has gone forever from these lands. Cougars have taken him away."

It so happened that right at that time of the year the sporting community was preparing for one of its great annual events. "Cougars" was the name of the most popular city football team, slated to play at home against its great rival team from the Okanagan Valley. A local newspaper, in an effort to demonstrate hometown loyalty, decided to drop its masthead to a lower position on its front page, and to run an encouraging single-line banner across the top of the front page that read: ***GO, COUGARS! GO!***

Unfortunately the editorial room, not entirely aware of this supportive declaration for the home team (it was more the decision of management than of the city editor, after all) determined the months-old story of the missing boy, along with the mystic divinations of the old shaman who appeared to have some idea of what had become of the little fellow, was an interesting yarn, but nonetheless fell short of the greatest and most important news of the day. (Nobody in their right mind believed in shamans anymore, anyway.) There was an opening for the story along the top of the paper's back page so the city editor, at the behest of his boss, slapped it in there – along with a suitable headline that took up the paper's entire eight-column width. The size and type of font matched exactly that which had been chosen for the slogan printed above the masthead.

It was unfortunate, indeed.

Seated on a park bench, or at a table in the Overlander café, or in the dining lounge of the Plaza Hotel, anyone snapping the paper open to its full extension would see the single-line message running clear across the top:

COUGARS CARRY OFF LITTLE BOY IN NORTHLAND – GO, COUGARS! GO!

St. Paddy's Night

Eventually I moved to the coast at Vancouver where, to earn my daily bread and attempt to take care of a growing family, again I found myself writing advertising inanities for one of the city's radio stations. It was a thankless occupation both financially and spiritually. The object, whether one cared to admit it or not, being to cram into a thirty- or sixty-second spot of broadcast air time sufficient gibberish to numb the brain of an ox – this in order to sell anything from toothpaste to automobiles, hotel accommodations to winter tires to pop concerts. Often this befuddlement would be set to Charlie Harper-style jingles – tinkling rhymes that, on rare occasions, might rise to the level of clever. As it turned out I was reasonably good at producing this sort of drivel. Although I despised what I was doing, I had moderately well-developed senses of both whimsy and humour, and the occupation did have a certain advantage: it was excellent training for a wordsmith.

I had been well-trained for the military in Britain so thought that now I had returned to Canada it might be useful to augment my daytime activities at the radio station by joining a militia unit that met once or twice per week in the evenings. I had joined the Rocky Mountain Rangers in Kamloops, so now transferred to the Irish Fusiliers of Canada (also known as the Vancouver Regiment) and spent a year or so listening to quaint – occasionally embroidered – Old Soldier stories in the officers' mess of the barrack building on Georgia Street. The building was a magnificent three-storied wooden headquarters complex that covered most of an entire city block at the entrance to Stanley Park. It contained all the paraphernalia of a working militia regiment: drill square, messing facilities and instruction rooms, parking space for all of the regimental trucks and guns, plus an armoury. The officers' mess consisted of a spacious lounge-cum-bar and dining room that fit comfortably into an upstairs corner of the barrack building. At this level there was one of the finest regimental museums in the country, and also an interior balcony that overlooked the parade square on the lower main floor.

The most memorable of the old soldiers who dropped in at the mess to regale us with incredible stories of derring-do was a friendly giant of a fellow – well clear of six feet four inches – who had fought with the Canadians throughout the First World War's notorious Passchendaele offensive in 1917. Being so large he was, naturally, awarded the nickname "Tiny" S –.

In the days of the First World War the soldiers in the trenches, like their comrades in the navy, were given a daily rum ration to keep them warm and bolster their fighting spirits. It was a soldier's entitlement, so if perchance he had not received his tot for any given period of time, be it a day or a month, he could ask for – and receive – his arrears. Tiny had been absent from the trenches for several days in a row, so when he asked for his arrears he discovered they now amounted to two clay-stone bottles of sweet Jamaican rum. He accepted his prize gleefully but, at the moment of receiving them the order went out to prepare to "go over the top." Quickly Tiny decided to bury the bottles in the bottom of his trench, and as he did this he used his compass to take the bearings of a prominent hill off in one direction, and a church steeple in another. This way he reckoned he would know exactly where they were located, and that he would be able to pick them up after the impending action – if he survived it.

As luck would have it he survived the battle alright, but he never returned to his trench. The heat of the action swept him and his comrades across the countryside – and at the end of the war he returned to Canada.

"I've still got my notebook from the trenches, and my bearings on those stone crocks," he told us one evening as we crowded around him in the mess.

"I've booked my flight," he said. "And I'm going to go back to see if I can find them ..."

Forty-five years after the fact – good luck, Tiny!

A few weeks later the friendly giant was back in the mess, and again he was holding forth. This time, however, he was recounting the adventures he had had on his most recent visit to the old battlefield. At his feet were two grey stoneware bottles.

"I found them exactly where I knew they'd be. Quite far down, and we had to dig a bit – but they were there, alright ..."

Somersaults

Tiny unsealed one bottle on the spot and proceeded to pour out a tot of deliciously well-aged Jamaican rum for each man in the mess.

"The second bottle's for my son," he told us.

Built entirely of lumber in 1909 as the city's horse show venue, the barracks of the Irish Fusiliers of Canada – the Vancouver Regiment – had served in its earliest days as one of Vancouver's grandest centres for all manner of social and cultural events. Originally the structure had had a capacity for some three thousand five hundred people seated in its bleachers and galleries. There was accommodation for another seven thousand on chairs set out on its main floor when there were concerts or fashion shows.

The building became known as the Stanley Park Armouries during the First World War, and was thereafter used pretty much exclusively for military purposes.

March was an important month on the regimental calendar. Each year the officers held a special dinner to mark the regiment's greatest moment of glory: the Battle of Barrosa, fought during the Peninsula War, on 5 March, 1811, when the combined armies of the British, Spanish and Portuguese managed to relieve Napoleon's siege of the small Spanish town. As the story was committed to legend, Irish troops fighting for the British were obliged to shoulder aside the sluggardly and hesitant Spanish troops in order to move to the front and get at the French. They did this with the cry *"faugh e baluch!"* – "clear the way!" – a slogan that was thereafter adopted as the motto of several Irish units. (Insolent and irreverent members of Britain's other rank and file regiments quickly transformed this famous cry to "fuck'n'bollocks!") The celebratory dinner in 1960 was necessarily held on 12 March. At one key point of the evening, the most junior officer present was required to stand on his chair and, with one foot on the dining table before him, recite the glories of the battle at Barrosa concluding by calling out in his strongest voice, *"Faugh e Baluch!"* Everyone then cheered, toasts were drunk – and the most senior officer at the head table presented the raconteur with an inscribed beer mug. Mine now lingers unused under its tarnish at the back of a kitchen shelf, courtesy of Honorary Colonel H.R. Fullerton, CD.

J. J. Hespeler-Boultbee

Five days later – on St. Patrick's night, 17 March, 1960 – there was a big celebration in the officers' mess. The regimental officers, this time with their wives in tow, gathered for yet another annual function, the dinner and dance in celebration of Ireland's patron saint.

When the meal was over, everyone retired to the lounge for drinks and, of course, throaty rounds of mournful Celtic ballads – voices well-lubricated by nips of Irish milk. All of us had to face the rigors of a work schedule the next morning, so the group started to disband around eleven o'clock. My wife was three months pregnant; we felt we needed to get home to West Vancouver where our small son was in his grandmother's care. Great party, but we left with others shortly after eleven.

The following morning it took an inordinately long time to drive across the Lion's Gate Bridge to get to work at the radio station. Clearing Stanley Park and entering the downtown area via Georgia Street, I learned why:

The armoury on the right-hand side, the first substantial building one would see coming out of the park, had been reduced to ashes by one of the greatest fires in the city's history. The heat had been so intense there was nothing to be salvaged; telephone poles on the opposite side of Georgia Street had been set ablaze like candles. One heck of a party; one heck of a hangover. Total destruction.

With nowhere to go on 18 March, the Irish Fusiliers of Canada was soon disbanded – and shortly thereafter I was to continue my eastward meanderings across the nation's wide prairie ...

Big Freeze – Regina

There was a defrocked Anglican minister on staff at the Regina newspaper – an addict of booze and drugs, a dissolute pedophile, yet a brilliant jurist, reporter and writer. He sat at a desk pushed off into a corner of the editorial room because he stank so bad his colleagues could not work near him. He was perpetually unwashed, though word was that his rooming house landlady occasionally scrubbed him down herself. Even so, there was a stench about him of rancid clothing emanating from an assortment of vestments he never removed when he came in from the cold, nor in fact ever appeared to change, winter or summer. The smell of liquor seeped from the pores of his grimy skin; the surface of the backs of his hands had about them a permanent shiny layer of scum, like that which collects over a period of time around the interior of an unwashed bathtub. His fingers were stained nicotine dark; his razor scraped his throat and jowls but once a week at most, leaving behind a variety of tell-tale nicks and blood-stained gouges where his unsteady hand had slipped.

Nowadays this reporter would likely be languishing in jail, but in the early 60's the laws were such that it would have been difficult to prove his culpability, and pedophiles like him were fairly free to indulge their ghastly predilections. It is not necessary for this accounting to name the s.o.b., so for this account I shall call him Jarrod Tarface. Despite what he was, he had a brilliant mind – and was an uncanny expert at unravelling intricate court protocol and jurisprudence. For this the newspaper editor assigned him to the famous Rasmussen case – the trial of one of the city's leading lawyers who was accused of having gone bad and embezzling huge sums of both government and private investment monies. The proceedings required a "trial-within-a-trial" for the examination of certain evidences, and Tarface was the one reporter on staff capable of comprehending what was going on. His reports flowed in unbroken prose from the courtroom to his notepad, and thence into his copy – which the editors claimed it was totally impossible to edit. His writing was judged so tightly composed and so accurate the newspaper staff did not dare touch it for fear of altering its meaning in some minute fashion and thus incurring the wrath of the court. They opted to let the reams of Jarrod's copy flow into the paper precisely as he had written them, along with a disclaimer (which in all likelihood would have proved no protection whatsoever had the reporter's words actually provoked further court interest).

Jarrod Tarface used to do most of his drinking in the bar of the LaSalle Hotel, its Hamilton Street entrance being directly opposite the main door of the newspaper offices. The hotel was also the favourite watering hole of most of the newspaper staff, but no one from the office would deign to sit and drink with this particular colleague; he was always to be seen seated in a dim corner, either alone or with one or other of an assortment of male companions considerably younger than himself – some of them mere boys by comparison. Regina was by no means a large city. Isolated as it was on its wide prairie expanse, a young and dynamic place with a population that at the time would have barely topped 120,000 souls, none of the newspaper staff could imagine there was any particular segment of it devoted to an alternative lifestyle – particularly of the sort espoused by Tarface. We were repelled by him, but at the same time acknowledged the man was an intriguing mystery. Both his brilliance and the reasons for his fall from grace were clear.

Late one afternoon when spring nipped at the edges of the daylight hours but fell to a point or two below freezing after the sun had set, a group of reporters leaving the hotel came out onto the sidewalk to find their disreputable colleague lying between two parked cars in the slush at the side of the road. He had been thrashing about, possibly in an attempt to get to his feet, so was about the same overall colour as the muck in which he was now lying unconscious. He was all but invisible to people hurrying by on the sidewalk, too preoccupied with where they should be placing their own two feet to notice anything untoward in the gutter. On this occasion the newsmen dispensed with their customary disdainful conventions and decided to exercise a little human compassion. They tried to get the wretched fellow to his feet, but he stretched out in the muck unable to offer them the least assistance. It seemed he was content to continue wallowing in the gutter. No one was strong enough, sufficiently charitable or particularly inclined to lift him bodily; it would have meant grappling at too close quarters with someone whose outer layers were as slippery as a greased pig. Yet he could not be permitted to continue lying there. Two of his colleagues managed to grab him by the collar of his filthy overcoat, two others to secure a purchase on the slippery fabric of his trouser cuffs. Like this they dragged him across the pavement into the lea of the hotel wall so that at the very least he would be spared getting crushed by unsuspecting automobile traffic – or the indignity and danger, as temperatures plunged, of being frozen into the gutter's slush within an hour or so. The police were called and he was manhandled into the back of a squad car.

"My god!" panicked the city editor when he learned of his ace reporter's circumstances. "Who the hell is going to cover for him in court tomorrow morning?"

The editor himself rushed down to police headquarters to see if he could somehow extricate Tarface from the drunk tank.

"We'd be delighted to let you have him," the desk sergeant commented sardonically, for Tarface was well known to the police.

"But we don't have him. When a man's so blotto he can't make it to the tank on his own feet, even with a station officer under each armpit, we take him to the hospital …"

It was there that the editor found Tarface strapped to a gurney, and elected to remain with him all night in an effort to get him to work when the court session began in the morning.

In the small hours the wretched fellow, drunk but responding to an intensive regimen of enforced sobering, was returned to his long-suffering landlady for a shower and a clean set of clothes. By ten o'clock, when the court was once more in session, Jarrod Tarface was seated at his desk in the press box, scratching his inimitable shorthand prose onto the pages of his notepad.

It was years before I was to learn the trial outcome. Rasmussen was cleared of all charges against him. However in an effort to research these events and Jarrod Tarface's part in them, so that I might present a fuller account of both him and his extraordinary feats of reportage, I have run into a block. No one is any longer able to remember the case, or the protagonists. Years have elapsed since that time. People have moved on or died, records are spotty. Memory plays its tricks and I am left wondering whether any of it actually happened – except that it did, and I know it because I was there.

Many young people are glad to escape the rigors of a Prairie winter, and I was no different. I spent two years in Regina and, although I can honestly claim the countryside and the vitality of the city's cultural activity were rich and enticing, and that I have always looked back on that time with a degree of nostalgia, I was glad to be able to quit the place when I did. Possibly I remember it best for the degree of fun I had there – not during winter's exceptional aggression, but certainly during the delights of the prairies' summer sunshine. There were several excursions to the delightful city of Moose Jaw, and as far afield as Saskatoon on the banks of the South Saskatchewan River, where its university offers one of the finest agricultural courses in the world. Towards the end of our first summer on the Prairies, I ventured out with my small family on a camping holiday in the Cypress Hills, the geologically unique region of picturesque and rolling countryside with its rivers, lakes and forests, unmolested by the Ice Age, an area that forms a major drainage divide between waters flowing north to Hudson Bay and those headed south to the Gulf of Mexico. This magic area is located right on the border that separates Saskatchewan from Alberta, a spit north of America's wide border state of Montana. In another direction, the Qu'Appelle Valley to the east of Regina, though bitterly whitened by its winter weather, is like an artist's palette once the snows have gone. Its lake and river are a welcome freshener in the extreme heat of summer.

For a time, then, Regina was my hub, the centre of a rich Saskatchewan cultural and outdoor life, but also one of those places where one remembers certain oddities in colourful dimension. Tarface was one of them.

There was, for instance, and this also comes vividly to mind, a wild and not altogether unpleasant journalist from New Zealand (we called him Kiwi, of course) who was the political representative for the Associated Press in Saskatchewan. The province was undergoing the final years of its great socialist experiment – the first political movement of its stripe in the country able to demonstrate its considerable success, powerful and threatening enough to induce paranoia in the minds of Canada's southern neighbours and coax them at one time into holding troop manoeuvers along the North Dakota border.

Kiwi was the political animal chosen by his U.S. news agency to keep an eye on the delicate heaving and ho-ing between the heavies of left and right in the province's legislative assembly. Although he had a desk in the press room, he was an earnest back-slapper, and was usually to be found prowling about the corridors of the parliamentary building where it was thought he was on personal good terms with practically every member on both sides of the house.

However, Kiwi had a monumentally bad temper. Returning to his desk after one of his morning walkabouts in search of worthy copy, or a politico whose back required buttering, he found that someone in the office had been using his typewriter. Whoever it was had removed from the machine's roller the story on which Kiwi himself had been working, placing the unfinished page of Kiwi's prose on the desk to one side in order to use the typewriter him (or her) self.

Kiwi's offended shouts and red-faced anger bounced off the gallery's ceiling. He picked up the typewriter and, screaming abuse like a two-year-old, launched it out through the open press room window. It fell two storeys to the tarmac car park below – where it landed on the top of socialist Premier Tommy Douglas' car.

Informed of the damage he had caused, he stepped into the hallway screaming even more offensive borderline fascist-tinted epithets at the premier for being so stupid as to park his car in that spot. This action hardly went over well among supporters of Canada's first socialist premier. The sergeant-at-arms entered into the fray and Kiwi was forthwith expelled – permanently – from the assembly building.

From that point he was of little further assistance to his agency's editorial and political interests in Saskatchewan. For all the ruckus he had made, his actual departure from the scene was quiet. He disappeared and we never saw him again.

At this point one should be assured that the hurling of typewriters is not necessarily a journalistic expression of pique – although it is true a typewriter, once hurled, does seem to be a signal expressive of anger. At least the clatter it makes upon landing tends to indicate a degree of fury more or less in keeping with the occasional frustrations of a journalistic calling.

For a few weeks that first winter, before the arrival of my family from the coast, I shared a rental house with a rowdy bunch of bachelors, three of them members of a local rugby club. There were five of us, which made for a full house in one of the city's residential neighbourhoods, but there was room enough and we were comfortable. Two slept on fold-out beds in a basement rumpus room, where there was also a bathroom, and one each in the three bedrooms on the main floor. Also on the main floor there was an entry vestibule and hallway just inside the front door, a large living-and-dining room area, a kitchen and pantry and a large bathroom. We took turns doing the chores – shopping, cooking, washing-up. One of the five was a colleague of mine at the newspaper, and it was he who had signed the rental agreement with the landlady. He and I were the only ones in the house with respectable jobs, which meant we had to get up and get going at some point of the day. The other three seemed to prefer spending their time drinking and chasing after the companionship of whatever ladies choose to accompany rugby players. Unfortunately there were precious few places for these fellows to romp when there was snow on the ground and the temperatures seldom above -20°C.

It was a long winter. There had been lots of parties during those interminable weeks, and by and large they had all gone well and with minimal damage. The house belonged to an amiable elderly lady who fled to Florida every winter. She would not return until mid-April. We kept a replacement tin stocked with sufficient funds so that the occasional breakage could be speedily replaced, but overall we all got along well and had no major disagreements. We felt a sense of responsibility towards the landlady, but in hindsight it was only a sometime thing.

My family was due to arrive, so on the eve of my departure from the house my companions decided a farewell to me was sufficient excuse for that particular weekend's rumble. Unfortunately it went sideways – the way things go when matters are left to young bachelors hell-bent on having a good time, and control scurries out of the control of young men who think they possess it. One of our companions had invited the rest of the rugby team.

Fortunately we had had the good sense to pack away all of the landlady's small breakables, but that did not pertain to the larger items of furniture in the living and dining room area.

The first hour was loud: lots of clanking glass, raucous laughter, thumping of chests and bragging. Then a taxi-load of young ladies showed up, and then another – and the pitch increased. At that point the whole room became a pitch – a rugby pitch.

When one cannot play rugby outdoors, the rules alter a smidge and play is resumed indoors. It was called "touch rugby" but the touching was intentional, and could hurt. To avoid being touched, the player with the ball will leap on furniture, be it sofa or coffee table, scuttle under the dining table, or fend-off with a heavy glass-framed picture yanked from its wall mounting. Some of us were trying to cool things down when an armchair was hurled through the glass of the living room's picture front window, and one of the players involuntarily followed it.

It had been warm indoors, but the outside was a frigid scape of snowbanks and drifts that covered what, in the warmer summer months, would have been one of the more delightful gardens on our street. A blast of twenty-below air put a momentary chill on play – until some wag, really wanting to put a damper on things, hooked a long hose to a basement tap and ran outside with it. Through the open front window he started to douse everything and everyone inside.

Suddenly it was no joke. The party came to an abrupt end and everyone left.

There was little any of the five householders were capable of doing right then and there. The house was suddenly emptied, and all of us were drunk. We did not have anything useful with which to close the gaping hole in the front of the house where the window should have been, and none of us was in any fit condition to figure out what to do or how to manipulate tools. So we simply left things as they were, closed the doors to the living and dining room areas and went to bed. I recall hearing the basement furnace operating on its thermostat and blasting away all night in a vain attempt to do what it was supposed to do. In my own room I lay a-bed, huddled in my overcoat with all of my blankets pulled about my shivering body.

The next morning we had to face the extent of what had been done. It was a catastrophe. There had been a snowfall during the night, and there was now a large drift in the front room that entirely covered the three-place sofa. Before the party began we had pushed it over against the interior wall separating the living room from my bedroom. The carpets of the living and dining rooms were sheets of ice. The drapes were frozen stiff, the weight of them catching at the pelmet and pulling it off the wall above the open gash of the non-existent window. All the fabrics were like boards; the cushions were ice blocks frozen to wherever they had been placed on the sofa or chairs. The top of the dining room table, having received a liberal dousing, was now (like the floor itself) a skating rink – the padded seats of its matching chair set like winter wonderland sculptures. The most startling sight of all was the way in which the water had soaked one of the living room walls, freezing where it had hit so that the weight of ice pulled several layers of wallpaper and gyproc away in a thick sheet. The whole thing then fell forwards, a hardened ice sail that leaned into the centre of the room as if beckoning the drunken party to continue.

"Khee-rist!" said all five of us, surveying the wreckage – though not all at the same time. Some had permitted themselves to sleep late as a means of escaping what they must have known they would be facing.

Having made the agreement with the landlady, it was my fellow journalist who immediately took charge.

"We're going to have to fix this," he said. "And we're all going to have to pay for it."

We had to seal up the window space as quickly as possible, so the very first order of business was a carpenter – followed by a glazier. The carpenter arrived almost right away and got to work closing the room off from the elements; the glazier came and took measurements, but it was several days before he was finally able to replace the window.

Next we had to thaw the place out, shovel the snow and loose wreckage into bins and attempt to gather together whatever was salvageable. These operations, and mopping up the melt that flowed through the floorboards into the basement, took us the best part of a week. The sofa, two large armchairs and all the cushions and fabrics were done for, so we pitched them into the front yard to merge with the winter landscape until the snows had thawed, at which time they could be gathered up and carted away to the dump.

The walls of the living and dining rooms had to be repaired and re-papered. New carpeting had to be purchased, along with new drapes, and we had to buy a new sofa and two armchairs that fairly matched the style of the ones destroyed. Pictures were repaired and replaced on the walls, most of the dining room furniture could be saved, but the padding on the seats had to be replaced, the woodwork polished.

I had moved into new digs shortly after the party, but I felt obliged to be at the old place whenever possible during repairs. To their credit, all of the members of the rugby club that had helped with the destruction were on hand to chip in with their share of costs. We divided the sum of the damages equally between all of us; my own share came to the equivalent of a month's salary. It took over a month, but the house was ultimately restored to a newer version of what it had been – and when the sun finally warmed things up, the landlady returned from her winter hideaway.

My colleague and former roommate knew he could hide nothing, so made his confession most humbly. He told his landlady the whole story, expecting a tongue-lashing – or even a lawsuit.

Not a bit of it. The old girl laughed and laughed, and from that moment on the two of them were the very best of friends. She forgave him his youthful shenanigans, and then offered to give him permanent lodging in her re-modelled and not altogether uncomfortable basement. To the best of my knowledge he was living there a year or so after I finally quit the city and moved to Toronto.

That turned out to be one of the coldest winters on record for Regina. For a two-day stretch, the radio informed us, the wind chill (a what-it-feels-like figure, derived from the combination of the winter wind's velocity as it blows across the landscape's still air temperature) had been -72°C – cold enough, as the saying goes, "to freeze the balls off a brass monkey." Local police walked the streets dressed in buffalo hide coats and hats, each man surrounded by an opaque haze of wintry vapours given off by his body heat. The wheels of those vehicles left at the sides of roads during some brief prior period of slush-thaw were now locked in a deep freeze that clutched at every indentation and crevasse of metal and rubber, holding them firmly in place. Not knowing the extent to which he was cemented in place, one truck driver revved his engine to pull away – and found his tractor simply powered itself out of its tires, ripping the rubber to shreds. Any car that had not had its block heater plugged-in continuously would have had its oil frozen to a molasses-like goop in the engine pan. Even in those instances when engine heaters were connected, the thin heat would not have been able to percolate into the interior of the cab; the padded dashboards of some stylish automobiles, even the fabric covering the seats, could shatter like crystal if the vehicle had been left standing long enough in the cold. One newspaperman, returning to the office after a visit to the LaSalle Hotel barbershop, had asked for a treatment of his preferred oils; when done, and in the time it took him to cross the road from the hotel's front door to the front door of the newspaper office, the hair on the man's head froze snow white. Another staffer was leaving the building at that very moment and caught a glimpse of his colleague in the foyer, his shock of normally dark hair now the colour of snow. The staffer reached up as he was passing to go outside. "Look at blondie, here ...!" he said, and playfully brushed his fingers across the man's head. Embarrassingly, the brittle icicle hair broke off at the scalp.

Art Critic

Regina's principal newspaper office had once been on Hamilton Street, right in the heart of the city's downtown core. In the last days of what might be called hard-nosed letter-set journalism it was not uncommon to have members of the public wander in off the street asking to see a reporter or an editor, usually to voice either congratulations or (more frequently) castigations, but occasionally for no other good reason than to jaw with an old friend or colleague. Senior citizens most frequently took advantage of this liberty; they appeared to find a newspaper office more readily accessible than a regular business office. The very nature of newspapering, as they saw it, was the handling of the daily goings on about the city and the world at large. If a man had a friend in the newspaper business he would be in a position to discover all kinds of useful information ahead of time, even skip out of the office with a free copy of the latest edition hot off the rumbling presses. Perks always included some useful element; they might save a fellow making a cross-town journey to the outlying railway station to purchase a ticket to the other side of a blizzard front, when all train services had been halted; or maybe dropping by the newspaper office would supply him with advance warning of a failing stock before he committed a wad of money he couldn't really afford. People at the newspaper office were on top of things, knew how the nation was ticking over. They knew how to put people in touch with people. The newspaper office was, in essence, a convenient and even sophisticated drop-in centre – provided, of course, no one dropped-in right on deadline.

Newspaper offices are not quite the same anymore. Now they are digital, high tech – and less friendly. They have certainly ceased to be drop-in centres. The Regina paper moved its offices out of the city centre many years ago, but in the early 1960's its editorial office frequently hosted the newsmakers of the day. If they had come in for an interview they might be ushered into a comfortable inner sanctum where there were a few well-worn easy chairs and a coffee machine …

One frequent visitor to the *Leader Post* office was the Lieutenant Governor of the Province of Saskatchewan, the Honourable Frank Bastedo. He was an elderly gentleman who walked with a cane. The stairs to the editorial office were a formidable challenge to him, but if he had something to say, a question to pose the newspaper staff, or if he simply felt in need of a chat, he would manage the climb without ado. He was an opinionated man, and one of the subjects about which he had strong views and a lot to say was the whole world of the visual and plastic arts. At that time in Regina's history the city was enjoying a richly deserved reputation as one of the nation's leading art centres. Indeed, there was hardly a well-known artist in the country who had not at one time or another been associated with the artistic goings-on of the province and its capital city. The broad landscapes, the gigantic sky along with the harsh winters all combined to summon scores of artists – every one of them feeling the potency and power of the unending prairies. It was as if a magnet drew the artistic to the city and they were all mesmerized by it and by its surroundings.

Somersaults

The Norman MacKenzie Art Gallery on Regina's College Avenue was the city's great pride, and on its walls one might have seen any number of outstanding works by Canadian artists. It, too, has changed and expanded enormously over the years, moving to a greatly improved location in the city – but even in the 1950's and 1960's being invited to exhibit work at the old gallery was a flashy feather in any artist's bonnet.

Frank Bastedo knew all this, of course. He knew that his capital city was an important art centre, but he was a conventional and very conservative man and in his newspaper office conversations he liked to express his distaste – nay, loathing – for most of the modern work Canadian artists were producing at the time. He felt bound to participate in some way; it was possible he saw it as an essential part of his job. But his own knowledge of the arts was restricted – some would have said lamentably so – by his own meagre understanding of the subject, his difficulty in grasping "symbolism," let alone "meaning." Maybe representational forms were clearer to him in their message; their images were fairly easy to read, so it followed that a lack of representational form must harbour some hidden – and therefore nefarious – meaning. If that was the case, Frank Bastedo was definitely having difficulties latching onto so esoteric a cultural area, and he would have none of it. According to him skies were supposed to be blue, clouds white and grass green. The cows depicted munching that grass had to have the unmistakable appearance of cows; most assuredly they could not be pink or purple in colour, nor could they be permitted to have two heads or their eyes in the "wrong" position.

Frank Bastedo's visits to the newspaper office might have been amusing had they not invariably devolved into tiresome lectures that pinned polite office staff to the walls, unable to break away from what the old buzzard, babbling on and on, considered "good art" and how it was being usurped by so much "bad art." Bad art, he said, was nothing less than an assault on the purity of good Christian teaching and was indicative of modern society's sliding moral values. It was the civic responsibility of people like the newspaper's editors and staff to assist in halting this clear debasement of society. On occasion he would even bring into the office examples of what he considered to be "good art" – sometimes even "bad art," if he had not already tossed it into the wastepaper basket – in order to use them to augment his viewpoints. On such occasions he would attempt to thump home his strategy (the editorial staff proved awfully dense) for combatting society's tragic downhill slide into a decay of biblical proportions. From time to time he would even leave pieces in the editorial room to be photographed, and he would attempt to coerce the editors into taking up and disseminating his argument.

Because he was the queen's chief representative in the province the editors would occasionally feel obliged to publish his views – but this usually tumbled Frank Bastedo into considerable trouble with the local art establishment. The op-ed writers had to be extremely careful not to allow the paper's columns to become a sounding board for any one individual's strongly held – often whacky – opinions. To their credit the editors did try to encourage debate – though the Lieutenant Governor was adamant his viewpoint was all to the public good and thus unassailable. God, he appeared to be telling us, was on his side …

But although he would talk and talk, some would say rant and rant, Frank Bastedo was absolutely no match when it came to a real debate with some of the finest artists and some of the finest minds in the land – though he would not have seen it that way. Time and again he was shown up as someone whose views and artistic convictions were intensely hackneyed and narrow and who, when confronted by the strong opinions of people who might have preferred to paint a cow's eyes on its rump, lost all patience and even his temper. His opponents in these discussions would tell him in no uncertain terms that he did not know what he was talking about – to which he would retort equally forcefully and with angry huffings that he did, too. Discussion would go on and on until everyone but Bastedo could not help but recognize the nauseous vortex, and so quietly withdraw. When finally left to addressing nothing more formidable than the wall before him, Bastedo would at last fall silent – convinced he had won the argument.

The old MacKenzie gallery building was extremely long, front-to-back, its interior a bit like the nave of a basilica, with smaller individual exhibition halls leading off either side of it. In the building's foyer, right inside the main entrance, was a large bronze Moore-like sculpting possessing a title that required considerable imagination to match it with the work's actual form – a rounded mass of shiny hollow bronze, a smaller mass bubbling out of its side, and the whole perforated by a sensuously generous orifice. It was truly a magnificent work, whatever it purported to be, but in reality not a lifelike representation of anything more than itself – a gigantic and altogether delightful metallic presence that simply sat and was, and had a silent way of shouting its existence to anyone who happened to be passing by. It didn't do anything but occupy the floor space on which it had been placed, and anyone entering through the gallery's main door could not help but notice it. Indeed, to proceed from the entry any further into the exhibition space one was obliged to walk around it. Standing at the very back of the building it was possible to look down the full length of the main hall, all the way to where the front entrance was partially obscured by this quiet giant whatever-it-was.

I was in the gallery late one afternoon to look at a temporary exhibit in one of the rear rooms of the building. It was closing time, and an announcement went out over a speaker system asking patrons to leave. People started to file out and an eerie stillness fell over the premises. I thought I must have been one of the last to leave. Stepping out of the exhibition salon into the main chamber – the "nave" – from the very back of the building I was able to see its full length and was just in time to observe the Honourable Frank Bastedo and his wife exit a hall at the front, right next to the main entrance foyer. Mrs. Bastedo was on her husband's arm assisting his slow progress; in his other hand he carried his walking stick. The pair shuffled over to the large bronze with clear deliberation, and there they paused. Bastedo hunched his shoulders and glowered at the work, then slowly the two of them walked all the way around it. Completing a full circle, Bastedo again paused. Letting go of his wife's arm, he stepped forward for a closer examination, his head jutting pugnaciously as he seemed to be making a thoroughly confrontational re-examination of the piece.

Without warning he raised his walking stick, and with all the force he could muster he struck the side of the bronze sculpting a single angry blow. The sculpting's hollowness caused it to boom like a mountain gong – the noise resounding throughout all the salons of the gallery as though rising from the depths of a great valley.

Satisfied, and no doubt considering his action a justifiable expression of his moral rectitude, and that he had satisfactorily expressed this to the object sitting silenced before him (the Great Bong's sudden fading hush was about as audible as its sudden clamour), Bastedo took his wife's arm anew and she hurried him out through the main door onto College Avenue. It was as if Mrs. Bastedo, at least, considered her husband's viewpoint expressed in this manner a little bit naughty.

Micky Canter

Most people in the city seemed to know who Micky Canter was. They may not have known him personally, but if they spent any time at all in the downtown area they would certainly have caught a glimpse of him – and having heard stories of his character, the reputation that preceded him, it would not have taken long to put two and two together. He was a difficult character to miss or to forget, early-thirties, wiry in build and bent over like a wattle stick so that he appeared to be a small man. This was a misconception; on rare occasions when Micky stood up and uncoiled himself to his full height, one would see him come close to six feet. He had noticeably quick movements, a tinselly-too-loud voice, and wore bottle-bottom glasses that gave him licence to poke up to within fifteen centimetres of the face of whomever he happened to be addressing. He would listen intently to whatever the other person had to say, then burst like a vomit of machine gun chatter all over them. People would become embarrassed and attempt to avoid him. At this point, noting their embarrassment, he would cling all the harder, forcing the person he was addressing to back away from him towards whatever exit came readily to hand. He tended to swamp, so was not the easiest person to get close to.

No one knew his detailed story, but it was not hard to guess some of the outstanding details. Micky's father was a Jewish greengrocer, the one man in town able to guarantee a supply of bananas in the city's mid-winter (there were few food courts or supermarket chains in those days). For this old Mr. Canter was known locally as "the banana man," a tyrant towards his son and customers alike. Those making a purchase from the shelves of his store would feel almost obliged to place their money directly into the old man's hand at the check-out counter – otherwise he would shake his palm under their nose and their compliance would be acknowledged by a dismissive grunt that would follow them ("Come again, or not, as you please!") until the store's outer screen door (winter and summer, a screen door) had banged shut.

Micky slaved for his father, hefting boxes and shuffling them about the store, putting out displays, taking them down, running errands, all the while the old man shouting an incessant string of whining and criticism. As a result Micky was as skittish as a chipmunk, and had a perpetual nervous rash on his neck and the backs of his hands. His face was red and pocked, prone to break-out in sores and pimples. While talking to him, his eyes would dart from side to side away from you, or he would sneak a quick look over his shoulder to see who might be there to poke at him. He exposed a sad self-image but, for all that, he was sharp and quick-witted; there was not much good or bad about himself to which he would not readily admit. He wished he was different, and would say so.

"It would help me get the girls," he would say, giggling and usually far too loud. I am not aware he ever succeeded with the girls. He would have embarrassed them.

Somewhat to my own surprise I found myself befriending Micky. One hot summer evening in 1961 I was sitting on the front porch of our house as he was passing, and he stopped at my gate to chat. I invited him to join me for a beer. He accepted. Then my wife invited him to stay for dinner, and again he accepted. Later we moved back out onto the front porch and talked, and by this juncture he understood that I had served two years in the British Army. He wanted to know which regiment and, when I told him, he pulled a sketch pad from his shoulder bag and with barely a comment or question, drew the figure of a soldier in my old regimental uniform.

"Is that about right?" he asked.

I was surprised.

"That's extraordinary ...!"

"Oh, I know them all!" he replied.

It seemed a bold response, so I was prompted to dig a little deeper.

"You mean all British Army regimental uniforms ...?"

"British, Canadian, American, you name it ..."

"All of them?"

Micky smiled, like a small boy who has triumphed at a game of checkers. Yes, he said, he knew them all – all regiments, all countries, all periods of history. It appeared military uniforms were his "thing." He had a whole library of books on the subject, he said, had committed their entire collections of illustrations to memory – and then some. His research had been thorough, and was ongoing, he claimed. If someone needed to know the number of buttons Napoleon's 11th Invincibles had down the rear of their jerkins, Micky could tell them.

Before he left us that evening he promised to "pay" for his dinner by painting a watercolour for me, and would drop it off in a day or so. I said he did not need to pay us, and put his offer out of mind. But he kept his word. A couple of days later he came by the house and withdrew a small card, twenty-four by eighteen centimetres, from a canvas shoulder bag. It was a very polished colour version of the sketch he had made for me on his first visit – a very precise rendering of a lieutenant in my former battalion of the King's African Rifles.

J. J. Hespeler-Boultbee

Micky Canter's sketch of a lieutenant in the uniform of 26th Battalion, King's African Rifles. He subsequently 'paid' for eleven more dinners with eleven more sketches of military uniforms drawn from the First and Second World Wars.

Dear Micky – he was so delighted with the way my small family accepted him, and our interest in his passion. The feeling went both ways. My wife and I warmed to this tormented and most unusual man. He came to the house for dinner several times after that – eleven more, to be precise. I know because he "paid" for each meal with a military watercolour; in addition to the KAR lieutenant, he painted a Japanese soldier, a Russian soldier, a French colonial trooper, a Hungarian artillery officer, and several others – twelve in all. The series has been framed and now hangs in the hallway of my apartment, each figure the receipt for one meal. Years later, on one of my cross-Canada journeys, he drew for me, in ballpoint and on lined paper, a soldier of the Peninsula War. This, too, is now framed and hanging with the others – the lucky thirteenth.

Micky's talent was so obvious both my wife and I had urged him to follow through, to continue some form of artistic study, to leave the drudgery of his father's grocery store, lift his sights and seek out an institute of fine arts – somewhere – that would be able to appreciate his abilities. It seemed to us essential he make use of both his painting skills and his exceptional knowledge of military uniforms and equipment. I had never encountered such a thing before; the nearest thing to it I could think of was my step-father's photographic memory and skill with languages. None of us was sure how or where Micky might start, or where he should apply. Such a place did not exist in the city at that time, but Regina was a centre of the arts; surely there would be someone available who could counsel him. Perhaps he should venture further afield ...

Micky was hesitant. Both my wife and I could see his quandary. Any such move would clash with his other life – the fury and bullying demands of his father, the banana man. Micky had never known an alternative; it was by no means a sure thing he could summon the confidence to break free of such a domination.

Carefully wrapped, I carried his paintings with me – for years – until the day I was finally established in a home in which I could display them in a manner that did them the justice they deserved. To me they are very special, not just because they are works of high quality in their own right, and demonstrate their artist's remarkable talent, but as memento of a very special "little guy" for whom I had and still have the highest regard. The work is a record of Micky Canter's exceptional ability. I would like to think – in fact I am quite sure – he would appreciate being remembered in such a way. He tried hard to be accepted, to "make good," as he would say – and with us, certainly, he succeeded.

I was on a cross-Canada lecture tour in 1977, and passed through Regina. I had originated my tour in Portugal, so when I met up with Micky I was able to present him with a postcard collection of Portuguese military uniforms and costumes – illustrations of everything from the era of the Discoveries right through till the present day. There must have been two hundred cards in all – the complete set on sale at Lisbon's military museum. Micky danced a jig, he was so ecstatic.

It was on that visit I learned he had, several years earlier, entered the fine arts programme at the University of Regina – had managed to earn himself a degree in art history and was currently working in the costume design section of the university's theatre department. He could not have landed in a more appropriate situation, and his renewed spirit showed. His mottled facial complexion had cleared, as had the backs of his hands and forearms, he spoke with confidence in his voice and as a man who knew his place in the world. His happy air was catching and I, too, felt I should dance a jig.

In 1980 I repeated the lecture tour, and eagerly anticipated seeing my old friend when I passed through Regina. I wrote to him giving the dates of my intended arrival, but had received no reply by the time I was booked to leave Portugal. Once back in the city I had some difficulty finding his house, so checked some of his colleagues at the university.

"Hadn't you heard?" they asked.

Micky had died of heart failure a couple of months earlier – right about the time I had left Europe, but not before he would have received my letter.

Some weeks later, returning to my home in Portugal and going through the mail that had accumulated in my absence, I found the letter I had sent Micky before leaving on my trip. Although I was able to confirm it had been sent to the correct address, it had now been returned to me – all the way back across the Atlantic Ocean. Someone at the post office in Regina had decided a mere street address, even though correct, was insufficient. There was a large and angry red stamp on the back of the envelope with check boxes to explain:

"Incorrectly addressed – no postal code."

Micky's heart problem was no great secret, which was at least one of the reasons I wanted to see him again. I have often wondered if Canada's postal system had been a mite less impersonal – had it exercised heart in place of such a rigid bureaucracy – had it made a little more effort to deliver my letter letting my friend know I was on my way, thus giving him the heart, so to say…

There are always "ifs" to contend with. If we are so cautious that we stop to consider them all we simply won't get where we're supposed to go.

To return to the original thread of this narrative, from Regina I made my way to Toronto. I still thought of making a splash by writing for the Big Papers. I had written a major story for one of the Toronto slicks, and it paid me more money than I had ever received before. It went to my head and I fooled myself: "I can do this again – and again and again and again …"

It didn't work that way. I found myself battling as never before, and having to take jobs I didn't want in order to stay alive.

This isn't the way it's supposed to be, I thought. But, indeed, it is what there was.

Euro-Junket

Assignments for a variety of publications, and my by-now well-developed inclination for submitting to a survivor's fugitive instincts, took me overseas at various points during the next several years – to London at first, then to Paris and Lisbon and Portuguese Africa – but during this period I would also return to Canada and spend stretches of time in British Columbia. There was even time to complete a university degree.

In the UK I was unemployed for almost half a year, but eventually managed to get work for a company in London doing industrial surveys. I had never done this sort of work before, but it was akin to the reporting I had been doing in Canada, inasmuch as I had to ask questions and obtain as accurate information as possible. For a time it was fun, and I was more than happy with the pay. The job involved office work, mostly, but occasionally I was called upon to make trips out to such centres as Sheffield, Manchester and Cardiff. I also went up to Newcastle, but there found the language of the Jarrow shipbuilders almost totally obscure. Me, not them, I told myself, but felt I still failed to achieve anything of consequence.

Cardiff I had known well from trips I had made there when courting my wife, and I was grateful for the opportunity to revisit one or two of our old haunts. But I had never been to Newcastle, Manchester or Sheffield before. In addition to my work, Sheffield provided the opportunity to reconnect with an old school chum from public school – Roger Viner, by now heading the cutlery factory that had been his family's concern for generations.

Newcastle may have been a washout, but my excursion to Manchester was a surprisingly different experience.

Most of our work was conducted from a bank of telephones in the London office, but for my trip to Manchester I was required to attend a conference in company with another man from our office – a West African by the name of Oto. The two of us arranged to meet at our office the day before our departure to sort out expenses for train travel and discuss the manner in which we would tackle the highlights of the meeting.

I had checked trains connecting London and Manchester, matching their timetable against the hour we had to be in the Manchester conference room. It turned out to be an extremely tight schedule, and that there was only one early morning train we could catch.

"Don't you worry about me, man," said Oto confidently. "I'll be there on time."

"Well," I encouraged, "how about we meet under the station clock at …"

I suggested a time.

"No," he replied, "don't you go waiting for me. I'll be there on time. You make your own way, and don't worry about me …"

"How will you be travelling? Have you got a car …?" I was thinking maybe I could catch a ride with him ...

"No. No car. But I'll be there …"

I knew that at the hour we were holding this discussion it was already too late for him to catch a train to Manchester, and that the earliest train the following day would be the only one he could possibly catch in order to be at the conference on time. So I was both curious and insistent:

"Well, *that* is the train – the only train you can catch. You had better be sure you're at the station on time."

The following day he was nowhere to be seen on the station platform, nor on the train once it was underway, and I had a few angry visions of myself having to make excuses to cover for his absence. In fact, on the way up on the train by myself I managed to work up quite a righteous lather. I was absolutely sure that when I arrived at the Manchester office I would have to start the proceedings by making some sort of grovelling apology for my associate's tardiness.

So I was surprised to enter the conference room and find Oto sitting there, ready for business. He was alert, well-rested and a deal more composed than I was.

"Good morning!" he greeted me, bright as a guardsman's polished button and smiling at me a whole mouthful of scrubbed white teeth.

We sat in conference throughout the morning but, at lunchtime, when the two of us were alone together, I had the opportunity of asking him how he happened to make it up to Manchester on time.

"Well, I came by my own …" he offered evasively.

Somersaults

"Of course you did ... But how? By car?"

"No. No car ..."

"So you were on the train ...?"

"No. I didn't come by train ..."

"Well, excuse me, Oto, but how the blazes did you manage to get here on time?" I asked.

"Ah!" he exclaimed, his eyes laughing at me. "You know we Africans have ways to get around that you know nothing of ... You may ask questions of me, but you will never be satisfied by my answers, so it's best we don't go into the matter further."

With that he clammed-up. Indeed, I ascertained that unless he had received a lift by car or flown – and I was sure he hadn't – there was absolutely no way at all he could possibly have made it to the conference on time. The bus timetable had not suited, either.

At the end of the conference we walked away from the Manchester office in the direction of the train station. We were close enough there was no need to take a taxi.

"Are you taking the train down to London ...?" I queried.

"No," he replied. "I leave you here."

And with that he bid me a very polite goodbye and peeled off along a side street with that grin of his, and a cheery wave.

The following morning, bright and early, he appeared for the conference debriefing at our head office near Victoria station.

Never an explanation. Short of "African magic" I am unable to think of one.

In Paris I taught "Executive English" – a pretty broad term if, indeed, members of the group I was teaching were executives. As a classroom assembly they were difficult, their individual levels of English language competence all over the map. But they were a cheerful bunch, all shapes and sizes, some in suits, some in dungarees, some clearly management, others as clearly shop foremen. They were about fifteen in number – staff at an aircraft production centre south of the city not far from Fresnes. The factory was making the seating for the Concorde. Rain or shine, I made the run down to the works five days a week on my motorbike, nipping in and out of traffic with what I imagined was the prowess of a Parisian dispatch rider.

My accommodation in the city (it is hard to imagine it now, as I understand the area has been extensively transformed since I lived there) was on rue de Birague, north from Rue de Rivoli – the last house on the right next to the archway entrance to Place des Vosges. People with a more up-to-date knowledge of the city have informed me that Place des Vosges has moved upscale, is now extremely chic and extremely expensive.

I lived there with a lady named Françoise in a cramped bed-sit on the ground floor of a shabby and rundown house. Our sole window looked out onto a busy residential street, its late afternoons and evenings a colourful promenade of hookers scouting for clientele. Most had staked-out regular positions – their beats – and their own strict code of conduct forbade encroachment. On occasion the *gendarmerie* was summoned to referee a scrap that had developed over some infringement of the unwritten rules and was threatening to morph into serious turf war. Such instances could be vicious, but paddy wagons were always close by.

A very pretty young lady in net stockings, a thinning boa about her bare shoulders and calling herself Céline, had laid claim to a position right outside our window. Most evenings throughout that cold winter Françoise and I would brew up a pot of chocolate milk on our hotplate, a treat at the end of a working day. We would always make sure there was sufficient for Céline, too, if she happened to be on station. Our landlady would not have approved had we invited her inside, so we would pass it out through our window to where she was standing and shivering against the wall.

On occasion Céline would decline, saying: "I have a client coming in a few minutes. Better not to accept a hot chocolate now, but may I knock on your window when I get back? I don't expect to be more than half an hour..."

By early spring Céline had gone. Françoise said she thought she was getting married. Her place below our window was occupied by a somewhat less appealing individual.

Visuals Fey

Françoise went off to spend a long weekend with her family in Tours, leaving me on my own in the city for several days. Late on one of these evenings I found myself walking alone outside the Louvre and, feeling exhilarated, decided to return on foot to our quarters at the entrance to Place des Vosges. I chose a route running through the Left Bank. Crossing the River Seine by way of Pont du Carrousel, I looked over the bridge's parapet into the dark waters below. City lights had already come on, and the rippled surface of the river sparkled and flashed their reflections, dancers on a broad ballet stage.

There was a book I wanted to buy, and thought it might be found at Shakespeare & Company, on Rue de la Bûcherie, so I made my way in that direction along Quai Voltaire, and so along the other *quais* – Malaquais, Conti and Grands Augustins, to Saint-Michel. Narrow backstreets and alleys in that area were laid out on a pattern more complex than a honeycomb (it seemed that way in the dark), the high grey stone walls of the buildings sensuous invitation to my curiosity. I have a good nose for direction, so dived in and a few wrong turns later came upon the bookstore from behind.

I found the volume I'd wanted, stopped for a few minutes to chat with the proprietor, then continued my way homeward – south around the expanse of René Viviani park and into back streets off Quai de Montebello, generally heading in the direction of Pont de Sully.

Streetlights were few and far between in this particular area, so I had to move cautiously. Rounding a corner made by two narrow alleys, I was unexpectedly confronted by the floodlit façade and flank of Notre-Dame de Paris. The magnificent old cathedral, rising into the night from its position across the narrow southern channel of Île de la Cité, was brilliantly alight. It looked for all the world like a gigantic Gothic wedding cake. I stopped, breathless at such a visual spectacle. This jewel of gold against the black of the night made its sudden appearance as if I had just that instant made my grand entrance into some children's fairyland. I sucked in my breath, I was so enchanted by the sight.

It was midnight. Custodians had their responsibilities.

Suddenly the lights went out and I was surrounded by an alarming inky blackness.

My feeling then was one of infinite sadness, a moment of paranoia, the sense that my precious only-seconds-long vision had been purposely and spitefully withdrawn.

Stumbling out onto Quai de la Tournelle, victim of what in that instant appeared to be an intensely personal sleight, I rushed back north across the river, coming onto Boulevard Henri IV and so via more narrow backstreets to Place des Vosges and my room on R. de Birague. For a long time after I got in I lay back on the bed and stared at the ceiling, unwilling but also unable to expel from my mind the sight of Notre-Dame as I had just seen it. There would have been others who witnessed the extinguishing of the floodlights on the cathedral that evening, but I was utterly convinced no one had witnessed it the way I had. My vision had lasted no more than seconds, but it is as fresh in my mind now as it was then, over forty years ago.

I really do believe that some people – maybe *most* people – sail through their entire lives without ever taking stock of the images and sensations that continually bombard them. Perhaps they are frightened by them or don't know how to react – as if confronted by a scary ogre that pops out and brushes their skin or hair as they rattle past in one of the rickety carriages of a ghost train in the dark tunnel of horrors ... People may scream when they are surprised, but there are many who have developed immunities to looking and feeling. Either they were never taught to look or to feel, or else they have become so busy they have developed a sort of natural breaker, like a fuse, that serves to flick off that (or any) particular *wow!*

Case in point:

Françoise and I had driven with friends one weekend to Limoges, for centuries considered one of the world's leading hubs in the manufacture of earthenware faience and porcelain. We stopped outside one of the city's central hotels, and a young fellow who had been travelling with us announced that he would like to use the washroom facilities.

"You go find out where it is, and report back. I'll follow you after you're done ..." I told him.

He ran up the steps of the hotel and disappeared inside. The rest of us waited in the car and chatted until he reappeared some minutes later. Climbing in, he said to me:

"It's on the first floor at the top of the stairs. First door on the left. It's marked. You can't miss it."

I walked into the hotel, up the broad stairway and, sure enough, on the left of the corridor that led off the landing there was a door marked with the universal W.C.

The bathroom was large, considering its use and contents: about five metres by five metres. The toilet itself was plumb in the middle of the wall opposite the door, a water tank directly above it, with a pull-chain hanging down, a handle on the end of it. There was a wash basin against the wall just to the right of the door as I entered the chamber. Perfect symmetry!

So much for the base description of the room. But what really caught the eye – *my* eye:

The whole space – every inch of it – was an example of exceptional ceramic artwork, and should more appropriately have been in a museum.

The floor of the chamber was covered with Limoges tiles – a tasteful and beautifully decorated motif of intertwined vines and flowers. The same design, somewhat elaborated, was on the wall tiles that had been laid up to shoulder height on the room's four walls – all of it the very finest of XVIII century Limoges porcelain tile decoration.

The same design was followed on the ceramic wash basin by the door, and the handles of its hot and cold water taps. The bowl of the toilet, the ceramic water tank above it, and even the porcelain handle on the end of the chain – were all in the same delicate pattern of exquisite Limoges porcelain.

I have an interest in ceramics and tile decoration, so I took my time appreciating it. This place was no mere toilet. It was an homage, a temple to celebrate the age-old tradition of the city's principal industry, one of France's most expressive and revered art forms.

When finally I returned to the car, my friends asked what had kept me so long.

"My god! What an incredible place!" I exclaimed, and I turned enthusiastically to the man who had preceded me there.

"Have you ever seen anything like that before?" I asked him.

"Like what?" he asked.

"Why! The tilework, man! The tilework! The entire bathroom was a work of art …"

"Oh!" he grunted. "You mean the bathroom tiles? Yeah – well, I didn't really pay all that much attention …"

Well, that's what I mean about people going through their lives without reacting to the things that are right around them. For me that Limoges bathroom is not the only memory I have of my time in France, but it is certainly one of the most outstanding …

The Captain's Table

My wife and I were married for seven years, but throughout this time had been together and apart so frequently our friends were confounded, and had lost count. One of their first hesitant queries on encountering us was: "Are you two together …?" Totting-up the various "on-again-off-again" periods of our relationship, of the total time married we actually lived together a little over two years. Our last attempt at anything resembling reconciliation was when I was living in Paris, by which point we had been apart for almost four years. No doubt it was madness to think it would work, but both of us believed we should make the effort, and that is what we did. It crumbled quickly – within a couple of months of my return from Europe to Canada.

The intent was that I resettle in Canada. I had an accumulation of gear I wished to keep and take back with me. Packed into various suitcases and army kit bags, it would have cost more money than I could afford in overweight by air, but I heard about a Yugoslavian shipping company that offered an exceptionally cheap passenger rate on their freight ships running between Lisbon and New York. Choosing this means of travel for the most complex portion of the journey – crossing the Atlantic – meant that I would not have to worry about extra expense for the amount of baggage accompanying me; all I had to do was look after it, and muscle it between stops and stations at the North American end. Nothing I felt I could not handle.

I booked passage out of Lisbon aboard the Kraljevica for mid-January, then caught an immigrant bus leaving Paris, and was in the Portuguese capital in less than three days. Staying at a small *pensão*, I passed a pleasant couple of weeks in my favourite European capital visiting with one of my dearest friends, wining and dining in the small eateries of Bairro Alto and Cais do Sodre, and shopping for at least another suitcase full of clothing, shoes and presents. Despite the fascist dictatorship of the *Estado Novo*, I was able to suppress any inclination to talk politics and so avoid clashing with the country's political and secret police. Mid-January in Lisbon can prove to be overcoat weather, but the skies were clear blue and people walked the decorated paving of the city's streets as if the trees were about to blossom.

In addition to a massive cargo of containers, both in the hold and on deck, the Kraljevica carried sixteen passengers in what, by any standard, was luxurious accommodation. The cabins were sizeable self-contained staterooms, each consisting of sleeping quarters with two bunkbeds, a comfortable bathroom and a separate living room. The furniture was well-anchored. In addition, there was a central lounge area with well-cushioned seating, and a small library containing an eclectic mix of books in a variety of different European languages. These were stored on shelves in two or three glass-fronted cabinets. There was also a gaming table for those wanting to play cards. The dining area was a separate salon located off to one side of the lounge.

Mealtimes, necessarily set to a specific schedule, might well have become uncomfortably stiff and formal affairs – at least at the start of the voyage when no one knew anyone else. However, this danger had been cleverly avoided by the seating arrangement. The dining salon was a spacious and well decorated hall that contained a single long table, which obliged anyone in conversation to address everyone else at the table. The captain himself, seldom absent, presided at each meal from his position in the centre of one side of the table as host of the assembly, his senior officers seated on either side of him according to rank. Seating for passengers was marked by small name plaques before each place. Officers always rose politely from their chairs if they happened to have been seated before the captain entered, or if one of the female passengers came in a few minutes late. It was not an altogether unpleasing formality and the male passengers quickly caught on – their table manners a mimic of the ship's officers. Conversation once the meal got under way, though, was noticeably informal. This seemed to be as the captain wanted it, and he went out of his way during mealtimes to make his guests feel at ease at his table. He was Yugoslavian, of course, but spoke quite excellent English and French, and he made it a point to address each of his guests with a measured and good-natured courtesy. A notice in each cabin set out a further matter of shipboard dining room etiquette: passengers were requested not to attend mealtimes in their pajamas or sleepwear, but that otherwise should feel free to attend breakfast and lunch in as casual wear as each found comfortable. Dress for the evening meal, however, was different: passengers were asked to come to the captain's table in "casually formal" attire. This quaintly polite edict had the effect of encouraging jackets for the men, skirts or dress pants for the ladies – and a not unpleasant atmosphere of civility at mealtimes.

As with most freighters, quarters for crew and passengers, as well as all the functional areas of the bridge, were located in the after section of the ship. Cargo was stored below the deck; I had no idea what it consisted of, but assumed it was all in containers rather similar to the scores of those we could see secured on deck. The visible central and forward areas of the ship were devoted entirely to cargo containers. They were stacked double and ran in four long double columns along the full length of the ship from superstructure to bow. A narrow passage ran between them up the middle of the deck to permit hands to move all the way to the prow if they had to.

Passengers boarded the ship in the dockside area of the Tagus River, between the city and Belem. Once under way, Lisbon fell behind surprisingly fast. In no time the ship was well out to sea, bound almost due west for New York. The captain had made a point of inviting all passengers up to the bridge "at any time you wish, night or day."

It was an invitation I remembered with gratitude when inevitably we ran into a North Atlantic winter storm. I felt safe on the bridge; it seemed to cure my nausea. Hanging onto the various grab handles and railings within the bridge house was calming. I could not tell exactly where we were headed, but it was not too hard to develop the notion I was in control – at least of myself. I hate to be seasick. Occasionally I have suffered the sickness so badly I thought it would be a mercy to have been thrown overboard.

Seasick though I was, this storm was so terrifying it dismissed all thought of my physical misery and gripped my whole being in the teeth of such a vice that my breath was squeezed from my lungs. I might have howled but had insufficient air. Had I remained in my cabin, my nausea would have taken hold of me, I knew it, and I would have spent my time miserably, groaning and vomiting into the wastes of the toilet or the bathtub. The ship was both rolling and pitching with extreme violence, so that negotiating the passages and companionways was a tricky labour. Once I had decided to go up to the bridge, it took a good ten minutes to arrive there. The captain was present with several of his officers, so calm and measured in the way he gave orders that I was assured in an instant he had faced this sort of situation before and knew what to do about it. I positioned myself quite close to him, and he turned to give me a reassuring smile. He must have recognized the questioning and terror in my eyes.

"A little rough this evening," he commented evenly, and with such magnificent understatement I felt immediate reassurance.

Our position on the bridge was so high above the waterline that the rolling and pitching of the ship below our feet was hugely exaggerated. Everyone there had to secure himself one way or another, and did so by wedging in next to a stanchion, or by holding a rail or some projection or other. Fortunately there was plenty to hang onto. The helmsman used a strap to lash himself to a compass housing.

The ship's movement formed a kind of logic in my head once I could see from the wheelhouse windows. My nausea vanished instantly. The massive sea was roiling, and we were bobbing along on top of it the same as a cork will stay aloft of a water-flow gushing through the plughole of a wash basin. The movement of the waters below us was a terrifying thing to see. It was not a stream; I could see no flow, and there was no visual sensation of the direction of a current – none of the normal things one might encounter standing, say, at the side of a river bank, or even at the seashore on a tempestuous day. Instead, there was the feeling that some angry giant had been aroused right underfoot – a giant covered in the enormous black quilt of the sea – and that he had been roused to fury by the presence of this pitiful little insect of a ship daring now to leave port and come crawling across its back. The captain had reduced speed to a minimum, slow but sufficient for us to make headway directly into the oncoming surge. It was difficult for me to gauge the height of these waves, but they must have been at least twice that of the bridge. Chugging up the steep front face of each oncoming wave, the ship would crest at the top, her bow rising well clear of the waters directly below it. Then the length of the ship would breach its fulcrum, and the bow would smash down onto the top of the on-rushing waters so they would cover both it and the foremost of the secured containers – flowing aft halfway along the length of the ship's deck. Each time it did this, the stern would rise out of the water, just as the bow had done when the ship crested, the screws revving violently on their shafts as the aft end lifted clear of the sea. This would cause a shudder to run throughout the hull, shaking it like a dog shakes the rabbit it has just brought down. When the stern fell back in again, the ship would power forward – downhill now, plunging into the deep saucer of surrounding waters so that once more they would engulf the prow. Then the ship would rise and level off as it began to make its way across the bottom of the trough. At this point I could look out from the bridge windows, and my gaze would be forced upwards – to the surrounding far rim of the saucer we were crossing, seemingly a hundred or more feet above our heads. Then we would begin to climb again – up and up to the apex of the rim – then over it to start the whole process again. This exhausting cycle went on for hour after hour, the captain never budging from his place beside the helmsman.

About mid-morning of the storm's second day I was once again on the bridge, and heard the captain let out a burst of surprised expostulation as he raised his binoculars to his eyes.

"Who is that?" he demanded to know.

Below, on the tempestuous deck right in front of us, a man was slowly making his way forward between the lines of containers. The movement of the ship was so violent that his progress was slow and laboured. He would take a step, then secure a handhold onto some strap or projection of one of the containers before taking his next step. He was dressed in jeans and a jean jacket, but walked barefoot.

It was one of our fellow passengers – an independent-minded fellow from New York who wore his hair long, his beads conspicuous, and was particularly loquacious at mealtimes. There was no mistaking him, nor his intent to move as far forward into the prow of the ship as he could.

"The man is risking his life," the captain said. "I will not risk the life of one of my crew members to go forward and bring him back …"

He took a microphone in hand, switching to a band that broadcast over forward-end speakers, and ordered the man to return at once. The man ignored the order and continued to move ahead until he finally attained the deck rails at the ships prow. As that end of the vessel ploughed under the surface of the raging sea, the man would hunker down, wrapping his arms and legs around the bars of the rails. Each time we went under we expected to find he had been swept away, but he managed to hang on until, soaking wet and probably very cold, he made his way back as carefully as he had gone out in the first place.

"He is very foolish," was all I heard the captain say.

The captain's more precise thinking was expressed at the next evening meal. An extra small table was set a short space apart from the main dining table at supper hour. The American's name plaque was set in the middle of it. The chief steward informed him he was no longer welcome at the captain's table, and would henceforth be served his meals alone and apart from the rest of us.

Funerals

Mother was married three times and divorced three times. She was an alcoholic and lived the last fifteen years of her life in Spain, where she died and is buried. Although at the time my home was close-by in Portugal, a few hours away by car, I was not near a telephone when she died. Her friends and lawyer were unable to get hold of me to tell me what had happened. In fact, I was taking a leisurely round-trip into Spain, and had planned an unannounced visit to be with her. I arrived six days too late. In the meantime, those who had been trying to reach me managed to connect with my brother then living in Britain, and he flew down to oversee the funeral. He was still in town when I arrived and was able to bring me up-to-date.

"Where is she buried?" I asked, naturally anxious to visit her gravesite.

"She's up at the Spanish cemetery ..."

"In one of those filing cabinets?"

Yes, he told me. She had been buried, as are millions of Spaniards, in a wall that is reminiscent of a filing cabinet in that such walls, although thick and substantially-built, are divided into numerous small "caves" only big enough to receive an adult coffin. After interment these spaces are sealed with mortar and a slab stone, usually a flat and inscribed marble plaque.

I happened to know, as my brother did not, that Mother did not wish to be buried in this fashion. I had visited her the year before, and she had taken some pains to explain to me precisely what she wanted, and that under no circumstance was I to allow her to be interred in a Spanish cemetery wall.

"I can't abide those things!" she had said. "I won't rest easy if my grave is in a wall ...I probably wouldn't even know my neighbour, let alone be able to have a drink with him ...!"

Then she told me how she had purchased a plot in the Protestant cemetery.

"Stick me in there, dear. It's at the top of a hill, but you shouldn't have too much trouble pushing me up in a barrow to where you need to tip me out. It's all paid for and I'll have a lovely view over the ocean. Besides," and she winked, "all my good friends will be there, and we'll be able to natter away with one another into eternity."

When I related this to my brother, we agreed to go to the authorities the following day and have the matter settled as Mother would have wanted. The man we needed to see was her lawyer, and he told us he would do what he could, but that we may run into bureaucratic trouble – which is precisely what happened. In Spain, other than in special circumstances usually involving police investigations, it is forbidden to disinter and move a body once it has been buried – for a period of five years. So that was that; dear Mama would have to remain where she was – turning over and over, no doubt, for the next half-decade. My brother returned to London; I waited a month at Mother's tiny apartment, packing and tidying up her numerous affairs, then returned to continue my life in Portugal.

I returned to Canada for brief visits, rebuilt my old stone house in Portugal, and five years later made arrangements to return to re-inter my mother in her own small plot on the hill of the Protestant cemetery. My brother was unable to attend. There was a protocol, of course, papers to be filled out and signed. Spanish bureaucracy can be every bit as convoluted as it is anywhere in the world. When I arrived I found a rosy-cheeked English minister, Mr. Hooper, was in charge.

"Oh dear!" he said, hanging his head and shaking it sadly. "I'm so sorry about your dear mother's passing. Oh dear …! So sad, so sad!"

"It's alright, Mr. Hooper," I encouraged him. I was afraid he might burst into tears. "Mother died five years ago, so I'm fine with it now. She had arranged and paid for a plot here, so we need to put her where she told me she'd like to be."

Seeing as I was so composed about it all, Mr. Hooper decided he could be, too.

"Very well, then," he said most matter-of-factly. "Would you be wanting a burial service here in the cemetery chapel, or would you prefer a prayer at graveside …?"

"Well, Mr. Hooper, I'm pretty sure Mother wouldn't choose to be found dead in a church – or even a chapel, for that matter – so I think a graveside prayer or two would be quite adequate …"

We made arrangements to meet early the following morning for the disinterment at the Spanish cemetery, and to convey the remains to the

Protestant cemetery. It was an hour of the day Mama would not have witnessed in the last half of her life, but a pleasant morning for all that, and I was more than a little curious as to how I would feel about seeing my mother's coffin.

As it happened, there was virtually nothing there. Mother's tiny space had been three tiers up, so it was not possible to see inside without a ladder of some kind, and that was the sole province of the Spanish graveside attendants. A gum booted worker with a rake climbed up unceremoniously and proceeded to pull out all that was inside, dropping it into a tarpaulin on the ground. Mama.

The coffin had completely disintegrated, as had her remains. Bones, nothing more. I saw her skull, how the top of it had been sawn open for the requisite autopsy the Spanish authorities demand for all foreigners who happen to die on their hallowed ground. I saw the silvered-metal joint Mother had had implanted some years before when she had fallen and broken an elbow – it, and her teeth, were about all that remained for me to recognize as the remains of my mother. All of her fitted with room to spare into the new coffin we had brought to the site – a small black box, two feet by two feet, that had a delicate silvered cross attached to its lid. I laid her bones gently onto the fabric inside the box, and closed its lid.

So we carried Mother across the city from the Spanish cemetery to the hillside of the Protestant cemetery in a big black hearse, and there a small group of her friends had gathered at the side of her new resting place – eight or ten people in all. Notable among them was Tim Mortimer, who came there with his wife, Rita. The two of them were very special to Mother. They operated a popular bar-cum-restaurant at the back of the beach near her apartment building, and it was there, for the most part, they all developed a close bond between them – a friendship that dated back over the entire time Mother had lived in Spain. Now Tim, a big man with a huge belly, stood with his feet planted purposefully on the ground beside his friend's grave, looking solemn with his bottom lip pushed out and clutching a bouquet of flowers in one big hand. His presence there was reassuring somehow. I knew he and Rita had been on hand for Mother's initial funeral five years before, and to have the two of them now take the time to turn out for her re-burial was indicative, I thought, of their love for her. Indeed, I felt the same way about everyone who had come that day – dear friends, all of them.

We were joined by Mr. Hooper in his simple Anglican vestments, who began to intone the words of last rites. Unfortunately, as the little black box was being lowered into the deep hole that had been prepared for it by the gravediggers, it got stuck. The dimensions of the hole were insufficient, and the little coffin simply could not be coaxed into settling onto the bottom.

Tim Mortimer glowered down at the black box across his ample stomach.

"Oh, Stephanie! You've done it again!"

We all laughed, except Mr. Hooper. Flustered, he stopped his intonations, his rosy cheeks turning a bright red as he looked at me in consternation. He felt badly for me in particular; surely no one had ever before laughed at one of his funerals.

It was necessary to relieve his embarrassment with some sort of explanation.

"Please don't be upset, Mr. Hooper," I said to him. "Mother spent her entire life causing trouble for other people and drawing attention to herself. Here she is, as you see, returning to us for her show-stopping second performance – and somehow again causing trouble. Absolutely in character."

"Exactly!" chimed Tim. "Stephanie to a tee!"

Mr. Hooper smiled uncertainly as he looked at each of those gathered around Mother's grave. Everyone nodded their encouragement to him, and he understood. Even in Mother's most solemn moments, there was room for fun, for humour and laughter. The situation she had created now was exactly the sort of slapstick she would have loved immensely – the very kernel of Mack Sennett's Keystone Kops, or of Buster Keaton, the gift of poking a hole in convention and pulling it down a peg or two, maybe even giving it a black eye. Mother, absolutely.

"Oh well, then!" said Mr. Hooper brightly. "Haul the box out, then. Everyone, relax for a few moments and we'll get the gravediggers to assist us…"

Two cemetery workers (it is a profession that requires gum boots) were produced, one an old gaffer, the other a younger fellow short a few marbles.

"Here!" scolded the older man in uncouth graveside Spanish, and he produced a tape measure. "I told you to dig the hole sixty-by-sixty, and look! It's fifty-five-by-fifty-five! Gimme that spade!"

The younger one floundered about uselessly, and finally produced a spade so that the senior gravedigger could get to work and open up the hole a bit.

We all stepped away while the two of them got on with it. Tim lit up a smoke. He was still clutching onto the bouquet of flowers, which were straining a bit, and bending over in their effort to wilt.

Somersaults

Finally all was ready. We returned to graveside and Mr. Hooper resumed his intonations. Tim laid his flowers on top of Mother's shiny black coffin as it was lowered into the earth, and in the end the gravediggers returned to fill in the hole they had dug only short minutes before. Then they tamped down the earth.

At last Mother was gone. She had been dead the past five years but it was not until this moment that I truly noted her passing and felt I was able to say farewell to her. Mr. Hooper put his arm awkwardly across my shoulders, and the assembly worked its way downhill.

"Drinks on the house at our place," offered Tim – so we all reassembled on the beach in front of Tim's and Rita's bar and settled in for the balance of the afternoon. Mr. Hooper gamely trooped along with us, kicked his shoes off and paddled for a few moments in the shallow Mediterranean eddies that lapped the seashore. Among us he was the only one who had never known my mother, so over a pleasant afternoon of beer and camaraderie – just as Mother might have wanted – we were able to tell him a little bit about the extraordinary lady over whose burial he had just presided.

Here lies Stephanie Hespeler,
Then Boultbee, then Freeze, then Benn.
So many men, never The Man ...
Arg-h, men!

Within the year my father also died. I had been living in Portugal for some years by 1980, and had been invited to participate in a cross-Canada speaking tour scheduled for the fall of that year. I decided to travel to Canada in the late summer so that I could visit friends and enjoy the countryside before the weather turned spiteful. I flew to London in the closing days of July and went straight to my brother's house off Maida Vale. He was working on the Continent that week, but had instructed me as to how I could obtain his front door key, and told me to wait for him until he returned in a few days.

On the morning of the first day at his house a colleague called my brother from their London office.

"He's not here," I said. "His boss had him go to Brussels for the week. Did you not know about it?"

The man on the other end of the line expressed surprise. No, he said, he had been away from the office himself and had not heard. In any case, he needed to speak to my brother personally.

"Well – I'm his brother. I arrived yesterday from Lisbon, and I'll be staying at his house until his return. If you tell me your name I'll be sure to give him the message …"

"You're his brother …?"

"Yes."

"Well …" There was a moment of hesitation. "I guess the message I have for your brother will be of concern to you, too. Your sister called this office from Canada a little while ago. She was trying to locate your brother to tell him his father had died … Your father, too, I assume? Did you already know about it?"

Yes, I thanked him, he was my father also. And no, I had not received any notice of his death till now. The voice on the end of the line was kind and concerned. He apologised for being the one to break the news to me.

By chance my brother arrived home the following morning, a day or so ahead of schedule. He immediately telephoned our half-sister in British Columbia – two brothers, five half-sisters – and learned that our father had died while on holiday in Barbados. His second wife, the girls' mother, was delayed in the Caribbean with her husband's remains, wrestling with the local bureaucracy entailed in getting him home for his funeral – and the threat of a brewing Hurricane Allen.

As it turned out the delays were of some value, for they allowed a little extra time for the gathering of the clan. I was scheduled to fly out of London ahead of my brother, so we agreed to meet up again at the home of one of our sisters in Kamloops. The date for our father's funeral had been set for about ten days following his death.

In Vancouver I stayed overnight with friends, made a few telephone calls to Victoria, then accepted a ride out onto the highway which led to the interior of the province. It was a warm and sunny August morning, and I had decided to hitch-hike the three hundred and fifty kilometers to Kamloops. I wanted to see the Fraser Canyon again, so deliberately took that route.

My first lift took me through the farmland of the lower Fraser Valley as far as Hope. The driver was kind enough to see me through to the far side of the town so that I would have a chance to catch a ride going all the way north through the canyon.

My second ride, however, was a strong and unusual experience for me.

The driver of this ride pulled to a stop beside me about fifteen minutes later, and I could see immediately he was homosexual. However, it was not his sexual proclivity that bothered me particularly at first; he was offering me a ride all the way to Kamloops, which would have suited me very well. He said that he lived there and was going there himself. But I was thrown when he initiated an insistent and obvious come-on as I sat in the seat beside him. I was not sure how to deal with him, found my ineptitude unnerving to the point of embarrassment, and even thought to ask him to let me out on the road. I was bothered by the idea that picking up hitch-hikers might have been his *modus operandi*, and I was fearful (albeit the middle of a bright summer day) that we were heading into a long and lonely canyon. I thought to demand he stop, but as we had both announced to each other that Kamloops was our goal, it would have appeared churlish – even rude – for me to want to back out. It would have been like announcing, "I don't feel comfortable among gay people," – which I didn't, but I didn't want to admit it – and even admitting that I did not want to admit it caused me some turmoil.

Over the course of the first few kilometers I tried to take the measure of the fellow, but decided that for all his presumptuous in-your-face approach, he was just a lonely fellow on the make. He was no threat to me – probably no threat to anybody.

Maybe I could make headway with some forthright talk ...

I was not comfortable. It was an irrational feeling, one I couldn't deny, yet I knew it was due entirely to my own attitude towards his open homosexuality – which I was sure he sensed. It was a throwback to that dominant segment of my childhood personality: my fear of the "other," of my confusion at being obliged, right here and now, to deal with what was in reality a new and strange thing for me. Never before had I been obliged to confront – within myself – precisely this sort of situation. A first.

Yet getting into the fellow's car was, precisely, what brought it about.

It took some inner strength I did not know I had, but I decided right there and then that the best way of dealing with my idiotic heebie-jeebies was to talk about them.

I opened by telling him I feared his sexuality, and this appeared to be a correct move. He listened and, when he was sure he understood what I was talking about, he responded in kind and forthrightly. He was honest and open, a witty and intelligent fellow.

"You don't know how good it is until you have tried it ..." was one fairly obvious comment he tossed out at me.

"No – don't try that one on me," I told him. "If ever I am tempted to go down your street I'll do it of my own volition, not because of some curiosity, or simply because I've been invited. Of this I am quite sure, and am sure you also can understand and respect this viewpoint. I noted your homosexuality right away; were you not able to see that I'm straight? I mean, you put yourself out there – but surely you would not be tempted to force yourself on someone against their will?"

He actually apologised to me at that point.

"No – I had not specifically noticed you were straight. Not right away. And no, I would not force myself on someone against their will. In your case, I misjudged. My bad. I'm sorry if it has upset you ..."

By and large it was a useful conversation – certainly for me, quite possibly for him also. We were total strangers yet here, on this winding road through the Fraser Canyon, we talked on matters I could never have imagined it possible to broach with a member of my family or friends, let alone a stranger. After we had cleared the air and established who we were, it seemed the discussion took an almost academic turn, and we chatted away the kilometres. Having made it quite clear to him my sole reason for being in his car was my need to get to Kamloops as quickly as possible, we found we could laugh and enjoy the spectacular scenery – no discomfort.

True to his word he dropped me at my sister's front door. It had been good of him to bring me so far along my way, and I bid him an amicable goodbye – knowing full well (as did he) it would be most unlikely our paths would cross again. Useful lessons.

My sister was clearly taken aback. She met the fellow, and I am sure she saw him as I had when he first stopped his car outside Hope. She made no comment. I'm sure she was happy to see me again, though I think she was a little surprised by the manner in which I'd hitch-hiked my way to my father's funeral.

It was a morning church service. As with my mother, I had never seen my father in a church before. The man had sired seven children, yet the first time they had all managed to gather around him was at his funeral. Strange, that, and a great sadness. But for me personally the greater sadness was that my father and I should have been at such loggerheads.

Afterwards it was agreed we would all gather at the summer home owned by one of my sisters and her husband – a splendid place in a quiet line of houses that spread themselves along the northern shoreline of Shuswap Lake. My step-mother decided she wanted to be at home alone; the rest of us made our separate ways to the lake in separate cars. The seven siblings plus various members of their families amounted on that occasion to some thirty people.

While most of us romped in the water and successfully managed to douse the sombreness of the day, my sisters grouped together and busied themselves preparing a feast. Tables were dragged out of the house, or borrowed from neighbours, and so placed end-to-end in the yard-space between the house and the lakeside to form one long banqueting board, with chairs set in place for each one of us. We sat down to eat about five o'clock. The conversation, of course, revolved around our father and the life the girls shared as they were growing up. There was little mention of either my brother or myself, or where or what we had been doing all those years with our mother. For my part, I felt subdued, as though placed there as little more than a spectator.

The wives of two couples staying at one of the houses in the line happened by, and learned of our family's gathering – although I do not believe anyone actually explained to them why we were gathering. It would have been heavy information for them to digest on such a beautiful summer's evening. Their husbands, they explained, were out fishing on the water – and in fact, we could hear them well. They had taken a box or two of beer with them in case the fishing wasn't up to par; and if it was, then the beer would be ready at hand to assist in celebration ... They were laughing and joking out on the water, and presently they answered their wives' summons to come in for supper. The most convenient landing spot for their boat was on the narrow beach right below where all of us were seated.

"Ho! Ho!" they both exclaimed as they gathered their gear together out of their boat. "The entire neighbour clan gathered together ... Ha! Ha!"

Their high spirits had been augmented by whatever it was they had consumed while out on the water. They laughed and joked, and the presence of all of us there seemed to push them a little bit higher. There was no reason why they would necessarily have been informed of the somberness of our party's get together – and actually no way of telling. At the end of a day playing in the water, and now sitting down to a first rate meal, we were in pretty good spirits ourselves ...

"Hey!" one of the fishermen laughed. "How can we show our appreciation of such an illustrious family ...?"

"I know!" exclaimed his friend.

Unbuckling his belt, he turned around, downed his trousers and wagged his bare bum at us. Seeing what his friend was doing, the other fellow followed suit. The pair of them laughed till tears rolled down their cheeks. Raucous humour. What an opportunity to gag it up!

"There you are! We'll never have a chance to do this again! Here's to you lot!"

Still shouting and laughing, the two drunken fishermen-neighbours threw their arms about one another's shoulders and staggered back to their own house for the meal their wives had prepared.

"Goodbye neighbours! Good people, the neighbours!"

The thirty of us – maybe not the full family complement, but all of us intimately connected with the head of the local clan whose funeral we had attended that morning – sat and looked at one another, in surprised bemusement. The two men, obviously, had not been informed of our father's funeral, and probably did not even know he had died. Our father had been an alderman of the city and was a significant social figure in Kamloops, so they most certainly would have known who he was – but they were drunk, they knew my sisters well enough to feel free to make such a ribald joke of the chance encounter ... It was an insult, but not one that was maliciously intended ... They were simply having fun – at our expense. Our discussion about it went back and forth for the remainder of our dinner.

"We should retaliate in some way ..." one of us suggested.

"In kind," I suggested – and that was the decision we made. After we had all finished eating, the lot of us, men, women and children, stood up from the table and sauntered amiably, two houses over, to where the fishermen were now having dinner on the porch with their wives. We formed a wide semi-circle in the yard below them. Then, on a word, we all turned about, downed our drawers and bent over.

"Message from us to you lot!"

Once more, roars of laughter from the smaller group on the porch.

"Do it again! Do it again!"

We might have obliged, except that one of the fishermen said to his wife:

"Hey, honey – go fetch the camera …!"

With that, in an instant, the entire family had straightened up, zipped up and turned to face the jokesters. Everyone on both sides had a good laugh, and we walked back to our portion of the lakefront. I don't believe any photographs were taken of the incident. And as a matter of fact, I'm not entirely convinced that everyone in our party actually downed their pants. One or two of my little nieces were pretty upset by what the rest of us had done.

However, I did hear, the following day before I left town, that profuse apologies had been offered when the fishermen and their wives finally came to a full understanding of why our family had been assembled. As friends and lakeside neighbours, they were mortified by what they had initiated.

My father's ashes were scattered at the ranch in the Caribou country north of Kamloops where he and my step-mother had raised their five daughters.

PART III
Smorgasbord

Part III – Smorgasbord

Effix	233
Fat Injun	237
Kidogo	241
Kincolith	242
Damned Dam	246
Prince Rupert	250
Philosophies	252
The Leather Jacket	259
Padre José Mojica	263
Ralph	270
Toronto the Good	273
Road South	277
Southern Warp	284
Birmin'ham	288
The Operatives	295
Kan-aid-ia	301
Beer Run	305
Peter Pinsway	308
MLK – "We shall win"	322

Effix

I was already into my thirties when I started attending university, and decided to spend a summer in British Columbia's north central region – at what turned out to be a successful effort to raise funds to pay my tuition and board – by working as a labourer on the Peace River dam. A road had been built from Hudson's Hope to the dam-site some thirty kilometres away, so I drove up, and there joined a group of about ten young men – mostly university students – all of us held in check by our lack of union memberships. It was one of those idiotic situations where we could not get work because we were not in the union, but could not get into the union because we did not have work. We were determined to break the deadlock, pester those in the company's office until we could get promises of work, then present this *fait accompli* to the union. It seemed about the only way to force our registration and so get work on the project. We pitched our collective lot together in a makeshift camp in the forest very close to the construction company's labour camp – and held on. Anyone with money would buy food to share with the others. Sometimes we would break into the camp kitchen to steal loaves of bread, or even whole pots of soup or dinners, which we would share between us. After a few weeks one man eventually got himself hired, and was thus in a position to put in a word with his shift boss to help the others.

It was not a comfortable camp. We did the best we could with fires and shelters, but our conditions were basic and rough, and boredom was a continuous problem. With little food, practically no money and the very harsh conditions, people's nerves were easily frayed.

One weekend towards the end of April, when the ice in the river was groaning and on the point of breakup, several of us decided we would cross the river on top of the floes – just for the adventure, and to be able to say we had done it. Fights had started to break out between some of the lads, and having a project of this kind seemed like a good way to relieve tensions.

It was an incredibly stupid and dangerous escapade. There was a bridge, but we decided not to use it. We were warned that at any moment one of us could fall through, that what might appear as firm footing could be otherwise. We went ahead anyway, each man carrying a long plank that, hopefully, he could use to brace himself if he felt the ice giving way under him.

There were nine of us, and we made it across, alright. But when we looked back from the far bank we could see that our footprints in the snow on the river's surface had already shifted dramatically – those in mid-river quite in advance of those we had just made close to the banks. At that point the height of our foolishness dawned on us. There was no question of trying to retrace our steps. Rather sheepishly, we returned to our camp by crossing the bridge. The very next day the ice in the river exploded with reports that sounded like canon fire. Great jagged ice cubes, some the size of a bungalow or a good-sized truck, popped out of the centre of the river as if dynamited, and the floes started heaving and grinding together as they moved and quickly picked up the speed of the current under them.

It was shortly after this idiocy, and before I was taken on by the company, that I had the opportunity to join a riverboat excursion upstream on the Peace above the dam site. It was probably one of the last opportunities anyone was ever to have to see the original riverbanks before the flow was closed off and the level of the water started to rise. We passed a cattle ranch towards the end of the first day – magnificent establishment consisting of a two-storey polished log house, with log barns and work sheds to match. Its owner, an elderly gentleman named Williams, asked us to give him a hand with demolition on our way back downstream, which we were happy to do some four days later. On our return his farm presented itself like a ghost town, a shell, an empty stage, just shadows in place of the activity that had been going on there when we had passed up-stream days before. The cattle had all been trucked out, the main house was empty, and everything had been removed from the barns and sheds. Mr. Williams was there with cans of ignition fuel and we helped him douse every one of the buildings.

Then we stood back with him to watch the whole place go up in flames.

"Thanks, boys! You'd best be off now," Williams said when the place was ablaze. "I've been told the dam is necessary, but for me it's a damned shame. My grandfather built this place. I was born and raised right here. They've given me acreage for the cattle, and a house to live in – all a couple of valleys over. But it's not the same. I'm eighty years old now, so it's not as though I'm in good enough shape to start anew ..."

We left him among the flaming and smoldering ruins of his homestead, puttering about with useless final chores before getting into his truck to drive over to the place an hour distant that had been assigned to him as compensation. The end of a life. We all felt it.

I could have sworn two years later I saw the old fellow, forlorn and bedraggled, standing on a street corner in Victoria, but did not have the heart to stop and make sure it was really him ...

Every day without fail, twice a day – morning and afternoon – we would present ourselves at the dam site's company employment office, bright-eyed, smiling and insistent. The company officers must have been sick of the sight of us, but it worked. By the first week of May we all had jobs. Work meant decent bunks in company accommodation – and meals in the dining hall; but the work itself was shovel and gumboot, hard and dirty. Most of us wound up as "muckers" in the power house or tail races – some four hundred feet under the level of the riverbed.

There were over four thousand men working on the dam – tough northerners on their umpteenth attempt to make a grub steak so they could marry their sweethearts, buy a house, seek some imagined Paradise – or else, like our chief cook, buy a Camaro and then a second one when he had smashed-up the first on the short road up to camp from Hudson's Hope. There seemed no shortage of money, nor of ways to blow it.

One day at lunch I found myself sitting with a small gang of the fellows with whom I had been working the past couple of weeks. I did not know any of them, but we had a rough camaraderie and a banter between us that fitted. I tried not to tell them I was doing this work in order to pay my way through university; for all that each of them was clever in his own way, they were not a schooled bunch, so without my telling them they soon had me figured out. They sought any and every occasion to rib me about it – a cause for great jocularity. I wanted a second helping of the lunch being served that day, so picked up my plate and shoved back my chair. As I turned to go, one of them said:

"Tip your chair up ..."

"What?" I queried. "Why?"

"Tip your chair up – save your place ..."

I must have looked quizzical.

"Yeah!" one of them said to his buddies. "You can sure tell he's never been inside ...!"

That's right, they all agreed. It was obvious I had never been inside, and they laughed uproariously among themselves.

One of them felt it best to explain:

"If you don't turn your chair up, the rules inside say it means you're not coming back, see ... someone else can take your place."

I put on my most innocent and surprised face, addressing my table chums with mock solemnity.

"You mean to tell me you've all been inside?" I asked incredulously. "Inside prison? Inside the pokey? Goodness me, what next!"

They all turned to one another to confirm the uppity-ness of my questioning, my ignorance, my brazen naïveté.

"Yeah!" they agreed. "You can sure tell he's never been inside."

It was a bit risky, but I decided to take the play a notch further:

"What were you in for?" I asked, looking innocently from one to the other of them.

This was gross impudence. It was almost as if I was accusing them all over again … One or two pushed their chairs back in order to get up and deal with me appropriately. A good thumping was in order. Luckily the one who had decided to explain to me the action indicative of all their past indiscretions held up his hands to quell his buddies' rising indignation at such disingenuous ignorance. Luckily, too, was the way in which all of them were evidently beginning to look on me as the nincompoop they suspected I was …

"That's sumpin' you don't arsk," another explained to me with great patience.

But I wasn't quite finished.

"Don't ask? Really I mean no offence," I said sincerely. "But why shouldn't I ask?"

Yet another, conceding that I was such an ass that maybe I really didn't know, decided to give me a clearer explanation.

"It ain't effi-kal," he replied.

Perfect! We all needed to break a bit of ice, and this provided the very best of excuses. We all put on big smiles of understanding. Nodding my head, I carefully tipped my chair forward as I went up for a second helping. Someone picked a chunk of food off their plate and threw it at me.

"Fuckin' jackass!"

Fat Injun

A four-year-old boy went missing. He had been staying with his parents in the married quarters of the camp. His father and two of his fellow workers decided to go hunting one weekend, and took the little fellow with them. Their transport was an open four-wheel-drive vehicle. The youngster was told to stay unattended in the car while the others scouted the thick bush in which they found themselves. When the men returned to the car some minutes later, the boy was gone.

The following day work on the dam was stopped immediately so that four thousand men could form shoulder-to-shoulder search gridlines and comb the dense bush. They kept up the search night and day for four twenty-four hour periods. Friends at one of the Vancouver newspapers told me that never before had there been such a large manhunt in Canada – adding he thought the whole exercise was probably useless. The bush was too thick, he said; the boy could not have survived one night in such a harsh wilderness, let alone four-going-on-five. Bears or coyotes would have finished him off by now – he must be dead.

The United States Air Force was called in from one of their bases in Alaska, and supplied sophisticated heat-seeking equipment. Aerial photographs were radioed from the patrol plane to HQ in Alaska, where they were copied and faxed along with an interpretive report directly to the construction camp's administrative office. We had workable copies on the search site within an hour. They showed tiny white dots wherever there was body temperature greater than the temperature of the ground. By the movement of these dots over a period of time, experts at reading air photographs were able to say what each one was – a bear making its way through a ravine, a caribou on higher ground, fast-moving small packs of coyotes or wolves fleeing from the presence of men on the ground. There was one little white dot that did not move, and was quite close to where the child had gone missing. The ground searchers, who had already combed the area thoroughly, were alerted and they took another look. The boy was found late in the evening of the fourth twenty-four hour period. He was weak and hungry, and sleepy – but he was alive. He later told his father he had been afraid to show himself for fear he might get a licking.

The four thousand workers went back to their jobs on the dam. I was sharing my camp quarters with a former convict, an enormous First Nations fellow, round all around and jolly-faced, who happily answered to the name Fat Injun.

"Surely I can call you something else," I had said to him.

"Nah, fuckit!" said Fat Injun. "My ma used to fuckin' call me Fat fuckin' Injun, and I've never fuckin' known 'nother fuckin' name – so you better call me Fat Injun. That way I'll know who the fuck yer talkin' to …"

"How'd you lose your front teeth?" I asked him when we were sitting in the room we shared. It was a weekend, and we both had time to kill.

"My fuckin' missus knocked 'em out. We got into a fuckin' fight one time, see, and she fuckin' done this t'me. I beat her for it, took a fuckin' knife to her. That's why the fuckin' police put me away last time …"

"Good God!" I said. "Did you kill her?"

"I might-a done, but I didn'. I done fuckin' six years fer that bitch – 'cos I been in before, see. Got a fuckin' rap sheet, an' I was on parole from before…"

I examined this huge man, tried to imagine what he might have been like when he'd been liquored-up, the sort of damage he might have inflicted on his wife. His voice was gentle and matter-of-fact as he explained the simple details to me – how the two of them had been drinking all day and an argument started over who had paid for the bottle from which they had been drinking, and who should pay for the next one. It didn't seem to me he understood what he might have done when he was "mad." Relatives found the two of them passed out on the kitchen floor.

"Six years?" I asked.

"Yeah. Time off for good behaviour …"

Fat Injun, sober, looked bewildered, a bit sad and not in the least dangerous. Drunk it was probably a totally different story. Screaming drunk (a thin line between drunk and screaming drunk) he would certainly have been anyone's nightmare.

"Fat Injun," I told him, "I have to take a drive down to Chetwynd. There's somebody I have to see down there, and then I'll be coming back. You want to go along for the ride?"

"Sure, what the fuck …!"

He meant yes.

He exchanged his hard hat for a toque, one of those people who remained incomplete if without some sort of covering to tamp his shiny bald head. Off we went, Fat Injun in great spirits as we fled the camp on the road to Chetwynd. It was pleasant to get away, and Fat Injun chattered amiably throughout the hour-long drive, finding beauty in all the landscapes surrounding us – craggy mountains, and kilometre after kilometre of dark forest that extended forever beyond his fuckin'orizon. We drove on good surface all the way, no other traffic. Like the covering on his head, the word "fuck" appeared to be a given, a necessity.

We had been driving the length of Moberly Lake's northern shore, and were almost at the eastern end of it where the road turns south again towards our destination, when I told Fat Injun about the friend we were going to visit.

"Who's yer fuckin' friend?" he had asked.

"His name is John Hannen," I told him. "He's a priest."

"A fuckin' priest …?" he exploded. His expression, one point off panic, was a mix of disgust and terror verging on hysteria. His face was alive – the sort of expression I might have expected from Father John Hannen his very self, had I led him to the edge of Chaos through the palace gates of Slaanesh.

"He's just a man," I tried to assure Fat Injun. "A good man. He's a friend of mine. You'll like him …"

It didn't work.

"Yeah – but a fuckin' *priest* …"

"There's nothing supernatural about a priest," I said. "A priest is a man like you or me. He has certain beliefs, that's all …"

"Argh, man! Y'shoulda fuckin' told me before we started out …"

"Look! We haven't arrived yet. If you're so upset by the notion, I could let you out of the car right now, if you like …"

We were in the wilds. There was no end to the hungry and curious bears or cougars that might have taken an interest in an unarmed Fat Injun complaining about a priest he didn't know as he walked along the road by himself.

"Nah! I'll go along with'yer … But a fuckin' priest! Sheesh!"

I pulled up in front of Father John's house.

"You coming in?" I asked Fat Injun.

"Nah! I'll stay here till yer done …"

Father John was expecting me, and gave me a hearty greeting at his front door.

"I brought someone with me, but he doesn't want to come in," I explained.

"But I was hoping you'd stay for tea …" the father said, distressed.

"I will. But Fat Injun, there, says he'd prefer to remain in the car. He has an aversion to priests …"

Father John glanced beyond my shoulder at Fat Injun studying his feet as he remained seated in the car, eyes averted. Moving around me, the priest stepped up to the car window and bent down to talk. He had said no more than a few words when Fat Injun stepped out, a big toothless grin on his fuckin' face. The two men shook hands,

"Good! Now we'll go in and I'll put the kettle on," said the priest crisply, and we all trooped into the house.

It was impossible for me to hear what Father John had said, but suddenly Fat Injun had become all soft butter and smiles – loquacious. It was amazing to hang back and see how he could hold forth on the pleasantries of life outside the pen – the weather, the forest, the river, the dam. He had removed his toque and was all 'Father This' and 'Father That' – conversational in a way I'd not heard before. As we sat in the comfortable chairs in Farther John's living room, the priest worked his charm on Fat Injun, and I listened to each telling stories relevant to life in this remote section of British Columbia. It occurred to me that, different as each man was from the other, they were yet somehow connected by the landscape and the familiarities of this extraordinarily rugged location each knew so well. I was the outsider, up in that region for the summer with no motivation nobler than making a buck so I could move on. Father John and Fat Injun, both of them, were of this land in a way markedly dissimilar one from the other, but more notably from myself or anyone else who might have been flitting by for a month or two.

We drank our tea and I became aware of how Fat Injun seemed quite at home balancing his cup and saucer in one hand and eating a cookie at the same time with the other. Almost dainty, I thought, with his woolen toque laid across one enormous knee. Then Father John got up and went into the kitchen for some more hot water.

"Fat Injun!" I said, mock scolding him. "You've been talking a blue streak since we got here, and you haven't once resorted to saying 'fuck' – not once. What's with you …?"

Fat Injun looked almost hurt.

"I don't fuckin'ave to say fuck if I don'wanna!"

The priest returned from the kitchen, and it was soon my turn to tell a story. Halfway through it I was stammering as I sought a word in English to denote 'nonsense' – but for some obscure reason had decided instead of actually saying 'nonsense' to use the little-known phrase in English, 'horse feathers' – nonsense because feathers don't grow on horses.[5]

I was stumbling in my attempt to find the right expression ...

"... Horse-um ... Horse ...uh ...Horse-horse ..." I was stuttering.

Polite as the vicar himself, tea cup and saucer in hand, Fat Injun leaned forward to assist:

"Shit ..?" he offered, with neither hesitation nor embarrassment.

Thank you, Fat Injun. Thank you very much ...

The direct simplicity of the English language does not require cleansing or embellishment. It is what it is, and it is sufficient. In our citified and totally imagined sophistication, we attempt to polish our language, beautify it and lacquer it with gallons of gobbledygook and prudish smarm ... then ooze it out like toothpaste from a tube so we run as little chance as possible our words might offend anyone by dribbling down their front, or slopping up their boots ...

Horse feathers, indeed!

Kidogo

After a time I moved from the comfort of the construction camp into a camp I pitched for myself in the forest, near the construction site but a couple of kilometres up a track off the main road. I slept under the canvas of a roomy tent, had a cot and a washstand, and made shelves, a table and stools out of sturdy green branches growing nearby.

A chipmunk I named Kidogo befriended me. Tiny, cheeky little fellow, with bushy tail, yellow-brown body, black and white stripes covering his back – from the moment he entered my tent his voice would nitter-natter at me like an outboard motor that conked-out every now and then, causing me to look about to find him and catch up with the full drift of his chatter. Usually food. He would leap to it, wide-eyed and sparky. I would place a cookie where he could jump up and take it or, the little creature's special show-stopper, he

---

[5] The expression is taken from the title of the 1932 Marx Brothers film, *Horse Feathers*.

would claw his way up my trousers and shirt front or spring onto me from my table top to take a cookie or a cracker from between my teeth. I kept my bread in a special wire basket I hung from a tree branch – but one day returning late from work, I found slices of white bread suspended from the branches of every tree around my tent. The door to the basket was wide open and Kidogo was angrily scolding me from a tree branch above my tent. When he wasn't chasing food, he would sometimes curl up and sleep in the woolly lining of my coat, or occasionally in its pocket.

I was promoted from mucker to scaler – a job that required climbing up the interior rock walls of the dam's under-river power house and, with a long metal pole, chiseling out any loose rock. This had to be done before the walls and ceiling of the cavern were *gunnited* with about six feet of reinforced concrete. The job paid well, but it un-nerved me. I am not fond of heights, nor do I like falling rock. By mid-September I reckoned I had earned enough – by then sufficient to see me through a year of university. I had to say goodbye to my wild little friend, but the evenings had become noticeably cooler and he was coming round less often. In the end I left Kidogo a loaf of bread, some nuts and the rest of my granola, and headed south.

In my first year I took courses in anthropology and classical history; from my second year on I continued with classical history, but dropped anthropology in favour of courses in fine arts, and art and architectural history. These studies seemed better to complement the ones I had completed in architectural history some years before in Britain. Although family and close advisors informed me I was wasting time and money, all of this study served me well a while later – another reason, I reckoned, for trusting one's gut over listening to the advice of others, no matter how well-intentioned the interference.

Kincolith

I was to head north once again within a year or two – as before, about halfway up the province towards its northern border with Yukon, so not actually all that far north. Father John Hannen had by now moved west across the province, and had taken up his new duties at the Anglican church in Kincolith, a First Nations village at the mouth of the Nass River, within

Canada but right off the tip of the Alaska Panhandle. He had written to say the village school required a substitute teacher for a couple of months, and that I could be a candidate for the job if I would get up there. It suited me very well. Right at that time I was sorely in need of replenishing my bank coffers, and reckoned I should take a full year to do it, so such a job – any job – up in that region of the province (the assemble-your-grub-steak region) could prove very useful. While itself not paying particularly well, substitute work in the village school could be a worthwhile experience, and it would provide me a good reason to head north again.

Coastal British Columbia is well served by all kinds of boats, large and small, so I started off by hitch-hiking to the north end of Vancouver Island to see if I could catch some sort of transport out of Port Hardy. Sure enough, there was a fishing boat headed up through the coastal islands all the way to Prince Rupert – a congenial boat owner estimating that with an early start it would be a two-day run, perhaps three – "depending how much beer you pack along with you." Three twelve-packs of beer was my fare, so I brought four – the additional paying for my food en route. Pretty quickly we found ourselves dealing with rough seas as we crossed from Queen Charlotte Strait out into the open waters of Smith Sound, so we put in at Goose Bay. That way the boat's cook-cum-first mate could find his footing in the galley and serve us up a superlative steak'n'mushroom dinner. We set out again in the evening, calm waters and good visibility once we were within the shelter of the Fitz Hugh Channel, and so we chugged along until late into the night, throwing out our anchor at Bella Bella. The whole of the next day we followed Tolmie Channel to Graham Reach, which in turn led us into the Grenville Channel – and so to Prince Rupert. For most of the trip we were able to travel what is known as the "Inside Passage," a course that led through a maze of waterways that ran between coastal islands and the B.C. mainland, thus avoiding the notorious winds and waves of Hecate Strait and the areas open to the North Pacific. It is a trip made today by cruise ships charging, when ticket and additional expenses are totted up, several thousands of dollars. Cost to me: four dozen bottles of beer.

As yet I had not reached my final destination, but the bulk of my travel so far had been by fishing boat so I saw no reason for not continuing in the same fashion. I holed-up a few days in Prince Rupert, knowing that I would be coming back this way in a month or two looking for work, and in this brief timespan made what I thought might be several useful contacts. Then I set about looking for another fishing boat operator to take me up the coast to Kincolith – which is how I met Charlie.

Charlie was a member of the Nisga'a First Nations, and came from Kincolith (since renamed Gingolx). He, his brother, and a nephew would be heading back to the village in a couple of days, and sure I could go with them. Bring a bottle of rum.

To complete this leg of the journey, up Chatham Sound, did mean exposing the boat to the northern end of Hecate Strait where its waters merge with those of Dixon Entrance. The map shows Dundas Island might have provided a bit of shelter, but in truth the waters were open, the wind came in from the southwest, and there was nothing to hide behind when the weather picked up. Which it did. Charlie braced himself behind his wheel, and I was able to wedge myself into a tight space next to a ladder. I heard the captain's brother and his son working down in the engine compartment, but saw virtually nothing of them the entire trip.

"Whar's yer rum?"

"Got it right here," I offered.

He took it, deftly uncapped it and helped himself to a mammoth gulp before handing the bottle back to me.

"Drink up! Might as well. It's gonna be a long'un."

By now we were well clear of Prince Rupert and the storm had picked up in ferocity. The little boat – it was a forty-five foot seiner – pitched about like a piece of driftwood.

"Any chance of going back?" I asked.

"Nah!" said Charlie curtly. "Can't bring 'er broadside to the waves. Gotta keep going. Hang on! Either we make 'er, or we go down – hee!-hee-hee!"

Nine hours and three bottles of rum later, giggling like truant schoolboys, the four of us crawled out onto the dock at Kincolith. Father John Hannen was there in his priestly garb, throwing holy water onto the waves at the mouth of the Nass River and saying prayers of deliverance. He had heard our alarmed voices on the ship-to-shore radio, and sprang immediately into priestly action.

There are them wot says Yea, and them wot says Nay. I could barely stand up or see straight, but on that occasion I was happy to cast my vote with the Yeas.

Teaching First Nations third-graders was not my forte. I think I made a valiant effort, but cannot make the legitimate claim that I actually enjoyed them; they were tolerable when they refrained from peeing in their pants or chattering among themselves in Nisga'a. I always suspected it was about me. Instead of putting up a hand and asking, "Please, sir, may I go to the toilet," some little ruffian in the front row would look me straight in the eye, put up his hand, giggle and say: "Hey, white man, I just peed ..." And I would feel obliged to suggest he go immediately to the washroom and clean himself up. There would be general laughter throughout the classroom when my eyes, streaming tears, would burn closed at the stench of urine. Peeing their pants was a cause of great hilarity, so I think they all did it.

The federal government in Ottawa would provide teaching materials for First Nations classrooms, and among these was a book, a reader distributed throughout the class, containing the story of Dick and Jane as they made their way to school with their little dog, Spot. The story told how they would stop at the curbside when the light turned red, wait for it to change to green, then – looking first to the left, then to the right – would step out and cross the road, walking. "Don't run!"

The story baffled them. The bank of little faces in front of me was a study in still life. What the heck was this guy reading us? White man stuff ...

Roads were tracks in Kincolith, and they were not paved. Curbs and traffic lights didn't exist. There were no roads into this place in those days, so no one could get here by car. Thus no cars.

A hand crept up at the back of the class:

"Hey, white man – you call a little dog Spot?"

"Well, yes," I replied. "It's one name that's common for a little dog ..."

"But Spot? A Spot is dirty! I wouldn't call my dog Spot ..."

"Oh?" I hesitated. "What do you call your dog?"

The boy puffed out his chest manfully.

"I call my dog Sigadumnak!"

"And what is the meaning of Sigadumnak?"

"Sigadumnak is the god of our river," replied the boy.

Then I realized we had been discussing an animal. Every kid in the class was descended from an animal. I was talking to Running Bear. Behind him was Frog. Next to him was Eagle Feather, and behind him were Killer Whale, Fox, Raven and Swift Deer ...

I felt small, thick, un-savvy.

To escape the stench of urine, I would take the class outside into the surrounding forest to play cowboy and Indians – but it was clear who was the cowboy. Mistake. The little rascals had disappeared without even the snap of a twig ...

Silence.

"Okay, class – back we go. Let's go. Class ...! Class ...!"

More silence.

Surely this was the unique teacher in school districts far and wide who had ever managed to lose an entire class within the time it takes to run from classroom to forest edge – a twenty-second sprint at most.

I traipsed back to the school house alone. When I reported the disaster to one of the parents, I was met by laughter so raucous I decided not to mention the event to anyone else, but to wait instead to see who would appear the next day.

They were all there, stone-faced as if nothing had happened.

"Alright, you guys. Get out your readers. We'll start with Spot the dog..."

Groans.

I fear I taught nothing of worth to these children. For me it was an experience in learning, not in teaching. I felt a curiosity concerning the region and the people, but found no joy in what I was supposed to be doing. Being teacher at the school for such a brief span of time counted for little, I thought, and if I was left feeling my efforts were insignificant then the whole exercise was unacceptable. I was gone from that school the instant a replacement was found.

Damned Dam

One incident did grab and hold my attention: Kincolith had a bridge, a log structure that was washed out by heavy rains and flooding during the months when I was substituting at the school. The band council had made application to the federally-financed Agricultural and Regional Development Association, and a new steel bridge had been promised. But the story behind this story turned out to be the most interesting, as is so often the case.

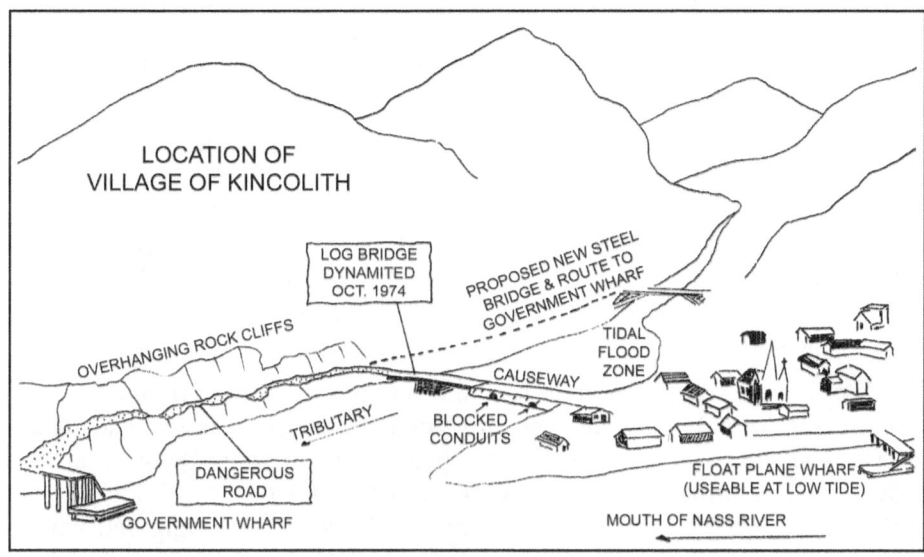

Diagram of the Kincolith bridge debacle

Gingolx as it is known today is connected to the rest of the province by a long and winding road leading to Terrace, but at the time of this incident it was not. It was an isolated community at the mouth of the roiling Nass River, its access to the outside world either by boat or by float plane always "weather permitting." It had been a fishing village for over one hundred years, its essential supplies brought in each week by a coastal freighter. Because of tidal problems, the ship had to be unloaded at a government wharf about one mile west of the village.

Inadequate and unsafe, the wharf should have been replaced long before I happened along; in fact, the band council and the government had been negotiating for a matter of years, with the government continually promising to commence work, and even making positive noises the previous summer. But to date it had failed to live up to its word.

Between the village and the rickety wharf was a fast-flowing stream – tributary to the Nass, entering the larger stream behind the village and in such a way the village itself was situated on the low-lying finger of land that had formed between the two waterways.

To reach the government wharf in prior years, the villagers had been obliged to cross the smaller stream by skiff, and so to ferry their supplies across into the village each week. Normally there had been no problem, but in bad weather – and in that region of British Columbia there is plenty of bad weather – this short voyage had proven dangerous. Not a few lives had been lost over the years.

Not unnaturally the band leaders had felt the easiest way to reach the wharf would be to build a bridge and blast out a roadway. After repeated requests, the matter had become a political issue during one of the previous provincial elections. No politician wanted to be caught denying such a reasonable request – but it is also clear they wanted to devote as little money as possible to the project. It was not the sort of issue that would garner large numbers of votes.

The riding's right wing contender was anxious to collect Nisga'a votes so as to unseat the left wing's incumbent member, so gave his promise to supply both bridge and road. The election was held in the previous October, and the provincial Department of Highways moved to construct the bridge in the spring preceding my own visit – total cost: $129,000. Right wing, left wing – it was hardly relevant; it was still a time in the province's history when both wings were willing and able – and frequently – to shaft First Nations peoples.

The Nisga'a band council was furious. There had been no substantial talk between government and the band about the type of bridge required, or its location.

"Never were there any consultations with us about the type of bridge, or where it should be placed," said band Chief Nathan Barton. "Not once did department representatives come to us and ask our advice. On the contrary, we went to them. We told them not to place the bridge where they seemed intent on putting it, for we knew if they did so, it would certainly be washed away… We told them – they didn't want to listen."

Insensitive government bureaucracy, the Department of Highways chose not to listen, and went ahead with their own plans. Its representatives built a bridge the Nisga'a felt was both inadequate and unsafe. The government team blasted out a road to the wharf – but never graded it properly, nor did they seal its upper walls against the fall of loose rock and dangerous overhangs. However, an election promise had been made and, as with so many promises of the kind now that it was time to make good on it, no one really wanted to get too involved. Thinking on the matter seems to have been: let's keep the promise, but strictly low-budget, and so get this matter out of the way as quietly as possible.

Sure enough, as the Nisga'a had predicted, the bridge did start to wash out. Shortly after it had been completed, a total of $18,000 was required for its repair – and the Department of Highways signed over $5,000 as its contribution towards this sum – the balance being made up by other federal agencies through the band itself. With expenditures now reaching $147,000, no one wanted to take the rap for what finally happened.

It would have been better, for sure, had the bridge been washed away. As it was, it simply became unsafe and un-useable. River silt, boulders, logs and uprooted trees jammed in behind the structure and the causeway leading onto it in such fashion that tidal waters and storm-driven river flow was held behind a substantial but unstable quasi-dam. It was the pressure of this back-up behind both causeway and dam that threatened to flush the entire village of Gingolx out to sea.

This time the council was not about to seek anyone else's advice. They simply called for an explosives expert to be flown in from Prince Rupert – and the bridge debris was dynamited clear of the main channel. It saved the village from certain disaster.

Rock falls and water flow had made the road to the wharf impassable to any traffic, and even walking on it had become hazardous.

When I talked to him in Prince Rupert, the district Department of Highways manager said the whole thing had been "regrettable," but that really it was not his department's responsibility. A department spokesman in Victoria, contacted by telephone, termed the bridge and its road had been a "gratuitous" offering to the village – a gift – and he was quick to claim it was not a "public" road, anyway!

Some gift – for a non-public!

Nevertheless, the entire construction of the project had been undertaken by the department, and it was the Prince Rupert manager's crew that had overseen the work from start to finish. In fact, this same manager had visited the site several times during construction.

Was the bridge especially designed for its intended purpose?

Well, not exactly, was the manager's response. It was a standard log stringer type of bridge, built on log cribs filled with rocks – two spans of approximately seventy feet each. Material for the construction consisted of "native" beach-combed logs. The bridge was of such a standard design, in fact, that it might as easily have been ordered from a catalogue. The two seventy-foot spans were sufficient to clear the stream, but not the tidal flood zone. The solution to this problem, the department appears to have reasoned, was to build a causeway across the flood zone in order to make the bridge fit. In addition to the debris from the collapsed bridge, however, along with the logs and trees that during the rains had washed downstream behind its wreckage, the causeway itself acted as a dam that trapped a dangerous great lake of water behind the village. Conduits leading under it were not big enough to take all the runoff, and were quickly choked so that the causeway itself became a major contributor to the threat of flood.

"Was the project a complete waste of money?" I asked Chief Barton.

Yes, he replied, adding he could see the Nisga'a were on the short end of a political stick. More, he felt the lack of consultation should be construed as a gross insult to the band and its council. It was nothing new, he told me. His people are habitually treated this way.

And while they appear to forgive such treatment surprisingly easily, they nonetheless pushed ahead with demands for a new bridge – this time one of steel, to be properly surveyed and designed for the space it would occupy, and where the Nisga'a council knew it should have been built in the first place.

But now, instead of costing the $147,000 the project had consumed up to the time of the washout, the new bridge and re-graded roadway to the wharf would cost $300,000, and then some.

Prince Rupert

The teaching situation was completely different a few weeks later when I began substituting for the Grade 12 history class at Prince Rupert's high school. The regular teacher had gone away for a couple of weeks and had left an assignment for his class: to study their text books concerning the Second World War. That was all the class had to do, and all I was required to do was to babysit. It was as dull for me as it was for the students. They lolled in their desks, rested their heads on their arms, or tried to talk to one another without me seeing them.

Walking up and down between the rows of desks on the first day, I glanced over the shoulder of one student to see the title of the chapter she was reading – "The Second World War." I excused myself, and picked up her book. The chapter prior to the one all of the class was required to read in that two-week period was entitled "The Period Before the War;" the chapter that followed was "The Period After the War" – a total, if memory serves, of eighteen pages – text plus liberal quantities of photographs – devoted to the Second World War.

"Is this the extent of your assignment?"

It was, and I was incredulous.

"Nothing else?"

A few film clips.

"Alright!" I said, as threateningly as I could. "I have an additional assignment for you – all of you, listen in. I want you to put your noses into that book and have this chapter completely read before the end of class today... Tomorrow we talk. Jump to it!"

The following day, meeting with the same group, I sat in front of them and quizzed them on their understanding of the text. They had a fair grasp of it, but not a lot beyond what had been written, mashed up with what they had seen of any number of Hollywood blockbusters. So I talked and I talked – and they listened, story after story after story. I supplemented my storytelling with pictures and maps and diagrams, I made sketches on the blackboard, presented them with stories pulled from my own experience, stories I had read and film documentaries I had seen, stories I had been told by a host of family and friends. For two weeks I cobbled together an amalgam of all they had read up to this point, lacing it with details of more recent events they would have known or heard about – using a "cause-and-effect" pattern that jogged a few "ah-ha's" from them as they noted some close experience garnered from the daily news, or the recollections of some story they had heard. Some of them told of tales they had heard from their parents, their aunts and uncles and grandparents.

The net result was a class that sat up and paid attention for the duration of the lessons we had together. A few students approached me after our time was up. Others would meet with me in the school library or canteen. I have never thought of myself as a particularly good teacher – but I am quite sure that a good teacher (at least of history!) must also be a good storyteller.

All aspects of history fascinate me, not always because of Burke's adage ("Those who don't know history are doomed to repeat it.") – but because no matter how often it appears to be repeated, it is unique. There is simply nothing, no occurrence, no story, more fascinating or stranger.

And there are few substitutes for a good story well-told.

Philosophies

Ming Lee was the cook aboard the supply ship that plied up and down the British Columbia coast, putting in at Prince Rupert every other week or so and allowing him a short break from his shipboard duties. We became friends over a period of several months, and I learned that in addition to being the cook, he also had his doctorate in philosophy from Beijing University, and was more than passingly acquainted with the classical literature of ancient China. Ming liked drinking beer, so when he was free we would often meet up in one of the town's beer parlours.

He found me particularly pensive one day, down and depressed. I felt I had been in Prince Rupert long enough and wanted to be on my way. Ming Lee asked me if I was familiar with the I Ching – the Chinese book of Changes. It was the oldest known example of Chinese literature, versions of it dating back to hundreds of years before Christ.

Yes, I told him, I had heard of it, but was not at all familiar with it.

"Well, let us consult it. It is entirely possible we might find in it the answer to your current disaffections ..."

He pushed three old Chinese coins into my hand. I looked at them uncomprehendingly – three flimsy-looking round coins with square holes cut in their centres, and stamped on both faces with Chinese characters. I could not guess at their age, but their tarnish had turned to a patina as though the seasons knew what to do about grime and how to create and preserve them.

"Hold these in your hand for a moment, and concentrate on the matter that gives rise to your concerns right now. Think of a short phrase that describes your problem – and then write down on this sheet of paper the one word that is the key to that phrase."

He pushed a blank piece of paper and a pen across the table.

"Don't show it to me. I don't need to see it, but writing the word will help you focus. Take your time …"

I was still clutching the coins he had given me, holding them in the same hand with which I took up the pen and thought about the phrase describing my state of mind: will I have funds enough to do the travelling I want? Then I wrote the single word "travel" onto the paper.

Then Ming Lee told me to shake the coins like dice and throw them onto the table. Examining them carefully, as if he was reading from inscriptions on the surfaces of them, he turned over the sheet of paper and started writing. What he wrote down were hexagrams, each a bank of six lines comprised of long and short dashes. He explained the long dash represented Yin, the short Yang. As I cast the coins over and over again, he would study them and then form a corresponding hexagram on the page. At the same time he would consult a book he had pulled from his satchel – the I Ching. It was much-used and clearly much-revered. Once a hexagram had been formed, he would turn to the book, thumbing through it carefully in order to select some special Chinese character. This he would write into my own notebook, then nod at me to throw the coins again.

"Each hexagram – there are sixty-four of them, and they work in an infinite number of combinations – will inform me what part of the I Ching to go to in order to call up the correct Chinese character," he explained.

"As I write each character into your book, a poem is being created, and this poem will provide a response to the question in your mind that caused you to write the word you have put on the other side of this sheet. You'll see…"

He worked like a squirrel feverishly storing nuts – from reading the coins I was throwing, to jotting down the correct hexagram, then to thumbing through the I Ching to find the precise Chinese character called for. All the time he was doing this I was trying to concentrate on the word I had written on the paper – "travel."

To undertake the travel I had in mind, I would need a considerable sum of money and, in order to obtain it, I was mulling a proposal I had received from a group of people in the town I had met within the past few weeks – to buy and resell a huge quantity of hashish. My cohorts had already set the whole operation in motion; a sure thing, I was told. A pushover. They assured me they had a vital role for me to play in the deal, and wanted me to commit to joining them. The money for my part in the operation was tempting – but I was very much aware of what looked like a hair-brained proposal, the obvious illegality of it, and of the consequences if the whole thing went sideways. The wide-eyed enthusiasm of my acquaintances was anything but convincing, but really I was not so afraid of these as I was of being obliged to make a commitment of trust to people of whom I knew nothing at all. On top of this, I had also heard stories that Prince Rupert was a centre of training for officers in the narcotics squad of the Royal Canadian Mounted Police.

I have often been open to adventures over which I have little or not even a modicum of control, but hopefully I also tend to draw the line at abject stupidity. There can be no denying I had initially allowed myself to be led on by the thrilling bubble of instant riches, yet somehow I knew I was now persisting beyond the point at which the idiocy of the scheme was actually measureable. It was a matter of curiosity to know where such clandestine efforts might lead.

My friend was concluding the poem – first in its Chinese form, and then translated into nine lines of cryptic English. In essence it read:

Go on your travels, if y'wishes, but ditch the idea of hasty riches ...!

On quite another occasion Ming Lee listened carefully, inscrutable smile dancing in the depths of his penetrating eyes, as I told him about an experience I had had some months earlier with a group of young Nisga'a men I had met in the city. They had invited me to accompany them for lunch at a house some of them had rented at the extreme eastern end of the town where it overlooked the waters of Tuck Inlet. From a balcony hanging almost above the fjord one could see where the eastern flank of Kaien Island cut away towards the south, and the bridge of the Yellowhead Highway that connected the island to the mainland. To the northeast was the seemingly unending length of the inlet where it disappeared into the forests of British Columbia's interior.

It was a congenial group. We drank a few beers, swapped a few yarns, and then one of the men offered me a small handful of dried-up psilocybin mushrooms.

"Three or four – try them ... Should be enough to lift you off ..."

I popped them into my mouth, imagining such a small quantity of them might give me no more than a pleasant buzz. They tasted leathery and bitter, so I worked up a saliva and swallowed them whole – then stepped out onto the balcony with a couple of the men.

Ming Lee was nodding his head.

"Interesting experience, no?"

It certainly was! There was no effect for maybe fifteen or twenty minutes, and when one of my companions pointed up the inlet I was more than able to follow his direction with perfect clarity.

"See that eagle flying towards us ...?" he queried.

I could not take my eyes off it.

Perfect clarity, indeed – the enormous bird was yet a long way away, but the sun caught its movements and flashed them to me in a golden Morse. I could see its beating wings, and the power of its strokes caused my own shoulders to flex. I could see how its movements through the rushing air ruffled the tips of its wings and the fluffy feathers about its neck. My vision astonished me, but still I felt my judgement of reality in no way compromised. Alert, I was cognizant of all that was happening and quite able to assign the keenness of my vision and awareness to the drug within the mushrooms I had consumed. They in no way hampered me; on the contrary they immensely stimulated me, giving me a feeling of empowerment. There was a tightness in my belly and my legs had become taut like springs, my thighs hardened as if cramped – but it was with the sureness of my capacity for action, not the painful crimping of chains.

The eagle passed right in front of the balcony, and I could see every feather on its body. Drawing level, it cocked its head and seemed to look straight at me.

At this point I felt myself lift off and join in the flight. I was not riding on the bird's back. I *was* the bird.

Prince Rupert is a town that stretches itself along the northern coast of Kaien Island, from the position where we were standing on the balcony, all the way to the docks at the island's extreme northwestern tip. Along the length of this narrow urban strip the streets, houses and structures follow the contour of the fjord. From my lofty position, flying parallel with the line made by land and water, the entire town as I had come to know it was laid out below my left wingtip. In the streets I could see some of the people I had come to know.

Don Lyons, one of my roommates, was about to enter the town's principal supermarket, and there were others whose faces were familiar to me: the projectionist from the local movie theatre, one of the students I had seen in the corridors of the high school, a group of First Nations men I had noted earlier milling about on the wharf next to a moored seiner. I saw the house in which I lived, and with a few strokes of my wings passed over the fish factory where I had been working at packing herring roe for export to Japan. I left the town behind me and flew quickly over open waters, northwest towards Metlakatla, the First Nations village on a bulging isthmus of the mainland to the north of Digby Island.

There is a dock at Metlakatla, and implanted into the soil at the head of it there were – maybe still are – three totem poles, one of which had settled into a noticeable list towards its companions. All three poles had long since lost their original colouring, their surfaces now bare and cracked. I chose one that was upright and perched on top of it, Metlakatla stretched below my talons.

I had never been to Metlakatla. I knew nothing about it beyond hearing the name, yet now I was looking at it – a First Nations waterfront settlement of simple houses and unpaved roads set against a backdrop of dark forest, green mountains and a brooding sea. I am told there has been considerable modernization of the place, that there are now one or two paved roads – but at the time of this visit the roads were unpaved, most of the houses appearing unpainted as though they had been deftly constructed out of shoreline driftwood and found materials.

An elderly lady stepped out from the doorway of the house closest to my perch. She was chunky of build, and tended to waddle when she walked, her long dress reaching almost to the ground. Her hair hung in long unkempt strands of silver-white. For a moment she stood in front of the door of her house, looking out over the inlet. Then she glanced up, her eyes squinting against the light, and she seemed not at all surprised to find me on the pole above her head. She studied me for a few long moments, almost as if she knew me and expected me to be there. Then she flicked a shawl across her shoulder and turned back into the darkness of her house.

"Greetings, eagle ..." she said, before closing the door, as though this was what she habitually offered up at this time of the day.

I perched a little longer, but soon spread my wings and made my way northwards towards the islands and mountains of southernmost Alaska – and I recall nothing more of my persona as eagle.

In time I opened my eyes from what must have been a deep slumber, perhaps even coma. It was dark outside, and I was sitting on a sofa in the living room of the Nisga'a household I had earlier come to visit.

"You done pretty good!"

My Nisga'a friends surrounded me, a small and casual group – one on a stool quite close to my head, the others seated on chairs at the table that stood by the now closed balcony door. All of them were smiling, the man next to me rocking back and forth as he waited for me to acknowledge him.

"You bin on a journey. We seen it," was all he said, and the others nodded their heads knowingly.

So did Ming Lee.

"You were with good people, and it is most necessary in instances like the one you describe. Had they not been with you, watching over you, it might have been an unpleasant thing. Man may live alone and unto himself, but to move forward with conviction – even when his noble act appears solitary – he requires the support of others. The Nisga'a were your friends. They were your team."

Three weeks after the event I describe, Ming Lee and I had the opportunity to travel together by boat to Metlakatla for the first time. As we pulled up to the dock, I could see the three totems – one of them distinctly listing towards the others. We walked together to the head of the dock and, with shivers running through me like an electric current, there was the house that belonged to the elderly First Nations woman I had seen from the top of the totem. I knew it because I had seen it before, and knew the woman herself would come to her door. She was closer now, and she examined the two of us – her head rolled back and her eyes combing us up and down through slits that resembled the dry wood of her house.

She adjusted her shawl as she turned to re-enter the darkness of her home, and she spoke to the two of us seeming to pronounce her words clearly – but not in a language I knew.

Ming Lee whispered in my ear as she disappeared.

"Did you understand …? Did she speak in English …?"

"I think I understood what she was saying," I told him, "but it wasn't English, nor was it any other language I know …"

It was possible to comprehend the fullness of this experience by acknowledging the depth of the peoples who surrounded me at the time, the character of their honesty.

Coastal peoples with ancient traditions and knowledge, they were bound in their very souls to the mysteries of the life and lands and waters of their region. I desperately wanted to know it, to be included and accepted – and I was … And yet it was beyond my ken. It was not the first time I had been touched by a mystery beyond my culture, but I knew that I had been taken on trust by these young First Nations people, and that it was their trust that permitted me to enter their circle as an outsider. I would never have been accepted had I attempted to crash the party. It was grace that greeted my coming, quiet, sincere and open. I was pulled into this select group, and quietly welcomed at its table.

The coastal First Nations revere their nature. The white man who came so recently into this land has often marvelled at his encounters with the stories told by his hosts – how there has been a sharing of flora and fauna that has been the way of the world since the beginning of their time. From their lips one will hear countless stories of birds and beasts, stories that can best be told by a people intimate with a life intricately-shared between man and his surrounding nature. I have been obliged to consider that my experience as an eagle was not so wild or unknown to people who could relate how the killer whale feeds in the depths of the waters, how the wolf prepares his winter lair, or how the bear knows exactly where to seek the best berries in spring.

Happily, Ming Lee was also a significant member of my team – witness to both the story and its conclusion.

The Leather Jacket

My mother was living in Spain and, on a trip there to visit with her, she presented me with a magnificent gift – a soft leather jacket made by the famous Spanish house of Cortafiel. It was a thoughtful and expensive gesture and, although I could not have known it at the time, it was the last gift she ever bought for me. I was extremely pleased with it, and found occasion to wear it a lot.

Returning with it to Canada, I moved into a house beside a lake in a forested area to the north of Victoria on Vancouver Island, and during that period befriended a young First Nations man by the name of Gary Lightman from the Brentwood band.

Lightman came to the house one afternoon in my absence. Hans, my housemate, did not know the man but figured if he was the friend he claimed to be there would be no harm in letting him come inside to wait for me. Hans talked to him for a while, then excused himself and went outside to chop firewood.

"I heard him go into your room, and thought it a bit strange, but I also thought it would be alright; he might have had some kind of arrangement with you. He was confident, had a pleasant approach. The guy said he was your friend, even told me his name – Gary Lightman. I wrote it down …"

I ran upstairs to my bedroom. The fellow had gone through all of my belongings and the place was in turmoil. I did a quick inventory; the first and most obvious thing I noted was the absence of my precious leather jacket. A home-knit sweater, a pair of good boots and another pair of shoes were also missing. A subsequent survey revealed the additional absence of clothing – shirts and trousers, mostly – and a duffle bag, which he probably used to cart away his booty. On my bed, as if in fair trade, were two monotone and (to my thinking) inferior prints of First Nations faces, the coiffures of which were decorated with feathers. I recognized the work of Gary Lightman, for it was our beer parlour conversation about art that had brought the two of us together in the first place – and when Lightman had learned where I lived. But this arrangement was hardly a fair trade, I reckoned.

The thief was gone, and he had not left by the front door, otherwise Hans would have seen him. In exiting by the back door, often left ajar, he would have been closer to the concealment of the forest that surrounded the house.

With not the least hesitation I drove directly to the police station to report the incident. About as rapidly, the police sent a radio despatch to the police at

Brentwood. That same night I was informed by the police they had been unable to make contact with Lightman; they said he would be interviewed as soon as he could be found – but by that time I was having second thoughts. I revisited the police station and asked them to drop the matter. No, they replied, they would not do that. I had reported a theft, and they would investigate a theft. If they discovered a theft had not been committed, then they would investigate me for making false accusations and wasting precious police time.

For some idiotic reason I thought I could help matters by driving up to Brentwood myself and trying to find the culprit. His house was not hard to locate, but when I got there and tried to explain my business to the young man's mother I was given short shrift.

"The police have been here once, looking for him, so we can expect them to come around again, eh?"

"Maybe not, if I could speak to your son. Can you get a message through to him for me, tell him I'd like to speak to him …"

"He's not here, and in any case I don't think he will want to speak to you."

At that point it seemed best to let the matter drop. Lightman's mother was not about to assist in any way. But several days later, at the beer parlour where he and I had first met, I ran into another man who knew him.

"Do you know where I could find him?" I asked.

"He went over to Vancouver. When he got back, the police went calling and beat the hell outta him. If it was you who put them onto him, you'd best stay well clear," he cautioned.

Yet another day or two passed, and the police came to the house to inform me that Lightman did not appear to have my gear. He had been to Vancouver, they told me, and had he had my things in his possession at the time he would probably have sold them for "beer money." I said nothing to the police about their visit to his house, and that I already knew they had beaten him. I decided it was best to accept my loss and let the matter drop. I had some stern words for Hans about letting the fellow into the house in the first place. Poor Hans was mortified; he had been completely taken in by Lightman, and readily admitted his gullibility in being so easily outwitted by a scoundrel. In the end it was a lesson for the two of us.

But in fact I had not quite let the matter drop. Some weeks later I found myself driving through Brentwood, and I passed right by Lightman's house. I wanted to say something about how I now felt sorry about the whole thing, that I wished I had not gone to the police and thus been responsible for them going to his house and beating him, and that I would much prefer to forget the whole unfortunate affair.

What was unfortunate was that again Lightman was not at home, and I again had to deal with his mother.

She was stone-cold. She glowered at me with hatful eyes as I spluttered my so well-reasoned explanations, apologies and lame excuses. Finally she turned her back and closed her door in my face.

I left and never saw Lightman again. I was not the thief, but for some reason I was the one feeling guilty.

Two years passed. I left Canada and went to Europe, remaining there a further two years before returning by ship, then another year passed while I went to work in northern British Columbia. In all there had been an interval of close to five years since this most unpleasant robbery.

But then one day I was walking on lower Douglas Street in Victoria, passing the Strathcona Hotel, when a young man swung out of Big Bad John's bar and started walking up the street in front of me. He was wearing my leather jacket. I caught up to him.

"Excuse me!" I said, and he turned to me affably. I had never seen him before. He was not Gary Lightman.

"You are wearing my jacket," I told him. "Could you tell me where you got it?"

Oh, he had had it for years, he said. He had bought it from a second-hand store on Robson Street in Vancouver …

"How can you prove it's yours?" he laughed. My claim was ridiculous.

I told him about the Cortafiel label under the collar, so he removed the jacket and, sure enough, there it was.

"I'd never really noticed that. Even so, it doesn't prove it's yours," he said.

By now we both knew we were on the fringe of an extraordinary coincidence, and he was every bit as curious as I was.

"Well, look on the inside of the left jacket pocket," I told him. "You will find there a spare button matching the others on the front of the jacket. That button had initially come in a tiny plastic bag inside the side pocket, but I was afraid to lose it – so I sewed it in there with red thread."

We checked – and sure enough there was the button sewn in place by red thread.

The poor fellow's face was a study in bemusement. He shook his head and laughed, so I told him more – how the jacket had been a precious gift from my mother, and that it had been stolen from my home five years earlier.

"I recognized it right away," I told him.

"So, I'm in possession of stolen property!"

"Yes!" I said.

He was a most reasonable fellow, and I liked him right away. He readily accepted the jacket had been a valued gift from my mother, and that it would have had sentimental value to me. Both of us understood he had bought it in good faith, paying what he thought was a fair price for it. Without any argument he agreed to return it to me. But then he reasoned with me:

"Look, it's a chilly day and if I give it to you right now I'll be feeling the need for it. Would you mind me keeping it for the rest of the day? We could meet – say, right here at the hotel? – tomorrow. I would be more than happy to return it to you then ..."

We agreed on a time ...

The next day I kept the appointment – and so did the fellow who had been wearing my coat. I watched him park his truck and get out, but then he walked up to me, sheepish and most apologetic – and without the jacket.

"Not a word of a lie, my friend: I purposely put your jacket on the front seat of the truck cab last evening ... This morning my little boy jumped in, and upset a can of burned motor oil – all over the jacket. I would have brought it to you, but really you would not want to see it now. It has to be thrown out. It's absolutely unwearable now – by either of us. I'm so sorry ..."

There was nothing I could say. I was sure he was telling me the truth; why would he have bothered to come out today to spin me a story like that? He might have been a scoundrel, but I don't think so. I reasoned that he had had possession of the jacket and worn it far longer than I had. It was more his than mine, now, anyway. I prefer to imagine Karma had a hand in this strange circumstance – that it brought the two of us together at this point in order to confound us with the knowledge that the jacket itself – the Thing that both of us wanted – was of no great importance. It makes a better story.

The two of us laughed, a little bitterly maybe. Then we shook hands, parted and went our separate ways as if the incident had never happened.

J. J. Hespeler-Boultbee

Padre José Mojica

Sometimes the very best of stories don't happen as a result of any particular journalistic winkling, but instead evolve and over time poke themselves above the run-of-the-mill.

This was to be the case one Sunday morning as I wandered through a market area of San Miguel de Allende, the heritage XVI/XVII century town in the mountains northwest of Mexico City noted as one of the principal arts centres in the country. The place boasts scores of churches. As I was passing one of the smaller ones, a delightful old stone structure, I noticed a sign on a board outside written in English: Sunday Mass & Homily to be in English. It was almost the appointed hour so, curious but without a whole lot of thought, I entered. I enjoy the silence one generally finds within houses of worship, and on this occasion it was a pleasing curiosity to discover a mass being offered in a language I could readily comprehend.

The congregation was small. There was no printed matter other than the barebones information written on the board outside, and I had forgotten to note the name of the homilist, but I took my place in one of the pews and waited. The mid-morning temperature in the street had already been rising noticeably as I had entered; the church's cool and darkened interior was a notable contrast.

Presently an unusually tall man entered, suntanned and with a full head of snow white hair. He stood before the congregation to offer us a blessing – in a voice that was seductive in its mellow simplicity, yet seemed to boom through all corners of his church. He spoke in clearly enunciated and faultlessly grammatical English, but there was a slight and unavoidable lilt to it that almost all Spanish-speakers have difficulty disguising. His use of language was entrancing, apart from its charming accent; a pitch to it that might have enticed a flock of recalcitrant sheep to stop wandering about the hillside, to gather round about and pay attention to what he had to say. He was dressed in the plain rough-woven brown wool habit of the Franciscan order, tied about his waist with a cord as white as his hair. Over the top of this habit he had thrown an additional cloak of bright green cotton. His feet were pushed into simple sandals that were secured about his heels and ankles by leather thongs. They could have been homemade.

Somersaults

I am not a Roman Catholic, so was somewhat lost in trying to follow the ritual of service – but when this priest rose to his feet to deliver his homily I was well focused. He spoke of the blessing of humility and in such a way that, had he not used words at all, I would have grasped the gist of his theme through his use of tone, body language and the expressive use of his hands. English speakers tend to flap their hands about in a generally meaningless pantomime when they are talking, no doubt convinced they are adding emphasis to their words – but they have a great deal to learn from the eloquence of a Latin who instinctively knows how to talk with his hands.

At the end of the service the congregation was invited to join the priest for coffee and cakes in the church's vestibule, and it was here that I learned his name: Father José Mojica, originally from San Miguel de Allende, but now in charge of a mission station for orphans in Lima, Peru. One of the congregation told me he was known as "the singing friar," a description to which I was to add further detail later in the day, but which for the moment seemed to fit my impression of his voice.

When I had a chance to talk to him in person I told him I was a journalist, and that I would like to interview him in greater detail. His reply was to invite me to his home at three o'clock that same afternoon. He gave me a paper with the address written on it: La Granjita. Then he said:

"Come by taxi. Every driver in the city knows where it is …"

So I found the one driver who had never heard of the man, and had no idea where to take me. We seemed to drive around for a half hour looking at unmarked streets. In the end, rolling down his window countless times to ask people passing on foot, we were able to discover the priest's street. It was an unmarked lane headed out of town stretching forever into the surrounding countryside. Moreover, it was bounded on either flank by high walls over which it was impossible to see anything at all except the blue sky. In the length of the entire wall I was able to see only one narrow door.

"There …!" I pointed, anxious by now to rid myself of this befuddled cabbie.

He dropped me at the door and sped away as though also anxious to dump such a feeble-brained gringo, one who apparently had no idea where he was supposed to be going …

I was by no means certain I had arrived at La Granjita.

At first I tried knocking on the door, but the silence from the other side of it was solid and prolonged. Then I spied a half-concealed bell-pull, so gave it a yank. I thought it might have clanged. It was a tinkle – coming from somewhere far away. I stopped and listened. Nothing. Mistaken.

Then I tried a simple manipulation of the door catch and it swung open like Sesame, as if my coming had been anticipated all along. Inside a garden spread up the side of a small hill for two hundred metres, with a large well-built and white-washed house at its crown. What could be seen of the lower reaches of the garden consisted of a sizeable pond surrounded by growths of tall grasses and rushes. A pathway led past a pleasantly landscaped area of patios with benches and a grass-roofed gazebo, and passing up towards the house there was a snow white donkey that ee-ored its welcome – or warning – at the approach of a stranger. His racket worked better than the bell-pull. Padre José Mojica came hurrying down a set of stairs from the veranda that surrounded the house, holding out his arms in greeting.

Behind him, on the veranda, guitars accompanying the unmistakeable cadence of Mexican song rose in harmony from a half dozen fine voices – baleful Latin ballads of allegiance perpetual for loves and lands. I was introduced to those present, six or seven young men rising to greet me, the residue of a football team that included the padre's nephew; he and his companions had defeated their opponents at a match in the town stadium that afternoon. They were all bound for their various out-of-town homes, and had come for a feast and a blessing from the priest. On several tables there were platters of the remains of at least three chickens, empty beer and wine bottles. As if in finale before their departure, the guitar was passed a final time to Padre José Mojica himself. He took the instrument in his hands, rapping his fingers carelessly across its strings to see if it was still in tune, then started to play a melody requiring the most intricate finger work. He played and sang like a professional – his voice issuing up from somewhere deep within his barrel chest. Someone quietly passed me a bottle of beer.

I was mesmerised, as if the sole observer at a private concert. I had neither asked for this, nor paid for it – but most certainly I was being treated to a very special event.

The padre laughed as he thrummed out the final line of the song.

"You like that?" he asked me.

I did, but my answer, really, was far better expressed by the applause of the priest's nephew and his companions. One by one they stood and hugged their mentor and champion then, gathering their belongings, they began to filter down the veranda stairs into the garden and across it towards the doorway by which I had entered from the street.

"I'll accompany them to the gate," the priest said to me. "Please – go into the house and feel free to look around. I think you will find it an interesting little museum."

The design of the house was the first thing that caught my attention, even before I set foot inside. Its main section was square-shaped and consisted of just two rooms – a large rectangular dining room and a sitting room of the same dimensions. These were side-by-side and formed a unitary square block. These two rooms were connected by a wide arched opening, and both in turn were linked by glass doors to a surrounding corridor, which also had exterior glass doors giving onto the veranda. The veranda completely encompassed and belted the central nucleus. Thus, like Russian dolls one inside the other, the square veranda enclosed a square corridor, which enclosed the square space comprising the dining and sitting rooms – and the whole was sheltered under one gigantic square roof. It was a strange design, but not unpleasant. There were no windows – just glass-panelled doors leading onto the veranda, similar to the glass-panelled doors that let into the central core. The other working parts of the house, the bedrooms and bathrooms, the kitchen, pantries and workrooms, were all tucked away in a separate wing, lower and to one side of the main social centre. This add-on wing, its flat roof at the same level as the deck of the veranda, was on the opposite side of the house, unseen from the garden through which I had made my initial approach.

The corridor surrounding the dining and living rooms was indeed a small museum gallery. Its walls were a mass of framed photographs, drawings and caricatures – no paintings – and it was like a Who's Who of all the big names of the era of the '20's and '30's – starring Padre José Mojica. In the first photograph I looked at, the padre was seen towering over Mussolini, with the Duke of Aosta at his side. Then there was the padre with the Prince of Wales (later King Edward VIII), then another with Adolf Hitler. Charlie Chaplin, Rudolph Valentino, Greta Garbo, Coco Chanel, Isadora Duncan, Katharine Hepburn, Walt Disney, Dolores del Rio, Gary Cooper, John Wayne, John Huston, Scott Fitzgerald, Somerset Maugham, Ernest Hemingway, George Gershwin, Pablo Picasso and Sidney Bechet – all of them also adorned the walls of this extraordinary corridor, almost all of them including a younger but very recognizable José Mojica smiling beside them. Sometimes they were dressed most formally, sometimes informally gathered outside restaurants or clubs, or seated at tables laden with glasses and bottles. In several of the photos there would be a group of people, always including José Mojica, standing on docks or at marinas, sailboats or flying boats in the background. The picture that finally stopped me short was a fine pencil drawing, a caricature of José Mojica himself. It was signed "Caruso."

The padre had caught up with me by then, and I heard him chuckle at my reaction to the cartoon.

"Excuse me," I blurted, "but who the devil are you …?"

Padre José Mojica's story was an unusual one. Born on a coffee and sugar plantation in San Gabriel, Jalisco, he studied agriculture in Mexico City, but found his real interest was at the Mexican Conservatory of Music where he took lessons in voice and guitar. In addition, he took drama lessons, was an athlete and equestrian, and mastered English, French and Italian. Finishing his school studies, he became an operatic tenor in Mexico City, moving to New York towards the end of the First World War. It was here he met and befriended Enrico Caruso, who helped him win a contract with the Chicago Civic Opera company in 1919. Broadening his artistic contacts, he sang as a lead tenor at the Metropolitan Opera House in New York, and worked in Hollywood as a leading actor for early Fox musicals.

La Granjita, the Antigua Villa Santa Monica, was part of an estate dating back to the era of XVI century Spanish colonialism. Mojica acquired it as a ruin and rebuilt it as a home for his mother about 1930. Most of the estate was given over to the church, but the house and garden was retained as a family residence.

The story he told me there in the corridor varied somewhat from his official biography. He said that he attempted marriage three times and, after the third failure to acquire a wife, returned to Mexico feeling depressed and sorry for himself. His mother had little patience with him, considering him a dissolute, for all that he was wealthy. One Sunday morning, on her way out to church, she berated him for his reluctance to accompany her. Not to disappoint her, he went along – and in the same church in which the two of us had met that morning, he decided he would follow a less profligate path, become a true Christian and enter the priesthood. In 1942, at the side of his mother's deathbed, he made her a solemn promise to follow through on this decision, and he promptly retired from Hollywood and all his North American theatrical pursuits.

Very shortly after that Mojica entered the monastery of San Francisco in Lima, and became a Franciscan monk, later a priest. He continued to sing, but now his very substantial recording royalties were given over to his mission. His superiors ordered him to write his autobiography, *Yo Pecador* (I Sinner), which was published in 1956. It sold three million copies in Spanish before being translated into English. It was made into a film in 1959, all royalties going towards the Lima monastery, an orphanage and school which the priest had founded. He would come back to what was now his family's *hacienda* for holidays every now and then. He told me he would be returning to Lima within the next few days.

The padre told me this story as we walked through the corridors of La Granjita, and I was impressed. I have never forgotten it, nor was I to forget what followed.

Taking me by the shoulder, José Mojica led me into the dining room. On the wall behind the chair at the head of the table was a large print that I recognized immediately as the Virgin Mary. I had seen the image before.

"Do you know who that is?" asked the padre.

"Of course. It's the Virgin Mary," I responded.

"Yes. You are right. But it is more," replied the priest. "This print depicts Nuestra Señora de Guadalupe – as she was after her miraculous appearance to the peasant Juan Diego in the year 1531. The original of the painting is at the Basilica of Our Lady of Guadalupe in Mexico City. She is the patron saint of all the Americas."

He paused to let his information sink in. He could see that I knew nothing of any of this.

"This was the first of Our Lady's appearances," the padre continued. "Juan Diego was a simple peasant walking with his donkey in that area of Mexico City, the Hill of Tepeyac, when he met a young maiden by the roadway. She told him she was Mary, the mother of God, and asked for him to oversee the building of a church at this place where they met.

"Juan Diego insisted that he was a nobody, that he had no authority to build such a church, but he nevertheless approached the archbishop of Mexico City, Juan de Zumárraga – and it was he who asked Juan Diego to return to the young lady to seek a sign proving her legitimacy."

Padre José Mojica continued his story, claiming Mary ordered the peasant to climb to the top of Tepeyac Hill – the place where they were – and to gather the flowers that were growing there. Tepeyac Hill was normally barren; flowers did not grow there, and Juan Diego knew it. However, he did as he was told and climbed to the top – and there he found a mass of Castilian roses, a flower not native to Mexico. He gathered them up and, in order to carry them without crushing them, he placed them into the apron of his *tilma*, or hemp cloak. He carried them like that to the archbishop, who was astonished to recognize the type of flower they were.

When Zumárraga demanded to know what the lady looked like, Juan Diego became shy and looked down at his *tilma*. There he saw the imprint left by the flowers; the pollen had stained the rough cloth, creating the image of the lady.

"It was a miracle!" exclaimed José Mojica. "And it is that same *tilma* that is hanging above the altar of the church later built at Tupeyac. Ultimately the image was venerated and adored, and colours were added to the original – but the basic image is as it appeared. The fabric has been scientifically tested, and there is no explanation for the basic pigmentation of the cloth. It is, indeed, the image of Our Lady."

I must have looked sceptical – or at least quizzical.

"And that is not all!" said the padre triumphantly. "At the very time of this holy apparition, the Aztecs were about to rise up in rebellion. It was all organized – they were going to rise en masse and slaughter every Spaniard in Mexico. The date had been set, and it was almost the eve of the uprising when this miracle happened. And do you know, word went out very fast, and the rebellion was checked. The entire tribe of Aztec people converted instead to Christianity, and bloodshed was averted."

This extraordinary story stayed with me as I drove north again to British Columbia. I deliberately passed Lafayette in Oregon, so was able to visit the nearby Trappist Abbey dedicated to Our Lady of Guadalupe – this at Padre José Mojica's suggestion. On that occasion I remained for two days, but some months later returned with my eight-year-old son – who brought along his bow and arrow, and a football.

Early on the first morning after our arrival, I was woken by my son shouting like an irate coach in the courtyard below my window.

"Don't hog the ball to yourself! Pass it out …! Over here! Over here!"

Poking a sleepy head above the sill of my cell window, I saw four Trappist monks, their white robes gathered up about the shins as they ran about the cobblestones kicking my son's football from one to the other. They said not a word, their grunts and the scrambling of their feet on the quadrangle paving indication a tournament was in progress. Occasionally there would be a whap! as the leather ball connected with someone's well-sandaled sweet spot.

My son stopped when he saw me.

"Dad – how come these guys won't talk to me …?"

I had no ready answer at that hour of the morning, but later over breakfast I was able to tell him that the silence of nature is one of mankind's greatest joys. I don't think he fully understood; next he wanted to set up an archery contest.

For me, though, apart from providing a few days alone with my son, it formed some kind of continuum in my spirit – not a particularly religious thing for me, but the extension of a brand of contentment I had seen in a man like José Mojica. Encountering him had been a rare privilege. It was very plain to see how this kindly man's simplicity had afforded him a peace that so greatly exceeded whatever he might have bought when he had millions.

Ralph

Rev. John Hannen needed to go to Montréal, and so did I. The priest was in Kincolith and I was in Victoria, but our time schedules coincided, so we decided to meet up in Calgary and travel east together by car – a large station wagon.

Father John was not alone. He had in the car with him both a cat and a dog – the latter a gentle creature that went by the name of Ralph. The cat had a name, for sure, but it mattered little on the day (or was it night?) we were cruising at the posted speed limit across the flatness of Saskatchewan and discovered the poor animal was missing. When we looked for him to give him his dinner, he had simply vanished. He had fled, certainly, for Ralph was far too tender and well-bred a companion to have dined on him. In any case had such a thing been attempted, it is likely we would have heard the cat's expostulations. The animal's disappearance remains a mystery to this day.

There was nothing about Ralph, however, that could be construed as mysterious; nothing at all out of the norm – except for his size.

Ralph was an Irish wolfhound, the largest breed of dog there is.

Moreover, he was an exceptionally large wolf hound who, before or since, remains quite the largest dog I have ever seen in my life. When I stood beside him, his shoulders were level with my elbow. If he stood on his hind legs and playfully rested his front paws on my shoulders, my nose would be pushed into the expanse of grey hair that spread across the huge bulk of his chest. His head was fully two feet – even three – above mine, which would have measured him at well over eight feet tall – just shy of two and a half metres.

From time to time it was necessary to stop the car and allow Ralph to jump out and run. Most dogs would be quite happy to chase rabbits if they could, but Ralph chased and played with horses instead, galloping along beside them. After stretching his legs and exercising himself across a wide expanse of prairie, he was happy to jump back into the rear of the station wagon, curl up and go to sleep.

Father John gave Ralph bones to chew on – great shanks that Ralph would reduce to unrecognizable and smelly mush-rubble over the course of the journey. We drove for the most part with the front windows wide open. In the heat of the prairie summer the scent of dog-plus-bone created a rank atmosphere almost as strong as the interior of a Nass River school room.

All went well until we were driving on the road that runs around the northern flank of Lake Superior and pulled up to the pumps of a gas station at Marathon, Ontario. The owner of the franchise had taken great pains with the decoration of his workplace. There were carefully-tended flower beds on either side of the station house, and numerous flowers and potted plants dotting the entire premises. The place was a work of art, and it would not have been a great surprise to learn that the manager was in line for some kind of prize for his colourful creativity.

We opened the door for a sleepy Ralph to emerge and, like Ferdinand the Bull, to meander about casually soaking up the delicate fragrances of the flower beds. Clearly he had found himself in some sort of heaven, and was enjoying his walk-about immensely. He hadn't yet chosen a place to leave his calling card, but was circling about while his master stood by with a plastic bag to pick it up wherever he dropped it. The gas station attendant was coming out to us to take our order when, from behind the station building there erupted an enormous German shepherd, barking, snarling and flying at Ralph's hind quarters. The attendant tried to grab his dog, but his effort was of no avail. The angry shepherd snatched at Ralph high on his hind leg.

Now angered himself, and terrifying, Ralph rose up to his full height, opened his cavernous jaws, and dropped with all his force onto the back of the shepherd's neck. In one movement he effortlessly picked up the smaller dog

Somersaults

and shook him like a housemaid shakes a mop from the window.

Yelps of pain and anger were added to the shouts of the priest, the attendant and myself as blood flew in every direction, splattering the pumps and our shirt fronts. The attendant grabbed a length of hose and attempted to flog Ralph's flanks, but that made the wolfhound angrier and he began to shake the shepherd with even more ferocity. Finally one of us thought of using water, managed to find a hose and so give Ralph a thorough wetting. He let the shepherd drop in a mangled and bloody heap by one of the pumps.

The attendant was furious and wanted to attack Ralph. Father John talked him down, apologized and managed to explain he did not believe Ralph was at fault. Obviously the shepherd was intended as a guard, but equally obvious was that he should have been tied up at a time of the day when the station was likely to be serving customers.

We spent time exchanging names and addresses, but left quickly when we could see the shepherd was still alive, and that the attendant needed to be on hand to receive the vet he had telephoned.

We gassed-up at another station. Ralph remained in the car, dozing and once more his gentle giant self. I couldn't help but wonder whether or not dogs have emotions or memories, and how they might stack them away in some area of their brains we don't know about – that thing we call instinct.

There was no further major incident until we reached downtown Montréal and parked the station wagon in the Canadian National Railways parkade. The car was well shaded, but even so we rolled the windows down a few inches so there would be a small circulation of air for Ralph's comfort. Then we left to go about our business – probably no more than an hour.

Ralph was gone when we returned. He could not possibly have climbed from the openings we had left in the windows. We had purposely not locked the doors, so our logical assumption was that someone passing by for some reason, or maybe just for the hell of it, had decided to let the dog out.

We thought immediately to go to a radio station and ask for assistance.

"What sort of a dog is he? What's his name? How big is he …?" Father John was asked.

A description was not difficult, but somewhat embarrassing. After all, how does one manage to lose in a downtown parkade a pet pooch the size of a baby camel?

Father John was questioned closely. In the end we settled down to listen to the presenter's announcement.

"Unusual notice here ... little doggie lost ... playful and loving pooch, but somewhat larger than most, and in need of four pounds of beef per day ... loves to chase deer ... and horses ..."

The announcer was having fun – but it was to our advantage.

Within a half hour there were a number of phone calls. We would find Ralph down at the shunting yards of the Canadian National Railway, the callers said, not very far from the parkade where we had left him. We ran over there as quickly as we could – and there was Ralph, having a high old time chasing locomotives up and down the tracks and barking at them.

Houdini ...

First the mystery of how the cat had fled the car. Now Ralph, too, presented us with the mystery of how he had managed to escape. Father John who, after all, had been considering the greatest of all mysteries his entire adult life, managed a shrug. We have talked of this and other deep matters at various times in the intervening years.

It is a fair assumption: some mysteries are for accepting and living with – not for solving.

Toronto the Good

I moved from Regina to Toronto in the early spring of 1962.

For the previous six years I had travelled large portions of western Canada as a journalist, gradually working my way east, and I was keenly aware I had been on the move for most of my short life so far – schools in Australia, the United States and Britain, learning quite a smattering of geography as I passed on my way. Then there had been military service in Africa and the Far East, trying to excuse – or make sense of – a disintegrating British Empire. There had been visits to many of the lands that lay between these definitive ports of call. Schooling in Britain afforded holiday adventures throughout various parts of the European mainland. But in all this movement I never really touched down in the United States, although I had been there, lived there, even attended schools there for a time.

At the conclusion of a fairly traumatic two years of active military service

I found I was not one of those with a tendency to polish doorknobs or duck my head when a car backfired, but there is no doubt I suffered the twitches of a soldier re-entering civilian life. It was a malaise that bordered an ill-concealed mania. I was nervous and jumpy, viewed the stimulation of my Canadian existence akin to watching the snow static on an old black and white television screen. No doubt I showed ingratitude for a number of the good things that came my way, but the truth of it was that I was most disenchanted with the pace of life I was living, and felt the need to inject it with a large dose of verve – and even more movement. A paycheque was necessary, and there was never enough of it, but neither was it in any way my prime motivator.

It was not long before I was concluding my first year in the Public Relations department at the Head Office of a major bank in downtown Toronto. The work itself held not the least appeal, and I felt I was going crackers. There was no energy. No pizazz. No whumph. None. Though fleeing my post periodically to catch a breath of cool street air or to snatch at my challenged wits, daily I was expected to sit nine-to-five behind a desk with a break at noon for lunch. My job was to churn out endless press releases that, to me, consisted of mundane and inconsequential promotional material, its sole aim to bundle into any given text, and as frequently as possible, the name of the institution that was becoming more odious to me as day followed day.

The question of gratitude for the work did not occur to me; I was bored stupid, alarmed by my colleagues of more or less equal rank who had set up a bar behind the boilers in the building's second basement, one level above the bullion room – the great secret of the bank's middle and junior assistant general managers. Numbers of them were alcoholics – or fast headed in that direction; enthusiastically they enjoined me to kibitz. I was amused at first, but not seriously enticed. Instead, hopelessly and stupidly, I frittered away time and energy chatting up the hordes of young ladies who worked in various offices throughout the building. Some of them presented themselves for giggles and titillation both during and after hours; but I found the best looking of them vapid, the not-so-attractive not so attractive. I wanted to kick myself for even bothering, to concentrate instead on thinking of myself as a journalist. For me the bank was a dead end.

Desperate to liven up a life fast fading to grey, to lace it with meaning or whumph (it was difficult to know whether or not they were the same thing) I had applied for a job at every "big time" news outlet in the city – and by peculiar accident, while still employed full-time by the bank, found myself accepted and signed-on as freelance stringer for two of the city's major daily newspapers. I was able to talk my way onto an editorial floor because of my previous experience on news beats out west; I could write reasonably well, so I was qualified.

The skills of journalism take years to develop, and prior to coming to Toronto to work as a public relations representative for the bank, or as a reporter on any of the city's papers, I had had to put in time on smaller provincial newspapers, or working for radio and television. Prior to the early 1960's there had been only one so-called "communications school" in the English language: Toronto's Ryerson, when it was still an institute of technology. By the mid-1970's that situation had changed, and journalism was being offered as a course of studies at virtually all colleges and universities across the country. Editors did not at first favour the product of these schools. One senior staffer once growled at me: "Nothing replaces experience … if you sent me one of those ninnies from journalism school, I'd kick his butt downstairs!"

Each of the two papers was at that time competitor of the other, and both had entertained my bid on a strict let's-see-what-you-can-do understanding. On that basis I was able to conceal important aspects of my full identity, and heard affirmatively from both papers on the same day. I could handle the extra work; the bank was a daytime job, whereas the papers required me to work in the evenings. I saw no particular conflict of interest so long as I had my regular daytime work. Even so, and before knowing precisely where I was headed, what was expected of me or how I might fare, I was not about to deny one paper in order to favour the other – so I worked for both. I could, so I did, and I decided right from the start to use a different name at each. I have four names if they're strung out in full, so at the one paper I used my first and the third names, at the other I wrote under the second and fourth. As long as I had my bank job, I could rationalize my situation was not unadulterated opportunism, although I finally had to admit that it had become precisely that the moment I became more involved with journalism than the bank. Quite consciously, about this time and with no small shred of guilt, I resolved to take great care upon entering the Press Club where personnel of either paper might have been able to make embarrassing cross-identification. It was an edgy sort of game, but I took a chance; I had joined the club as a press writer for the bank, but it still gave me a rush and I took a veiled pleasure in trying to avoid being discovered. On quite another level (a shade of rationalization my mother might have recognized, no doubt) I convinced myself I was simply trying to shove my foot through the doorway of what presented itself as an exclusive big city professional arena. I saw no reason why I should be excluded; felt my reporting skills were every bit as good as the best of any of my colleagues and that all I had to do was prove it. I wanted to perform work I would find pithy and exciting; and, not least, to be recognized and suitably compensated for my efforts. Though it is certain I missed it in these glorious first moments of self-absorption, it is also very likely I was simultaneously honing the razor edge of an insufferable arrogance.

I enjoyed good lunches at the Toronto Press Club, but I was sailing close-hauled against a fickle wind, to be sure, and it would take no more than a small puff to see me toppled over. It seemed wiser to sit in the shadier corners of the dining room. Yet within a short span of time it became obvious through the dimness of my egotistical short-sightedness that, while I was probably not doing any damage to either newspaper, it might not be long before I could mess up, cross my wires and cause considerable harm and embarrassment – to both papers and myself. By what mechanism would I cope in the event each of my editors required me to cover the same event? It took diligence to work out a *modus operandi,* because it did happen on at least a couple of occasions. I had been overweening to the point that in the rare moments that I stopped to take stock of my situation I could recognize in myself excruciating pretensions. Such contemplative musings caused considerable discomfort because I knew, deep down, that cocky really did not fit me. Each of the editors for whom I worked, and from whom I had carefully concealed my duplicity, was showing growing confidence in my work. I genuinely liked both of them, felt grateful for the opportunities each had given me. The fact each was coming to trust me appeared to germinate a speck of decency that floated to the surface of my personal ambition, presenting itself as Conscience. I had even made a couple of friends among the two editorial staffs, and had successfully kept my secret from them. (I wince as I think back; I have winced a lot in eighty years.) My opportunism and dishonesty sucked at me. It would only be a matter of time, surely, before my falsity would be discovered; neither paper would want such a right prat on staff if that were to happen. If the axe fell I could wave goodbye to a budding career in journalism. Worse: I would probably have to remain on at the bloody bank. The mere thought of it brought me up sharp, and I resolved to change my ways as quickly as possible before someone challenged my concept of professional ethics. How? Having wormed my way in, it would not be so easy to wriggle my way out.

After almost a full year of editorial dodging, and continuing to hang on while becoming daily more unhinged at the bank's head office, a regular holiday break provided opportunity to make my escape from a frantic lifestyle that, though it put a welcome and slightly fatter pay packet on my plate each month, was nonetheless seriously challenging my scruples. It was not that there was anything wrong with being a news and/or public relations writer working several outlets; but there was certainly something wrong when it became necessary to hide my actions from anyone, when my sense of loyalty was so divided – when I was so clearly deceiving some people to whom I felt a growing sense of attachment, even responsibility.

Events of the epoch came to my rescue. Martin Luther King set fire to America's southern states. Alabama was exploding. Desegregation. I knew nothing about it, but decided to go.

Road South

I had no clear idea what was going on, or where Alabama was. I did not understand the situation, nor could I measure the intensity of whatever it was that was happening there, but I resolved to leave the bank and travel to Alabama in my car to find out. This time I would concentrate on feeding my prime journalistic output to a single news outlet. With these noble aspirations in mind, I managed to secure a letter of credential as freelance correspondent – which I was anyway – from the managing editor of the paper for which I had been writing the most. I made my peace with the editor of the second paper, bowing low and walking backwards from his office. Surprisingly he bore me no grudge. Most happily I accepted the notion all these decisions would ensure the end of my banking career.

In an effort to cover my journalistic nakedness I bought maps, visited libraries and did some concentrated reading in the newspaper morgue. I needed to background myself quickly, and with more than a mere passing knowledge of the subject area; my aim was to reach a considerably deeper understanding of these momentous events than the man reading his newspaper on the subway heading home at the end of a day.

But the more I dug the more I needed to dig, and in the end had to get going long before I felt myself ready. There was no time for all the research that had to be done, so I told myself to go look at it, learn from the experience. Dig later.

What was occurring throughout that spring and summer in Birmingham – and all across the southern United States of America – was an inferno touched off by years of enforced racial degradation and separation, the demand for equality between the races, the inevitable struggle for the emancipation of African Americans after hundreds of years of slavery, humiliating servitude and second-class citizenship. African Americans would no longer accept without question their shadowy second class status, segregated and denied use of the same facilities and spaces as their Caucasian brethren. They were being led by a Christian minister named Rev. Martin Luther King, Junior. He was the man to watch. If possible I would find him and talk to him.

The story was the big headline of the day – and yet, as I was later to become aware, it was lamentably covered in the Toronto papers. Every news source in the world was taking the story seriously and treating it with *gravitas*. The Toronto papers naturally, and like news outlets everywhere in North America, latched onto the story's sensation. In a blinkered and fair-minded Canada, where a critical spectator population likes to champion an underdog and is ever intrigued by the ways in which our southern neighbours appear so easily to lace themselves into Gordian knots over issue after issue, it was necessary to access alternate news sources to come close to the actual on-the-street story. It was hard not to have a social conscience concerning the African Americans, who daily had to face all manner of harassment from their white countrymen. Southern Ontario had been one of the principal northern terminuses of the Underground Railway that had ferried runaway Afro-Americans to safety in the middle and latter portions of the XIX century so, to my reckoning, this was a Canadian story as well. However, that would have been a difficult assessment to make if one read what was written in Canada's major English-language dailies. It was not until later that I was able to make some reasonable comparison between Canadian coverage and the way the story was treated almost everywhere else; there was an abundance of self-righteousness in Canada's news commentary.

Even in polite conversation the underdogs in this confrontation were referred to as Negroes. They themselves used the word. Dr. King himself used it. It is a recent phenomenon, but we have all had to learn how to say Afro-American. One day, as we learn more about brotherhood, maybe even that designation will fall away, too; politically correct terminology – even a commonplace designation for an idea – has a way of readjusting itself over time. The more repulsive epithet, "Nigger," always has been a strong pejorative, definitely not acceptable by anyone possessed of sensibilities towards those at whom the word is aimed, and who most detest it. Soon apparent to me was that this alone was the one substantial reason such a word lived so persistently among the racist white population. This group looked upon their dark-skinned fellow countrymen as sub-human, and its militant viewpoint was that the Afro-Americans were neither requiring nor deserving of more attention than the vilest of slurs.

Birmingham – sixty percent white, forty percent black – was sensationally splashed in ninety-five-point headlines, and I was determined to get there. With a cot rigged beside me in my little car in place of the regular passenger seat, it took me three days to make it south from Toronto to Birmingham. Heading first into the upper northwest corner of New York, then into Pennsylvania and Ohio, I turned south through Kentucky and Tennessee.

On a sunny early morning in Kentucky I stopped at a local farm to ask if I could use the wooden outhouse visible from the road, perhaps shave at the pump in the front yard. The farmer looked quizzically at my foreign car and circled it slowly while I availed myself of his proffered facilities.

"Beautiful morning," I said to him when I was done. "I've been driving non-stop from Toronto. May I take a walk through your paddock to stretch out my legs?"

"What kind of a car is that …?" he asked, a look of disdain on his face.

It was a German-built DKW, I told him – front wheel drive, three-cylinder two-cycle engine that wound up and screamed like a high-powered leaf blower at full throttle. Indeed, its fuel was a mix of gasoline and oil. If ever I had a breakdown it was likely as easy (and cheaper) to have it serviced in the shop of the local lawn mower repair man than at a regular automobile mechanic's. On the highway it could cruise comfortably at one hundred kilometres an hour, and do it at a cost of little more than ten dollars for all of that distance. Well – exaggeration: I'd have to stop for lunch, and the sandwich would cost me two dollars.

"Hm-m-m!" grunted the farmer.

I think Toronto foxed him somewhat. Maybe it was the Ontario plate. In any case, he shrugged and gave me the nod.

"Go ahead," he replied.

His fields were enclosed by rough-cut wood rail fencing. I ducked through into fresh green meadow and paced myself out, kicking off shoes and socks, stretching my arms and stretching my trunk as I bare-footed swiftly towards an area of forest on the far side. Again ducking under fence rail I entered among the trees and felt the glorious exhilaration that comes from filling lungs with the pure airs and scents of early morning woodland, feeling Mother Earth and her soft grasses padding my feet and filling the gaps between my toes. But there were also twigs and small stones that attacked the soles of my feet as I walked barefoot into the trees, so I had not gone very far and was happy to stop when I came upon a small clearing in which there was a large and highly polished metal sculpture – brasses and bronzes and gleaming stainless steels worked into a fantastic and bulbous shape some ten feet high. There were pipes that curled and embraced the thing – and a tap.

Whatever it be, it be beautiful, I thought. My tactile senses were tweaked, my artistic penchant for the three dimensional. I walked around it, stopping to examine my newly-shaved jowls in the object's mirror-like surfaces. My image bounced back like a carnival distorting mirror, and I extended my arms and laughed as I did a pirouette and glanced back over my shoulder at its cockeyed reflections. I resisted the temptation to clamber up to the top of it.

A sense of childlike joy courses my veins when I spy something eye-catching and mysterious, a *thing* in some way exotic that someone has taken the trouble to make, no matter what it is. I might also confess such feelings are inclined to come wave-like and can be accompanied by a bewildering naïveté. My acceptance of *sculpture* is a cavernous bucket – but naïve.

In Ontario's Georgian Bay area, miles from rampant civilization, I walked my two dogs one afternoon across an immaculate greensward surrounded on all sides, I thought, by welcoming expanses of woodland where, as is natural in such abundant countryside, I imagined there romped all manner of fauna that might interest my mutts. However, at the moment of crossing the green, a sudden deluge of tiny hard yellow balls emanating from beyond the top of a high convex hill hailed down upon our heads. It was a veritable bombardment. The dogs were alarmed and I was offended – the attack seemed to me willful and deliberate. I had with me a plastic raincoat so, when there was a pause in the sally, I spread it on the ground and scurried about hither and thither, gathering up the missiles like other-worldly mushrooms. Once they got my drift, the dogs likewise assisted. We made a game of it and very soon the ground about us had been totally cleared of all the yellow projectiles. Pulling together the extremities of the raincoat, I slung it sack-like over my shoulder and so walked off into the trees to continue our outing. Later I took the bundle from the front seat of my car and displayed its contents before my friends at the local café, eager to show them I was not exaggerating when I related how I had been so outrageously assailed while out rambling with my dogs. Even so, I attempted to tell them, they were pretty things. Maybe I could make some artistic display out of them …

My companions thought that screamingly funny. They hooted with laughter. They could not believe I had never seen a golf ball before. And, indeed, I had not.

"I thought golf balls were white, and bigger ..." I told them, perplexed.

They laughed all the more.

Golf balls on a training range are generally yellow, they scoffed, and they further advised the whole collection – I had picked up more than a score of them – should be returned forthwith to the local club. They were convincing, so this I did with considerable embarrassment. The club steward said he was satisfied with my delayed honesty, commented briefly how certain members had been mystified by the disappearance of all the yellow projectiles they had launched over the hill – but from the corner of my eye I saw him shake his head incredulously at having to address such a buffoon.

This exhibition of my naïveté was embarrassing enough; it might have been far more so, I dare say, had the steward accused me of theft and summoned the police.

It was the same level of applied naïveté relating to the object presently under scrutiny, this woodland sculpture. No stranger to moments of extended vacuity (some young people tend to enter this blissful state quite frequently), I had not the faintest idea what I was looking at.

Once having acknowledged this, however, I was not about to waste time and energy trying to figure it out. Clearly it was a most accomplished abstract sculpture placed where it was out of the artist's (or owner's) projected sense of whimsy. I was content to revel in the piece for itself; its shapes and textures were immensely pleasing and its contrast to the surrounding light-speckled greenery little short of uncanny. Whatever it was, it appealed to my wide acceptance of such oddities in this whacky world, so long as they caused no harm – and this thing did not look as if it was about to explode. It sat there, shiny and incomprehensible, like some strange kind of bus from a distant star. I listened to its silence. Not even a hum.

I was still looking at it when there came an ominous and metallic click from the bushes behind me. I turned to face down the long black tubes of a twelve-gauge shotgun and, beyond them, the glowering countenance of the Kentucky farmer. He had crept up to within ten paces behind me and had the gun to his shoulder. What I had heard was the snapping of the breach as it closed over the shells he had loaded into its chamber.

"What the hell you doin' here, boy?"

I held my shoes and socks out at arms' length on either side of me, crucifix-like, confused that I should be thus accosted at gun-point after receiving such affable license to tramp his lands.

"Sorry, eh?" I stammered innocently, at the same time mustering what I hoped was a winning smile. "I have no wish to offend ... I thought I had your permission ..."

"Yeah? Well, you can think your sorry ass off of my land."

I had judged him a reasonable man, and couldn't really understand why he would want to shoot me. So I sat myself on the ground at the foot of the sculpture and began to pull on my footwear.

"Sorry," I said again. (Canadians might like to think "sorry" is disarming; it's often the first thing they say. Disarming people, Canadians.)

"It's really a misunderstanding," I told him. "I thought you said it would be alright if I stretched out ..."

"In the paddock," he replied. "OK in the paddock. I didn't say you could climb no fences and come nosin' about over here ..."

He had lowered the gun, so I felt a little easier.

"That's a beautiful thing you have there," I said cheerily, nodding at the metal contraption behind me. "What is it?"

He sneered at me, but there was a quizzical sort of smile concealed behind his most serious countenance. I knew he was assessing the naïveté thing.

"Don't you have no never mind 'bout that," he said deliberately. "I guess you ain't no reven'oo-er, that's fer damn sure ... but you git your goddamm ass outta here anyways."

And so I left. Shame that I couldn't have stayed and talked to the man a little longer; I would have liked to have asked him questions about his farm and about Kentucky. For all his initial gruffness, he had seemed like an intelligent and understanding sort of fellow. I was already in what constituted "the south," so thought he might have had a useful viewpoint about what was happening in Birmingham. But I never got the chance. He had a gun, and I had no wish to push my luck. Discretion superseded all – twin-barrels and twelve gauges being a none-too-subtle nudge of encouragement to put considerable distance between self and the farmer's fields as quickly as possible.

I was alone on a sunny but empty highway with my thoughts and injuries – for indeed I felt the prick of a personal injury at the farmer's stern attitude. And the shotgun – I could not figure out what had made him so angry he had felt it necessary to level the thing at my head.

No matter how hard I knitted my brow, my mind's wick would not fizz. No spark at all.

But then the car zipped past a roadside hoarding that promoted "Corn Likker" – and the penny dropped. Lights twinkled on in my befuddled morning mind, then flared.

At that point I had to pull the car to a stop by the side of the road, I was laughing so hard.

Adventures of the roadway were not at an end. Later that day, driving through the Tennessee countryside, I stopped to pick up a young sailor hitch-hiking at the side of the road. Serviceman on his way home on leave, I reckoned ... He serves his country; it's no trouble for me to do him a good turn. Very naïve.

He was not very communicative, grunted at me unintelligibly when I tried to draw him out. We had been travelling about half an hour on the highway, but there was little traffic.

"Take a right!" he ordered me all of a sudden as we approached a turn-off.

"No," I replied. "I'm not headed that way. I can let you out if you like ..."

"Take a right, I said ...!" And he pulled out a long knife.

I tried not to show my alarm. Instead I put my foot to the floor and raced up a ramp to the right that was a mere few metres past the turning he had indicated. My passenger obviously did not know the vicinity well, for the ramp onto which we turned led directly into an urbanized zone, and the very first thing I spotted was the blue light above the door of a police post. Without hesitation I drove – fast – to the door of the station, slammed on the brakes so hard that the sailor, sitting beside me on my makeshift bed with his knife drawn, was thrown against the dashboard and the inside surface of the windshield. He had not been wearing a seat belt. At the same time I sounded my horn, so long and so insistently that, within seconds, there was a policeman at my window asking me why all the fuss?

The sailor had neither the time to tuck away his knife nor the balance he needed to recover himself from being thrown against the dashboard. I opened my door, stepped out and jerked my thumb over my shoulder.

"That hitch-hiker has just pulled a knife on me!"

"Goddamn!" was all the sailor had time to say before two burly policemen dragged him from my car and frog-marched him inside the police station.

The incident delayed me for a few hours while I made out a report to the police, and they measured the length of the miscreant's knife-blade. I explained how, as a working journalist, I needed to get down into Alabama as quickly as possible. They were kind, even indulgent, and soon I was on my way again – the cautions, the nodding and knowing heads of the police officers predominantly in mind. There and then I made a resolution to be careful about picking up hitch-hikers – though admitting foreknowledge of some vagabond's bad intent would be hard to surmise. To the moment of this writing I can say I have had no further problems with occasional hitchers. There has to be, I rationalize, some delicate balance in these matters – between caution and kindness – and stupidity. So far so good, and I'll be eighty-one when this opus makes its way to market.

Southern Warp

A few miles short of Birmingham I turned into a service station thinking to gas up the car. There was a diner, so I parked and stepped inside for a bite to eat first.

The DKW drew immediate attention. At that time and in those parts Americans drove big cars. "Dollar grins," we used to call them – a reference to their size, chromium-plated and toothy grillwork, and the cost of running them. The size of my little rig presented an oddity, its Ontario license plates stamping its driver an outsider. Curious northerners – those from north of the Mason-Dixon Line, at any rate – were none too welcome among southerners. They had no business messing about in Alabama. My presence among the café's clientele was instantly noted, its affect as instantly negative.

The crew-cut owner-cum-cook-cum-server on the other side of the counter looked more like a bouncer. He flicked a toothpick from one side of his mouth to the other as he re-rolled up his sleeves over burly arms. He wore a soiled no-nonsense apron. His silent unwavering scowl followed my every pace into his bailiwick. A sign tacked to the wall behind his shoulder read: "Management reserves the right to refuse service ..." to any patron it thought objectionable – which, no ambiguity here, I understood referred to anyone of the wrong skin colour, as well as anyone else who might proffer objectionable appearance or utterance of differing opinion ...

Straddling a stool at the counter, I flashed the man a merry smile, nodding my head at the offensive sign.

"That intended for me?" I asked him.

"Yep."

His response was arresting. A punch on the nose could not have brought me up faster. Idiotically, and far too late, I realized my question alone revealed all of my relevant northern bias – to him and to everyone else in the café. There was a distinct movement at one of the tables behind me. A group of five or six white men, beers uncapped, had ceased their conversation the moment I had stepped into the place. They had been sullenly watching both myself and their host. Nary a word exchanged, but the messages were clear.

I stood up.

"Thank you," I said, nodding my head, bowing ever so slightly at the waist and making for the door.

I heard the scraping of chairs across the floor. It appeared the men were pushing themselves away from their table, intent on seeing me out.

Seconds ahead of them, I bolted to my car, leapt in and started up the motor just as the first of the toughs crashed his full weight into my door and tried to open it – to pull me out, I guess. Someone kicked a fender as I spun out of the parking lot, and in my mirror I saw the lot of them turn and pile themselves into a pick-up. It was about fifteen kilometres to Birmingham, and I drove as if competing in the Indy 500, figuring I could lose my pursuers in the streets of the city – if the gas held out. I had not had the chance to refill the tank. The gods smiled on me: my little bomb outpaced my pursuers' truck. They abandoned the chase after a kilometre or two. I could see them in the rear-view mirror as they pulled off to the side of the road.

I had encountered racial hatred before, of course, but of a quite different aspect and intensity. There had been a ghastly colour bar in Kenya when I had done my military service there with the British colonial army during the so called "emergency" occasioned by the Mau Mau. There and at that time it had been all too easy to justify such appalling attitudes by claiming native workers were lazy, or filthy dirty, or ornery, or stupid – anything to augment a discombobulated reasoning that would excuse racialism and its consequent tensions as the result of carefully manicured antagonisms deemed necessary in order to confront and defeat an implacable enemy. Those Africans who adhered to the British line of propaganda, "loyalists" and "good Africans," were favoured by the whites (albeit at arm's length) in an effort to keep an essential element on side – the "hearts and minds" bit – but they were by no means "equal," and never exempt abuse. At all levels, from the minions on the farms and in the ranks of the police and Home Guard to the highest grade of British-appointed Kikuyu "chiefs," the Africans were disdained by settlers and military alike, held in contempt, insulted and sneered at both behind their backs and to their faces. Many whites claiming to like blacks were, under it all, insufferably paternalistic towards them, talking about "my" black boy, or "our" Kikuyu farm hands, seldom if ever coming closer to "them" than an employer to a menial servant. For self-preservation or gain, no matter the motive, lots of Africans would quietly and obsequiously accept gross maltreatment as fair price for what small favours they received. In America these would be named "Uncle Toms." The worst treatment of all was reserved for those "bloody insolent Niggers" (the Kikuyu were called "Niggers," but were also referred to as "Kukes" – which was possibly even more derogatory) who stood up to the British or "answered back" if and when they thought they had a valid complaint. Generally, though (for the sake of examining racial hatreds with dispassionate disconnect) the antagonisms in colonial Africa of a white man for a black man, or by a black for a white, presented a certain twisted but understandable illogic. There were white apologists for the blacks, but they were suffered as a minority so small they could be ignored; they were, in any case, clearly "wrong-headed."

But the racial hatred I was to encounter in Alabama had no logic to it whatsoever. It seemed to be a channel, an excuse, for blind violence and wanton hooliganism, as if giving vent to the basest need of human nature to seek out a difference and then make an enemy of it, destroy it utterly (even though "it" had the semblance of a human being) and to do so in a manner so cruel that the man who screamed inhumanity brought that same inhumanity down upon his own head. Logic, never!

Racist laws were concocted, carefully mapped out on paper, to justify utterly anti-social behaviour. A white man's antagonism for another white man on the mere suspicion that the second could harbour sympathies for a black man, or that he (a white) should be threatened or possibly beaten into some form of submission for querying the reasoning behind such feeling – for being a "Nigger lover" – was a madness quite alien to my experience. To my naïve calculation this was the random and unreasoned idiocy that accompanied some frantic attempt to justify guilt. It was a kind of uneducated jailhouse stupidity. Why should I have been so surprised to encounter these currents of hostility, to be so taken aback by their virility?

Looking back, my brutal encounter with Alabama, however, was an occurrence thought at the time to have been peculiar to that set of circumstances and that geography – when in fact it was an isolated but expanding phenomenon of global proportions, as yet a small portion of a rising crescendo of ill feeling for "the other" that lent its impetus to extraordinary political aggressions; these would continue to be unleashed in ever-expanding bursts of viciousness throughout the balance of the XX century and well into the XXI century. Though totally irrational and acknowledging nothing of more substance than the basic uniform of an adversary, racism was not a *cause* so much as it was a convenient *excuse* that helped to delineate people on opposing sides of ferocious argument, each of whom saw their individual positions as utterly desperate – virtually no space left in which to manoeuvre. In Alabama and throughout the southern United States the opponents in the confrontation were, on the one hand, a huge African American minority who felt their lives had become an unjust and intolerable form of imprisonment within their own rapidly developing society, and an even larger southern American white majority who preferred the status quo and was clearly neither developing so rapidly nor particularly cared to, or even knew how to – and, moreover, a poorly educated group that historically had stood aloof and considered all persons of colour inferior to itself. Theirs was the unfeeling attitude left over from the days of slavery inculcated through a gruesome history into their present-day culture and collective barbarous psyche. On both sides one could gauge the anger brought on by sheer desperation – the Afro-Americans because they had had enough, and saw their liberation as a "now or never" human right; the whites because they understood that their domination and control, their status, over what till now had been their servant population, was slipping from their grasp. This latter group despised the veneer of "uppity black" insubordination such slippage implied.

Of course I knew that desperation was nothing new in the history of human conflict, understood it very well as kernel to what I had long ago come to recognize as the "empirical life," the very foundation of fascism. I had never been so completely naïve as to misunderstand the concepts of entitlement possessed by ruling classes worldwide when they are not tempered by a basic intelligence, effective unions or effective Human Rights organizations. But by marching head-up and so unprepared into the very midst of this level of the Alabama confrontation was nevertheless indicative, on my part, of naïveté a-plenty.

Many activists and supporters of the African American freedom movement were being beaten up or even killed in those days. Vigilante groups or police would enter homes in force on the flimsiest of pretexts. Floggings and arrests were common. The Ku Klux Klan was active, as were lynch mobs and shootings. Bombings in and around Birmingham had become so ubiquitous that between the end of the Second World War and 1962 more than fifty of them were unaccounted for, and the city itself had become known as Bombingham. Center Street in the Smithfield district, white on one side, Afro-American on the other, was devastated by unrest. Bombings and shootings in this area were intended to intimidate whites wanting to sell their properties to Afro-Americans, and the Afro-Americans who were willing to buy them. This and a string of gun battles served to earn for the area the nickname Dynamite Hill.

There is not the least doubt in my mind that had I been caught by the thugs who chased my car that afternoon on the road into Birmingham, my life would have stopped or dramatically altered course right there – and the events of the story that follows would never have taken place. A single and sobering thought. Throughout the course of my life I have been obliged to take note of a number of sobering eventualities.

Birmin'ham

For the next several weeks I was witness to an extraordinary assortment of banal savageries and the kind of unnecessarily vile language, demeaning and insulting, that had no other purpose than to undermine self-esteem – and this in a place where the majority of the inhabitants otherwise considered themselves members of a civilized, even genteel, society. White authority (seeing itself as representative of a superior culture that espoused what were claimed to be democratic principles, indeed represented a people convinced their white skins were proof of their evolution to most lofty rank) deliberately lowered themselves into a cesspool of self-righteous brutality. It was hard to take it all in, to witness it, let alone make sense of it.

The very day after I arrived in the city, on 2 May, 1963, I witnessed the launching of what was later to become known as the Children's Crusade – a mass demonstration by hundreds of the city's school children.

Then I watched as policemen in service who, as the children's supposed guardians, and by-the-by guardians also of the laws one could reasonably have expected would protect the weak and vulnerable, set their snarling attack dogs onto the peacefully demonstrating men, women and children who had rallied in the streets. These "authorities" used the authority of their nightsticks to club to the ground and break the bones of any demonstrator, or anyone with a dark skin expressing a contrary opinion – or, for that matter, anyone with a dark skin who was simply passing by and happened to be caught unaware. There were hundreds of children; they were organized, highly motivated and disciplined. And they were courageous. They did not confront authority with violence, but marched towards the violence like martyrs. They sang: "We shall overcome!" – and were met by attack dogs, water cannons and clubs.

I watched as teams of white-skinned firemen shouted racial obscenities at virtually anyone on the streets they considered "Nigger" and, with unconscionable relish, turned the full pressure of their fire hoses on both peaceful demonstrators and spectators. They not only wetted down their victims, but battered them so violently with the water jets that even a strong man would be instantly knocked off his feet. It was an easy and effective way to wash demonstrators along the roadways and across the rough paving of the sidewalks like so much garbage. It was no timid bathing. Invariably it entailed broken bones, lacerations and abrasions, concussions and hospitalization.

An Afro-American schoolgirl, fourteen or fifteen years of age, rounded a corner of the street to be confronted unexpectedly by a full phalanx of firemen and their hoses. She tried to run away.

"Hey! Get that Nigger bitch …!"

The team of firemen wheeled and played their jet of water onto her, so strong, so violent it ripped the flimsy cotton dress from her body. Her school books were torn from her grasp and destroyed in an instant. She fell naked onto the roadway.

"Look at the dirty black whore!" hooted the firemen, laughing at her nakedness. "Give her a bath!"

They played the immense power of the jets onto her body and legs, tumbling her across the tarmac like a rag golliwog. She would be knocked down again every time she tried to stand up, but miraculously managed to grab and hold onto the metal rail of a fence surrounding a small front garden.

In an interval when the firemen had turned their attentions elsewhere someone rushed from the house and took the girl, hurt and bloodied, into the shelter of a friendly home.

An old man, shuffling along the sidewalk with the aid of a stick, had attempted to pick up his feet and scurry across the street to avoid the imbroglio. His way was barred by police dog-handlers who held their animals in short check at the ends of long leashes – but abruptly let the leashes out to their fullest extent when their dogs were within inches of demonstrators. The result was certainly intentional; the dogs would lunge forward and bite. The old man could not escape. One of the dogs flew at his thigh wrenching him to the ground, gnashing first at his leg, then his stomach, and finally the arms with which he attempted to defend himself. The dog's handler made not the slightest move to haul his animal back until the man's screams were reduced to whimperings.

That very night, and at the supper hour on numerous nights that followed, such images were broadcast on the nation's television screens – peaceful unarmed marchers and protesters savaged by the authorities in the streets of their own city; school children beaten and bloodied by nightsticks; dogs and water cannons used indiscriminately as weapons on young and old alike before they were arrested and carted off to jail in paddy wagons or school buses. The outraged shouts of the Afro-American multitude bellowed the slogans of the nation's civil rights movement; from inside the vehicles transporting them, the children laughed and called out their derision of white authority, their defiant voices singing their freedom songs above the din of the streets as they were taken away. Throughout the nation the violence against these citizens, the children in particular, caused such an uproar of disgust that the following day, May 3, even more children skipped school to swarm out onto the streets and participate in the marches – and they kept this up until May 5.

The response of a racist authority was predictable: the school board, sympathetic to racist administrations at municipal and state level, suspended or expelled over one thousand children.

This decision was immediately put before the state court, which also favoured the racists – and so promptly and deliberately upheld the school board's edicts.

On May 10 the state court's decision was overturned by the U.S. Supreme Court, and the children were returned to their classrooms.

The very next day Col. Eugene "Bull" Connor who, as the city's

Commissioner of Public Safety was also the de facto chief of police and the fire brigades, was forced to resign his post. Col. Al Lingo, director of the Alabama Department of Public Safety and the State Highway Patrol, answering directly to State Governor George Wallace, was initially in a position to continue Connor's unsavoury work and to wrestle with the civic authorities who were beginning to buckle under the enraged onslaught of those seeking desegregation.

These were the tumultuous events in motion during the first days after my arrival in the city. As a visiting outsider it was difficult to grasp the full picture, or to comprehend the nuances of any single action I might have viewed on the street. It was as if I was riding a rickety narrow gauge train into the dark tunnel of a spectacular Mardi Gras horror chamber – unable to stop and get off, yet unable to see anything until the wobbly rig in which I sat spun around a corner, and the lid lifted on a black coffin or a skeletal head glowed behind a net interwoven with unimaginable human trauma. It was not hard to understand that Birmingham was only one element of a far wider problem, but my full attention was riveted by the corruption and dark injustice of what I was witnessing and it was impossible to expand my view to encompass the entire show. I had had no experience of prior desegregation manoeuvres. I learned that there had been sit-ins in cafés, and that management of roadside diners were refusing service to Afro-Americans, that there had been supportive challenges to segregated buses throughout the south, strong resistance to laws requiring Afro-Americans to ride in the seats at the back of a bus and to accept that all public utilities, from drinking fountains and toilets to libraries and the schools themselves, must be separate. Until I entered Birmingham I had seen none of it. Nor had I seen the effectiveness of the retail boycott of the city's stores. I knew nothing of the hatreds all this had engendered prior to the city's uprisings, and that the situation had been simmering long months, even years, prior to my own arrival in Birmingham. I had no concept of other movements and negotiations, or what had happened previously in other locales such as Albany or Montgomery – or the sort of violent confrontation that was later to occur in Selma. But it was plain that if the trauma that was Birmingham was indicative of a wider conflict, the entire south must surely be about to burst into flames. I knew it, could feel it but couldn't see it – until suddenly I saw it.

What I could see, the virility of a horrendous white-on-black cruelty, adversely coloured my view of the United States of America. Imperialism as practiced by the British, and in which I had had my own nose rubbed so resoundingly only short years before, had been a clear demonstration of abhorrent crimes against humanity, and it was largely the reasoned anticolonial voice of the Americans – in the United Nations at the time of the Suez invasion in 1956 – that had brought this home to me. And yet here, in the streets of a city in the country that had always held itself to be the finest model of civility and democracy – and thus above all others – I was witnessing a level of deliberate vulgarity and barbarity that appeared to exceed anything I had previously seen – even during the Mau Mau emergency in Kenya, and in the war against the communists in Malaya.

What is the scale for a measurement of disgust? My naïveté, indeed!

In America, surely, we are supposed to see the culmination of the highest echelons of Civilization – of Justice, Honour, Brotherhood and, maybe most important of all, face-up and honest Fair Play.

If these couldn't be secured and defended on America's own soil, where could they be?

A news reporter, we are told (especially by editors), is supposed to remain a neutral observer of the events surrounding any story he or she is covering – and as a rule of thumb that is indeed a most majestic target. It is also nonsense. By nature I believe most journalists are actually sensitive creatures, flatly unable to witness the agony and predicaments of others at close quarters without assuming at least a portion of their suffering – and that, frankly, is how it is meant to be. How can I be expected to write accurately about a man's pain if I am so distant I cannot feel it myself? Journalists are constantly told by their editors "be objective," which would be all very well but for the fact that journalists are human, subjective by nature – no matter how cold and distanced he or she pretends to be. Aha! You counter – then account for the cold-blooded and intrusive mind of the *paparazzo*!

Well, yes, there are exceptions to my refined thesis, as there are exceptions to all rules. We know very well there really do exist sons of bitches in this world – people who do not give a tinker's damn about what you think or how you feel, and who will stick the camera in your face anyway, or publish your words verbatim even though, for very good reason, you may have requested otherwise; or preceded them with qualifiers. Callous editors love them because they always get "the story."

But the truth is, they don't really get *the* story – they get *a* story, enough to fill a column in a dollar rag, or even enough to sell that rag.

Surely it is sensitivity to the story that gives the story its truth? To my way of thinking, sensitivity is the single most important quality that permits a ready comprehension of any "story," and I believe any news reporter worthy of the trade would agree it is a most necessary trait if he really wants to understand the events he is covering – and impart the essence of his understanding to the story he is telling. Cold truth is the paramount ingredient permitting a connection between story-teller and story-reader – and any child will tell his grandpapa, instantly, the moment the fairy tale being read to him veers from the line of truth by even the smallest detail.

The down-side of truth-telling is that a summer-long event like Birmingham (the agony that had started long prior to my arrival continued long past my departure) tends to pulverize the mind. Short weeks, and my own mind was in utter turmoil. My naïveté was not the fault. What I saw, clear as if it had been carved deep by the stonecutter shaping the cruel smirk of his gargoyle, was a whole society – a white society – that simply did not give a damn. Not about others, white or black, and not even about themselves. Not really. I saw a whole depraved and zombie-minded society absent genuine creativity, who could give nothing because they had nothing to give but malice – an entire society now faced with the inevitability of right over wrong and the possibility of performing a noble and constructive act, instead prefer to sit itself in a corner and masturbate. What greater signal of hatred – of others and of self – can there be? And this was long before Donald Trump turned himself loose on America.

Looking back over fifty years it is easy to understand how the events of those short weeks in Birmingham marked me as surely as if I had been branded. There was no quandary as to my feelings then, and even now it is easy to see and recreate them – an ocean as wide as all my horizons. Attempting to explain them is akin to trying to fit the sands of an entire panorama into a child's beach pail. Although I had allowed myself to be seduced by America before, in Birmingham I was seeing the nation disrobed for the first time. It was a distasteful shock, as though I alone was witness to this monstrous pornography, this great growling bombastic giant of tinsel and glitz, noise and incredible achievement, turning over in fitful and nightmarish slumbers. Could this great dame's unsavoury urges satisfy sufficiently the lusts of those who had opted to bed with her and succumb to her ravishing?

If America is the crucible of modern democracy, as she so persistently claims, if America is the custodian of all that is fine and sacred, and represents The Best to which Humanity can aspire and thus be blessed with a God-given right to play the world's *amah* with big stick and commanding voice, then also she is the saddest and most glaring example of mankind's worst traits and unutterable failures. I began to see the United States of America as both the school and the arena, training ground and showplace, of the Great Corruptor, the playpen of the cigar-chomping diamond-ringed gangster, a carnival show of arrogance and vice, the bawdy house of brittle tragedies in which could be found the full lexicon of blasphemous heresies, samplings of all the squalid excrement of mankind's rampant excesses – and thus a negation of history's continual cycle of lessons.

Is there not a more positive truth to be told? Is there nothing that can be said to rise above such extraordinary profanity?

In Afro-American Birmingham in 1963, yes.

In white supremacist Birmingham in 1963, no.

In my heart I had always known (a blind faith) the list of fine values to which America has claimed at least an intellectual adherence. One does not have to be an American to have a passing knowledge of the Constitution's lofty language, to have heard the National Anthem, or have hummed along to the stirring verses of the Battle Hymn of the Republic. The noblest of human values and freedoms are inscribed on a plaque at the Statue of Liberty in the lines of Emma Lazarus' poem *"The Great Colossus"* offering succor to the "huddled masses," and so on and so on.[6]

These are the ideals by which America has chosen to be judged, which were and which remain intentionally noble, setting for the nation as a whole, and for all the world to examine and judge, the very highest standards of moral behaviour. Unfortunately this makes them all the more readily noted when they are not attained.

Well I remember how, as one of my grade school teachers was penciling livid red castigations into the margins of my classmates' workbooks (mine, too, was there), I ventured a query of remonstrance:

"You are quick to mark us down for our mistakes, Ma'am," I told her boldly. "When we try hard and do well why don't you award us praise, and paste gold stars at the tops of our best work?"

She glowered and raised the finger of admonition.

"I expect you to try hard at *all* times, young Master Jeremy. Your

---

[6] Following the unveiling of the statue in October, 1886, the Afro-American newspaper, *The Cleveland Gazette*, in reference to Emma Lazarus' poem, *"The Great Colossus,"* editorialized: "'Liberty enlightening the world,' indeed! The expression makes us sick. This government is a howling farce. It cannot, or rather *does not,* protect its citizens within its *own* borders. Shove the [Frédéric August] Bartholdi statue, torch and all, into the ocean until the 'liberty' of this country is such as to make it possible for an inoffensive and industrious colored man to earn a respectable living for himself and family, without being ku-kluxed, perhaps murdered, his daughter and wife outraged, and his property destroyed. The idea of the 'liberty' of this country 'enlightening the world,' or even Patagonia, is ridiculous in the extreme."

excellent work should be brighter than any gold star I can award you. You yourself should know that anything less than your best, at any time, is simply not good enough!"

It would seem reasonable to suppose if the lesson in this was sufficient for the comprehension of a grade schooler, then it should also be clear enough for anyone giving a tacit nod towards the American Constitution. It is a document Americans love to quote, and some can spout lengthy chunks of it along with convincing interpretations.

Like others who confess naïveté, and ever the optimist, now in Birmingham I was feeling anger oozing through my confusion concerning a Constitution I knew barely at all, and which in any case was not mine. Optimism was a poor fit in face of the brutality I was discovering. It was not merely that I was the witness to some abhorrent political movement, and thus to feel personally its imposition of violence; it was as if a smothering blanket had been laid over a perpetually cowed people, such as had been the case in Axis-Europe, Japan, South Africa, and in so many countries in Central and South America short years before – people who had spent their entire lives at the butt-end of a colossal mendacity. Here in the Deep South of the United States of America fascism, pure and unadorned, was ingrained within the blind and selfish spirit of the privileged – people for whom the Constitution was little more than a concoction they had selectively mixed for themselves in order to permit the luxury of experimenting the giddiest freedoms of a giddy Cyrenaic hedonism. Here in America, there was not a doubt in my mind, fascism had been diligently constructed on solid foundations.

The Operatives

Arriving in the city, I had taken a room at the Dinkler-Tutwiler Hotel, thrown my bags onto the bed and left immediately to see if I could locate Dr. Martin Luther King. He had set up his operational headquarters in the Gaston Motel, right across the road from the park in which the police had established their headquarters in a series of trailers. It was easy to find the motel, and even Dr. King himself. Leaving my car in the hotel parking lot, my route to the motel was a short walk across the downtown. Within a half hour I presented my credentials at the motel's reception desk and was ushered into a first floor room to be seated at a table with other newspapermen. Dr. Martin Luther King, Jr. himself was presiding over a general question-and-answer session concerning street strategies. I could hardly believe my good fortune, but the fact of my nationality seemed to count as useful.

"We need the press," said Dr. King when I stood and introduced myself. "We need all of you to carry our message far beyond these city limits – and the foreign press is especially welcome here."

I tried to write everything down. When the meeting broke up, I went downstairs to the motel café and kept writing. The one name with which I was even remotely familiar was Dr. King's, but suddenly others crowded in and I was at my wit's end to sort out who was who, or to which particular organization each owed allegiance. For the first time I was hearing an encyclopedic list of initials and acronyms – organizations that had mustered their forces of men, women and know-how in order to combat this accursed racial segregation.

A partial list:

ACMHR – Alabama Christian Movement for Human Rights (1956 – Rev. Fred Shuttlesworth)

LCCR – Leadership Conference on Civil Rights (1950 – Philip Randolph, Roy Wilkins)

NAACP – National Association for the Advancement of Colored People (1909)

NASW – National Association of Social Workers (1955)

NOI – Nation of Islam (1930 – Elijah Muhammad)

SCLC – Southern Christian Leadership Conference (1957 – Bayard Rustin, Ella Baker, Rev. Dr. Martin Luther King, Jr., Rev. Fred Shuttlesworth, Rev. Ralph Abernathy)

SNCC – Student Nonviolent Coordinating Committee (1960 – Ella Baker)

Operation Breadbasket (1962 – Rev. Fred Bennette)

There were others, and yet others were formed in the months and years long after this Alabama adventure. The list has grown every year since …

Attempting, now, to place my own activities within the context of the story I was trying to cover I am forced to admit to an embarrassment of breaches in detail. But the shenanigans of a solitary young reporter who entered that tumult as witness by no means constitute the compelling story. The events themselves and their aftermath were the story, then as they are now. Any reporter entering that arena cold, without a strong background in race relations and an innate comprehension of what was going on, could only render a scant interpretation of what was unfolding. At any given moment events were so widespread and of such magnitude, one reporter alone would be quite unable to divide him/herself into enough parts to measure its impact throughout the land.

Conscientious reporter though I'm sure I was, pad and pen ever at hand and scribbling, I was quickly aware of my inadequacy. At night, back in the hotel, I would piece together my scraps of paper, my take on the different elements of the overall scene as I had jotted it down, trying to understand it. As time would permit I would write the events of the day and my thoughts about them into a better-kept notebook, more often than not pitching out the pocket worn, crumpled and virtually illegible bird-scratch leaves of the pad I'd used on the run. It was a mistake. I would have been better served with the hasty notations. My hope was that I'd be able to make fuller sense of the story by filling in detail – later – and then never did. The good intent was there, of course, but too soon there was some new aspect that required more urgent attention, an even bigger element of the assignment – and then it was too late to make amends. Huge gaps have developed, widening as memory fades.

In truth I had lost something of value. The bird-scratch notes possessed a spontaneity that may have failed the cut in the stilted prose of a more formal attempt at writing; but they also contained detail and names I would dearly love to recall.

As to personalities, throughout my days in Birmingham I would have been obliged to catch names on the fly and, to my chagrin, did not always note them down. Consequently I feel I owe a most humble apology to anyone who feels their history has been offended by my disorganization. Too many names now elude me. Some important ones remain clear:

I noted Rev. Dr. King's, to be sure, and likewise Whitney Young. Rev. James Bevel, Rev. Fred Shuttlesworth, and the fiery Rev. Dr. Wyatt Tee Walker all made themselves available with great courtesy. Arthur Gaston, the owner of the motel, and Rev. Bevel were present on numerous occasions, and I was able to converse with both of them. It was Rev. Bevel himself, chief organizer of what became known as the Children's Crusade, who explained to an upstart young Canadian reporter the significance of the NAACP of which, at that time, he was one of the principal leaders.

All were people I had never encountered before but who, during my stay in the city, showed me great kindness and respect. Dr. King, working tirelessly to keep hold of and lead his team in face of constant provocations to its non-violent aims, was a figure often glimpsed through a doorway, his head bowed over a desk or a city map, talking earnestly to his lieutenants. I had been hoping to sit down and interview him at length but in the end, apart from one brief casual encounter, I was limited to meeting with him and asking my questions during the tight scheduling of the several press conferences he held throughout the period I was there.

Whitney Young seemed to me to stand apart from most of the others. He possessed an august sense of command and air of steady statesmanship. I can also recall very clearly a winning sense of good humour, refreshing under the circumstances.

The one man at the Gaston Motel with whom I had most dealings was Andrew Young. He caught my eye immediately because he appeared to be so youthful, so vigorously alert and involved – not a whole lot younger than the others yet, to my inexperienced view, notably young to be participating in such monumental national events. He was one of those in the meeting room when I first showed up; I sought him out and was able to meet and talk with him on any number of occasions when I needed help; I felt free to stop him when our paths crossed. He possessed an informal and most tolerant manner with members of a clamouring press.

As the months and years of the desegregation fight proceeded, the names of scores of these famous and brave men were flashed before me time and again – along with a continuous stream of new ones. I was to hear over and over about literally dozens of those Afro-American leaders I had either met briefly, or with whom I had had passing acquaintance in the corridors of the Gaston Motel. I would see familiar faces in the daily press, in magazines and on television, and could associate these news makers with the events I had been covering. Except Dr. King, all of them had been totally new to me when I had first arrived there, but they became more than occasionally familiar long after I had left Alabama and as the desegregation process unfolded.

It was not unlike being the proverbial fly on the wall. Many times mine would be the sole white face in a sea of brown – which actually made me a conspicuous fly. I was present, but I was also cognizant this fight was not mine. It was possible to have strong and sympathetic bonds with my new friends inside the walls of the Gaston Motel or the 16th Street Baptist Church, but clearly I was not one of them. All I could offer to such a friendship was a promise that I would try my best to tell their story in Canada – and knowing my efforts would be circumscribed by the whim of an editor.

The pale hue of my Caucasian skin was the one thing I had in common with the street rabble outside the motel that was shouting for the blood of the Afro-Americans inside. On the assumption that "the friend of mine enemy is mine enemy" I had been anxious to remain apart – at least to give the appearance of impartiality. A northerner? A foreigner with contrary views? As surely as I had been rushed by the thugs at the roadside diner on my way into the city, I would have been singled out for roughing up, or worse. It was not hard to understand in an intellectual sort of way that the mob in the streets could have looked on me with jaundiced eyes, but I felt so utterly detached physically from the entire situation it was difficult to consider myself either the friend or the enemy of anyone. Interfering nuisance, maybe, but hardly a fifth columnist – and not at all a quisling.

Yet working these things over in my mind it occurred to me I had very rapidly done what no journalist is supposed to do: I had developed strong sympathies and taken a side. I was not so detached after all, and I had to take great pains to see this sentiment did not appear that way to the white rabble in the streets. Seeing me as an objective journalist daily entering their enemy's quarters, they might very well have demanded I demonstrate my neutrality – but by siding with them? That they didn't make this demand would seem to indicate they had some notion of my correct role. I told myself it would have been highly detrimental for me to let them know, through some inadvertent slip, that the detachment I attempted to portray was cover for a mindset opposed to their own.

Acknowledging the delicacy of my position, it made sense for me to present the face of total journalistic dispassion outside the motel; had I for a moment permitted my true emotions to be seen by those in the streets beyond the Gaston's walls, I would have been just as liable as any of the Afro-Americans inside to be picked on or picked off. It was a necessarily dishonest duality that did not bother me a whole lot, except that I had no idea how long I could keep it up. I realized the racists in the streets had no interest in me whatsoever as long as I stood aside – or beside them – and maintained silence. So taken up were they by the frenzies of their hatred it was easy for me to cultivate invisibility. Had I chosen to pronounce myself sympathetic to the views of the white Alabamans surrounding me, to express the idea that my real loyalties were in any way in line with theirs, I have no doubt they would have found a use for me – a foreigner able to wield sufficient and convincing journalistic clout to weasel his way into that headquarters "Nigger nest," and thus able to discover the programmes of the Afro-Americans inside and what their less than civic minds were plotting next. I felt comfort in my neutrality well knowing that to negate it would have been to confront great discomfort indeed.

On the other hand, and for totally different reasons, mixing daily with those who frequented the city's most infamously black motel, my Caucasian countenance was never once commented upon by the Afro-Americans. Within the walls of the Gaston I was at no time subjected to even the slightest humiliation of the sort that was being heaped daily upon the heads of the Afro-Americans outside. I felt myself totally welcome among them; I enjoyed the honour of being addressed as "Brother." They knew that to all outside their stream I was merely a reporter doing his job – that this effort in the end would in some way assist them.

On the drive south I had made the error of thinking this whole escapade had no coherent place for me, that at most it would test me tangentially.

Till that moment the glossy white pages of my life's copybook had been relatively clear, sullied a little here and there by my share in a few disastrous relationships and a two-year bout with the British Army, but by-and-large I reckoned the skirmishes of life had left me relatively unscarred, given little cause for a repentance requiring identification. Up to that point, and to the clear vision of my eye at the moment, I had sported through life a fairly solid sense of balance and fair play, so far avoiding any obvious damage. It was the happy-go-lucky viewpoint of my fairly confident twenty-seven years – more brimful of brass than intelligence. My time on active service with the military had been exciting, but on the whole probably less forbidding than for others I had known. As a soldier an enemy had been picked for me, which fact relieved me of the onerous responsibility of choosing one for myself.

But here in Alabama, having entered this zone of ferment of my own volition, it was clear I was being required to take a moral stance – not a thing I especially recognized as being required of the individual me before. The Fates had always permitted me to thrash through the days of my life in my own silly way – with vigour but blindly – and I had been fortunate. Charmed, in a way. But suddenly everything was different. Now, right and wrong could not have been presented in clearer light. There were simply no grey areas.

The leaders of the Afro-American movement were hugely impressive, as were the numbers of people I met every day who had somehow associated themselves with Dr. King's dream of unity throughout his country. Quite a few I had come to know as operatives on his team, people I had found in the rooms and corridors of the Gaston Motel. Their sense of purpose and control, their confident bravado, the bold humour each expressed in the face of the clear danger lurking in the streets outside the walls of the building – these could not help but impress a young reporter trying to set his feet down and secure a balance, even though so obviously an outsider floundering somewhat beyond his depth. It was difficult to tie together all the loose ends of this extremely complex story – and I had walked into it cold.

Kan-aid-ia

The people who were running this show wanted journalists on hand to write up the doings of their days and relate them to the world, but if truth were told they were far too occupied with their revolution to have a whole lot of time to talk to reporters and answer all the questions people like me felt needed answering. So I took to hanging out with whomever I could in the meeting rooms, and I would attend Dr. King's press conferences whenever he called them. My main source of substance and ambient beyond the basic comprehension of what the revolution was all about, was to be found in the streets or at the Baptist church. Everyone wanted to talk, and everyone had something to say. I did not have to travel very far, and there was a story to be noted down every time I turned around or spoke to someone new. When I needed to come up for air, or put my head down and write out my notes, I'd retreat to the Gaston coffee shop and take a table by the window.

"Hey, brother – you from around here?"

"No," I replied. "I'm Canadian."

My questioner had approached me from behind. He pointed to the handwritten pages of my notebook.

"You a reporter?"

"Yes."

"You from Kan-aid-ia?"

"Yes." This was amusing.

He wore a colossal shock of woolly black hair. I had never seen anything like it before, even in pictures. In due course I was to recognize the style as "afro," but I knew nothing of this at the time. My first impression was that he was wearing an unkempt guardsman's busby and looked a bit like a British government propaganda photograph of a member of the Mau Mau.

He wanted to talk, so merrily plonked himself down on one of the other chairs at the table and proceeded to launch himself into conversation – with another question.

"I've heard of this here Kan-aid-ia ... Where's it at?"

A couple of his friends sat at a nearby table and looked over at us. They were grinning – and not a little curious as to what progress Afro was making with me. They had probably set him up. There were no other white people in the café; it was not at all usual to see a white man and a black man sitting together at the same table in friendly conversation. But this was the Gaston, and I knew I was on safe ground. This story was one of white on black, not black on white.

At first I thought his question some kind of joke, but the look of earnest inquisitiveness in his eyes very quickly informed that the fellow really did not know. A happily unschooled kind of bumpkin, his query was fetching in its simplicity.

"It's quite a ways north of here," I hesitated. "Big place ..."

"North of the Mason-Dixon ...?" He was all attention.

I was still unsure whether or not he was pulling my leg. One of the fellows at the other table started to chuckle gleefully. He had been listening in, but now moved over and joined us.

"He don't know nut'in from nut'in," he chided good-naturedly.

Afro was not in the least humiliated. On the contrary, he smiled a row of magnificent white teeth, and gave his friend a mock punch on the arm. The friend feinted sideways as though falling from his chair.

"Woe, man!"

"Never was much at knowin' geography'n'stuff," said Afro, holding up a hand in case he had to fend off retaliation from his friend. "You tell me where this place is at."

I pulled over a paper placemat and at this point several young men in the room, all Afro-Americans who had been paying attention to us, curious as to what was going on, moved in and looked over my shoulder as I sketched a rough map of North and Central America. I wrote in Alaska, all the Canadian provinces, the lakes – and Mexico. Then I indicated very roughly where

Alabama would have been had my map been at all accurate.

None of them appeared to have a great deal of schooling, but they seemed willing to learn. Afro, it was becoming apparent, was a leader of his group. He knew where he was "at," though clearly not in terms of geography.

"Hush-up!" he commanded as his companions noisily tried to move in closer. "We can learn somethin' from this gentle-man …"

Then he looked down at my map and studied it with concentration.

"This is America, right? And Alaska, okay – I got that. And all this is Kan-aid-ia …?" He swept his fingers over the paper from Vancouver Island to Newfoundland and Labrador.

"That's right. And all of it north of the Mason-Dixon line," I said.

He looked doubtful.

"But look-ee … All that there's north of the Mason-Dixon line, you say – an' you draw this place Kan-aid-ia bigger than the US of A. That can't be right …!"

"Well, it's not a scale map," I told him. "It's only a diagram to give you an idea because you asked. But Canada is, in fact, considerably bigger than your US of A."

He pulled his chin in and looked at me with a pair of googly pop-eyes.

"Ye-e-e-e!" he exclaimed, amazed. "Y'don't say!"

I didn't know if it was so very important to plot Canada on the map. It seemed as though it was one of those elements of minutiae that parlour games are made of, and within a moment or two the guest at my table abandoned my homeland and reverted to his original bumpkin guise. I started to feel finicky and altogether too clever. He wasn't done with me yet.

"An'say – you got problems same as us, up there in Kan-aid-ia? You got black folks up there, right? How them folks get treated up there where you come from?"

"I know what I've read in the newspapers about Birmingham, no more. And what I've seen in the streets these last few days …" I told him. "I've talked to some of your movement's leaders in their meeting rooms upstairs … Yesterday I saw the actions of the police and firemen in the streets facing off against some of your demonstrators – most of whom seemed to be black school children. I don't think I've ever seen anything like that. Not in Canada. Not anywhere."

Afro and his friends were listening carefully to what I was saying.

"We don't have the sort of divisions you appear to have down here," I continued. "We don't have a whole lot of blacks, anyway. We have Indians, so we discriminate against them instead …"

That really bowled over my audience. Guffaws of laughter all around. That was the best thing they had heard all day. Afro slapped me on the shoulder as he got up to leave, flashed me a broad smile to show off his spectacular teeth, gave me a thumbs up and an open palm wave.

"Hey bro, gotta go. You enjoy your stay in Birmin'ham, y'hear. Keep your eyes on them State Highway Patrol boys. Then when you get back to Kan-aid-ia, if you've learned your lesson well from our police down here in this fair city, you'll really know how to beat up on them Indians of yours. Ye-e-e-e!"

He swung out of the café, more like a dance, and I watched him from the window as he jumped over the door and into the front seat of his sleek electric-metal green Ford Fairlane 500 convertible. He had parked it outside on the street. His companions sat with me for a few moments longer at the table watching me watching him go.

"Jeez! He's the man!" said one, and they all laughed as the group of them got up to wander outside and mill about like wary conspirators in the street. Several policemen were eyeing them from their positions in the shadows of the park across the way.

I saw Afro only once more after that. A day or two later he cruised by the motel, the canvas top of his car peeled back. He saw me sitting in the window of the café, pulled over to the curb and parked. Jumping over the driver's side door, he loped inside.

"Hey, bro!" he greeted me, pulling up a chair and straddling it to socialize with me over its wooden back.

Then he bummed a dollar off me, said he needed to put some gas in the Fairlane 500.

Beer Run

There was an upstairs work room at the motel which was used for press conferences, but which at other times served for the movement's operatives working at an assortment of tables preparing pamphlets, circulars and press releases – generally attempting to cope with small mountains of necessary paperwork and answer incoming calls passed through from the switchboard. I went there from time to time, but late one afternoon during a rare lull in the action and a light turn of conversation I happened to mention that I was unimpressed with American beer. My comment drew instant attention, and so I felt compelled to offer up the two cases of good Canadian brew I had brought south in the trunk of my car. It seemed to be the right occasion. There was delight all around and a general consensus that fine beer should not be left in the trunk of a car in Birmingham's heat, that it should be fetched in as quickly as possible – indeed, within the hour – to stash such rare elixir in one of the motel's refrigerators.

Dr. King happened into the room right at that moment. Catching the good-natured theme of the conversation, he paused to join in the banter.

"If your Canadian beer is as strong as we've heard, Mr. Hespeler-Boultbee, you'd better not let any one person have too much of it ... I need these people with me one hundred percent!"

I was struck by his use of my surname. On my first day in the city I had attended one of his press conferences and, when asking a question, had introduced myself – a difficult name to catch when uttered only once on first meeting – and now he had used it correctly. It was indicative of one of his extraordinary traits: a keen memory. Most people will forget names or, in the case of a difficult name, ask for it to be repeated. Remembering names must be more a gift than a knack, and Dr. King appeared to have it in abundance – and not just a memory for names, but also for long tracts and accurate quotation. Several people drew my attention to this; if someone had said something, he was able to recall it verbatim and use it in its correct context.

But to the matter of beer: it was just before sundown when I left the hotel with the two cases I had locked in the back of my car and headed back towards the Gaston Motel, taking a shortcut through the Kelly Ingram Park. The motel was located across the street from the park where, plumb in the centre, the State Highway Patrol had pugnaciously elected to set up headquarters in a series of white trailers. I knew this. They were positioned so as to be seen and to intimidate, and for this reason I had carefully avoided approaching them till now. The beer cases were not heavy, but I had a shoulder bag as well so that the full load was a little awkward to carry over the short distance. They had been in my car since I had left Toronto and it made sense to get it stacked away in a refrigerator now that I knew where one was available. There should have been no harm in cutting across the park, walking past the police trailers ... There were numbers of officers in the vicinity but one in particular stood out for his size, clearly the boss. He had a white safety helmet perched like an egg atop his head. Holstered, hanging low down on each of his hips and intended to be noticed, was a pair of twin pearl-white-handled revolvers. He nodded at me as I walked by.

"Good evening," I greeted him in response.

"Hi, there!" he replied – and I kept walking.

Several metres past him, I heard:

"Hey, boy!"

Couldn't be me, I thought, and kept walking. Wrong.

"Boy! I'm talkin' to you! You stop right where you are ..."

I stopped, turned towards him, said nothing.

"Where you goin', boy?"

There was a beer case in each of my hands, so I inclined my head in the direction of the motel.

"Over there," I replied.

"To that Niggrah motel?"

"Is that what you call it?"

"What the hell you goin' there for, boy?" The anger in his voice rose quickly.

"I've been invited to join some friends," I told him truthfully.

"What kind of friends you got that hang out in a Niggrah motel?" His voice now was sneering and aggressive.

"Good friends," I said. "Honest folk."

"Ain't nuthin' good over there, boy. Nuthin' honest. Jus' them damn Niggrahs, an' they ain't no good for nobody," he cautioned. "Whatcha goin' over there for?"

"A breath of fresh air," I said, a little too testily.

He nodded his bulbous head, didn't take his eyes off me.

"You're pretty clever, huh, boy!" He came over and towered in front of me. He indicated the cartons of beer in my hands.

"Watcha got there, huh ...?"

"Beer," I told him.

"Well, you put it right there on the ground!" he ordered me, and at the same time he called to another of the police officers nearby.

"Take this uppity young fella back to the precinct. He wants fresh air, so you show him what we got. Give him a comfortable place to bed down for the night. Lots'a fresh air ..."

With that I was escorted to a nearby squad car and placed in its back seat. As the cop was driving me the few blocks to the police cells I asked him...

"Am I under arrest?"

"Guess so. Boss colonel don't like people like you."

"Why on earth not?" I enquired. "My skin's as white as his ..."

"Yeah, but you a Nigger-lover, an' you got a mouth, boy."

"Does he intend to keep my beer?"

"Forget your fuckin' beer. You don't need it where you goin'."

The Birmingham police precinct was probably little different from any other – cold walls painted cold pastel colours, an absence of anything remotely decorative, and a police staff on the stiff adrenalin fix that signalled the paranoia of the times. Clearly civility had become a lost art form on the likes of whoever they thought I was, along with the inability to deliver to anyone but their own kind even a minimal pinch of grace. To a man (I did not see or have contact with any female officers) they were brusque and ill-mannered. Every one of the officers coming into the reception area looked as though what he wanted to do most of all was to kick someone's butt, teach someone a lesson – and that his biggest immediate regret would be if his intended pupil was not held in confinement long enough to receive an adequate portion of his instruction.

My small pack, my shoes, my belt, and everything I had in my pockets at the time were placed in a plastic bin, and I was shuttled into a tiny cell with a single concrete bunkbed and a metal toilet.

"Can you tell me why I'm in here?" I asked the officer who was closing the steel door to my cell.

"Nope," he replied, and the door was slammed shut.

Peter Pinsway

It was a warm night, and I slept well without a blanket. In the morning, almost at first light, I was offered a cup of coffee and a dish of tasteless hominy grits. Both were foul.

"You're free to go," I was told, and at the front desk my belongings were returned to me.

"How about the two cases of beer taken from me in the park?" I asked.

"Don't know nuthin'bout that. They ain't on the list o'things you left at this counter last night. You best be on your way, fella, or you'll be spendin' a mite more time as our guest."

Blatant theft was cause for fair indignation, I reckoned, but I clammed up, at least savvy enough to keep the thought tucked in. It was not a good moment to pick a further quarrel with the Birmingham police department.

Returning to my room at the Dinkler-Tutwiler, I took a shower and climbed into a fresh change of clothes. The day was already hot, so I threw my light suit jacket over my arm. Intending to go straight to the Gaston Motel, I was in the process of handing over my key at the front desk when I glanced up and, to my surprise (and the surprise of everybody else in the lobby) saw Charlot alighting from a taxi and commissioning the hotel concierge to carry his bags through the front door. A small man, dapper and businesslike, strode quickly across the foyer. He was dressed – as if in pantomime – as a cleaner-cut version of Charlie Chaplin's little hobo in any number of his silent films.

Both the desk clerk and I watched blink-eyed and open-mouthed as the little fellow made his way to the reception desk.

"Good morning!" he hailed the clerk cheerily and, as I was standing awkwardly right beside him, he nodded a polite greeting in my direction as well. He placed a valise on the floor at his feet and hooked a tightly-rolled umbrella over his forearm, at the same time deftly doffing his black bowler hat and replacing it on his head.

"You have a reservation for me, I believe?"

Momentarily overloaded, the desk clerk fumbled into action.

The newcomer's accent was a vigorously enunciated Queen's English, commanding and confident, unusual enough and loud enough to ring like a crystal bell throughout the hotel lobby. A number of people looked up and appeared to take interest. The man was dressed in a carefully-brushed Savile Row black jacket, white handkerchief poking out of its top pocket, the white cuffs of the shirt (gold cuff-links) projecting the regulation one inch at the end of each black sleeve. He wore immaculately-creased pinstripe trousers (black and grey) and highly-polished black Oxford shoes, their toes peeping brightly beyond the stove-pipe ends of the trouser-legs.

The bowler hat and tightly-rolled umbrella were his most incongruous accoutrements, but possibly not more noticeable than the clarity, tone and timbre of his impeccable English accent. In the streets of the City of London at that time he would have passed unnoticed in a crowd, but here in the drawling surrounds of Birmingham, Alabama, he would have presented himself to locals as some rare specimen of primate escaped from a zoo. His manner, his extraordinarily confident Englishness, was in perfect sync with the man he indeed was, but the locale of his appearance was several thousand kilometres off centre, and the cultural setting he embodied clashed louder than London's bridge falling into the Arizona desert.

"Name's Pinsway. Peter Pinsway. London Daily Register. My office was in touch with you day-before-yesterday," he announced.

At that I stepped forward.

"Mr. Pinsway ... Couldn't help overhearing. Excuse me, but may I introduce myself?"

And I told him who I was and where I came from.

"Canada, a-ha! I'm so glad to meet you," he bubbled, his face lighting merrily. "Oh – what a stroke of good fortune! Let me do the doin's here and keep this young chap happy. Will you join me for a little breakfast? I didn't eat on my flight down from Washington ..."

He turned back to the desk clerk, finished signing in and summoned a porter to deliver his bags to his room. Then he turned and gave me his full attention.

"By George! How wonderful to meet a Canadian, right off the bat! I'm hungry, so let's find the dining room and get to know one another. Meeting you is really most fortuitous. Yes, indeed!"

Peter Pinsway addressed me effusively, and clearly could not have cared less that everybody we passed in the hotel lobby was gawking at him. He took me by the arm and thus we walked together into the hotel dining room.

He was considerably older than I was and next to the formality of his attire I must have looked like a southern hick. But nothing fazed him. His talk was expansive and egalitarian. Everything about his conversation indicated that at that precise moment I was the very centre of his attention.

"Look here," he said. "There can't be all that many of us Commonwealth chaps about, wot? We must stick together …"

"There aren't any at all," I told him. "At least, not now. No other Canadians that I know of, and I haven't met anyone from Britain, either. You're the first."

"Not quite," he told me. "We had our Washington correspondent down here for a couple of weeks, lady by the name of S –. Had dinner with her last night in Washington. Fine journalist but somehow she got herself into trouble, crossed the local police, and they booted her out of the city, out of the state. Highway Patrol drove her to the state boundary, told her to be gone and they wouldn't vouch for her safety if she came back. Extraordinary way to treat anyone, member of the press, and especially a lady. She had to leave, poor dear, but she wasn't a great deal of use to the paper after that, stuck way up there in Washington. So I've been sent out from London to replace her, if that's possible … Tall order. She's a good reporter, keen eye for detail."

He tasted the grits that had been set down in front of him.

"Local porridge, I suppose … Dreadful!" He pushed the dish away and turned his attention to a boiled egg that looked remarkably like the police chief's helmet.

Just into his sixties at the time of our meeting, Peter Pinsway was now a senior reporter for one of Britain's leading conservative newspapers. Prior to that he had served a full career with the Royal Navy, taking an early retirement from the service as a senior information officer. He was tough, highly disciplined, had an exceptionally quick mind, and appeared to take an interest in everything around him. As I was to discover right at the outset of our relationship he also had a winning sense of humour.

"We mustn't dawdle over breakfast, old boy. I have an appointment set up for eleven o'clock. You should come along with me… As you have already been here for a time, I am sure you would be a distinct asset."

"What's your appointment?" I asked him.

He drew a notebook from his jacket pocket and flipped it open.

"Chap called – amazing name! – Bull Connor … Head of the city's security apparatus, it seems."

I laughed.

"Yes, head of security – that's exactly who he is. There is a police chief accountable to him who goes by the name of Al Lingo, but Bull Connor is the city's commissioner of public safety. It seems he's the boss of most things around here. Lingo arrested me last evening, and ordered me off to jail for the night. The police let me out just before I met you at the front desk. You'll be seeing Bull Connor, and I don't suppose he'd know me from a sack of beans. But in the event a connection is made between the police and my stay over with them, and with you, it might be a good idea for me not to accompany you to your interview ..."

"You spent last night in jail? Good gracious! Whatever for?"

I told him about my shortcut through the park and past the police trailers, how I'd been stopped by someone I was sure was Al Lingo himself – that the man I had seen wore pearl-handled revolvers slung low on his hips – and how I had managed to wisecrack myself into having two cases of good Canadian beer confiscated.

"Twenty-four bottles of the best ...!" I expostulated.

"Well, we can't have that," said Peter. "You'd better come with me so you can ask to have them back."

"No, I'd best not. It could rile them, maybe spoil your own interview," I replied.

"Nonsense! The police have taken your property, and you have every right – indeed duty – to reclaim it. Besides, I am sure you can help me with my enquiries. You'll be able to think of questions for this chappie that I wouldn't think to ask on my own. You've been released now, so that's the end of the matter. No one has any cause to be offended. You're not going to be re-arrested, surely? The fellow's not going to say anything to me that he wouldn't also be able to say to you, so we can hear him out together. It's not up to me to ask him for the return of your beer. No, no! You should come, you must come. We'll go in together."

Peter had made up his mind. His confidence brooked no denial and I wanted my beer back, so there was no need for him to press me. The whole situation tweaked my sense of humour. I had heard a description of the police chief from people I had met at the Gaston, and was pretty sure it was Al Lingo who had arrested me the night before. If it had indeed been him he might have guessed I was a journalist, but he couldn't have known for sure. Now we were about to meet his boss. Maybe it would do no great harm if I tagged along. Bull Connor was on my own list of people I'd like to meet, so I was quite happy to accept the opportunity.

"Well, we'll go first to this Bull Connor's office, but we should try to make contact with your fellow, too – this Lingo chap. I'd imagine Connor's office is at City Hall, but we should first drop by the local police HQ, enquire there where we can find the Safety Commissioner's office … It would be a useful ploy to make ourselves known to that lot. They may recognize you, of course, but no harm in that – and they won't know me. It would be a good idea for you to go right back in and let them know who you are – and that you're looking for their supreme chief. Courage, man! Sometimes one has to play the one-upmanship game boldly, you see …" Peter Pinsway was thinking aloud.

He winked. I may have had doubts about my situation, but my companion was having fun.

An hour later we met again in the hotel foyer and together walked over to the police headquarters. Peter had had a shower and changed his shirt, but he wore the same dapper set of clothes – pin-stripe trousers, black jacket and black bowler hat tipped at a purposeful angle ever so slightly forward to give some shade to his eyes. He paced briskly along the pavement as if on an errand for Her Majesty, his umbrella swinging in time with his stride. It was scorching hot and rain had not the slightest intention of falling on Birmingham that day, or maybe for the next six months, but the umbrella and the manner in which it was so tightly furled, for all that it could be taken as incongruous nonsense, did set a sort of no-nonsense tone to our mission. Possibly for the very reason these accoutrements could be taken as superfluous pieces of otherwise utilitarian equipment (as was the bowler), there was a dash of the curious – even nonsensical – that could be usefully added to what otherwise might be considered a dissonance of uniform. The getup possessed a stop-dead impact, a surprise element that could be made good use of, if employed judiciously – and I was sure my companion would know how best to accomplish that. I felt confident matters were in most capable hands, and I had not the least doubt about Peter Pinsway's capacity to carry it off to our mutual advantage. My own part, it was clear, would necessarily be played out in the wings. Theatre, after all.

We took the front stairs to the precinct offices two-at-a-time at precisely two minutes to the hour.

"Good morning!" Peter greeted the desk sergeant. "My name is Pinsway. My colleague and I are both from the press. We have an appointment with

Col. Connor at eleven o'clock. Would you be good enough to tell us where we may find his office?"

The desk sergeant glanced at me. I had changed into a summer suit and looked considerably more presentable than when he had seen me a few hours earlier, but he recognized me and frowned his curiosity.

"Back again!" I told him, smiling, and before he could utter the obvious.

"His office is across at City Hall," the sergeant replied. "Take you two minutes to walk over there."

"And how about the police chief, Col. Al Lingo?" Peter said. "Any chance of a short visit with him?"

"Your friend here has already met Col. Lingo …"

"I had in mind something a little more formal," I ventured reasonably.

The sergeant managed a slow grin.

A group of officers in uniform entered the precinct reception area accompanied by a number of people in civilian dress. Without pausing, they passed immediately along a short corridor into an adjoining hall.

"Well, there go the very two gentlemen you're wanting to see …" said the desk sergeant.

"Excellent!" said Peter, setting off at a gallop in pursuit of the party just arrived. I was hesitant, but seeing the sergeant didn't make a move to block Peter's momentum I gathered my confidence and set off after him.

The double-door to the inner hall was wide open, and Peter had already crossed the threshold when I caught up to him. We entered a large room where it appeared an entire senior contingent of State Highway Patrol and city police officers had been arranged in a semi-circle to receive their briefing orders for the upcoming shift. Col. Al Lingo was standing with another man in civilian dress at the centre of the group, both of them with their backs to the doorway. Lingo's large physique, dressed in the uniform of the force over which he was commander, stood with legs planted firmly apart, arms and open ham-like hands held out to his sides in the manner of a storyteller imitating a gorilla, or perhaps as if about to snatch the twin revolvers he displayed in holsters at his sides. This was indeed the man who had arrested me the night before. His pistols were impressive. Slung low down on each of his thighs, they were long barrelled and had pearly white handles that glinted …

We had clear view of the faces of most of the officers, some of whom noticeably knitted their brows and scowled uncertainly in alarm as they saw us approach the back of their leader.

Somersaults

Peter quickly reached out with his umbrella as if to use its tip to tap the colonel on the shoulder and bestow upon him a knighthood. Then he thought better of the gesture. No doubt the pointy business end of his brolly appeared a trifle aggressive. So deliberately, almost theatrically, he turned the thing around and, holding it by its pointy shaft, delivered a confident rap with the handle on Al Lingo's epaulette.

The colonel grunted and spun around, at the same time lowering his helmeted head as if to charge. He squinted at Peter, clearly unable to assess exactly what he was looking at.

What he encountered was a disarmingly irresistible example of Peter's rhythmically-tuned fine timing. The Englishman bowed with superb grace as he doffed his bowler, hooked his umbrella over one arm and simultaneously stepped forward, hand outstretched, and effusively grasped Col. Lingo's pudgy right mitt. The colonel, caught with his mouth open, said not a word.

"Colonel, sir! Col. Bull Connor! I'm Peter Pinsway!" he announced. "What a delight it is for me to meet you, sir ... Your fame has carried afar, you know – to the very shores of Her Majesty's Great Britain, and I've come all this way to meet you in person. My office has been in touch, no ...? For our appointment here at eleven o'clock? Goodness me! What an experience this is, sir! What a great day, what a momentous day for me ...!"

Col. Al Lingo was clearly flummoxed, but automatically offered his hand to take Peter's, simultaneously waving his free hand towards the civilian standing next to him.

"Seems these gentlemen have an appointment to speak to you, Bull ..."

The real Bull Connor was also a large man, dressed in his shirt sleeves and a thin tie, with a fake straw fedora plopped on top of his head. The hat's narrow brim barely extended beyond its wearer's ears, serving to exaggerate the thickness of the Bull's neck and making him look every bit as absurd as Lingo in his white egg helmet. I wondered in a bemused way if either man ever removed his headgear or if in their respective parlours, at home perchance, they ate their suppers and went to bed hatted.

At that time I had lived long enough among Englishmen to recognize Peter was plying a thick layer of his Englishness, slathering the butter so to speak; but I also knew (and Peter must also have calculated this) there is no white gentleman from America's deep south who could possibly have had the least idea this Englishman was anything but genuine. The patter was impeccable and unstoppable. No one of substance would have been so gauche as to fault Peter's charm, the easy smile, the soothing caramel-rich earnestness of his words, the clear-browed honesty and intensity of his eyes; nor, most of all, his air of total authority. His words formed a web of silken threads, and both Al Lingo and Bull Connor were immediately enmeshed. It mattered not a whit that Peter had got his dignitaries mixed up. It later occurred to me he may have confused them deliberately in order to tweak their tails. Playfully English.

For a moment I thought I caught a glimpse of Lingo frowning at me askance. Or was it glowering? I could not have cared less. Peter was in process of consuming by far the greater part of his attention. I saw no reason why there had to be any smoldering resentment on the part of the State Highway Patrol chief. Evidently neither did he, and he made no special issue of my presence.

"Gentlemen, *my* name is Lingo – Col. Al Lingo. I am the head of the State Highway Patrol here in Birmin'ham. Seems you'd be wanting to talk to Col. Bull Connor, here, this fair city's Commissioner of Public Safety."

He indicated the gentleman standing next to him in shirt sleeves, wearing the idiotic hat.

"I have pressing business with these officers, here," Lingo continued, the sweep of his arm encompassing the half-circle of police patrolmen standing in front of us. "It won't take but a moment. Why don't you all use my office, and I'll join you presently …"

So it was Ku Klux Klansman Bull Connor who led the way into Al Lingo's office, and bade us be seated. He fitted himself comfortably into Al Lingo's chair.

"Well, gentlemen, what can we do for you …?"

All the man's swagger, his arrogance, the sour meanness folded into the wrinkles around his cold eyes and turned-down mouth were displayed in the tone of that first simple query.

Peter jumped right in like a warrior fit to take on the whole tide of battle, brolly in place of sword. He introduced the two of us, eliciting from Bull Connor a series of grunts informing that, as members of the press, he didn't give a damn who the hell we were. The colonel was far and away the most powerful of a troika of commissioners who ran the city under a figurehead mayor. As Commissioner of Public Safety for a total of twenty-six years, he was in charge of both the police and the fire department, as well as all hospitals, clinics and schools. Now his methods of dealing with a city torn apart along racial lines and clearly not working well were objects of closest scrutiny – by every thinking man wanting to inform himself as to the goings on in Alabama. There had been an election the previous year, however, and although Connor had been voted out at the time, to be replaced by a new mayor and a nine-member city council, he had refused (with the connivance of State Governor George Wallace) to bow out gracefully. He was not one to accept even a clear defeat, branding all de-segregationists as "communist stoolies," "liars," "fifth columnists" and worse. In effect Birmingham had two administrations. It was while Peter and I were still in Birmingham that a judgment against him was finally handed down by the Alabama Supreme Court ending his long years of almost absolute control over the city, but as we sat with him in Al Lingo's office that twist of events had yet to come to pass.

Exquisitely polite, Peter managed to trundle all over Bull Connor's muddy social terrain.

"My colleague, here, is yet another British Commonwealth representative present in the city, Col. Connor, and I'm sure you'll agree it is vital for all of us that we corroborate our findings and give our respective publics a clear view of what is happening here ... You'll appreciate that of course ... Very different from the way we operate in England, but I have to say, sir, one can't help but admire you Americans. No frills. You see what needs to be done, and you leap right to it. No nonsense ..."

Peter was offering the dimmest of faint praise to damn the fellow. His patter both surprised and stupefied the crafty old racist, coating this unsavoury southern white bulwark of self-righteous hypocrisy with smiles and layers of affably malleable Britishness. At times I wanted to laugh. Peter's artful theatre, so apparent to me, passed right over the colonel's head. Had I given the least display of my sense of mirth, I feared lest Peter's spell would have been broken – and was mindful, also, of the very real possibility of landing myself right quick back in the pokey. But it was not difficult to put the lid on my amusement; memory of the cell I'd occupied the night before had a dampening effect, and I didn't particularly want to repeat the experience. Beyond that was my amazement at the sheer skill of my companion's manipulation of this whacko brute – and the lesson in interview skill to which I was party. Listening to Peter, I found myself conjuring parallel images: a highly adept *banderillero* wielding his darts in torment of a bewildered bovine, or a Connor-jowled mongrel on the end of a chain accepting hard biscuit from the outstretched hand of Sweet Reason. Peter's was a potpourri of the finest stagecraft, every bit as mesmerizing as it was amusing.

I shook my mind clear and came back to the chief's office. As it turned out Connor gave us an hour of his time, explaining his strategies for containing these "Niggrah outrages." He was sure (Peter had told him) we understood the logic of his whips, his attack dogs, his water cannons, his continual stream of verbal abuse. Yes (Peter, unblinking eyes fixed on his quarry, was nodding his head) – all of these actions are a most necessary means of containing the mob and returning Birmingham to the serenity of the hospitable city it had always been prior to the excesses of these unruly black hooligans ... Surely the English of all people should be able to understand that? Why, lots of people throughout America – way beyond the borders of Alabama – were firmly behind the actions of Birmingham's lawful authorities. Desegregation, my ass! Where was the all-fired need for them damned sons-o'-bitches to mess up the streets of our city with their violations of just law...?

Who the hooligans – against whom the violations ...? These were factors not precisely defined.

Indeed, how just the laws?

Birmingham's school students had launched their Children's Crusade short days before. Their parents' activities in the streets were being hamstrung: police were threatening them with lengthy incarcerations, and employers were threatening sackings for absenteeism. Few could afford to sacrifice meager earnings. So now it was the children's turn. It was the antagonistic response they faced as they marched day after day in the streets in front of the world's press and television cameras – the violence of the police wielding clubs and breaking their bones, the viciousness of the police attack dogs, the force of the Fire Department's hoses, and the jubilantly confrontational way in which hundreds of youngsters had faced arrest and been packed into buses to be taken away to jail, singing! – that had finally brought Bull Connor down. The worldwide condemnation of Connor's bull tactics backfired on him, and both he and his overt form of racism were done. Within two days of Peter and I meeting with Connor and Lingo, the system of the city's administration was switched from a mayor-and-three-commissioners to the more democratic form of elected representation, mayor-and-council. Connor was given the boot – but none of these adjustments was sufficient to prevent the bombing of the Gaston Motel or blowing to smithereens the home of Dr. King's brother. Nor were they sufficient to prevent the bombing later that year of the 16th Street Baptist Church, in which four little girls lost their lives. The fight would continue over the months and years to come, but it was these events in Birmingham that led, later that same summer, to the famous mass "March on Washington," the largest ever seen to that date in the nation's capital, demanding meaningful civil rights legislation. It was the national disgrace of Birmingham's racists that proved the tipping point. It was this city that provided the name, the first of any number of backdrops against which the remainder of the desegregation fight would be fought and won throughout America.

That morning as Peter and I sat with him in Al Lingo's office, Bull Connor still figured he was on top. He blustered and fumed, cursing the "Niggrahs," inferior and dirty layabouts and communists, swearing none of them would ever fit comfortably into an Alabama he administered.

Finished with his instructions to the day's Highway Patrol detail, Al Lingo sauntered back into his office just as we were wrapping up our interview with Connor.

Given an un-harried moment to examine the small group invading his office, Lingo momentarily hung back from expressing the obvious contempt he felt for the press at large. But his eyes betrayed uncertainty. He was not about to warm to the London dandy who occasioned his city with bowler and brolly, but clearly he did not know what to make of him. And then there was this witless young prisoner of the night before ...

Col. Lingo hesitated, still somewhat befuddled by his initial encounter with Peter in the outer office. He appeared to mistake Connor's general and silent bewilderment as an all clear.

Peter leapt in immediately:

"Charming office, Col. Lingo, sir, charming ... I was saying so to your colleague, here, Col. Connor. Efficient, and not a superfluous frill anywhere to be seen ..."

He picked a framed photograph off the desk, then carefully put it back in its place.

"This would be your family, no ...?"

Col. Lingo still held back a moment, hesitating – but Peter gave him scant opportunity to avoid entanglement. The chief of the State Highway Patrol was obliged to glance down at the photograph of his family on the desk. There was an intense moment of silence as he and Peter examined the photograph together. By the end of it, however, Al Lingo had been wrapped-up tightly as if in the coils of a python, positively lathered with Peter's complimentary and honeyed butter. Had he but known it, the wretched fellow was dealing with a man of considerable and most persuasive authority, in every way superior to his own. It was a great performance, but Lingo missed it. Could not see it.

Bull Connor made no move to vacate Lingo's chair, and I also remained seated. Peter, however, who had stood up when Lingo entered, took a few quick paces to one side at the front of the officer's large desk, careful to be respectful of everyone's space and not to block my own view of the proceedings.

Then he indicated me and talked quickly as if, as a matter of course, he knew perfectly well Col. Lingo and I had had a prior encounter.

Lingo sized up a spare chair before pulling it over, conscious he would not have fitted into it comfortably had his revolvers remained anchored to his hips. He undid his gun belt, laid the twin six-shooters in their holsters on the top of his desk.

They were rare and beautiful pieces, and of course Peter did not pass up the opportunity to remark on their perfection.

"Magnificent!" he exclaimed. "The very finest I've seen …!"

Hands behind his back as he bent over them, he then glanced up – superb timing – at their proud owner. His remark certainly included the family photograph, but it was the guns that formed the focal point of attention, and Col. Al Lingo was inordinately proud of his guns.

"They were a gift from my daddy …"

Pause.

"I understand you met my colleague last evening and had occasion to relieve him of two cases of a very fine Canadian beer?" Peter was smiling affably, slipped the query most matter-of-factly, and had Al Lingo nodding his head in assent before he fully understood what was being asked.

"Uh-h, yes … the fellas, uh-h …"

"And of course there'll be no trouble returning it to him …? All of it?"

"No, no. I'll speak to the fellas and see to it right away."

All affability and smiles and understanding. By now Peter had a very clear picture and everything he needed in the way of quotes from both colonels. So did I. We rose to go.

"We're staying at the Dinkler-Tutwiler," I told Col. Lingo as we all shook hands. "Would you please have your boys leave the beer for me at the front desk …?"

"I'll do that. I'll do that," he said – and I never saw the man again.

Neither, as it turned out, did I ever again see my two cases of Canadian beer.

I did manage to see Bull Connor once more, though. He was packing up the desk in his City Hall office a day or two later when I popped my head round the edge of his door. I thought I heard him muttering to himself irritably.

"Col. Connor?"

He looked up, but did not seem to recognize me.

"Are you a newsman?" he enquired.

"Yes."

"Get out!"

It was the briefest of my social calls. My time spent with T.R. Wright, superintendent of the Board of Education, was politer but about as succinct. He told me he could not imagine what business it was of the foreign press to take such an interest in the daily deliberations of the board but, by chance – most fortunate coincidence – he did have a mimeographed paper to explain why over one thousand children had been suspended or expelled from their schools. By that time the details were moot: the children had been reinstated days before.

As a matter of convenience Peter Pinsway and I found ourselves a single working unit over the next couple of weeks. Bull Connor was gone; Al Lingo was promoted by State Governor George Wallace from Chief of the State Highway Patrol to Director of the Alabama Department of Public Safety. Events in Birmingham's streets were becoming less tumultuous but had not entirely calmed down, and both Peter and I had a few leads on stories we needed to chase down elsewhere. I had the transport and could get us about easily. Peter, being an older and far more experienced reporter than myself, was an ideal mentor. He had a degree of confidence and clout I lacked – a deftness and savvy I was clever enough to recognize came after long years of experience jousting with champions in the lists of human interactions. "London" had special meaning when he said the word; I couldn't say it – and "Toronto" packed nowhere near the same heft.

"London" seemed to ring the bell of recognition with even the dullest-witted policeman or firefighter and coupled with the name of the paper (a weighty title of renown, especially with "The" in front of it) wondrous things seemed to happen. I tended to hang back and let Peter "do the doin's" when it was necessary. He accomplished his doin's with superb aplomb, could charm doors open, woo barmaids or traffic cops, or send the sternest councillors into paroxysms of burbling and fluttering. I learned a lot, was having fun and loved it.

Before it was blown to bits Peter and I managed to attend several gatherings at the 16th Street Baptist Church to hear Dr. King's preaching. The place was always packed so there was barely room to move, but Peter and I were known and recognised by that time, and would be pushed to the front so we could have a first rate view of the proceedings. At almost every session a group of Afro-American women would come out onto the floor between the choir stalls chanting, singing and dancing to rhythmic Gospel music. It seemed the whole church was rocking its way to freedom – the salvation of everyone inside it.

Dr. King would hold up his hand to speak, and the whole place would fall silent:

"Brothers!" he would call out – then again: "Brothers!"

Each time he called out the entire congregation answered back: "Brothers!"

The vocal rally would go back and forth hypnotically, sometimes for what seemed to be several minutes, until it appeared the whole congregation was transfixed. Then Dr. King would hold up his hands and call for attention. When the place was silent, everybody at the very edge of anticipation, he would launch into a harangue of such eloquence that his audience would shake their heads in wonder at the promise and poetry of his words.

"One day …" he intoned – and it was as if he was reading from God's own heavenly agenda – blacks and whites would live together in harmony in America … Though he criticized his persecutors, never once did I hear him call them down, never once demean them.

MLK – "We shall win"

Sometimes meetings at the 16th Street Baptist Church would go on for several hours. They would finally break up into smaller groups that would filter into the streets still singing, so highly charged by what they had just seen and heard inside.

Peter summoned me quickly one morning. He had managed to arrange for an interview with Dr. Martin Luther King Jr.

Rev. Martin Luther King Jr. and civil rights attorney Arthur D. Shores
at press conference in the Gaston Motel

"He has limited time, as you know, so you'd best get a move on. Great opportunity for you, old fellow ... and I could surely use your skills. You'll be another pair of eyes and ears, and for sure you'll pick up easily on some point I could miss. It will give you a chance to get to know the man a little better."

We hurried off to the Gaston a few blocks away, and presented ourselves at the desk downstairs. Both of us had been in and around the motel almost daily since our arrival in the city, so our presence as journalists was already well marked and understood by those on the minister's team. Even so, on this occasion we were escorted upstairs to the room Dr. King used as an office and were shown straight in. He was sitting behind a makeshift desk, and rose to greet us warmly as we entered.

"You and I have already met, Mr. Hespeler-Boultbee. I'm glad to see you here at the Gaston. I hope you are findin' everythin' you need to tell your story – this great story …?"

"*Your* story," I corrected him.

"Indeed, sir!" he concurred. He was smiling as he turned to Peter Pinsway.

"You must be Mr. Pinsway? I have seen you here in the motel, and at the church, so I must apologize we have not been able to get together earlier. These are tumultuous days. All of us are obliged to complete two full days of work in a single day, and no one has the time to indulge our desires and needs to be with friends and loved ones. Welcome to Birmin'ham!"

Dr. King tended to drop the 'g' off '–ing.' As with so many others, he pronounced the city Birm-in-HAM.

Already the traumas that had filled the newspapers and television screens during the past days – the street demonstrations, the Children's Crusade and the violence that had accompanied these events – were now being eclipsed by the upcoming enrolment of two black students at the university in Tuscaloosa. According to federal law, they were entitled to take their respective places in class, but it had never happened before and now the state governor, George Wallace, had seen fit to take both a segregationist and political stand, vowing to block the students' efforts to register – with his own body, if necessary.

"This is not goin' to be an easy fight," Dr. King told the two of us. "As you know, Governor Wallace calls me a communist and has vowed, 'segregation now, segregation tomorrow, segregation forever.' He means it, not because he himself necessarily believes what he's sayin', but because he has to feed the white racists out there – the ones who elected him and are so desperately clingin' to power."

"How do you think it's going to work out …?" Peter asked carefully.

Dr. King smiled, exuding confidence.

"We shall win," he said. "We *shall* overcome. There is no question that we shall win this fight, for God is at our side. But I am worried about all of our brothers who will have to suffer because of the racist vision of such men. We have the federal government very active and lookin' over our shoulder, so now we must wait and see what transpires. No matter what – whether it's this comin' fight at the University of Alabama, or the fight that comes after that, rest assured we shall win."

It was not a long interview. Peter was point man in this, and I do not believe I said a word beyond the politeness of our greeting and farewell. My pad and pen were ready, but I am sure I failed to write a single word. There was nothing more than the obvious to note down.

"We'll try to get to Tuscaloosa tomorrow," Peter was telling Dr. King.

On June 11 Peter and I drove from Birmingham to Tuscaloosa to hear Governor Wallace take his stand at the door of the University of Alabama's Foster Auditorium. He had promised to "stand on the steps at the schoolhouse door" to prevent the two Afro-Americans, Vivian Malone and James Hood, from registering for classes. Hollow bravado – Wallace trumpeted his viewpoint to a crowd that realized federal agents were immediately on hand to take over and void whatever the governor proposed.

Deputy Attorney General Nicholas Katzenbach, escorted to the auditorium by federal marshals, told Wallace to step aside. The governor refused. Instead he gave a prepared speech about states' rights, forcing Katzenbach to respond – which he did by telephoning President John F. Kennedy.

The president promptly federalized the Alabama National Guard under General Henry Graham, who wasted no time ordering Wallace to step aside – a direct order from the President of the United States. Wallace blathered on for a short time, trying to explain and acquit himself – but in the end he had to comply. His show was of hesitation and reluctance, a sad attempt at face-saving he evidently thought might create a visual impact before the on-looking newspapermen and television cameras. No one paid any attention. His moment had passed; the story was now the enrolment of the two students.

Peter and I witnessed this burlesque, and the next day I headed back north to Canada, turning my back on the vulgarity of Alabama's bloody desegregation casino.

Fifty years on, as I write these lines, the show goes on and on like the slow-motion replay of a movie loop in which the bar-brawl never comes to an end. Societies beyond America's borders, stunned by the ways in which Americans pulverize themselves, look on as this once great nation, convinced it is still the leader of modern civilization, twists itself into a pretzel over the outcome of the latest white versus black case – or the scores of sordid gun-crazed incidents that kill Americans by the thousands every year. Pick one. Fanatics on all sides of the racial quarrel scream they are right, yet are unwilling and unable to compromise. Guns. As I write, it is for the most part an outraged black community that cannot accept the exoneration of some white man for what he claims is the self-defence killing of a black, a farcical trial that will never reach the core of the problem because neither side wants it to. All sides would prefer to scream their ire by forcing their unresolvable issues onto courts that have been constantly overwhelmed by the sheer size and tenacity of the situations they face – laws that were established in the first place to favour the lawmakers rather than tackle the complaints of the aggrieved. No matter the outcome, no matter the pronouncements, what emerges is totally irrelevant in light of the next crisis that has already arisen. So much suspicion, so much doubt, so much confusion – one wonders if there is anyone capable of pinpointing the problem, or if there is not some mass hallucination wandering the American landscape like a gargantuan Goya-like ogre devouring its frightened children. No one seems capable of lifting the finger of certainty – or stating precisely which certainty is the fulcrum of justice.

Meanwhile a worried world, as if watching the tantrums of a delinquent little brother, winces as the US of A once again divides itself along whatever lines or cataclysmic faults happen to be seething at the time, dissolves itself into dangerous conniptions, screaming and finger-pointing. Then out come the guns.

"Look me up when Sanity permits you to come to London," said Peter brightly, tipping his bowler. "We'll take a draught of a far finer brew than anything you left behind for that undeserving policeman!"

"Good idea!" I promised. Later, on the assignment that would eventually take me to my new life in Portugal, I was able to do just that.

www.ingramcontent.com/pod-product-compliance
Lightning Source LLC
Chambersburg PA
CBHW022050160426
43198CB00008B/178